Robert John Harvey-Gibson

A Textbook of Elementary Biology

Robert John Harvey-Gibson

A Textbook of Elementary Biology

ISBN/EAN: 9783743330986

Manufactured in Europe, USA, Canada, Australia, Japa

Cover: Foto ©ninafisch / pixelio.de

Manufactured and distributed by brebook publishing software
(www.brebook.com)

Robert John Harvey-Gibson

A Textbook of Elementary Biology

CONTENTS.

		PAGE
INTRODUCTION		1

CHAPTER
- I. MATTER AND ENERGY 7
    - SECTION i. Matter 7
    - ,, ii. Energy 12
    - ,, iii. Classification of chemical compounds . 21
    - ,, iv. Laws of chemical change . . . 22
- II. PROTOPLASM 25
    - SECTION i. Chemical composition of protoplasm . 25
    - ,, ii. Morphology and physiology of protoplasm 29
    - ,, iii. Phenomena concomitant with the manifestations of energy by living protoplasm 35
    - ,, iv. Physiological significance of chlorophyll 38
    - ,, v. Conditions of the environment necessary for the maintenance of life in animal and vegetal protoplasm . . . 41
    - ,, vi. The balance of nature 48
- III. INDIVIDUAL AND TRIBAL LIFE—DISTRIBUTION AND CLASSIFICATION 50
    - SECTION i. Individual life 50
    - ,, ii. Tribal life 52
    - ,, iii. Distribution 54
    - ,, iv. Classification 54

CHAPTER				PAGE
IV.	THE MORPHOLOGY AND PHYSIOLOGY OF THE SIMPLEST LIVING ORGANISMS—PROTISTA			55
	SECTION	i.	Protista—*Protamœba*	55
	,,	ii.	Protista—*Protomyxa*	57
	,,	iii.	The relation of unicellular to multicellular organisms	62
V.	UNICELLULAR PLANTS—PROTOPHYTA—*Protococcus*			69
VI.	UNICELLULAR ANIMALS—PROTOZOA—*Amœba*			73
VII.	METAPHYTA—NON-VASCULARIA			76
	SECTION	i.	Fresh-water Algæ—*Spirogyra*	76
	,,	ii.	Salt-water Algæ—*Fucus*	83
	,,	iii.	Fungi—*Penicillium*	91
	,,	iv.	Musci—*Polytrichum*	101
VIII.	METAPHYTA—VASCULARIA			113
	SECTION	i.	Filices—*Pteris*	113
	,,	ii.	Ligulatæ—*Selaginella*	131
	,,	iii.	Monocotyledones—*Lilium*	143
	,,	iv.	Dicotyledones—*Ranunculus*	178
	,,	v.	General physiology of plants	189
	,,	vi.	Carnivorous plants	213
IX.	METAZOA—INVERTEBRATA			219
	SECTION	i.	Hydrozoa—*Obelia*	219
	,,	ii.	Vermes—*Lumbricus*	233
X.	METAZOA—VERTEBRATA			251
	SECTION	i.	Cephalochorda—*Amphioxus*	251
	,,	ii.	Amphibia—*Rana*	263
	,,	iii.	General physiology of animals	335
XI.	HISTORY OF BIOLOGY			345

ELEMENTARY BIOLOGY.

INTRODUCTION.

Errata.

Page 84, line 24, *for* spherical *read* oblong
 ,,   100 ,, 4, *for* what is known as *read* an imperfect
 ,,   174 ,, 7 from bottom, *omit* like the lily

appear late in the history of science, and, of necessity, their advent is preceded by a period during which the efforts of scientific workers are, consciously or unconsciously, directed chiefly to the accumulation of stores of information on matters of fact. Moreover, not only have those observations already made to be revised, corrected, and extended, but they require to be directly verified and amplified by experiment before the generalisations or inductions formed from their study can be said to be perfectly legitimate and trustworthy. Observations previously isolated become aggregated round these generalisations as centres, each generalisation being known as **a natural law**.

The relationships discovered to exist between individual phenomena were soon found to be capable of wide extension; for the various natural laws which expressed these

CHAPTER							PAGE
IV.	THE MORPHOLOGY AND PHYSIOLOGY OF THE SIMPLEST LIVING ORGANISMS—PROTISTA						55
	SECTION	i.	Protista—*Protamœba*				55
	,,	ii.	Protista—*Protomyxa*				57
	,,	iii.	The relation of unicellular to multicellular organisms				62
V.	UNICELLULAR PLANTS—PROTOPHYTA—*Protococcus*						69
VI.	UNICELLULAR ANIMALS—PROTOZOA—*Amœba*						73
VII.	METAPHYTA—NON-VASCULARIA						76

	,,	iii.	Monocotyledones—				
	,,	iv.	Dicotyledones—*Ranunculus*				178
	,,	v.	General physiology of plants				189
	,,	vi.	Carnivorous plants				213
IX.	METAZOA—INVERTEBRATA						219
	SECTION	i.	Hydrozoa—*Obelia*				219
	,,	ii.	Vermes—*Lumbricus*				233
X.	METAZOA—VERTEBRATA						251
	SECTION	i.	Cephalochorda—*Amphioxus*				251
	,,	ii.	Amphibia—*Rana*				263
	,,	iii.	General physiology of animals				335
XI.	HISTORY OF BIOLOGY						345

ELEMENTARY BIOLOGY.

INTRODUCTION.

THE study of natural phenomena has occupied the attention of mankind from the earliest times of which we have any record. That the observations so made should have been crude, incomplete, and often erroneous, and that the relationship of the several observations to each other should have been, in most cases, entirely overlooked, are results which are completely in accordance with what we know of the development of scientific thought. For generalisations appear late in the history of science, and, of necessity, their advent is preceded by a period during which the efforts of scientific workers are, consciously or unconsciously, directed chiefly to the accumulation of stores of information on matters of fact. Moreover, not only have those observations already made to be revised, corrected, and extended, but they require to be directly verified and amplified by experiment before the generalisations or inductions formed from their study can be said to be perfectly legitimate and trustworthy. Observations previously isolated become aggregated round these generalisations as centres, each generalisation being known as **a natural law**.

The relationships discovered to exist between individual phenomena were soon found to be capable of wide extension; for the various natural laws which expressed these relationships were themselves found to have a genetic connection. Natural laws were found to be capable of being systematised into bodies of truth, or **departments of science**, more commonly, but with less accuracy, termed **sciences**.

One step alone remained in this process of unification of knowledge, namely, the determination of the inter-relationships of the various departments of science. Hence arose the various attempts which have been made within comparatively recent years to formulate a **classification of the sciences**. It can scarcely be said that a uniform agreement has been come to as yet upon all points with reference to that classification, but the general order of relationship and development of the several sciences may be said to be now beyond controversy.

A careful distinction must be drawn at the very outset between what constitutes the **subject-matter** of the sciences themselves, and the **methods** or instruments which are employed in their study. These methods are two in number, and entirely different in their nature—**qualitative**, embracing the methods of inductive and deductive Logic, and **quantitative**, or mathematical, embracing that section of mathematics usually known as Pure Mathematics.

All scientific knowledge rests fundamentally on the belief in the 'order of nature;' that is to say, on the belief that **under the same conditions the same cause will produce the same effect**. The basis for this belief is the universal experience of mankind, obtained by **observation** of and **experiment** on natural phenomena, and formulated therefrom by inductive reasoning, the induction going by the name of the **law of causality**.

In attempting to classify or arrange the sciences in their natural order, regard must be had to the several conditions of a natural classification.

Firstly, the sciences must be arranged in the order of their complexity; that is to say, sciences which involve simple and definite generalisations must precede sciences built out of generalisations involved and complex in their nature. Manifestly, therefore, if we accept this as a principle of classification, the sciences will arrange themselves in order of their difficulty. Further, the sciences dealing with generalities must precede those dealing with specialities, since the latter are dependent on the former for proof. The science, for instance, dealing with the subject of chemical decomposition in general must precede the science which discusses the phenomena of life, amongst which the laws of chemical decomposition play so important a part.

If the sciences be classified according to such principles, they will be found, generally speaking, to arrange themselves in the order of their own historic development. Naturally, therefore, the classification will indicate the order in which they ought to be studied. The absurdity of endeavouring to grapple with the principles of Biology without a preliminary acquaintance with the facts and laws of Physics and Chemistry, for instance, becomes at once apparent ; nor will the absurdity be diminished, and the misconceptions which result be less pronounced and mischievous, when attempts are made not only to become acquainted with, but even to teach the principles of the higher sciences of Sociology and Ethics without even an elementary knowledge of the facts and conclusions of Biology.

The most general of the sciences is manifestly **Astronomy**, since it treats of the universe in the widest possible acceptation of the term. Astronomy may be defined as the science which discusses '**the distribution, motions and characteristics of the heavenly bodies.**' Astronomy requires for its proper study an accurate and extensive knowledge of qualitative and quantitative methods, but its conclusions are independent of the special conclusions of the other sciences.

The first limitation to the scope of scientific enquiry is, naturally, accessibility to the subject matter of science. An extensive acquaintance with matter so far removed as the fixed stars, or even the planets of our own system, is a manifest impossibility. Consequently, when we define the next three sciences of **Physics, Chemistry,** and **Biology,** as '**the sciences of matter and energy,**' we mean it to be understood that they are limited to a consideration of the phenomena of matter and energy as manifested, for the most part, on our own earth. We say, 'for the most part,' for within recent years the method of spectrum analysis introduced by Bunsen and Kirchhoff have enabled physicists and chemists to make considerable progress towards the attainment of a knowledge of the composition of the heavenly bodies ; whilst our belief in the universal applicability of the laws of Physics has become so firm that, although not submitted to the test of actual experiment or even actual observation, we have no hesitation in affirming that they hold sway in the farthest removed of these bodies known to us.

Physics may be defined as '**the systematic exposition of the phenomena and properties of matter and energy, in so far as these phenomena and properties can be stated in terms of definite measurement and explained by reference to mechanical principles and laws**' (Daniell). Physics is usually divided into two sections, the one dealing with the phenomena and properties of masses of matter, the other concerned with matter in its molecular aspect, and termed molar and molecular physics respectively. The department of molecular physics leads up to, and in some measure overlaps, the science of Chemistry.

Chemistry may be defined as **the science which embraces the study (1) of the properties of chemical elements, and of the compounds formed by the union of two or more of them ; and (2) of the laws which regulate the mutual action of elements and compounds on each other.**

We shall have occasion to discuss more fully in Chapters I. and II. the general scope of Physics and Chemistry, more especially with reference to the last of the three sciences of matter and energy, namely, Biology.

Biology, being '**the science which deals with the**

matter and energy of living things' (using the term 'living thing' in its ordinary acceptation), manifestly rests on Physics and Chemistry, since it involves the application of the laws and principles of these sciences to the special case of living matter, whether plant or animal. Contrary, perhaps, to our first anticipation, we find that the phenomena of Biology, complex and involved as they admittedly are, are generally speaking capable of expression in physical terms, while the changes that take place in the animal or plant organism are found to agree in all important points with those which form the subject of chemical and physical investigations. Even mental or psychological phenomena, although the nature of their connection with the chemical and other changes taking place contemporaneously in the brain, has not yet been determined, are undeniably accompanied by some such change, and cannot be said to be independent of the physical and chemical basis on which the science of Biology, as a whole, is built. The dependence of Biology on Chemistry becomes still more evident when we learn that no constituent of living matter is incapable of being classified among chemical substances; that, in other words, the substances which enter into the composition of living things are among the commonest constituents of the minerals of the earth's crust.

It is usual to classify such departments of knowledge as Geology, Mineralogy, Botany, Zoology, Anthropology, and Sociology as distinct sciences. They cannot, however, claim a higher rank than that of sub-sciences, while some of them are merely special departments of the four great sciences already mentioned.

This discussion regarding the position of Biology in a classification of the sciences leads us, therefore, to the conclusion that Biology has for its subject the matter and energy of living things, and is, therefore, dependent on the more general sciences of Physics and Chemistry, and itself forms the starting-point for a series of special sub-sciences, such as Botany, Zoology, Anthropology, and Sociology, all of which are dependent on it for their fundamental basis. We have also seen that a study of the more general sciences of Physics and Chemistry ought to precede the study of Biology, just as the discussion of the principles of Biology forms a necessary preliminary to the proper understanding of the phenomena and laws of Psychology, Sociology, and other related sub-sciences.

The first chapters of this text-book are, therefore, devoted to giving a short account of the principles of Physics and Chemistry, looked at mainly in the light of their application to Biology ; whilst the chemical and physical characters of protoplasm—'the physical basis of life'—led up to by a brief discussion of chemical compounds in general, forms the natural introduction to the subject-matter of Biology itself.

CHAPTER I.

MATTER AND ENERGY.

SECTION I.—MATTER.

WHAT is **matter?** What is **energy?** must of necessity be the first questions asked in a survey of the sciences that deal with these two subjects. A categorical answer to either query is, however, an impossibility. We know matter and energy only as revealed to us through their properties ; nor is there any likelihood of our ever attaining to a knowledge of their essential nature. In order to define the terms 'matter,' 'energy,' therefore, it is necessary to enumerate their properties in some detail.

Fundamental properties of matter.—Matter obviously exists in measurable quantities, each quantity occupying a certain volume or bulk. Matter, as occupying a certain volume of space, must possess appreciable length, breadth, and thickness ; that is to say, each volume of matter must possess a definite form. Moreover, in virtue of the universal applicability of the **law of gravitation**—viz. that every particle of matter in the universe attracts every other particle with a force directly proportional to the mass of the attracting particle, and inversely proportional to the square of the distance between them—every particle of matter must possess weight, that is, a tendency to rush to the centre of the earth, as the nearest great attracting body.

Matter exists in a variety of states. We are familiar more especially with the solid, liquid, and gaseous states and others intermediate between any two of them.[1] It is a familiarly known fact, moreover, that the same kind of matter may exist in different states, under different atmospheric and other conditions—i.e. we may have transformation of matter from one state into another.. Water is probably the most familiar instance of this. Fluid under ordinary temperatures, it becomes solid when the temperature is sufficiently reduced, or gaseous when sufficiently augmented. Matter in its manifold state possesses the same fundamental properties.

Matter is divisible, but not infinitely so (save in imagination). Practically, and even theoretically, there are limits to the divisibility of matter. The practical limits to the divisibility of matter are soon reached ; but, theoretically, matter is believed to consist of extremely minute and perfectly invisible particles, or **molecules**. Matter is, therefore, not absolutely continuous ; the molecules of which it is composed are an appreciable distance apart, i.e. matter is porous, and therefore penetrable or permeable. For it is conceivable that smaller molecules of another substance might be insinuated between the larger molecules. Molecules themselves are, however, supposed to be impenetrable.

The number of molecules in a given volume of a substance varies according as the substance is in the solid, liquid, or gaseous state. Observation and experiment teach us that the molecules are relatively close to one another in the solid and liquid states, and that they are further apart in the gaseous.

Defined physically, **a molecule is the smallest particle of a substance that can possess the properties of the whole**;

[1] No reference is made in the text to the recent interesting speculation of Crookes and others on the possible existence of a fourth state which matter is believed to be capable of subsisting in, when the tension of its gaseous state is reduced to one-millionth of an atmosphere, as being out of place in an elementary sketch like the present. See 'Radiant Matter,' by W. Crookes, F.R.S., *British Association Report*, 1879.

or, from a chemical point of view, **the smallest quantity that is able to exist in a free state or take part in or result from a chemical change.** Molecules of the same kind, i.e. of the same substance in whatever state it may occur, agree in possessing the same weight, size, and properties, differing in these respects from molecules of all other substances.

Constitution of matter.—Molecules by the employment of certain agencies, chemical or other, are themselves capable of division. Their constituent parts are termed **atoms**. An atom may therefore be looked upon as the ultimate chemical particle of matter, as distinguished from the molecule, the ultimate physical particle. The atom, as its name indicates, is itself indivisible by any means at present in our power. Nearly every molecule is composed of two or more atoms. In a very few cases the molecules consist of one atom only, e.g. the metals mercury, cadmium, and zinc, and in these cases the ultimate physical and ultimate chemical particles may be said to be identical. If all the atoms going to form a molecule be identical, then the molecule, or ultimate physical particle, is an elementary molecule, and a substance composed of such molecules is termed a **chemical element**. If, however, the atoms going to make up the molecule differ in size, weight, and other properties, then the molecule is compound in its nature, and the substance formed of such molecules is known as a **chemical compound**.

Molecules vary in size according to the number of atoms entering into their composition—that number ranging from one (in a very few cases) to several hundreds. In the case of elementary substances the terms monatomic, diatomic, triatomic, &c., are used according to the number of atoms going to make up a molecule of the element in question.

At the present time about seventy different kinds of atoms, or elementary forms of matter, are known.[1] It is

---

[1] Since the above sentence was written Kruss and Nilson announce the discovery of twenty new elements in rare Scandinavian minerals.

possible, however, that that number may be increased as new methods of investigation are discovered. The method of spectrum analysis, for instance, already alluded to above, has added many to the list. Since not a few of the elements have been discovered by the decomposition of substances which were believed, in a less advanced condition of the science, to be themselves elements, it is by no means improbable that continued research in the same direction may prove productive of further results of a similar nature. Indeed, the suggestion has been thrown out by some bolder speculators that all the elements are simply different modifications or conditions of one primary elemental form of matter.

We have hitherto purposely omitted to mention one property of matter, namely **inertia**, which is defined by Newton as '**the tendency of every body to persevere in a state of rest, or of uniform motion in a straight line, unless in so far as it is acted upon by an impressed force.**' We are thus introduced to two new ideas—'motion' and 'force.' The conception of 'motion' is one so familiar to us, that it does not require further definition. Like 'matter' and 'energy,' the essential nature of force is unknown. It may be defined, however, from a study of its effects, as that which produces, arrests, accelerates, retards, or changes the direction of motion.

We have already seen that the same kind of matter may exist in the different states known as solid, liquid, and gaseous, and in intermediate states. We have also seen that these states of matter are transformable, the one into the other. The transformation is possible only in consequence of the application of a certain amount of force.

When left alone, the solid is bounded by definite free surfaces, often, as in crystals, natural planes. Liquids have one free surface, namely, that exposed to the external atmosphere, and other surfaces which are in contact with the containing vessel, in number and nature corresponding to the sides of the vessel. The one free surface is always horizontal, and is constantly changing owing to the escape of molecules from the surface into the air. A gas has no free surface. The molecules, freed from mutual influence, are constantly tending to become farther and farther separated from each other.

It has been calculated that in a cubic inch of air the number of molecules can be expressed only by a row of figures twenty-one in number. This calculation can give only a very faint conception of the number of molecules in a given mass, or of their extreme minuteness. Each molecule is believed to be in perpetual and extremely rapid motion in straight lines in all directions, and to hit against its neighbours on every side at the rate of something like 18,000 million times per second.

In addition to this motion of translation, molecules are believed to possess intrinsic motions of vibration and rotation, dependent for their intensity upon the temperature of the substance.

As already stated, an application of heat to a solid has the effect of transforming it into the liquid, and through that state into the gas, or, in some cases, into a gas directly, the molecules of which can by further application of the same force be made to recede farther and farther from each other. Change of state is therefore accompanied by change in the rate of motion of the constituent molecules, a high temperature being associated with a rapid motion, and a low temperature with a relatively sluggish motion. The converse is likewise true, abstraction of heat being sufficient to change the gaseous state first into the liquid and lastly into the solid. Water may be again cited as the most familiar example of this change.

The transformation of one state of matter into another is possible in virtue of a manifestation of **energy**.

Section II.—Energy.

Work is the production of motion in mass or molecule against resistance. Work is done when a mass of matter is lifted against the resistance of gravity; work is done when a chemical compound is decomposed, for the resistance of the peculiar form of attraction known as chemical affinity is overcome and the molecules are separated from each other.

Energy is the power to do work. It must be carefully distinguished from force, the existence of which it, however, implies, and from motion which, as being produced by force, indicates the presence of energy. Thus, force is exerted when a weight is lifted in virtue of the arm of the labourer possessing a store of energy, a certain proportion of which energy is used in the act of lifting the weight. Force is similarly exerted when a compound is decomposed in virtue of the agent in the decomposition possessing a store of energy, some of which is expended in the performing of the work of decomposition.

When a mass of matter rests on the earth's surface, it exerts a certain force due to the action of gravity; but it possesses no energy, it possesses no motion of its own. When the mass is raised, say to the top of a high tower, the force of gravity has been, in accordance with the law of gravity, reduced, by an extremely small but calculable amount, because its distance from the centre of the attracting body has been increased. It has no motion of its own, but it has gained a certain amount of energy—**energy of position, or potential energy.** It is capable of doing some work; it is capable, for instance, of driving a pile into the ground if allowed to drop upon it. When the mass reaches the ground again, it has lost its energy. Its energy in the act of falling has become transformed into **active** or **kinetic energy.** Kinetic energy is therefore **energy of motion.**

Further, by the agency of, say, a steam engine, the weight might be again raised to the top of the tower, i.e. the kinetic energy of the engine may be retransformed into the potential energy of the raised weight.

Again, the weight at the tower's top is prevented from falling by the resistance of the tower. It requires an exertion of force to overcome this resistance. That counteracting force implies a source of energy which must manifestly be a form of kinetic energy. Imagine the weight referred to as suspended from a hook—the energy employed to liberate the weight from its support must be a kinetic energy. The **liberating energy** need not be by any means commensurate to the effects produced by the liberation. The old proverb, 'a small spark may raise a great conflagration,' accurately expresses this fact. Indeed, we may take this proverb as an illustration. A barrel of gunpowder consists of a mixture of a large number of molecules of different substances which under certain conditions have a very strong tendency to unite and form new combinations. So long as the condition of their union be absent, the molecules retain energy of position, and the barrel of gunpowder is a store of potential energy. The condition of their union is the production of a high temperature in their immediate vicinity. That condition being satisfied by the application of a spark to the mass, the affinities of the molecules become at once satisfied, and the store of potential energy becomes transformed into kinetic energy, accompanied by the usual attendant phenomena of an explosion, viz. sound, light, and heat.

It is necessary that we should trace this conception of energy a little farther.

Kinetic energy being energy of motion, the various modes of motion may be conversely termed kinetic energies. **Sound** is produced by the vibration of molecules, and is communicated to the organ of hearing by the sympathetic vibration of the molecules of the atmosphere between the ear and the source of the sound. Sound is therefore a mode of motion. **Light,** according to the undulatory theory first propounded by Huyghens, is to be considered as due to the vibrations of an imponderable medium termed ether, which pervades all space between the particles of matter, and which is by some eminent physicists regarded as in all probability forming the fundamental basis of matter itself. Light may therefore be considered as a mode of motion, though not precisely in the same sense as sound is considered to be so. Lastly, **heat** is undoubtedly due to the vibration of molecules of matter. Of course, on the assumption that the space between all molecules is filled by an ethereal medium, the vibrations of molecules mean also the simultaneous vibration of their ethereal surroundings. Now, we have seen that the potential energy of the gunpowder became transformed into kinetic energy, manifesting sufficient force to cause a considerable alteration in the distance relationships of surrounding objects. But the heat produced during the explosion, which we have just seen to be a form of kinetic energy, must have resulted from the transformation of a portion of the original potential energy of the gunpowder; similarly for the light and sound. We conclude, therefore, that all the energy of the gunpowder is not available for the production of ordinary motion of translation amongst masses. Part is transformed into forms of kinetic energy, probably not desired, but nevertheless invariably accompanying the chief manifestation. An extended course of observation and experiment teaches us that every transformation of potential energy into kinetic, or of kinetic into potential, is attended by one or more, what might be termed, by-manifestations of energy, the chief of these, and that form of kinetic energy into which all others ultimately become transformed, being heat.[1]

Heat, of course, as kinetic energy, can itself be trans-

---

[1] The rough determination of the source, destination, and proportional amount of the various forms in which energy manifests itself in

formed, though only partially, into potential energy. According to a law first enunciated by Carnot, it is only when heat passes from a warmer to a colder body, and even then only partially, that it can be converted directly or indirectly into mechanical work. That passage, however, cannot be interrupted. There is a constant tendency in nature towards the establishment of an equilibrium of temperature ; so that every transformation of energy is accompanied by the dissipation of a certain proportion of it into space in the unavailable form of uniformly diffused heat. It is to be noted that this does not involve a loss of energy ; it merely involves a **degradation of energy** from an available form into a form unavailable to man. **There is never any absolute loss of energy.** Like matter, it is **indestructible**. The relation between the amount of potential and of kinetic energy in the universe is constantly changing—the amount of the kinetic energy steadily increasing at the expense of the potential energy. But the sum of the two forms of energy is a constant quantity. This goes by the name of the **law of the conservation of energy**, and it is one of the most important generalisations to be found in the whole range of science. As stated by Clerk Maxwell, the law may be expressed as follows :—' The total energy of any material system is a quantity which can neither be increased nor diminished by any action between the parts of the system, though it may be transformed into any of the forms of which energy is susceptible.'

Although it is true that the sum of the energies of the universe is a constant quantity, yet it must be borne in mind that energy, as has been already stated indirectly, is partly available, partly unavailable, and that energy in its available form is continually becoming less in amount.

An attempt has been made to measure energy in terms

ordinary physical or chemical interactions, will form an instructive exercise for the junior student, and enable him to become familiar with the transformation of energy in all its aspects.

of the work done by its expenditure. The standard of measurement was first determined by Joule, by his discovery of the **mechanical equivalent of heat**. That discovery may be thus expressed :—the amount of heat-energy necessary to elevate the temperature of one pound of water through 1° Fahr., if converted into ordinary motion, is capable of lifting one pound of water to a height of 772 feet from the earth's surface ; and, conversely, a pound of water falling from a height of 772 feet has its temperature raised in consequence 1° Fahr. If a **foot-pound** be the unit of mechanical work, i.e. the amount of energy required to raise one pound to the height of one foot from the earth's surface, and a **pound-degree** be the unit of heat-work, i.e. the amount of energy required to raise one pound of water 1° Fahr., then a definite quantitative relationship is established between mechanical energy, or energy of visible motion, and heat-energy, viz. 772 foot-pounds are equivalent to 1 pound-degree.

All the available terrestrial energy is derived from certain stores of potential energy, and also from various forms of kinetic energy, which are constantly being manifested on the earth's surface. These different sources may be classified as being either directly or indirectly available, the latter class being that from which the direct sources are themselves derived.

A. Directly Available Source of Energy (Potential).

Fuel.—Under this term are embraced all substances used in the working of machines, whether these machines be animal, vegetal, physical, or chemical. One instance may suffice by way of illustration.

Given the elementary substances, carbon (C), hydrogen (H), and oxygen (O), it is possible, by the expenditure of a certain amount of kinetic energy in a manner which we shall have to consider later on, to build up a complex substance known as grape-sugar. Grape-sugar is a store of potential energy, for by the expenditure of kinetic energy in its formation, the atoms of carbon, hydrogen, and oxygen have obtained potential energy, because their chemical affinities are only partially satisfied (p. 20). It is found that in a molecule of grape-sugar there are six atoms of carbon, twelve of hydrogen, and six of oxygen, which chemists tell us are probably related to one another in the following manner :—

$$\begin{array}{cccccc} H & H & H & H & & \\ | & | & | & | & & \\ H-C-C-C-C-C-C-H \\ | & | & | & | & | & | \\ O & O & O & O & O & O \\ | & | & | & | & | & | \\ H & H & H & H & H & H \end{array}$$

the atoms of carbon being linked to each other, and to the hydrogen atoms. But the affinity of the carbon and hydrogen for oxygen is far greater than that of carbon for carbon, or carbon for hydrogen ; therefore, when grape-sugar is burnt or decomposed in the living body, every atom of carbon and of hydrogen immediately quits its former connection and links itself firmly to oxygen, producing in consequence a series of molecules of much simpler composition, known as carbonic acid and water, the excess of oxygen required being obtained from the atmosphere. The potential energy of the grape-sugar becomes transformed mainly into heat

B. Directly Available Sources of Energy (Kinetic).

From a purely biological point of view these sources are not of very great importance.

1. **Tides.**—Tides are sources of potential energy four times in the twenty-four hours, becoming kinetic at ebb and

flow. Tidal motion is a source of energy little used, although in many cases there seems to be no feasible objection to its employment.

2. **Ordinary water-power and falling bodies in general.**—This source of energy has been employed from very ancient times. The possession of potential energy by water depends on its being at an elevation, and its transformation into kinetic energy on its being allowed to fall or flow to a lower level. An undulating or mountainous country will be, therefore, a country with the greatest available water-power, not only on account of the many differences of level, but also on account of the greater rainfall in a mountainous country, and consequent greater absolute supply of water. The energy available by the fall of water from a height is of the same nature as that available by the fall of solids, for example, various forms of hammer, clock-weights, &c.

3. **Wind currents.**—Universally employed as a motive power in navigation, mills, &c., but a source of energy not always to be depended upon, and often adverse to the furtherance of the object for which it is wanted.

4. **Water currents.**—Ocean currents are, under certain circumstances, useful as an assistant motive power; whilst river currents are not infrequently employed for the carriage of material to the sea, e.g. the carriage of wood on the St. Lawrence.

5. **Hotsprings, volcanoes, and earthquakes.**—These sources, although prodigious in amount, in addition to being only locally developed, and in regions where their energy is, as a rule, not wanted, are so utterly unreliable, that they may be left out of account entirely, at least until a method of transforming their energy, by storage or otherwise, into reliable forms be discovered.

C. INDIRECTLY AVAILABLE SOURCES OF ENERGY (KINETIC).

1. **Gravity.**—The law of gravity has been already stated at page 7, and it is in virtue of that attractive force that we are able to make use of such directly available sources of energy as some of those already mentioned, e.g. tides, ordinary water-power, falling bodies, &c.

2. **Solar radiation.**—This is the first of the two great sources of energy looked at from a biological point of view. Its relation to plant and animal life will be discussed in detail afterwards. At present we need only direct attention to the irregular heating of the atmosphere by the sun's rays in relation to the formation of winds and of ocean currents. Its influence on the evaporation of water, &c. may also be specially noted.

3. **The rotation of the earth on its axis** causes changes in the direction of the atmospheric and oceanic currents, and thus, in conjunction with solar radiation, may be said to be the cause of them.

4. **The earth's internal heat.**—In accordance with the nebular hypothesis, now almost universally accepted in some form by physicists, the earth's internal heat is the residuum of the heat it possessed in its originally molten condition. It manifests itself chiefly in the forms referred to under the fifth heading of the class of kinetic energies entitled 'directly available.' It is a source of energy which must manifestly become gradually exhausted as the age of the earth increases.

5. **Chemical affinity.**—This is to be considered as the second of the two great sources of the energy of living things, and on that account merits fuller treatment.

We have already defined a chemical element as a substance homogeneous in itself, i.e. whose atoms are all of one kind. It has been already stated, that there are about seventy such elements at present known (footnote, p. 9). A compound has also been defined as composed of two or more elements. A distinction must be carefully drawn between a compound and a mixture. In a compound each element, or constituent, loses its own peculiar characters, whilst in a mixture each constituent retains its own characters. Thus, for example, hydrogen is a colourless, tasteless, odourless gas, extremely light and inflammable, and possessed also of certain other chemical peculiarities that do not require to be specialised here. Oxygen is also a colourless, odourless, tasteless gas, sixteen times as heavy as hydrogen, not inflammable, but a supporter of combustion. If certain definite quantities of these two gases be mixed in a vessel, it is found that the hydrogen in the vessel still retains all the properties of hydrogen, and the oxygen all the properties of oxygen. If, however, a light be applied to the mixture, an explosion immediately takes place, both gases disappear as such, and in their place is left a compound gas, water vapour, which on analysis is found to contain exactly the same amount of hydrogen and oxygen which went to form the mixture, but which differs entirely in properties from either of its constituents. The force which tends to bring about this union is known as the force of **chemical affinity**, and is one of the most important sources of energy known to us. It may be defined in the following terms :—the force which tends to make certain chemical elements or compounds unite with certain other elements or compounds in definite proportions, so as to lead to the formation of a new substance, or substances, with different properties from those of the individual constituents.

The original position of separation of the constituents of a compound, previous to combination, is energy of position, or potential energy. The supply of an equal amount of energy to that given off at decomposition is necessary to effect recombination.

Chemical combination, as a form of kinetic energy, is of course always attended by the evolution of heat, or other manifestations of energy resolvable ultimately into heat.

SECTION III.—CLASSIFICATION OF CHEMICAL COMPOUNDS.

The degree of chemical affinity between elements or compounds varies with the elements or compounds under consideration. For example, the affinity between carbon and oxygen is much greater than that between carbon and hydrogen; hence the potential energy in the separation of carbon and oxygen atoms is greater in amount than that in the separation of carbon and hydrogen atoms. There is a marked corresponding difference in the firmness of the resulting compounds. Indeed, it is possible to arrange the various, almost innumerable, chemical compounds in a long chain or series, beginning at the one end with those that require the expenditure of an enormous amount of energy to bring about their decomposition, and ending with those that can scarcely be got to hold together at all, that indeed require a constant expenditure of energy to make them do so. The former may be known as **stable** and the latter as **unstable** compounds. The classification is a useful one, but is one in which, as in most natural classifications, no hard-and fast line of demarcation can be drawn between the two classes.

Generally speaking, the more complex a compound is, that is to say, the greater the number of atoms entering into its composition, the more unstable it is, and the fewer the number of atoms in a compound the more stable it is; soda, water, carbonic acid, iron-rust, and such like, are examples of simple compounds, containing from two to five atoms each; whilst the majority of the unstable compounds contain twenty, fifty, a hundred, or more atoms. Hæmoglobin, the red colouring matter of blood, the most complex compound known, is said to contain no fewer than 1,897 atoms ($C_{600}H_{960}N_{154}Fe\,S_3O_{179}$).

The more complex unstable compounds are chiefly formed as products of the vital processes, and are found associated for the most part with living organisms. They have, therefore, been termed **organic**. Similarly, owing to the fact that the simple stable compounds are found, as a rule, in the outside world, and in great measure independent of living things, they have been termed **inorganic**.

The general tendency of elements is to unite to form, and of complex compounds to decompose into, simple stable compounds.

Section IV.—Laws of Chemical Change.

The chemical changes taking place in an organism are of three types, **synthesis, isomeric change**, and **decomposition**.

1. By **synthesis** is understood the building up of compounds out of elements, or out of simpler compounds, in obedience to their several chemical affinities.

2. **Isomeric change** frequently occurs in the plant and animal organism, and consists in the rearrangement of the atoms of a compound. Hence we have to distinguish between the composition and the constitution of a compound, i.e. between simply the number and nature of the atoms, and the relation of the atoms to one another.

3. **Decomposition.**—A compound is decomposed when (*a*) the complex molecule breaks up into two or more simpler molecules, the sum of the atoms in all of which is identical with the sum of those in the original molecule. Thus grape-sugar, when subjected to a certain treatment, decomposes or **dissociates** into two molecules of alcohol and two molecules of carbonic acid.

(*b*) By **dehydration**, or the separation of a certain number of atoms of hydrogen and oxygen in the form of molecules of water, some complex substances are reduced to simpler forms.

(*c*) Similarly, the addition of one or more molecules of water—**hydration**—may cause a complex molecule to resolve itself into several molecules, each having a simpler composition than that of the original molecule.

(*d*) Undoubtedly the commonest mode of decomposition is **oxidation**, that is to say, the constant tendency of the constituent atoms of complex molecules to give up their weaker affinities, and to unite with free or loosely combined oxygen. All the changes taking place in decaying vegetal or animal matter are dependent, more or less, on the oxidation and removal of the several constituents of the decaying substance in the form of carbonic acid, water, and other simple compounds. The principle at the bottom of disinfection is the supply of a large quantity of free or loosely combined oxygen which is available for the oxidation and rendering harmless of putrescent and injurious matter.

(*e*) **Deoxidation**, or the withdrawal of oxygen, is of much rarer occurrence, but does take place in certain cases.

Instances of these actions in plenty will present themselves to us as we proceed. They are omitted here, as they would otherwise be the means of introducing a larger number of new terms than it would be possible to pause to explain at this stage.

By way of recapitulation, we may classify chemical compounds in the following manner:—

Simple	Complex
Stable	Unstable
Inorganic	Organic
Found in the environment	Found in the organism

It must be borne in mind, however, that these different groups flow into one another, and are by no means perfectly distinct. A few illustrations will make this sufficiently clear.

Water is a simple compound; it is stable, and it is found in by far the greatest abundance in the inorganic environment, but it constitutes ninety-three per cent. of the turnip, for example, among vegetals, and forms about seventy per cent. of the weight of the human body. Salts of potash, lime, and soda, common salt, and other substances found in the environment in prodigious quantities, are nevertheless present in the organism in no insignificant amount. So also many oils and carbohydrates (or compounds of carbon, oxygen, and hydrogen), although probably the result of vital processes in some bygone period in the world's history, are nevertheless found existing abundantly, undecomposed, in the environment.

Many comparatively simple compounds are extremely unstable, such for instance as the compound known as iodide of nitrogen, which, although it consists of only four atoms, explodes at once on being touched. Many other examples will be noted in the sequel.

CHAPTER II.

PROTOPLASM.

SECTION I.—CHEMICAL COMPOSITION OF PROTOPLASM.

Protoplasm, the 'physical basis of life,' the granular transparent viscous substance present in all living things, and without which no life is possible, may be defined chemically as an immensely complex compound, or mixture of compounds, yielding on analysis [1] simpler chemical derivatives, which may be classified under the following heads :—

A. Proteids and albuminoids, containing carbon, hydrogen, oxygen, nitrogen, sulphur, phosphorus, and a variable amount of ash.

B. Amyloids or carbohydrates, containing the elements, carbon, hydrogen, and oxygen.

C. Fats, with a similar composition.

D. Water in large quantity.

E. Inorganic salts.

F. Many bodies which are regarded as stages in the formation or decomposition of protoplasm.

All these substances are of the highest importance in a study of biology, and we shall therefore devote some time to their discussion.

[1] The process of analysis consists in (1) desiccation, i.e. drying without combustion, removing all volatile matters, and leaving only non-volatile substances; (2) combustion or calcination, which by oxidation, dissociation, &c., removes all combustible bodies and leaves a mineral, incombustible ash.

A. **Proteids and albuminoids.**—Generally speaking, these are substances of unknown constitution, but with a percentage composition, varying in round numbers

	C	H	N	O	S
from	51	7	15	21	·5
to	55	7·5	16·5	23 5	2

They are all incapable of being crystallised. They are soluble in water, or at least swell up in it. When treated with nitric acid (HNO_3), they take on a yellow colour. They are decomposed by the acid, and the yellow deposit, or precipitate, formed dissolves into an orange-red solution on the addition of a solution of ammonia (NH_3H_2O). Polarised light is turned to the right when passed through a solution of a proteid.

Proteids may be divided into two chief classes— (*a*) **albumins** and **globulins**, which are distinguished from (*b*) **albuminates**, by the fact that when subjected, in solution, to a temperature of over 73° C. they are coagulated or rendered solid, whilst albuminates are not so affected. Albumins, moreover, are soluble in cold water, whilst globulins are not, unless some neutral salt be added, e.g. common salt (NaCl). It is from these two groups of substances that most of the proteid matter of the animal and vegetal worlds is derived. As examples of animal albumins may be mentioned egg-albumin, or white of egg, and serum-albumin, or the albumin found in the fluid portion of blood, whilst the main constituent of vegetal protoplasm is vegetal albumin.

Of globulins, myosin, the chief constituent of muscle, and glutin, which enters largely into the composition of seeds, may be taken as examples.

Casein, the chief constituent of milk in the animal world, and the principal source of nourishment in beans, peas, &c., may be given as illustrating the class of albuminates. The albumins become changed into albuminates if treated with an acid or an alkali, and receive the names of acid-albuminates and alkali-albuminates according to the nature of the agent employed to bring about the alteration.

Albuminoids very closely resemble proteids in general appearance and in chemical composition, save that some albuminoids contain no sulphur. They differ, however, in one point; they cannot be made use of by animals as food, on account of their sparing solubility in water and in the comparatively weak acids and alkalies of the organism. As examples may be mentioned mucin, the substance which gives the viscidity to saliva, gelatin, a familiar commercial product, and keratin, the chief constituent of horn, hoof, nail, hair, and such like.

B. **Amyloids** or **carbohydrates.** — These substances, when compared with the group of proteids, are comparatively simple in their chemical composition. They consist of the three elements—carbon, hydrogen, and oxygen, the hydrogen and oxygen being present in the same proportion as that in which they occur in water, i.e. two atoms of hydrogen to one of oxygen. The large amount of carbon and hydrogen in their composition gives them their name of carbohydrates, whilst a synonym of starch, viz. amylum, which is one of the chief carbohydrates, accounts for the term amyloid as applied to them. They are sweet to the taste, e.g. sugar, or are capable of being converted into sugar by treatment with a weak acid, or certain other substances found in the plant and animal organism. In addition to ordinary sugar and starch, glycogen or animal starch, milk sugar or lactose, muscle sugar or inosite, may be cited as examples of carbohydrates found in the animal world.

C. **Fats and fatty acids.**—These substances are closely allied in chemical composition to carbohydrates, from which they are partly derived. They are also largely formed by a transformation of proteids. They contain carbon, hydrogen, and oxygen, usually in the form of more complex molecules than those of the carbohydrate group. Their general characters are well known. When acted on by an alkali or superheated steam,[1] they take up water (hydration) and decompose into glycerin and their corresponding fatty acids (dissociation), which unite with the alkalies to form soaps. The chief neutral fats are palmitin, the chief constituent of palm oil ('railway grease'), olein, the principal component of olive oil, and stearin, of which beef and mutton fat mainly consists.

The fatty acids comprise a series of bodies which occur chiefly in combination with glycerin to form the neutral fats above mentioned, and with alkalies to form soaps. A number of them will call for special mention afterwards; at present it will be enough to refer to the fatty acids of the neutral fats, i.e. palmitic, stearic, and oleic acids.

D. **Water** (H_2O) is the chief mineral constituent of both plants and animals. It often forms a very large proportion by weight of the organism, constituting over 80 per cent. by weight of the kidney, and over 90 per cent. of many succulent plants, e.g. turnip. The well-known 'jelly-fish' of our seas are composed almost entirely of water, a mere film of solid matter being left after desiccation. Some parts of the organism contain very little water, as for example the enamel of the teeth, where it is present in the proportion of only 0·2 per cent.

E. **Salts.**—The chief inorganic salts are the chlorides, phosphates, carbonates, and sulphates of soda, lime, potash, and magnesia. Salts of iron, manganese, and other metals, also occur. These will call for special mention subsequently.

F. **Transition substances formed in the integration and disintegration of protoplasm.**—The nature and significance of these bodies cannot with advantage be treated of before a discussion of the chemical changes taking place in the organism during growth and decay. One or two

---

[1] I.e. steam treated under pressure to a temperature above 212° F.

examples of these transition-substances which are more commonly known may be given, e.g. urea, a nitrogenous derivative excreted by the kidney, bile-acids, ammonia, and various ammoniacal salts, tannin, wax, and many vegetal acids and alkaloids.[1]

Section II.—Morphology and Physiology of Protoplasm.

Protoplasm (πρῶτος 'first,' πλάσμα 'formed substance'), when examined in large quantity by the naked eye, appears as a colourless, more or less transparent jelly. In nature it however occurs much more frequently subdivided into extremely minute pieces, resembling each other in general structure and appearance. To study these separate particles, or **cells** as they are termed, high magnifying powers of the microscope are required. When so examined protoplasm is found to consist of a clear, glassy, or finely granular soft substance, in which there is frequently to be distinguished an outer layer or **ectoplasm**, always more transparent than the inner, more granular **endoplasm**. In consistence protoplasm varies very greatly.

In intimate structure it consists of a homogeneous portion or matrix in which are imbedded granules (fig. 1). Minute droplets of water also occur (more abundantly in plant than in animal protoplasm), which go by the name of

[1] It is to be distinctly understood that a memory-knowledge of the characters of the substances entering into the composition of protoplasm is of little value, unless coupled with a practical knowledge gained by actual observation and experiment in the laboratory. This synopsis of the characters of proteids and other organic compounds is intended for reference. It is suggested that one or two of the most striking peculiarities of the substances, once seen, should be kept in mind, and that the other characters should be learnt gradually and unconsciously as familiarity with the substances themselves is obtained. That knowledge consists in being able to repeat a list of peculiarities by heart is one of the most mischievous delusions of modern education.

vacuoles. There may be one or more vacuoles in each cell; indeed, in very many vegetal cells there is more of vacuole than protoplasm (fig. 4 c). Vacuoles are probably reservoirs for substances used in the manufacture of protoplasm or for products of its disintegration. After treatment with certain reagents, or in some cases without such treatment, the protoplasmic matrix is found to be composed of a sponge-like arrangement of threads or fibrillæ (fig. 2) interlacing with one another and forming a supporting framework, while the interstices are filled with a more fluid homogeneous sub-

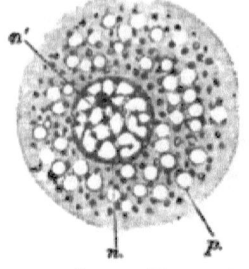

FIG. 1.—DIAGRAM OF AN ANIMAL CELL MUCH MAGNIFIED. (Schäfer.)

p, protoplasm, with vacuoles and granules : *n*, nucleus, with intranuclear network and nucleolus (*n'*).

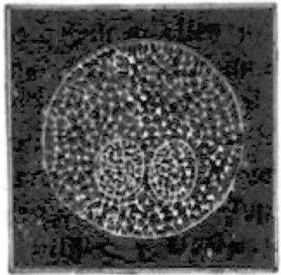

FIG. 2.—DIAGRAM OF AN ANIMAL CELL WITH TWO NUCLEI AND SHOWING INTRACELLULAR AND INTRANUCLEAR NETWORKS. (Klein.)

stance. Most recent investigators into the minute structure of protoplasm agree in thinking that the homogeneous matrix above alluded to corresponds to the interfibrillar matter, whilst the knots on the network, as well as the fibrillæ themselves when seen end-on, furnish the granular appearance. True granules are, however, also found in the interfibrillar matter itself.

In the great majority of cells, generally near the centre, is to be found an oval or rounded, rarely irregular, body termed the **nucleus** (fig. 1). It is usually inclosed in a definite nuclear wall or envelope. Like the cell itself the nucleus consists of a fibrillar network and an interfibrillar substance.

Protoplasm. 31

In consequence the nucleus presents the appearance, under a low magnifying power, of a homogeneous matrix with scattered granules (fig. 2).

Usually one or more granules of larger size are to be distinguished in the nucleus to which the name of **nucleoli** has been given, some of which are probably knots on the intranuclear network.

A mass of protoplasm possessed of these morphological characters may be 'naked' or without a cell-wall, and in that condition has a more or less irregular outline (fig. 3),

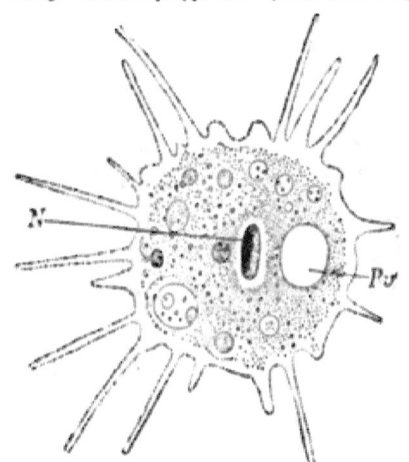

FIG. 3.—*Amœba polypodia.* (Max Schultze.)

N, nucleus ; *Pv*, contractile vacuole.

or it may be inclosed in a definite envelope or **cell-wall,** composed of substances formed from the protoplasm. Most cells when first formed are 'naked.' They may remain so during their whole existence, or they may become enveloped by a cell-wall of variable thickness and form. The cell-wall is much more extensively developed in the plant than in the animal organism (fig. 4).

Physiology of protoplasm.—Protoplasm and the various structures differentiated from it may be considered, however, from another point of view.

It is found that all cells undergo certain changes during their existence—changes concomitant with the phenomena known popularly as growth, reproduction, decay, and death

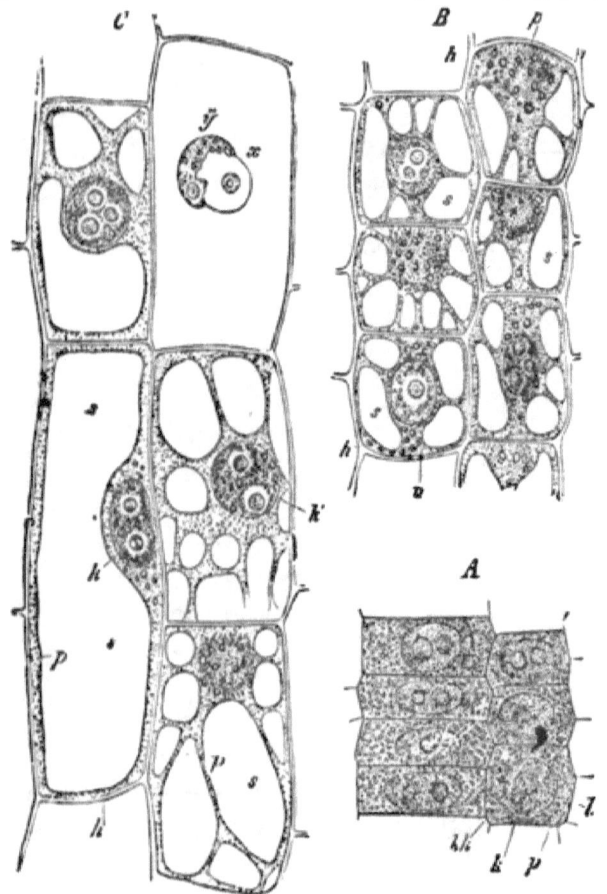

FIG. 4.—CELLS FROM THE ROOT OF *Fritillaria imperialis* (× 550). (Sachs.)

A, very young cells from near apex; B, from 2 mm. above the apex; C, from about 8 mm. above the apex. *h*, cell-wall; *p*, protoplasm; *k*, nucleus; *k k*, nucleoli; *s*, vacuoles and cell-sap cavity.

—changes in which the protoplasm and its modifications play different parts, perform different duties or **functions**.

The performance of any function, i.e. the doing of any work, as already fully explained (Chapter I., section ii), involves the expenditure of a certain amount of energy. Protoplasm, in virtue of its being composed of a number of very complex and unstable compounds, constitutes a large store of potential energy. In consequence of the transformation of part of this potential energy into kinetic energy the various functions of protoplasm come to be performed ; in other words, the various functions of protoplasm are manifestations of kinetic energy. In the expenditure of energy the complex compounds become broken down into simpler compounds and often into elements ; hence the presence of so many transitional substances and simple compounds in the chemical composition of protoplasm. We have now to consider what these functions are, and for that purpose we will consider a naked cell, such as that represented at fig. 3.

We note first that it possesses **contractility**—that is to say, that it is capable of motion as a whole or in certain parts. Protoplasmic motion may be definite or indefinite. **Indefinite motion** consists in the protrusion and withdrawal of finger-like prolongations of protoplasm from any region. The term **pseudopodium** is applied to such a projection, and the motion itself is usually known as **amœboid motion**, from its being specially developed in an extremely simple animal organism known as *Amœba*, the discussion of whose characters will occupy us later on. The mass of the protoplasm may follow the pseudopodium, and locomotion of the cell be effected. **Definite motion**, or motion always in one and the same direction, occurs only in cells which are more differentiated than those we are at present discussing (e.g. muscle). Reference to definite motion is, therefore, postponed.

Again, protoplasm is **irritable**—that is to say, if a stimulus be applied to the mass, such as a shock of electricity, an application of gentle heat, or certain chemical substances the protoplasm responds, shows irritability or excitement, local or general. For example, a shock of electricity immediately produces a general contraction and drawing in of all pseudopodia, amounting, if the shock be a strong one, to actual paralysis and death.

Motion, however, seems in many cases to be produced independently of external stimulus, and to arise as a consequence of some internal chemical changes taking place, not, as in the previous case, in response to stimuli, but automatically. Protoplasm is said, therefore, to possess **automatism**.

Other stimuli than those mentioned produce local irritability and motion of a peculiar kind. Contact with solid particles produces a movement of the neighbouring protoplasm, and results in the engulfing of the particles into the viscous mass by the protrusion of pseudopodia which surround and inclose them. The food-particles thus inclosed undergo certain changes in the interior of the cell during a species of circulation which they experience in its mass—changes which result in the absorption, alteration, and preparation of the particles into compounds from which new protoplasm is integrated—changes which are no doubt brought about by the chemical action of certain substances present in, and formed from, the protoplasm. In consequence of this power of absorbing or ingesting food particles the protoplasm is said to possess the power of **assimilation**. These primary changes are followed by others of a more complicated nature, in virtue of which new protoplasm is integrated or built up. It will be convenient to designate all chemical changes taking place in the organism as **metabolic** changes; changes concerned in the building up of protoplasm will therefore constitute **constructive metabolism** or **anabolism**; whilst the changes which take place in the decomposition of protoplasm may be termed collectively **destructive metabolism** or **katabolism**. The products of anabolism and katabolism will therefore be naturally termed **anastates** and **katastates** respectively.

The destructive changes to which protoplasm, when formed, becomes at once liable, result in the production of two sets of substances (*a*), **secretions**, and (*b*), **excretions**, which may be known therefore by the general name of katastates. Both series are chemical compounds, much simpler as a rule in their composition than protoplasm itself, but differing from each other in one important point, viz. that secretions are themselves necessary for the anabolism of food matters, whilst excretions are bodies which are useless and injurious to the organism, and must ultimately be got rid of. Excretions include not only the products of the katabolism of the protoplasm, but also of the secretions after they have performed their functions. They likewise include those portions of the food-material taken into the organism which are useless from a nutritive point of view.

It has been already pointed out that decomposition consists chiefly in the oxidation of the constituent atoms of the complex molecules. Further, on reference to the average composition of proteids (p. 26), it will be seen that carbon is by far the most important and abundant constituent. Manifestly, therefore, oxidation in the cell must mean chiefly oxidation of carbon and formation of carbonic acid (CO_2), the most abundant and most stable oxide of carbon known. Katabolism must, therefore, be accompanied by a plentiful production of carbonic acid, the process of excretion of which is known by the special term of **respiration**.

In addition to these changes, there are others which result in the separation of part of the protoplasm to form a young cell or cells. **Vegetative multiplication** and **reproduction** are the terms applied to such changes ; the discussion of both is, however, postponed for the present.

SECTION III.—PHENOMENA CONCOMITANT WITH MANIFESTATIONS OF ENERGY BY LIVING PROTOPLASM.

Having considered the various manifestations of energy in living protoplasm—viz. contractility, irritability and automatism, reception and assimilation of food, metabolism, secretion, excretion, and respiration—we have now to glance at the general result of these changes on the protoplasmic mass as a whole.

Commencing at any given moment in the life of a cell, we may find one of three things happening. In the first place, the chemical substances assimilated and undergoing constructive metabolism may be just equal in amount to the sum of the compounds used up in the concomitant destructive metabolism. In the second place, the amount assimilated and absorbed may be greater than the amount expended. Or thirdly, destructive metabolism may be in excess of constructive metabolism. In the first case the protoplasmic mass will be at a standstill—it will neither increase nor decrease in size; in the second case it will grow; in the third case it will diminish in size and decay.

Growth is accompanied usually by differentiation of parts or **development**. Development may be either morphological or physiological or both, and consists in the gradual adaptation of special parts to the performance of special functions.

Decay is generally ended more or less abruptly by **death** or the cessation of the various manifestations of energy; no doubt in consequence of a failure on the part of one or other of the functions already mentioned, and the consequent impossibility of maintaining a sufficient store of potential energy on which to draw for the performance of the various functions of the cell. As is to be expected, death is almost always followed by a general breaking down of the complex molecules through the unrestrained play of the laws of decomposition.

We have seen in the simple case which we have used as an illustration that the various functions were all performed by one cell. In other words, while we had physiological differentiation we had complete, or almost complete,[1]

---

[1] It is probable that the vacuoles may perform excretory functions (p. 73).

morphological non-differentiation. Every part of the cell is capable of taking in food-particles, the excreta being also ejected at any point. Emission of carbonic acid or respiration takes place over the surface generally, and so on.

By far the majority of plants and animals are, however, made of vast multitudes or collections of cells, some of which are specially differentiated to perform one function, whilst others are differentiated to perform another. All the cells have the general characters we have already described as belonging to protoplasmic units, but while their other functions are in abeyance, some one function—it may be the power of contracting or of exhibiting responses to stimuli —is very highly developed. Collections of such similar cells are said to be specialised for the performance of one function. Naturally, also, their form and structure becomes correspondingly modified. Such cell aggregates are termed **tissues.** Thus we have muscular tissue, whose special function is that of contraction; nerve tissue, whose special function is that of showing irritability in response to stimuli or automatically; connective tissue, where the cells are modified to act as padding or as connecting links between other tissues, and so on. Moreover, it is conceivable that different parts of the plant or animal may contain more than one kind of tissue. Such parts are termed **organs**; hence the term organic as applied to chemical compounds found in the cells and tissues composing such organs, organised as applied to the plant or animal possessing such differentiation of parts, and organism used as a synonym for living thing.[1]

A reference was made (at p. 35) to the power which cells possessed of separating a part of themselves for the purpose of reproduction and multiplication. When the organism consists of a single cell, separation of, so far as we know, any

[1] It must be borne in mind, however, that these terms are applied to many plants and animals which cannot be said to possess tissues, much less organs.

part of the cell is all that is required to form the basis of a new individual. In the higher organisms, where cells are specialised and differentiated, there are certain cells whose sole function in the organism it is to produce other cells capable, under certain conditions, of undergoing development and growth, and of forming ultimately a new organism.

In the lower organisms reproduction takes place just previous to death, and consists, so to speak, in the saving of the last remains of the store of potential energy of the parent organism.

Section IV.—Physiological Significance of Chlorophyll.

Hitherto we have spoken of protoplasm in general, but it will have been noted that throughout reference was made to the existence of two varieties of that substance—**animal protoplasm** and **vegetal protoplasm**. So far as the morphology of protoplasm itself is concerned, the details of difference between the two forms will be more easily understood after examples of the animal and vegetal worlds have been examined. At present it behoves us to notice more especially the peculiarities of a substance which is present in by far the majority of plants, and which is characteristic in great measure of vegetal protoplasm. That substance is **chlorophyll**, to the presence of which in certain cells the familiar green colour of most plants is due. Chlorophyll (save in a few rare cases) is not found uniformly diffused through the protoplasm, but in the form of rounded or (more rarely) of stellate or ribbon-shaped masses, lying imbedded in the protoplasm. These are known technically as chlorophyll bodies. Chlorophyll bodies consist of a green pigment, chlorophyll itself, united in certain definite proportions with definite masses of protoplasm. The chlorophyll itself is small in amount and can be extracted from the protoplasm by alcohol, ether, and several other allied substances. The protoplasmic residue, or vehicle, remaining after the removal of the chlorophyll, is apparently not diminished in amount, but has a vacuolated or frothy appearance.

Chlorophyll bodies grow and multiply like cells, though, of course, they are not to be considered as cells morphologically. The growth and multiplication are due entirely to the activity of the protoplasmic vehicle. The chlorophyll bodies, of which there are usually a large number in each cell, are formed from the general protoplasm by a process of differentiation. In the chlorophyll bodies themselves secondary products of metabolism are often found. The most common of these is starch, which is present at first in small quantity, in the form of minute granules, but afterwards increases in amount until the whole chlorophyll body becomes transformed into a mass of starch. Droplets of oil and other substances are also not infrequently found in

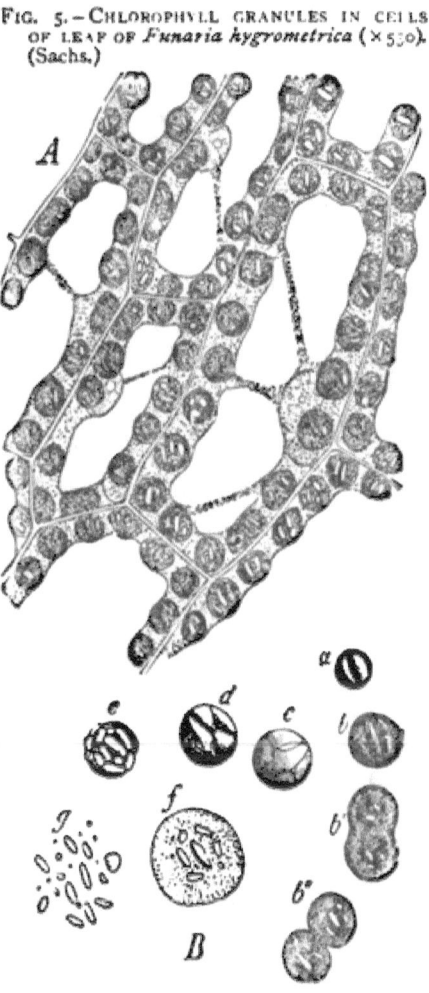

FIG. 5.—CHLOROPHYLL GRANULES IN CELLS OF LEAF OF *Funaria hygrometrica* ($\times 550$). (Sachs.)

A, granules of chlorophyll, with contained starch grains imbedded in the protoplasm of the cells; B, separated chlorophyll granules containing starch; a, b, young granules; b', b'', chlorophyll granules dividing; c, d, e, old chlorophyll granules; f, granule swollen up by action of water; g, starch granules remaining after chlorophyll has been destroyed by action of water.

the chlorophyll body. The significance of these changes in constitution will be discussed later on.

The percentage chemical composition of chlorophyll has been lately ascertained, and is as follows:—

Carbon	73·34
Hydrogen	9·72
Nitrogen	5·68
Oxygen	9·54
Phosphorus	1·38
Magnesium	0·34
	100·00

It has already been noted that in consequence of metabolic changes constantly taking place in organisms, large quantities of carbonic acid were continually being produced. Notwithstanding this fact, the quantity of carbonic acid in the atmosphere is tolerably nearly a constant quantity. The question immediately arises, What becomes of it? In brief terms it may be said that it forms the main constituent of the food of plants, although they themselves, in common with animals, excrete considerable quantities of it. Yet, generally speaking, the quantity they absorb is not only largely in excess of their own production, but balances the production of the same gas by the animal, on which it acts as a poison. Plants are able to make use of this gas as food in virtue of their possessing chlorophyll, which in presence of sunlight is capable of bringing about the assimilation of carbonic acid by vegetal protoplasm. It is evident, therefore, that chlorophyll is a substance of the very highest importance, not only in the vegetal economy but indirectly in the animal economy also.

Further, it is manifest that the absorption by the vegetal of large quantities of carbonic acid must mean the reception into the vegetal organism of an enormous amount of oxygen —far more than is necessary for the carrying on of the metabolic changes taking place in vegetal cells. As a matter of fact the oxygen is in great part given back into the atmosphere, in this manner keeping up that balance of gases in the atmosphere which is necessary for the maintenance of animal life.

Before the full bearing of these different phenomena can be seen it will be necessary to refer briefly to certain physical facts of the highest importance in the discussion of the relations of animal and vegetal protoplasm—firstly, to their inorganic surroundings, and, secondly, to each other.

SECTION V.—CONDITIONS OF THE ENVIRONMENT NECESSARY FOR THE MAINTENANCE OF LIFE IN ANIMAL AND VEGETAL PROTOPLASM.

A. **Composition of the atmosphere.**—An 'empty' room, 10 feet every way, contains 1,000 cubic feet of air, which, if dry and pure, is a mixture of nearly—

      790·2 cubic feet of nitrogen.
      209·4 ,, oxygen.
      0·4 ,, carbonic acid.

To such air the terms 'normal,' or 'fresh air' are applied. In addition to these, traces of other gases, such as ammonia (NH_3), and ammoniacal salts, carbonic oxide (CO) and certain other compounds of carbon. The atmosphere, moreover, always contains a certain proportion of water-vapour, which varies as is well known from day to day and from hour to hour. Normally it amounts to from 5 to 15 per cent.

If such a room be occupied by an animal, say an adult human individual, it will be found that after about two hours or so (provided there be no addition of fresh air), the atmosphere has become unbearable and highly injurious to life, from the presence in it of certain obnoxious gases. The alteration in the composition of the atmosphere is due to the addition to it of a large quantity of carbonic acid gas (and of other gases in less amount) produced in consequence of the metabolic changes taking place in the organism. Thus air expired from the lungs contains only 16 per cent. instead of 21 per cent. of oxygen, and $4\frac{1}{3}$ per cent. of carbonic acid instead of $\frac{4}{100}$ per cent. The amount of nitrogen remains unaltered. Expired air also contains traces of poisonous and fœtid organic matter, and a large amount of water-vapour. Such air is termed 'foul' air. If the atmosphere of such a room is to remain perfectly wholesome, about 20 cubic feet of fresh air per minute should be supplied for each individual in it.

Small as is the proportion of carbonic acid found in fresh air (only 4 volumes in 10,000), yet that proportion is amply sufficient for the supply of the carbon required by the vegetal economy; whilst if the proportion be increased beyond that amount, danger would ensue to animal life. The atmospheric conditions, therefore, necessary for the proper maintenance of animal and vegetal life are manifestly that the air should be pure and dry, with a proportion of carbonic acid present not over ·04 per cent.

We have hitherto considered the atmospheric conditions necessary for the maintenance of life in terrestrial plants and animals; we have now to glance at the conditions necessary for the maintenance of aquatic life.

No life of any kind could be possible under water were it not that all gases are soluble in water. The **solubility** of different gases, however, depends on—first, the temperature and pressure of the gas, and, secondly, the degree of inherent tendency of the gas to dissolve. The last, which is called the coefficient of absorption of the gas, varies very greatly. For example, at a temperature of 0° C., and under a barometric pressure of 760 mm. one volume of water will absorb, of—

Nitrogen	·02035 vols.
Oxygen	·04114 ,,
Carbonic acid	1·7967 ,,
Ammonia	1148·8 ,,

When a mixture of gases, such as air, is exposed to the action of a solvent such as water, the proportion of each gas absorbed will depend—first, on the coefficient of absorption of the gas, and, secondly, on the proportion of it present in the mixture, the temperature and pressure remaining constant. If the temperature vary, however, the amount of each gas absorbed will vary also, increasing as the temperature decreases, and decreasing as it increases. If the pressure vary, the amount of gas absorbed will be directly proportional to the pressure.

It will be seen that, owing to the very low coefficient of absorption of the three chief gases of the atmosphere, the total amount of the gases dissolved in water is very small indeed. Nevertheless, the oxygen present is sufficient for the maintenance of animal life, as the carbonic acid is sufficient to supply the carbon required by submerged plants. Ammonia, which we have cited as an instance of a gas with a very high coefficient of absorption, is present in such small quantity in the atmosphere that, notwithstanding its extreme solubility, the proportion present in water is quite trifling. Moreover, it is quickly licked out of the air by rain and carried down to the earth, where it at once enters into combination with other substances in the soil, to form ammoniacal salts, or becomes oxidised into nitric acid, this latter substance at once forming nitrates by combination with such bases as potash, lime, and soda. This 'nitrification' takes place also in the case of ammonia produced by decaying humus.

B. **Temperature.**—The extremes of temperature between which life is possible vary greatly according as it is vegetal or animal protoplasm that is under consideration. Generally speaking, life cannot be maintained in either kind of protoplasm under a continued exposure to a temperature of above 50° C., or below 0° C. In the case of certain extremely simple and minute organisms of doubtful affinities, and of the reproductive cells of certain groups of plants, these limits may be considerably extended, 100° C., or even 120° C., being insufficient to cause death.

Cold as a general rule retards, whilst gentle heat accelerates, amœboid and other protoplasmic movements. A species of coagulation, however, takes place if the temperature exceed 45° C.

C. Pressure.—The ordinary pressure of the atmosphere at the sea-level is about 14·73 lbs. on the square inch, which indicates the weight of a column of air of the same sectional area. Manifestly the atmospheric pressure will vary according to the height above the sea-level at which the observation is made. Atmospheric pressure also varies with the latitude and longitude, the temperature, the season of the year, and the hour of the day.

The total atmospheric pressure on the surface of the body of an average-sized human adult is about 14 tons, a pressure which is, however, equalised by the outward pressure of the air permeating the tissues. As a general rule, higher organisms are constructed so as to subsist under an atmospheric pressure not varying widely on either side of the average, viz. 30 in. or 760 mm. of the mercurial barometer. Many of the lower forms of life, however, can tolerate without injury a much higher pressure than that. With reference to aquatic, and more especially marine, animals the limits of pressure are much wider. Many fish, for example, live at a depth of from 300 to 2,000 fathoms, that is to say, they are capable of accommodating themselves to a pressure varying from one-half to two tons on the square inch. Fish living at greater depths must, of course, be subject to still greater pressures, amounting in some cases to as much as four-and-a-half tons on the square inch, always of course balanced by an equally great outward pressure of the water with which their tissues are permeated. These forms, when brought to the surface, are found to be greatly injured owing to the effect on their bodies of the removal of much of the external pressure at the surface.

D. **Light.**—(a) In relation to vegetal life, it has already been explained that the life of plants containing chlorophyll is entirely dependent on the action of light, inasmuch as the assimilation of carbonic acid is impossible without it. The higher metabolic processes can, however, go on equally well in darkness. It follows that while these processes are active in all parts of the plant, the assimilation of carbon takes place only in the parts which contain chlorophyll. Plants not containing chlorophyll, such as the parasitic fungi, are dependent on chlorophyll-bearing plants for the products of assimilation on which they subsist.

Sunlight, as is well known, is a mixture of a number of coloured rays. Sunlight may be readily resolved into its constituent coloured rays by passing it through a prism. In accordance with certain laws of optics, the light comes out of the prism at a different angle to its surface from that at which it enters. Moreover, each of the constituent coloured rays issues at an angle peculiar to itself. The rays are said, therefore, to be differently refrangible. The result is, consequently, that the broken-up ray of white light forms a band of colour known as the solar spectrum. The colours are red, orange, yellow, green, blue, indigo, and violet, and are arranged in that order. These colours merge gradually into one another; hence the term 'continuous' as applied to such a spectrum. The red, orange, yellow, and green are the rays of low refrangibility, while the refrangibility gradually increases through blue and indigo to the violet-end of the spectrum. There is abundant evidence to show that there are other rays, non-luminous, and therefore invisible, beyond the red rays on the one hand, and beyond the violet on the other.

It is found that these different rays have not all the same effect on vegetal life. For instance, the rays of low refrangibility are those concerned in the chemical changes in the plant, whilst mechanical changes are furthered by the rays at and beyond the violet end of the spectrum. It must be borne in mind in this relation that many chemical changes are furthered by the rays of high refrangibility. For example, the decomposition of silver salts in photography takes place under the influence of the violet rays of the spectrum. Probably special rays a l through the spectrum are capable of bringing about or influencing in some way or another special chemical changes, while only some (those beyond the red end of the spectrum) are capable of producing the sensation of heat, and others (the red and yellow) the sensation of light, in any appreciable degree.

In reference to the decomposition of carbonic acid by chlorophyll-bearing cells, it is found that the less refrangible rays are those through whose influence carbonic acid is decomposed and chlorophyll is produced, while the more refrangible rays have not that effect.

The influence of light on plants varies with its intensity. This subject is, however, still far from being thoroughly investigated, so that little may be said on this subject beyond the general statement that diffused daylight seems more suitable for the furtherance of plant life than direct sunlight, while assimilation ceases after sunset.

Manifestly this subject is closely connected with the depth to which the light penetrates into the plant tissues, since the light loses in intensity according to the thickness of the tissue through which it has passed. The rays of least refrangibility, that is to say those chiefly concerned in chemical changes in plants, are found to penetrate most deeply. The rays at the violet end of the spectrum are in great part absorbed by the chlorophyll and the colouring matters in the superficial cells. In regard to aquatic, and especially marine, plants, the depth to which light penetrates through water has to be considered. Experiments have shown that darkness prevails at all depths beneath 100 fathoms, and consequently that no vegetal life can exist beneath that depth, if, indeed, it ever exists so far.

(*b*) In regard to animal life, the presence or absence of

light seems to have little or no particular effect. Some animals live throughout their whole existence in darkness, and very many others in light so dim that they may be said to be practically independent of its influence altogether. The special luminosity known as phosphorescence, which many of these animals are themselves capable of producing, may in some part act as a substitute for sunlight.

E. **Food-supply.**—Since animals have no power of building up complex organic compounds out of simple inorganic materials, but are dependent directly or indirectly on the vegetal kingdom for their food, manifestly it is of the first importance for the maintenance of animal life that vegetals should have the means of nourishment in abundance and in an accessible form. The food of animals is extremely variable. Some animals are entirely herbivorous, others entirely carnivorous, while others still are omnivorous. It must be at once evident, in order that any group of animals may remain in existence, that a sufficient supply of that particular food on which they subsist should be available. In some cases that supply is extremely localised and small in amount. The larvæ of certain flies, for example. are dependent for the maintenance of their life on the larvæ of a particular species of bee.

The food materials required by plants are most easily determined by analysing the plant itself (p. 187). An examination of the products of desiccation, of calcination, and of the ash shows that the following elements are required for the maintenance of plant life :—

I. and chiefly,—carbon, hydrogen, oxygen, and nitrogen.

II. and less important,—sulphur, potassium, calcium, iron, magnesium, phosphorus, chlorine, sodium, and silicon.

The source of the carbon has already been sufficiently explained ; nitrogen is obtained by the plant from compounds of ammonia and nitric acid in the soil, and not as might have been expected from the enormous supply in the atmosphere; oxygen is obtained by the decomposition of water, carbonic acid, and oxy-salts; the source of the hydrogen is water, which is decomposed in the chlorophyll-bearing cells in presence of sunlight; sulphur is absorbed in the form of soluble salts or sulphuric acid; the other elements also are absorbed in the form of various salts from the soil or other medium in which the plant lives. The various sources of these different substances and the changes which they undergo in the plant organism will be dealt with more fully afterwards (p. 188). Reference is made to the subject at this point chiefly to show what are the main conditions of life in regard to food-supply.

In section iv it was pointed out that in consequence of the relationship of the plant world to carbonic acid and of the animal world to oxygen, a balance of gases was maintained in the atmosphere. Having now reviewed generally the condition of environment necessary for the maintenance of life, we shall be able to understand more readily the importance of the subject of gaseous balance in the air.

Section VI.—The Balance of Nature.

In explaining what is meant by the balance of nature it will be necessary to repeat certain statements already made, with the view of explaining the relationship in which they stand to each other.

We have seen that animals and plants or parts of plants not possessed of chlorophyll require organic compounds for their sustenance, as well as salts and water, the organic compounds being obtained directly or indirectly from the vegetal world. They remove oxygen from the atmosphere, and return carbonic acid with the evolution of energy; i.e. the solar energy originally stored in the organic compound manifests itself in the various phenomena of life, ultimately becoming dissipated as heat into space, the products of disintegration being at the same time returned to the inorganic world.

On the other hand we have seen that plants possessed of

chlorophyll are independent of organic compounds for their nutrition, since they seize the solar energy and use it to decompose the carbonic acid of the atmosphere. Oxygen is returned to the atmosphere, carbon is retained, and, uniting with the elements of water, is finally precipitated in the form of some comparatively simple organic compound. This being digested as required, and water, mineral matters, and nitrogen being obtained from the soil by the roots, the reintegration of new protoplasm is effected.

As explained in section iv., the same destructive metabolism exemplified by animals is also exhibited by plants, but masked in great measure by constructive metabolism where chlorophyll is present.

There is thus in the economy of nature a double balance :—

(1) **Between animal** and **vegetal life,** or more strictly between **colourless** and **green protoplasm** ; and (2) **between fresh** and **foul air,** or more strictly between **oxygen** and **carbonic acid.**

This subject is so important in Biology that it warrants repetition yet once more in the diagrammatic form appended beneath, which will be readily understood from the above remarks.

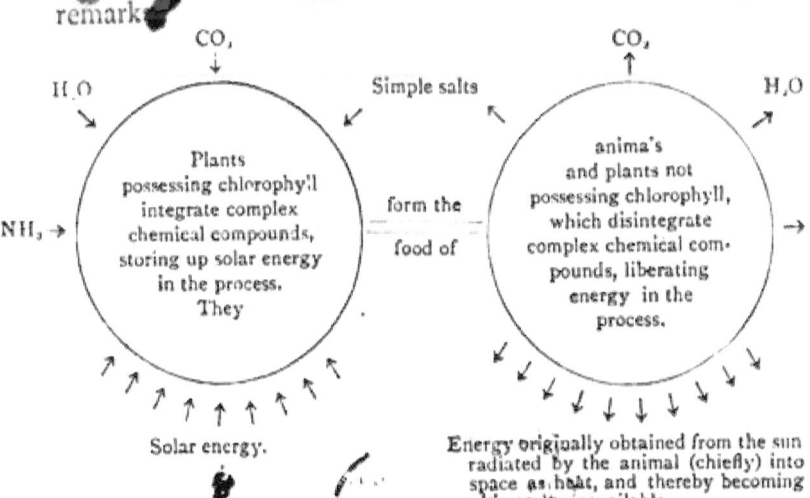

CHAPTER III.

INDIVIDUAL AND TRIBAL LIFE—DISTRIBUTION AND CLASSIFICATION.

SECTION I.—INDIVIDUAL LIFE.

THE transference of kinetic solar energy into potential energy stored in complex chemical compounds involves the necessity for the existence of collecting or preparing organs in the organism by and in which the food materials may be brought to it and elaborated for its use. These organs are technically called **organs of nutrition, alimentation, digestion,** or **assimilation.** Further, the food materials when prepared must be distributed to every part of the organism, hence the necessity for distributing organs or **organs of circulation.** The cells or ultimate constituents of the tissues to which the food materials are distributed then exercise a **selective action** on them, and new protoplasm is integrated, thus forming a store of potential energy in each individual cell. Liberation of this store of potential energy as kinetic energy is afterwards effected, manifesting itself in the various phenomena of life. The compounds are decomposed and the energy let loose by the action on the cells of a liberating energy from without, or in virtue of the property of automatism possessed by the cell itself. It still remains to be determined, however, how far automatism is dependent on, and influenced by, external changes not necessarily immediately precedent to the exhibition of automatism.

The ultimate results are seen in the various phenomena

of life, such as secretion, motion, nervation, &c., for the manifestation of which, special organs and tissues are set apart, as explained in section iii. Organs are consequently developed to fulfil these functions. The **muscular** or **contractile system** subserves the function of motion; some parts are specially adapted to **protect** the more delicate organs from external injury, whilst others are specially modified to act as a **supporting framework** to the same. Moreover, the **nervous system** with its accompanying sense organs, is that which is especially differentiated to receive and retain impressions from the external world, to regulate the due performance of the functions of the other systems, and generally, to instigate in the cells and tissues chemical changes which result in the several phenomena we have already considered. Lastly, it is necessary that certain organs should be set apart for the removal of the bye-products of the decomposition of complex compounds; these may be termed **purificatory organs.** Since it is manifest that the bye-products must consist either of solid, fluid or gaseous constituents, the purificatory organs will differ according as it is their function to remove solid, fluid or gaseous bye-products. The solid or fluid refuse matters are got rid of mainly by the **excretory** or **renal organs**, whilst the gaseous bye-products are removed chiefly by the **respiratory system.**

We have thus seen the individual to consist of a co-ordinated series of organs, or systems, each performing its own function, but all subservient to one end, viz. the proper maintenance of individual life.

We may arrange these organs and their functions in two parallel columns, thus :—

Morphology (structure).	Physiology (function).
A. Nutritive or alimentary system.	Nutrition.
B. Circulatory ,,	Circulation.
C. Purificatory ,,	Purification.
i. Renal (fluid &c. excreta)	i. Excretion.
ii. Respiratory (gaseous &c. excreta)	ii. Respiration.

Morphology (structure).—*cont.*	Physiology (function).—*cont.*
D Contractile system	Contraction—motion.
E. Supporting ,,	Support.
F. Protecting ,,	Protection.
G. Nervous ,,	Nervation.
Sense organs.	Sensation.

Section II.—Tribal Life.

The various systems we have already discussed are concerned entirely with the maintenance of individual life. One system present in the individual, however, we have yet to examine, viz. the **reproductive system**, which is concerned entirely with the maintenance of tribal life, i.e. the maintenance on the earth's surface of organisms of the same kind as that in which the special reproductive elements under consideration are developed.

Reproduction may be either **sexual** or **asexual**. **Asexual reproduction** consists in the separation of a part (usually a single cell) of the individual, which part is capable (without union with any other part) of becoming an adult organism like its parent.

By **sexual reproduction** is meant the production by the same or different individuals of two kinds of cells, one of which is known as the male cell (sperm or spermatozoon), the other as the female (ovum), the union of which results in a product (embryo) capable of forming, after it has passed through several developmental changes, an adult organism like one or other of its parents. It is worthy of note at this point, that the male reproductive cell is almost always in the animal, and very generally in the vegetal kingdom, an extremely minute and very active body, whilst the female cell in all cases (with a few exceptions in the very lowest forms) is comparatively large and immobile. After union with the male cell the female cell begins to undergo changes which are probably due to the instigating influence of the male cell. In other words, the female cell is a store of potential energy, while the male is a store of kinetic energy, which acts as a liberating energy on the female cell, permitting of the transference of its potential into kinetic energy.[1] In certain rare cases the female cell has the power of developing without previous union with the male cell. This is known as **parthenogenesis**.

These two methods of reproduction are usually conjoined, especially in the vegetal kingdom, save in very low forms of life, where, so far as we know, asexual reproduction alone exists. Sexual reproduction prevails more generally among the highest forms of life, especially in the animal world.

After **fertilisation** (as sexual union is termed) of the female cell by the male, the female cell may be considered as and styled an **embryo**. The embryo passes through a variety of stages, sometimes very extraordinary in their nature, before arriving at the adult condition. The history of these successive changes is termed its **ontogeny**, or individual life-history. It is, moreover, apparent that every organism must have a genealogy or tribal history in addition to its individual history. To the genealogical history the term **phylogeny** is applied.

As a result of the brilliant researches of biologists during the past century, amongst whom Lamarck, Geoffrey St. Hilaire, Hæckel, Darwin, and Wallace hold the first places, a definite relation has been established between these two histories. In an elementary text-book like the present, it would be entirely out of place to go into this subject with requisite detail; it will be sufficient to state briefly that there is abundant evidence to show that the **ontogeny of any organism is an epitome of its own phylogeny**, and that the various stages in its development indicate landmarks guiding us in the tracing of its genealogical history—each

---

[1] Probably the male cell at the same time brings to the female cell certain chemical compounds necessary for the further development of the ovum.

stage exhibiting, in a greater or less degree, a likeness to extinct or now existing organisms of a lower grade of organisation.

SECTION III.—DISTRIBUTION.

It may have been noted that in the preceding sections we have answered three out of the four questions which may be asked concerning every living thing. Morphology answers the question, What is it? Physiology answers the question, How does it live? Phylogeny answers the question, Whence came it? What was its origin? One query yet remains, Where is the organism found? An answer to that query is given by the section which treats of the **distribution** of organisms.

Any given group of animals may have a distribution in space, or a **geographical distribution**, and also a distribution in time, or a **geological distribution**. In the former case the habitat and distribution over the earth's surface of the members of the tribe is taken account of, in the latter, note is taken of the occurrence of remains of the same forms as fossils in the strata of the earth's crust.

SECTION IV.—CLASSIFICATION.

It has been already explained that organisms widely differ in the structure of their different organs. Hence we have varying degrees of likeness and unlikeness among organisms, and a starting-point is thus afforded us for classifying them. **Classification** consists essentially in the grouping together of like and the separation of unlike forms, not merely in their adult condition, but after taking into account their entire life-histories. Classifications may be either natural or unnatural. By an unnatural classification is meant one based on superficial or apparent resemblance, whilst a natural classification is one based, not only on accurate morphological investigation, but also on the story of relationship with other organisms told by ontogeny.

CHAPTER IV.

THE MORPHOLOGY AND PHYSIOLOGY OF THE SIMPLEST LIVING ORGANISMS—PROTISTA.

SECTION I.—PROTISTA—*PROTAMŒBA*.

IN the preceding chapters an account has been given of the main principles on which Biology is based, and of the chief aspects or ways of looking at the subject. We have in the chapters that follow to discuss the subject-matter of Biology, dealing with it in the manner already sketched out. We have seen that progress from lowly organised plants and animals to those of a higher grade in either kingdom, is marked by what we have termed 'differentiation of parts,' that is by the specialisation or setting aside of special organs, tissues, and cells in the organism for special duties the performance of which is necessary for the maintenance of individual and tribal life. It is natural that we should find that the lower we go in the scale of being the less differentiation we should meet with, until we ultimately arrive at forms that exhibit no structural or morphological differentiation at all, although they do show, as has been pointed out (at page 37), physiological differentiation, or division of labour. In order to understand rightly the principle of differentiation in the higher forms it is necessary that we should study the structure and life-history of one of the simplest types known to us. Such a form is that known as *Protamœba primitiva* (fig. 6). The utmost that can be said of it is that it is a microscopic speck of almost unmodified protoplasm, presenting at most a differentiation into a denser, more hyaline or glassy, outer layer or **ectosarc**, and a more fluid, and granular, inner portion or **endosarc**.[1] In form *Protamœba* is irregular, and varies from time to time, the ectosarc becoming produced into pseudopodia in consequence of changes taking place automatically in the organism, or in response to stimuli from without (page 34). The pseudopodia may vary in shape and size, being blunt or filamentous, and are capable of retraction. Frequently the pseudopodia, especially if filamentous, fuse with one another, forming a network, or a mass, at a little distance from the parent body (fig. 7).

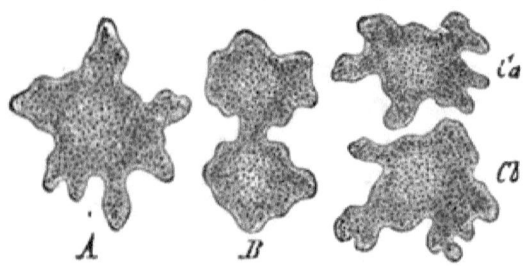

FIG. 6.—*Protamœba primitiva.* (Hæckel.)

A, before division ; *B*, in process of dividing ; *Ca* and *Cb*, two new individuals resulting from division.

The protrusion of a pseudopodium from the hyaline ectosarc is followed by the streaming into the pseudopodium of the granular endosarc. Locomotion is effected by the gradual movement of the entire body in the wake of a pseudopodium. Food-particles are taken into the protoplasm at any point, and the excreta, or indigestible and useless parts of the food, are extruded at any point. At a certain period in the life-history of *Protamœba* the protoplasm of the body becomes divided into two or more parts (fig. 6). The organism either separates into halves, either half receding from the other, or small portions of the mass are nipped off. These halves or smaller portions are capable of at once starting life on their

---

[1] These terms, ecto- and endo-sarc, must be carefully distinguished from the terms ecto- and endo-derm, mentioned at p. 220.

own account, engulfing food particles, exhibiting amœboid motion, and dividing just as in the case of the parent.

A simpler state of things than this could scarcely be imagined. Here we have morphological differentiation at

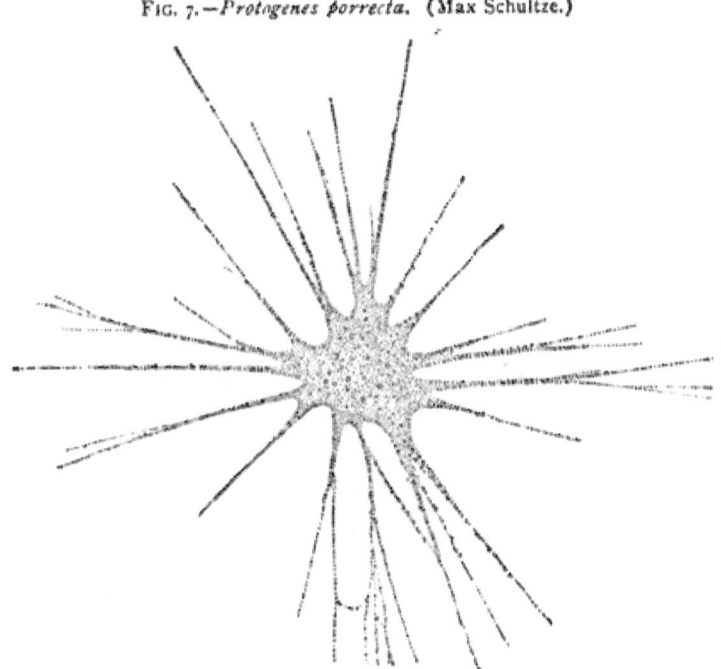

FIG. 7.—*Protogenes porrecta*. (Max Schultze.)

its lowest; whilst it is to be noted that all the various functions exhibited by higher forms are manifested by this exceedingly simple organism.

SECTION II.—PROTISTA—*PROTOMYXA*.

Closely allied to *Protamœba* we find another simple organism, with an even more instructive life-history.

Crawling over the shells of some dead molluscs in the Canary Isles, Hæckel found an organism, the study of whose structure and life-history has thrown a flood of light on the relationships of forms such as we are discussing to each other and to the higher plants and animals. That form Hæckel termed *Protomyxa aurantiaca* (fig. 8). *Protomyxa*

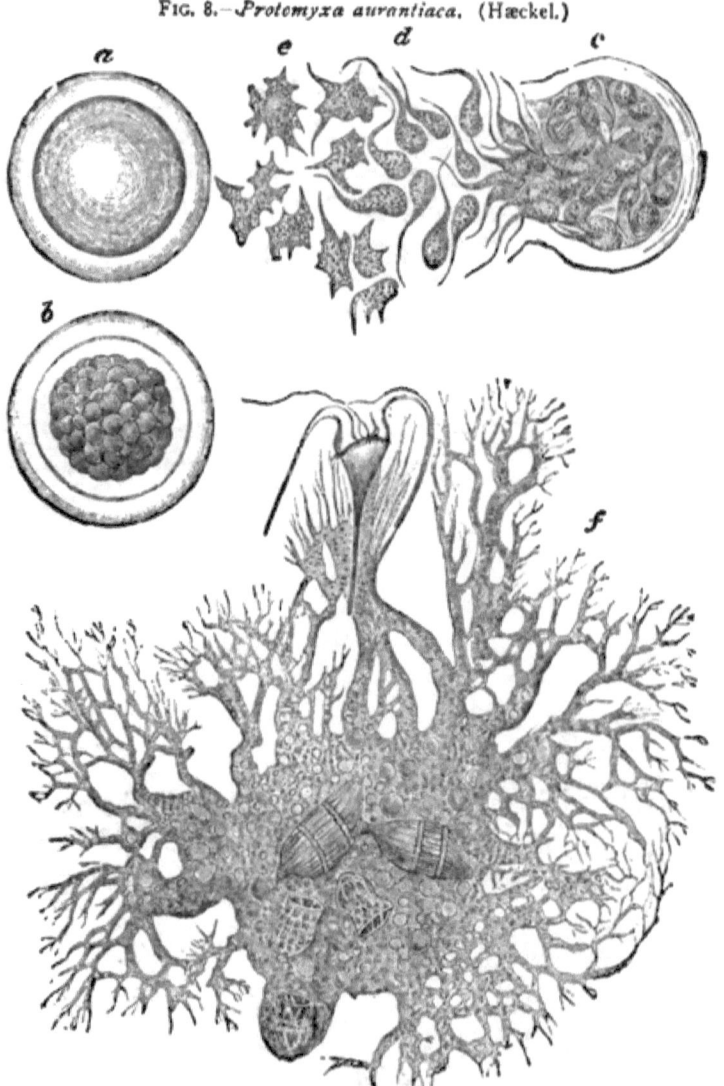

FIG. 8.—*Protomyxa aurantiaca.* (Hæckel.)

For explanation see text.

exhibits four very different stages in its life-history, each of which has a distinct significance.

At one period of its existence *Protomyxa* exists as a minute *Protamœba*-like creature (fig. 8*e*) possessing the general characters already described as possessed by that form. Numbers of these *Protamœba*-like bodies unite to form a large aggregation of protoplasm, to which the name of **plasmodium** is given (fig. 8*f*). The plasmodium behaves exactly like a large *Protamœba*, throwing out and retracting pseudopodia, engulfing food particles, &c. The individuals going to form a plasmodium cannot, however, be distinguished in its mass as individuals; their identity becomes lost. After a time, however, the plasmodium comes to rest and the pseudopodia are withdrawn. The mass collects into a round ball which soon becomes covered by a capsular investment or **cyst**; hence this stage is spoken of as the encysted stage (fig. 8*a*). Subsequently the protoplasm within the cyst becomes segmented or divided into distinct masses forming a mulberry-like bunch within the cyst (fig. 8*b*). Under certain conditions the cyst bursts and the separate protoplasmic masses escape (fig. 8*c*). Each unit is an actively moving pear-shaped mass of protoplasm, possessed of a fine flagellum or whip at the pointed end by the constant motion of which the little organism is propelled through the fluid medium. This motion is, however, transitory, for the flagellate mass speedily becomes more and more sluggish in its movements, and ultimately comes to rest, drawing in its flagellum and developing pseudopodia like those of the form we started with. Such are the stages in the life-history of this important type, and they are of sufficient interest to warrant more detailed treatment before we proceed to the consideration of higher forms.

In the first or **amœboid stage** we have to note especially the apparently exceeding simplicity of structure accompanied by complexity of function. In other words, we have in this stage complete physiological differentiation without corresponding morphological differentiation.

Passing to the second or **plasmodial stage**, we have

exemplified the union of a number of amœboid units after they have to a certain extent exhausted their store of energy by active motion. Evidence produced of late years tends to show that plasmodium formation, or the union of separate amœboid units, in other forms as well as in this, is an act intimately connected with reproduction. As explained above (p. 52), sexual reproduction consists in the union of a male with a female cell, followed by the development of the product of union into a new organism or organisms. Here we have union, not of two dissimilar cells, but of many more or less similar cells. Nevertheless there is evidence to show that the union, if it be not truly sexual in its nature, is, so far as we know at present, at least accompanied by several of the phenomena which characterise sexual union of cells. In other words, in the conjugation of the separate amœboid stages of this simple form we have probably the first appearance of sexual union in living things.

We have seen that the plasmodial stage is sooner or later followed by an **encysted** or **resting stage**, where the protoplasm contracts into a spherical mass, and becomes clothed by a capsule. In the period during which the protoplasm remains encysted, probably certain constructive molecular rearrangements are taking place in the protoplasm, which result in the revivifying or rejuvenescence of the mass, the energy of the various amœboid units originally entering into the formation of the plasmodium being, so to speak, concentrated. What meaning must we attach to the cyst? During active amœboid life carbonic acid and water were being abundantly excreted, as already explained. During the encysted stage, of course, the organism is still living, only the vital phenomena are not so actively manifested. There must, therefore, be a certain quantity of carbonic acid and water produced even then. What becomes of the excreta? During the active amœboid stage, owing to the constant motion and change of position of the different parts of the organism, the excreta escape easily into the surrounding medium; but during the resting stage, manifestly, the rapid escape of effete matter would not be possible. Hence the excreta would become more or less aggregated round the organism itself. The organism becomes, in other words, encrusted or enclosed by its own excreta. The fact that the cyst is at first wanting, then thin, and gradually becomes thicker, is thus explained. Further, when we examine into the chemical nature of the cyst we find it to be composed of a substance exceedingly common in the plant world, namely **cellulose**. Now, one of the most apparent physiological distinctions between animals and plants is, that while the power of motion is characteristic of the former it is not so of the latter. Hence we are not astonished to find that cellulose, which we have seen to be in some way associated with rest, is a substance of rare occurrence in the animal world; and that in those animals in which it, or some substance chemically allied, does occur the power of movement has been nearly or entirely lost.

Chemically, cellulose (which must be the subject of more careful consideration subsequently) is composed of carbon, hydrogen, and oxygen (the two latter in the proportion in which they occur in water). We have here the elements of carbonic acid and water, while the oxygen which the carbon has lost is probably used up in various concomitant chemical changes taking place in the encysted organism.

The first result of this temporary cessation of activity, represented by the encysted stage, is the formation of a store of energy (potential), which first manifests itself kinetically, under special circumstances, in the subdivision or **segmentation** of the protoplasm into masses, which by-and-by escape upon the rupture of the cyst (probably by internal pressure). The organisms which escape are actively motile masses of protoplasm, each provided with a flagellum by means of which motion is effected. Hence this may be known as the **flagellate stage**. As in the amœboid condition, it is possible, by the application of a gentle heat, to accelerate this motion, while excess of heat paralyses and kills the organism. After a time the flagellum is gradually withdrawn, the motion becoming slower and slower until the amœboid stage is again reached, and it becomes again necessary for the organism to take in a stock of food to make good the waste and enable it to remain in existence.

The importance of these four stages in the study of the interrelationships of the lower organisms, whether plant or animal, and indeed in a study of the physiology of the higher forms as well, cannot well be exaggerated. It will be necessary, however, to devote a special section to the discussion of the subject.

SECTION III.—THE RELATION OF UNICELLULAR TO MULTICELLULAR ORGANISMS.

On reviewing the multiplicity of forms which we meet with among the lowest plants and the lowest animals, together with those organisms which are doubtfully classified under either category, we soon discover that each and all live for a longer or shorter period of their existence in one or other of the four stages exemplified by the life-history of *Protomyxa*, while most, if not all, show some indication of a tendency to pass through a corresponding series of stages in their own life-histories. One, for example, lives during the greater part of its existence in the form of an encysted cell; but at another time, possibly only for an exceedingly short period, the protoplasm escapes from its cyst and becomes a motile flagellate organism. In other cases the plasmodium stage is the one emphasised. In many cases one or more stages of the general type of life-history (that of *Protomyxa*) are omitted, or slurred over very rapidly. Manifestly, if inquiry be made into the reason for this emphasising of some one stage, the explanation will be found in that adaptation of the organism to its environment which has already been discussed at some length in

Chapter II. section v. For instance, flagellate and amœboid motion are possible only in a liquid (water). If that were absent the protoplasm would dry up and shrivel, or the surface would become covered by a skin; in other words, encystation would take place. Those forms, therefore, which exhibit the complete life-history of *Protomyxa* are necessarily such as live in liquid media. It will be easily seen from this that the varying length in the duration of the several stages can be accounted for by the habits of the form in question, whether living all its life in a fluid, or only a part of its existence in such a medium.

In the cases hitherto discussed we have dealt with organisms composed of one cell only. To such organisms the term **unicellular** has been applied. Now, manifestly, the term 'unicellular organism' might be applied to organisms which were referable either to the plant or to the animal world. We have already seen (p. 38) that the green colouring matter chlorophyll is essentially characteristic of the plant as distinguished from the animal, and we have just learnt that a cellular investment is an additional characteristic of a vegetal cell. We are able, therefore, roughly, to divide unicellular organisms into vegetal unicellular organisms and animal unicellular organisms. To the former class we give the name of **Protophyta**, or 'primitive plants'; while to the latter we give the name of **Protozoa**, or 'primitive animals.' There are, however, many organisms which, as has been already indicated, cannot be said to belong directly to either group, e.g. *Protomyxa* itself. These are grouped along with the Protophyta and Protozoa in one general collection, to which the term **Protista**, or 'primitive living things,' is applied. A protist is therefore a unicellular organism, whether truly vegetal or animal or doubtful in its affinities; in other words, an extremely simple living thing. A protozoon is a unicellular organism, generally without chlorophyll, and without a cellulose investment; in other words, an extremely simple animal. A protophyte is a unicellular organism usually possessing chlorophyll and a cellulose cell-wall; that is to say, an extremely simple plant.

It is important to notice that this classification into unicellular plants and unicellular animals is a very loose one, and that no doubt many of the organisms at present classed as doubtfully vegetal or animal in their relationships, are in reality transition stages between the two types, or forms which represent the generalised type from which both animal and vegetal have been derived. It is further worthy of note that the presence or absence of chlorophyll is a more important distinction than the presence or absence of a cellulose capsule, since the capsule of cellulose, or of a substance chemically related to cellulose, is developed, at least temporarily, in not a few Protozoa. We have already seen (p. 38) that chlorophyll is far more important from a physiological than from a morphological point of view; hence we may say that the distinction between unicellular animals and unicellular plants is mainly a physiological one.

Unicellular organisms make up, however, only a small proportion of the organisms on the earth's surface. By far the majority of organisms are composed of a vast number of cells which are specially modified for the performance of special functions—that is to say, differentiated in the manner already fully explained. Such organisms are said to be **multicellular**, and among these organisms there are several well-marked differences which enable us at a glance to say whether any given organism is a plant or an animal. Such differences are the presence or absence of chlorophyll, the presence or absence of cellulose, the possession or not of the power of movement, the method of feeding, and character of the foodstuffs, &c. We divide these multicellular organisms into multicellular plants, or **Metaphyta**, and multicellular animals, or **Metazoa**. Even here, however, the lowest group of Metaphyta includes forms which, from their possessing the power of motion, have been often

Metazoa and Metaphyta.

classed with the Metazoa. Their metaphytal affinities are, however, now deemed indubitable.

It is necessary at this point that we should clearly understand the relationship of the Metaphyta and Metazoa to the Protista as a whole.

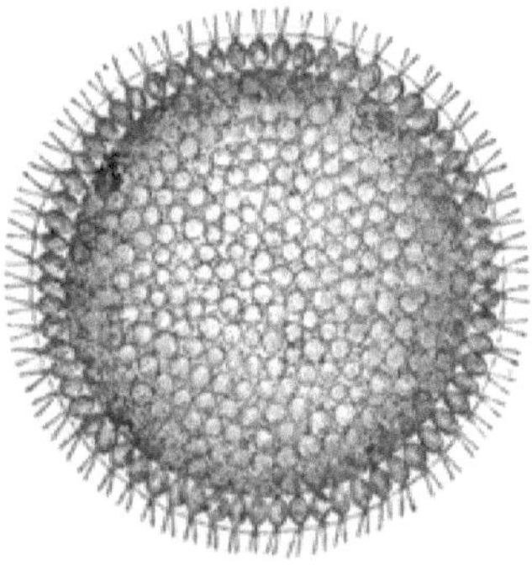

A metaphyte is essentially a vast collection of encysted cells, or cells invested with cellulose capsules (fig. 4). In *Protomyxa* the encysted protoplasm becomes segmented into a number of parts. Now if each of these parts were to develop round it a cellulose capsule, and to remain attached to the neighbouring segments, we should have formed an elementary metaphyte. Such elementary Metaphyta are found in great profusion; and no doubt we may look upon this as the probable way in which the group Metaphyta has

FIG. 9.—*Volvox Globator*. (Stein.)

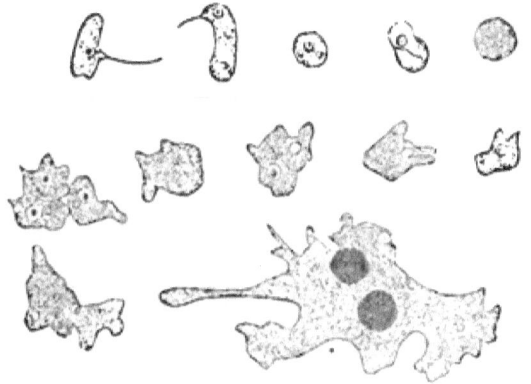

FIG. 10.—LIFE-HISTORY OF *Physarum album*. (Cienkowski)

originated,—namely, by the multiplication and cohesion of encysted cells. We have only a few instances of Metaphyta formed by the cohesion of flagellate cells (fig. 9), or of amœboid cells (fig. 15).

On the other hand, Metazoa may be looked upon as resulting from the multiplication and cohesion of cells in one or other or both of these latter conditions. In the multiplication of the amœboid stage movement is usually very much diminished, and is as a rule in one direction, i.e. de-

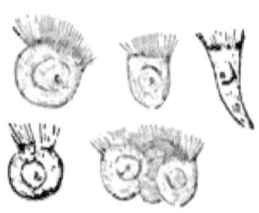

FIG. 11.—CILIATED CELLS FROM THE FROG'S MOUTH. (Sharpey.)

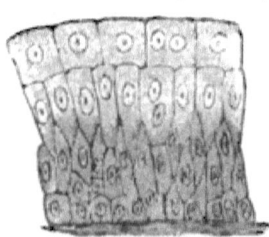

FIG. 12.—CELLS FROM THE LINING OF THE URETER. (Kölliker.)

finite. In most cases the amœboid condition is represented simply by the absence of the cell-wall (fig. 12). Flagellate Metazoa are of common occurrence among the lower groups

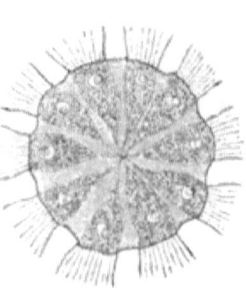

FIG. 13.—*Magosphæra planula*. (Herdman.)

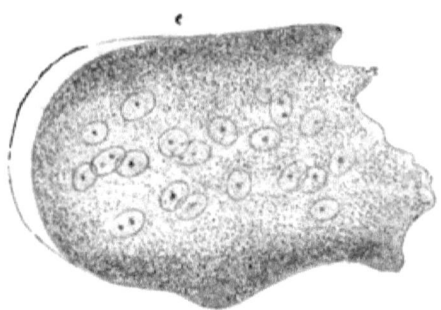

FIG. 14.—MULTINUCLEATED CELL FROM THE MARROW HIGHLY MAGNIFIED. (Schäfer.)

of that sub-kingdom (fig. 13); whilst masses of flagellate, or, if there be a number of small flagella on each cell, ciliated cells occur frequently scattered here and there in the bodies of the higher Metazoa (fig. 11). The plasmodial condition may be looked upon as in reality a multicellular stage in the life-history of a unicellular organism; but that condition is retained as the permanent adult form only in one or two aberrant groups of plants (fig. 15). In the sponge group and allied forms amongst animals the plasmodial stage is permanently exemplified; it also appears in ab-

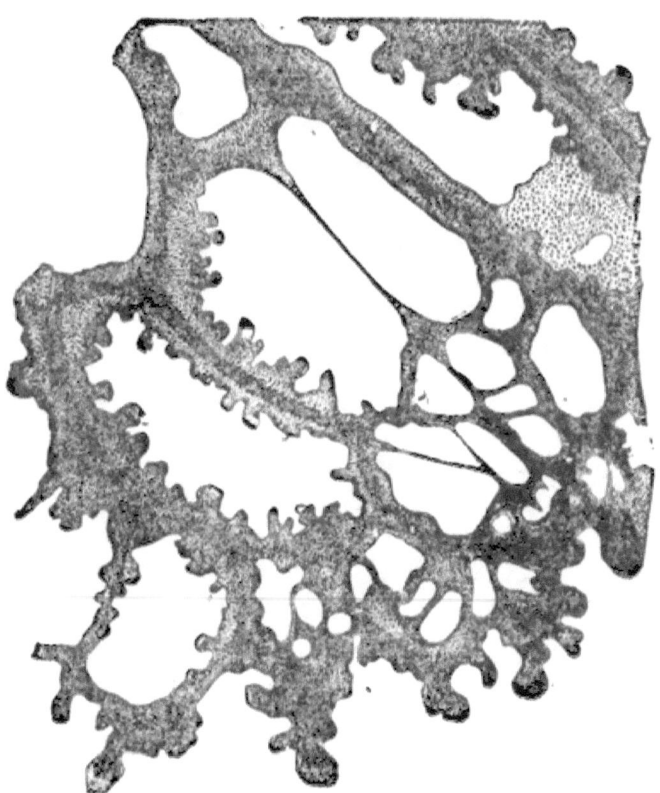

FIG. 15.—PLASMODIUM OF *Didymium leucopus*. (Sachs.)

normal (diseased) cells and, in certain cases also, normally in the higher Metazoa (fig. 14). In disease the ciliated cells are those which most commonly, losing their cilia, become plasmodial. Such collections of diseased cells are plasmodia in which the nuclei of the constituent cells are still visible, thereby at once indicating the multicellular origin of the mass. It must be clearly remembered that no hard and fast lines can be drawn with reference to such phenomena;

FIG. 16.—WHITE FIBRO-CARTILAGE FROM AN INTERVERTEBRAL DISK (HUMAN). HIGHLY MAGNIFIED. (Schäfer).

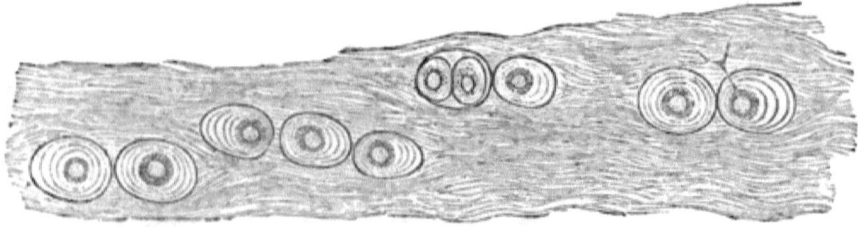

The concentric lines around the cells indicate the limits of deposit of successive capsules or cell-walls.

animal cells, for instance, especially those entering into the formation of the supporting system, have very distinct cell-walls, though not of cellulose (fig. 16). The absence of the power of motion in these cells is to be noted.

The author is indebted for many of the generalisations discussed in this chapter to the works of his friend Mr. Patrick Geddes, Lecturer on Botany in University College, Dundee.

CHAPTER V.

UNICELLULAR PLANTS—PROTOPHYTA.

PROTOCOCCUS.

As an example of the simplest form of plant known, we may select *Protococcus pluvialis*, one of the organisms which gives the green colour to damp wood and stones, and which is found also in large quantities wherever rain-water collects.

The plant is of extremely minute size, varying from $\frac{1}{10000}$th to $\frac{1}{400}$th of an inch in diameter. In shape it is ovoid or elliptical, and presents, when examined under a high magnifying power, a differentiation into protoplasm and cell-wall. The protoplasm has diffused through its mass or aggregated in the form of rounded masses the green colouring matter chlorophyll. In addition there may be seen a nucleus and granules. Some forms have, in addition to the chlorophyll, red colouring matter present, usually in the form of a spot at one end. The cell-wall is of an appreciable thickness, is colourless, and composed of cellulose.

Occasionally *Protococcus* becomes motile, and migrates from place to place in the medium (water) by means of the vibration of two flagella or cilia which are extruded from one end of the cell. Careful examination under a high magnifying power shows that the protoplasm has contracted generally from the cell-wall, but is continuous with the cilia. Not infrequently the cell-wall becomes entirely lost, and *Protococcus* moves about as a naked mass of protoplasm provided with the two cilia already mentioned. The nucleus and red spot are distinctly visible at this stage, usually close to the origin of the cilia. After a variable period of existence in this free-swimming condition the cilia are absorbed, the cell comes to rest, and the reformation of a cellulose coat takes place.

With regard to the physiology of *Protococcus*, being a plant possessed of chlorophyll, it decomposes water and carbonic acid in the presence of sunlight, and integrates new protoplasm, setting free oxygen into the air in the process. In this instance, of course, the carbonic acid is obtained from the rain-water. The nitrogenous elements in its com-

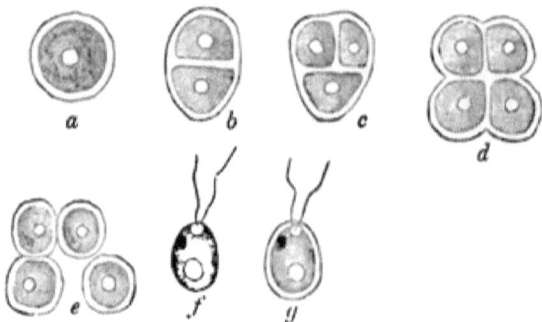

FIG. 17.— LIFE-HISTORY OF *Protococcus pluvialis*.

a-e, stages in vegetative division; *f, g*, motile stage.

position *Protococcus* obtains from the air or from the surrounding objects upon which it may happen to be growing. All the phenomena spoken of as characteristic of plants possessing chlorophyll are exhibited by *Protococcus* and therefore need not be repeated here.

When the plant is provided with the necessary substances for its nutrition and life, multiplication takes place. No sexual union or other phenomenon connected with sexual reproduction is, so far as we at present know, manifested by *Protococcus*. Multiplication is entirely a vegetative process. The protoplasm, when multiplication takes place, becomes divided into two parts, and a cellulose partition is formed between them (fig. 17). Each half may again divide, either simultaneously or successively, and the new cells become gradually detached to form new individuals. This process is known as cell-division or **fission**, and is the simplest known mode of multiplication. These new cells are naturally at first small, and have thinner walls than the older cells ; but increase in age is accompanied by increase in thickness of the cell wall, and increase in size as a whole.

Protococcus is very widely diffused, because of its power of migration by the possession of a motile stage. Such migrations, of course, take place only in a liquid medium. In addition, however, *Protococcus* has the power of retaining its vitality even though dried. The extreme minuteness and lightness of the dried plant manifestly permit of its being carried about by winds, and its area of distribution is thus materially widened.

There are many different species and varieties of the genus *Protococcus*, all more or less like each other, and all possessing the general features above enumerated.

Comparing the life-history of *Protococcus* with that of *Protomyxa*, we notice that we have represented the encysted stage in the adult plant, whilst the incipient multicellular condition resulting from rapid division indicates a transition to the Metaphyta, which, as already stated, are merely aggregates of encysted protoplasmic units. Further, the ciliated stage is represented in the motile *Protococcus*, whilst the amœboid condition is hinted at in the quiescent naked phase immediately succeeding the withdrawal of the cilia. The plasmodial stage is apparently wanting ; its absence may, perhaps, be explained by the presence of chlorophyll in the protoplasmic unit enabling it to replenish its store of energy directly, without needing to unite with other units, and to undergo molecular rearrangement.[1]

Protococcus is a true plant for three reasons : first, it is invested by a cellulose capsule ; secondly, it is possessed of

[1] It is to be noted that in the *Myxomycetes*, where plasmodium-formation is the rule, chlorophyll is wanting. Chlorophyll is also wanting in animals, where the formation of plasmodia is of frequent occurrence.

chlorophyll; and thirdly, it is therefore able to integrate new protoplasm from inorganic material.

The varieties of form and life-history exemplified amongst the Protophyta are very numerous. Although it is not within the scope of this book to enter into a description of these allied forms, yet mention must be made of the *Diatomaceæ*, of the *Saccharomycetes* and *Schizomycetes*, as examples of this important group. The unicellular *Diatomaceæ* are particularly remarkable for their variety of form, and for the great beauty of their silicious skeletons. It is possible that some of the types included under the Protophyta may represent stages in the life-history of the Metaphyta, and hence ought by rights to be considered in that relation. The *Saccharomycetes*, represented by the common Yeast-plant (*Torula*), are by many botanists looked upon as degraded Metaphyta. For further details with regard to these forms, however, reference must be made to such text-books of Botany as those of Gœbel, Strasburger, De Bary, and others.

CHAPTER VI.

UNICELLULAR ANIMALS—PROTOZOA.

AMŒBA.

IN order to emphasise the distinction between a unicellular animal and a unicellular plant, we devote this chapter to a sketch of the organisation and life-history of one of the simplest of the animal forms, viz. *Amœba*.

Much of what has been said of protoplasm in general is applicable here. Indeed, as will be seen on reference to Chapter II., *Amœba* was there instanced as an example of protoplasm in one of its simplest and most easily accessible forms. It may be well, however, to repeat briefly the main points there discussed in detail.[1]

Amœba (fig. 18), as there stated, has generally the appearance of a minute particle of transparent or finely granular jelly, having a nucleus, contractile vacuole, and granules, and showing an elementary differentiation into ecto- and endo-sarc. During its life it is constantly undergoing slow changes in form, due to the protrusion and withdrawal of masses of its own substance (pseudopodia). Its method of ingesting and circulating food-material has already been described (p. 34). Careful observation shows that the contractile vacuole undergoes periodic changes of form which partake of the nature of alternate swellings and contractions, known technically as **diastole** and **systole**. It is probable that the contractile vacuole is some sort of renal organ

---

[1] It is advisable that the student re-read Chapter II. in this relation.

whereby the water, and possibly also certain nitrogenous excreta, are separated from the protoplasm and ejected on the surface. The general physiology of *Amœba*, the effect of the application of heat, &c., has been already described fully above (pp. 33-35).

At a certain period—at present, so far as we know, undeterminable, but probably in some way related to the condition of the environment and the state of nutrition of the

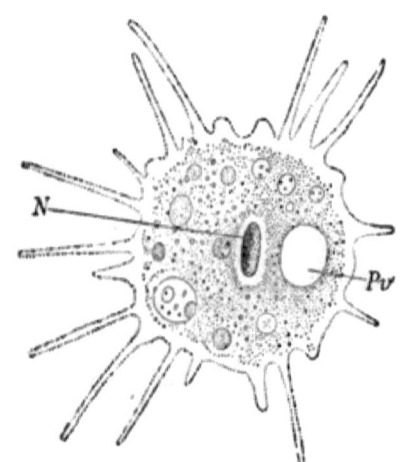

FIG. 18. *Amœba polypodia* (Max Schultze.)

N, nucleus ; *Pv*, contractile vacuole.

animal itself—the *Amœba* assumes a more or less globular form and becomes enclosed in a cellulose cyst. No segmentation, however, takes place as in *Protomyxa*. After a period of a few hours the cyst bursts and the *Amœba* escapes and becomes actively motile. This process is known as **rejuvenescence.**

Amœbæ are inhabitants of damp earth and stagnant water, and are decidedly local in their distribution, as might be expected from the absence of special possibilities for diffusion. They vary much in size, but a common size is from $\frac{1}{1000}$th to $\frac{1}{400}$th of an inch. Vegetative multiplication by fission is common here also, as in the case of *Protococcus*, although in *Amœba* no cellulose cell-wall is formed. As in *Protococcus* so in *Amœba*, division of the nucleus precedes division of the mass as a whole.

Amœba is an animal because it possesses no cellulose cell-wall ; because chlorophyll is absent ; and because the organism is for that reason incapable of using the carbonic acid of the atmosphere and the water and simple salts of the soil in the manufacture of new protoplasm, but requires to be supplied with organised matter or protoplasm already partially or entirely integrated.

As regards its physiology, it is to be noted (p. 35) that carbonic acid is constantly being produced, both in the dark and in sunlight, and thus it presents superficially a great difference to the plant where carbonic acid is exhaled in quantity in the dark only, whilst in daylight its exhalation is masked by the comparatively large amount of oxygen given forth contemporaneously.

CHAPTER VII.

METAPHYTA—NON-VASCULARIA.

SECTION I.—FRESH-WATER ALGÆ—*SPIROGYRA*.

IN the two preceding chapters we have discussed the structure and life-history of a representative of each of the two groups known as Protophyta and Protozoa, or unicellular plants and unicellular animals. We have seen, moreover, that at one stage in the life-history of the example taken to illustrate the Protophyta it assumed a temporary resemblance to a very elementary metaphyte. *Protococcus* was found to divide into three or four pieces, which for a short space of time remained attached to each other, forming a very simple multicellular organism. It is to be noted, however, that the cells are really physiologically independent of each other, being rather members of a colony than units in one whole. The organism at this stage does not exhibit that division of labour which has been already explained (at page 37) as being characteristic of multicellular organisms. It is quite true that many multicellular plants and animals do show only a very slight approach to morphological differentiation; and we cannot be surprised that it is so, since manifestly in the simplest beginnings of a metaphyte, morphological sameness must precede differentiation. Every plant and every animal has its cells at first perfectly similar. It is only after a period, varying in duration with the nature of the plant or the animal in question, that the cells begin to be differentiated and become specially modified for the performance of their several duties.

Metaphyta—Spirogyra.

We commence our study of the Metaphyta, or multicellular plants, by examining a plant which exhibits very little morphological differentiation. As an example, we take the common pond weed known as *Spirogyra longata*. In structure *Spirogyra* has the form of a green thread composed of a variable number of cells, placed end to end. The cells are all exactly alike, save for certain slight variations in size. Such a collection of more or less similar cells is termed a **thallus**, a flattened or thread-like cellular expansion. In some cases the thallus may be large, in other cases small. For example, the familiar seaweeds on the coast are instances of large flattened thalli, while *Spirogyra* itself is an instance of a delicate, narrow, and thread-like thallus.

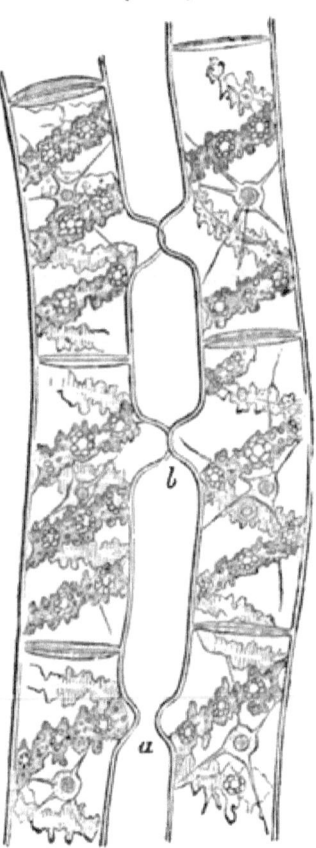

FIG. 19.—*Spirogyra longata.* (Sachs.)

Incipient conjugation. *a*, processes approaching each other; *b*, processes united.

We shall see in the present chapter that thalli differ very greatly in form and size. Each cell is composed of a cellulose coat, or cell-wall, with contents. The contents are granular protoplasm, a nucleus, a green spiral band, and a variable quantity of a watery substance known as cell sap.

Further details can be made out only by employing high magnifying powers of the microscope. When that is done it is seen that the protoplasm in the cells, at least at some distance from the free ends of the thread, exists as a layer lying immediately within the cell-wall. From this layer there stretch to the nucleus threads of protoplasm, the nucleus itself being surrounded by a layer of the same substance. The nucleus may, however, be found lying close to the cell-wall, but always separated from it by the layer of protoplasm above referred to. The cell-sap, a watery fluid containing certain organic substances which are probably products of the metabolism of protoplasm, varies in amount according to the age of the cell. *Spirogyra*, being an unattached floating plant, has neither apex nor base, though the terminal cells have rounded ends, and less cell-sap than other cells. The nucleus contains a nucleolus, and that again is said by some writers to contain a distinctly differentiated endonucleolus. The structure of the spiral band varies with the species of *Spirogyra* under consideration. In some forms it is single, in others double, but in all cases it possesses more or less irregular margins, is of a green colour, and contains starch granules, aggregated at definite intervals or scattered irregularly through it. The band itself consists of a protoplasmic basis and chlorophyll, which is in this case diffused in the protoplasmic band, and not in the form of granules as was the case in *Protococcus*.

Increase in length is effected by the division of a previously existing cell into two parts. Division takes place only during the night. The process of division is a somewhat complicated one, and is accompanied by a series of changes in the nucleus which have been the subject of much recent study and debate. Without entering into detail, it may be sufficient to indicate the chief features in the process as follows.

The division of a cell is preceded by division of the nucleus. The process of division of the nucleus is known as **karyokinesis**. The structure of the nucleus has already been described (p. 30), and it is necessary for the comprehension of the phenomena of karyokinesis to bear that structure in mind. The first stage consists in the partial or complete disappearance of the fibrillæ, or network, and the assumption of a more markedly granular character by the protoplasm; the granules then unite into the form of curved rods or threads and arrange themselves parallel to the long axis of the nucleus. This is known as the **spindle stage** in division (fig. 20, iv.). At the same time the protoplasm of the cell generally aggregates round either pole of

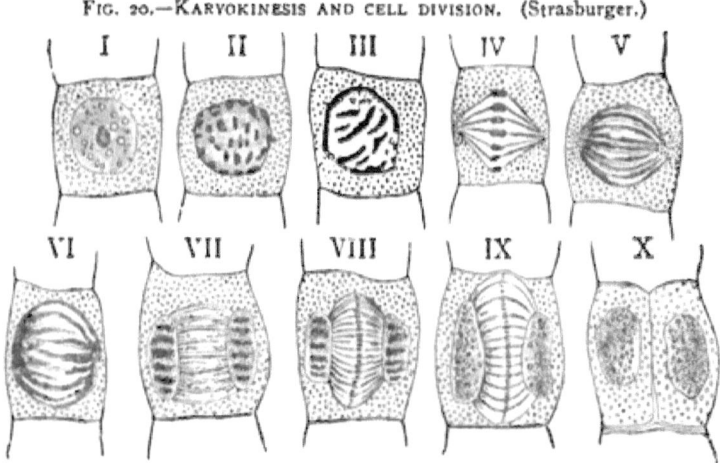

FIG. 20.—KARYOKINESIS AND CELL DIVISION. (Strasburger.)

the spindle and exhibits a radial arrangement of its granules. The next stage consists in the appearance of a plate or thickening round the equator of the spindle, known as the nuclear, or **equatorial disc**. The equatorial disc next splits into two plates, either half travelling to either pole to form the two new nuclei (fig 20, vi.).

The protoplasm of the cell itself has meantime been undergoing the preliminary alterations necessary to the formation of a new cell-wall between the two nuclei. These changes consist in the differentiation of a special plate of protoplasm across the middle of the cell. In this there appears a deposit of cellulose, which gradually increases in amount, until it ultimately cuts the old cell into two (fig. 20, ix.). The nuclei then take up a central position, and the two new cells gradually assume the characters of the parent cell from which they arose.

Spirogyra does not differ essentially in its physiology from the general type (Chap. VIII. sect. v.). The phenomena of constructive and destructive metabolism are the same as those exhibited by all green plants, save that its gaseous food is obtained from carbonic acid dissolved in water.

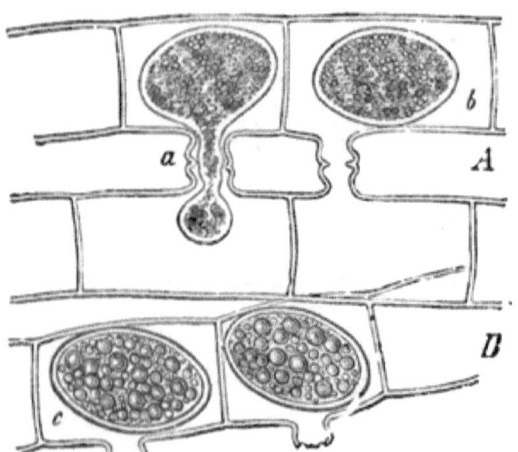

FIG. 21.—CONJUGATION IN *Spirogyra longata*. (Sachs.)

A, a, passage of the male protoplasm into the female cell ; *b, B, c*, embryos in different stages of development within the mother cell-wall.

A species of sexual union and reproduction prevails in *Spirogyra*, whereby new individuals are formed. **Conjugation**, as it is sometimes called, takes place between two cells of different filaments lying close to each other (fig. 19). It is to be noted that the conjugating cells are, to the eye, precisely similar, although doubtless there are molecular differences of importance ; the basis for that belief will be given presently. The first stage in the union consists in either cell sending out lateral protrusions or buds which grow towards each other (fig. 19), and increase in length and size until they touch. Fusion of the walls at the point of contact takes place, and a direct communication is established therefore between the two cells. Meantime the protoplasmic contents of both cells contract and withdraw from the cell-wall, forming a dense rounded mass in the interior of either cell. This contraction is accompanied and rendered possible by the expulsion of a quantity of water from the cell. The contraction may take place in both cells at the same time, or more usually in one cell before the other. This would seem to point to some molecular difference between the cells, probably of nutritive condition (p. 90). The next step consists in the passage of one or other of the protoplasmic masses into the other cell in which latter no doubt preparatory metabolic changes are taking place (fig. 21). This fact would again point to some molecular difference between the cells. Union of the protoplasmic masses follows, and results in the formation of an ovoid mass which is smaller in bulk than the sum of the two masses before union, doubtless owing again to the expulsion of water; such a body is called in most text-books a 'zygospore,' or 'resting spore.' The term 'spore,' as applied to such a body, is most undoubtedly inappropriate, if not positively wrong, because that name is applied to cells which multiply the plant asexually (p. 95), and which do not result from conjugation of two reproductive cells of different sexes.[1] Although the conjugating cells of *Spirogyra* are apparently alike, yet there can be no doubt that this is a case of primitive sexual union, and therefore if we decide to call the egg or female reproductive cell of a plant before fertilisation an ovum, this 'zygospore' is simply a fertilised ovum or embryo. It is true we cannot say beforehand which of the conjugating cells is the ovum, and which

---

[1] The term 'spore' is used by Vines in his *Physiology of Plants* to designate both the asexually produced spore and the embryo, or product of union of the ovum and sperm.

corresponds to the male element, until movement of the protoplasm of one of the cells takes place. Then, on the general analogy that the male element is usually the more active of the two (p. 52), we are able to guess that the more passive cell is that which corresponds to the ovum.[1]

After undergoing a short period of rest, during which, no doubt, various important rearrangements of the protoplasmic materials take place, the body resulting from the union of the two cells ('zygospore'), which has meantime obtained a thick cell-wall, bursts first its own special capsule, and

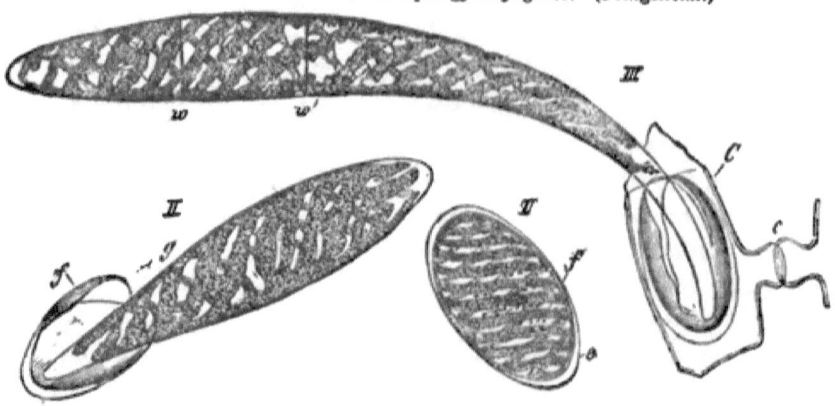

FIG. 22.—GERMINATION OF *Spirogyra jugalis*. (Pringsheim.)

I, 'zygospore'; *e*, *f*, layers of cell-wall. II, germination of embryo, *g*. III, young *Spirogyra*, with three cells already formed; c, cell-wall of parent (female) cell; *w*, *w'*, new cell-walls; *c*, conjugating processes.

afterwards the mother cell-wall, and pushes out a long filament, which develops gradually into a new *Spirogyra*.

Such is the life-history of *Spirogyra*, and it is to be noted by way of recapitulation that we have here an exceedingly simple thallus, producing two cells of different

---

[1] It is desirable that the student should as far as possible familiarise himself with the terms in use in other text-books, after he has, by means of a uniform terminology such as that adopted here, mastered the exact signification of the various parts of plants, more especially of their reproductive organs.

sex, which unite together, the product of union developing into a new thallus.

Taking a general view of the allies of *Spirogyra*, we find that they embrace a most varied collection of forms. The modification lies principally in the form of the thallus. For example, some take on the form of a hollow sphere, the component cells being provided with flagella, as in *Pandorina*. Others again, such as the *Coleochæteæ*, by successive division, assume the form of rounded or irregular plates built out of branched multicellular threads.

The familiar though aberrant *Chara* is more thread-like in form, but the delicate stem and branches into which the thallus is divided are more highly differentiated than those of the filamentous forms of which *Spirogyra* is the type.

All the forms mentioned are inhabitants of fresh water, and differ only in the structure of the thallus, as above stated, and in the nature of their reproductive cells and the parts of the thallus which bear them. All shades of differentiation are exemplified, from the simple form we have just examined to the fully developed sexual apparatus we are about to describe in the next vegetal type that falls to be discussed.

Section II.—Salt-water Algæ—*FUCUS*.

In this and succeeding vegetal types where the reproductive organs are distinctly differentiated, it will be most convenient to discuss the plant first from a vegetative point of view, and then to treat of its reproductive apparatus.

Vegetative organs.—To illustrate the group of salt-water Algæ, or seaweeds, and as giving a good instance of a typical plant of the lower or less advanced type of structure, no better example could be found than one of the common seaweeds—*Fucus platycarpus*. The plant consists of a much-branched and flattened thallus attached by means of cylindrical and branched roots to some fixed object. The dimensions of the thallus vary extremely; but it usually attains a length of from one to five or six feet in the group to which *F. platycarpus* belongs.

The branching is **dichotomous**—i.e. the growing apex divides into two nearly equal portions. All the branches lie in the same plane, and all more or less resemble each other. Each branch consists of a cylindrical core or mid-rib with a lamella on either side, both lamellæ lying also in the plane of branching. Every here and there along the lamellæ air-sacs or bladders are found, which are, morphologically, simply spaces in the cellular tissue.

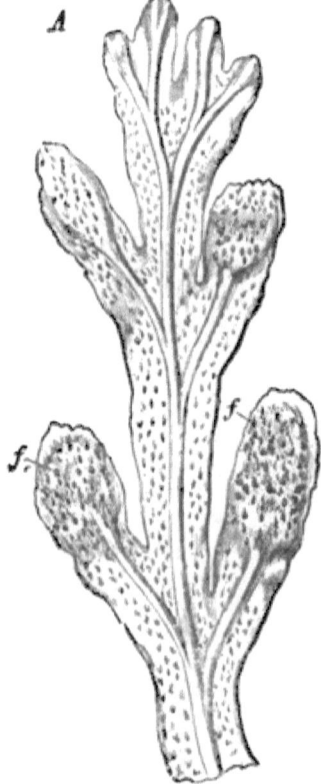

FIG. 23.—PART OF THE THALLUS OF *Fucus platycarpus*. (Thuret.)

A, dichotomous branc' ing; *f, f*, fertile branches.

If a section of the branch be examined microscopically it will be found to consist of cells which differ in shape and size according to the part of the branch under examination. On the surface the cells are small, spherical, and have no **intercellular spaces** between them; the cells of the centre are elongated and branched, and form a loose spongy mass, with necessarily large intercellular spaces. The cell-walls are very thick and mucilaginous in their nature, and swell up readily under the action of fresh-water. Hence the slimy character of the seaweeds when handled, and especially if examined after steeping in fresh-water, or preservation in alcohol or spirit.

Although the colour of *Fucus* is a dull brown it is not

to be supposed that there is no chlorophyll present. Its presence is masked by an admixture of a brown colouring-matter. It performs the same function as the unmixed chlorophyll of *Spirogyra*. The carbonic acid is, of course, as in the case of *Spirogyra*, obtained from the water (in this case salt-water), and the various physiological processes are conducted as in that type.

Reproductive organs.—The reproductive apparatus of *Fucus* is of a very complete and highly differentiated nature. At the proper season, certain (usually many) of the branches exhibit at their terminations swellings which are covered over with minute mounds or pimples. These are fertile branches, and the pimples represent the mouths of small depressions or sacs ('conceptacles') sunk in the tissue of the thallus. Each sac contains (in *F. platycarpus*) both male and female cells. If a vertical section of a sac be examined (fig. 24) it will be found to consist of a bounding wall of cells not unlike, and continuous with, the cells forming the superficial layer of the thallus, from which spring numerous hairs of variable shape – some long and branching, others thick, short, and in some cases almost spherical. These are respectively the **spermaria**, or sperm-producing organs, and the **ovaria**, or ovum-producing organs. The cavity of the sac is filled with sea-water, mingled with the mucus secreted from the slimy tissue of the thallus.

A more careful examination of the hairs in the sac discovers that they spring from the lining-wall of the sac, and that, since the sac itself is formed in all probability by an indentation or **invagination** of the superficial cells,[1] the reproductive hairs are really equivalent morphologically to superficial or **epidermal hairs**.

Taking the male elements first, we find that the **sperms** (fig. 25) are minute unicellular bodies without any visible

---

[1] According to Bower, Q.J.M.S. 1876, the formation of the conceptacle, at least in some forms, commences with the decay of a superficial cell.

nucleus, but each provided with a red spot of colouring-matter and two fine flagella, by the constant vibration of which they are able to move about with extreme rapidity. The sperms are developed in the interior of club-shaped

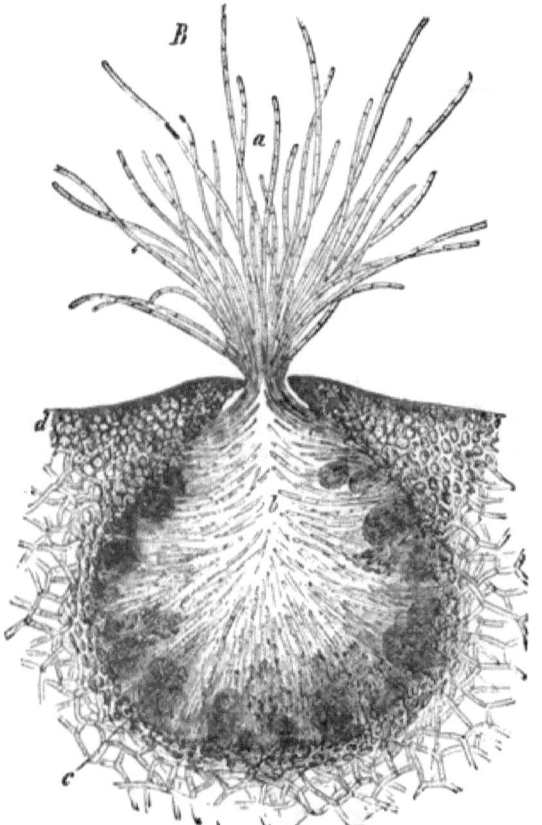

Fig. 24.—Section of the Conceptacle of *Fucus platycarpus*. (Thuret.)

a, *b*, sterile hairs ; *c*, ovaria ; *e*, spermaria ; *d* thallus.

branches of the male hairs, each branch being a **spermarium** (antheridium). Each spermarium consists at first of a cell-wall and granular protoplasm, which latter gradually becomes segmented and modified into the sperms already described, which escape on the rupture of the wall of the spermarium. Scattered amongst the male hairs are other hairs, which are unbranched, but destitute of spermaria. These are **sterile hairs**, which have been unable to develop into true sexual hairs owing to the pressure for space, etc. Some of these sterile hairs are very long, and extend out through the mouth of the sac to the exterior.

The **ovaria** are comparatively large spherical bodies resting on a basal cell which arises from the lining-wall of the

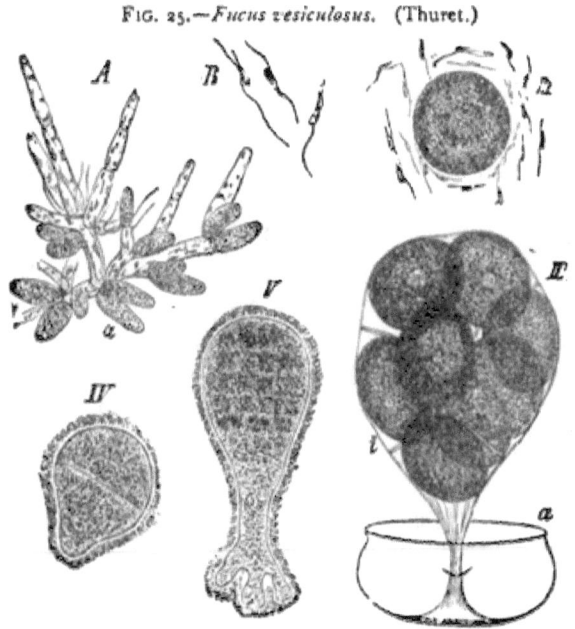

FIG. 25.—*Fucus vesiculosus.* (Thuret.)

A, branched hairs bearing spermaria. *a*. *B*, sperms. *II*, ovarium (outer wall. *a* ; inner wall, *i*) containing eight ova. *III*, ovum surrounded by sperms. *IV*, *V*, development of embryo.

sac. Each ovarium consists originally of a cell-wall which is composed of an inner and an outer layer, filed with dense dark protoplasm. The ovarium in *F. platycarpus* divides into eight **ova**, although in other forms a smaller number of ova are occasionally formed from the contents of each mature ovarium. The ovarium on bursting ejects its ova into the cavity of the sac, and from thence to the exterior, where they are fertilised by sperms which have meantime escaped from the spermaria. Although many sperms attack each ovum, and by their active motion cause the passive ovum to move also, yet probably only one sperm fuses with the ovum (fig. 25). Immediately after the act of fertilisation the ovum becomes an **embryo**. As the first consequence of union with the male cell, the previously naked ovum takes on a cell-wall and begins to **germinate**, elongating and dividing, at first transversely, and then vertically, or in the direction of the long axis of the embryo. Very soon after fertilisation the embryo comes to rest, attaching itself to some fixed body, whilst the free end develops by repeated cell-division into an organism like the parent.

To recapitulate, we have in *Fucus* a thallus giving rise to two undoubtedly sexual cells which after union produce a thallus like that from which they arose. There is thus exemplified in this form a certain amount of morphological differentiation. We find that a distinction can be drawn between the purely vegetative portion of thallus and the purely reproductive portion. That part which has for its duty the formation of cells which have to do with the maintenance of tribal life is altered in outward form and microscopic or histological structure from the purely vegetative portions of the thallus ; yet both the purely vegetative and the purely reproductive branches are modifications of the same type. It can scarcely be said that the thallus of *Fucus*, from a vegetative point of view, is morphologically differentiated ; since, although we find that there is an approximation to a stem, from which the branches spring, and to a root, yet these are not at the same time physiologically differentiated,—that is to say, they do not perform the functions of circulation and absorption respectively, which are the chief functions of the similar parts known by these terms in the higher plants. Probably every cell in the thallus performs for itself the important functions requisite for the maintenance of life.

Amongst the cells forming the thallus, however, we have a certain amount of modification of form. As already seen, the cells of the centre, or **medulla**, are different from those nearer the surface, or **cortex**; whilst those associated with the reproductive sacs are still more variable in shape. Collections of more or less similar cells are called **tissues**. Thus we may speak of **medullary tissue** and **cortical tissue**, or we may describe in general term the whole thallus as being made up of a **cellular tissue**. Organs, therefore, are made up of tissues, which are themselves collections of more or less similar cells.

It is important that we should pause at this point and endeavour to ascertain what is the rationale of the phenomena of true sexual reproduction which we have, in *Fucus*, met with for the first time.

In the first place, what is the connection, if any, between asexual and sexual reproduction? It was pointed out (p. 52) that asexual reproduction meant the separation of any cell from the parent, which, without union with any other cell, was capable of developing into an organism like the parent. A modification of this process is exhibited among the higher plants, and more rarely among the higher animals; namely, the separation of many cells in the form of a 'bud,' 'shoot,' 'stolon,' etc., which is similarly capable of developing into an adult organism.

The process of protoplasmic anabolism (p. 36) was seen to be one usually accompanied by growth in the early stages of a plant's or animal's life-history. The various phenomena of life are, of course, always possible only if the products of katabolism be got rid of. Now since the mass of any growing cell increases as the cube of the dimensions, while the surface only increases as the square (H. Spencer), katabolism must sooner or later overtake and outstrip anabolism, with one of two results to the cell,—namely, either it must be poisoned by its own excreta, or it must divide into two or more parts, so as to restore the proper proportion of surface and mass. Hence at the limit of growth, in *Protococcus* for example, division takes place. This division amongst the lowest types represents asexual multiplication.

It is conceivable, however, that the division might result in the formation of two cells not equally anabolic or katabolic. For instance, one half might contain an excess of protoplasm which had a tendency to break down, or exhibit energy in movement ; the other half might be more anabolic, passive, and sluggish. We should have thus formed an incipient sexual differentiation ; the more katabolic cell would represent the male cell, or sperm, whilst the more anabolic would represent the female cell, or ovum. Attention was directed in the case of *Spirogyra* to the difference in physiological activity observed between the two conjugating cells, and it was there pointed out that it was probable that the more kinetic cell represented the male and the more sluggish the female element in true sexual conjugation.

The kinetic or katabolic cell may be looked upon as the liberating energy which sets off, so to speak, the potential energy, just as the spark sets off the gunpowder; only in this case the conditions are more complicated. The kinetic energy must be energy resulting from the decomposition of special chemical compounds, and the products of katabolism must themselves be such as are able to stimulate the ovum to undergo those changes which convert it into an embryo. This subject will be referred to again when we come to consider the fertilisation of the higher plants and animals.

Amongst salt-water Algæ, as amongst fresh-water forms, we meet with great variety in the form and structure of the thallus. All agreeing in the general characters already described in the type discussed above, they yet present almost every conceivable modification of such a primitive type. The threadlike thallus is represented by *Ectocarpus*, which is otherwise specially interesting as exhibiting an incipient sexual differentiation among its reproductive cells. *Laminaria*, again, has a flat and much-branched thallus. Amongst the red seaweeds, or *Floridea*, there is great variety of form, and one large group—the *Corallineæ*—derive their name from the fact that they have an incrustation of carbonate of lime which covers the thallus and causes them to mimic in some respects the corals among animals.

The reproductive cells, the method of fertilisation, and the subsequent changes in the ovum are also somewhat different from the corresponding phenomena in the type selected; but nevertheless the essential points are precisely similar, and in such a text-book as the present it is not possible to do more than point out the general relationship amongst individual differences.

SECTION III.—FUNGI—*PENICILLIUM.*

We have now to direct our attention to a group of plants very different in external appearance and in minute structure from those we have been hitherto discussing, viz. the **Fungi**. Under this extensive class are included such forms as the common grey moulds, the mushrooms, and many others more or less popularly familiar. In microscopic structure and external configuration they present very great variety, but there are certain well-defined characters which they all possess, and which separate them from the Algæ on the one hand, and the higher plants on the other. It will be of advantage to briefly emphasise these characteristics and in some measure to account for them.

In the first place, it is to be noted that **the cells of Fungi contain no chlorophyll**, and in the second place that the Fungi live **parasitically on dead or living organisms**. Can we trace any relationship between these two phenomena?

It will be remembered that the presence of chlorophyll (Chap. II. sect. iv.) in the green plant was an essential condition of the decomposition of carbonic acid, and that by the assistance of chlorophyll in the presence of sunlight the green plant was able to build up complex organic compounds out of simple inorganic compounds and elements. Now a fungus lives entirely upon the already organised compounds found in the living or dead organism on which it is a parasite. The necessity for the complex anabolic processes above referred to is therefore in great measure avoided, and consequently chlorophyll is not required.

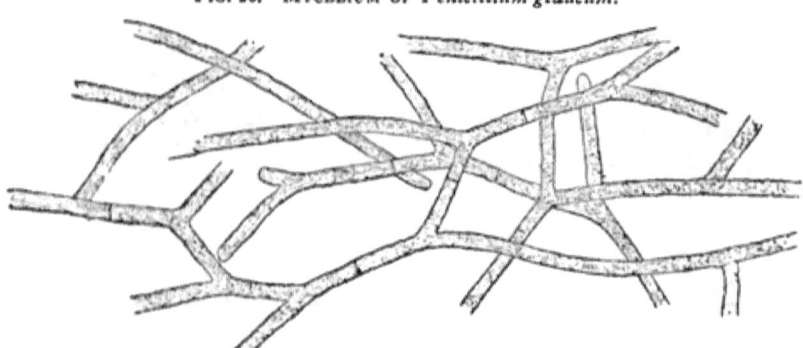

FIG. 26.—MYCELIUM OF *Penicillium glaucum*.

Hence we see that absence of chlorophyll in the Fungi is a result of parasitic habits.

Further, we notice that the form of the fungus as a whole is by no means definite; that there is to the naked eye a want of that individuality which we see developed in such a form as *Fucus*. Indeed it will be found that many of the moulds form colonial masses, varying in extent with that of the nutritive surfaces on which they live.

It will be best at this point to describe a typical fungus, availing ourselves, as far as we can, of the knowledge of vegetal life-history we have derived from a study of the immediately preceding type.

If any moist organic substance, such as a piece of thin

bread, be exposed to air and light for some days there will usually be found over its surface at the end of that time a dense white felt-work, which forms a tolerably firm covering to the underlying organic material. This is the so-called 'mycelium' of *Penicillium glaucum*. We will assume that the cultivation has been obtained pure, that is, free from admixture with other moulds—a result not always obtained.

Vegetative organs.—The felt-like mass (fig. 26), when examined under the microscope, is discovered to consist of

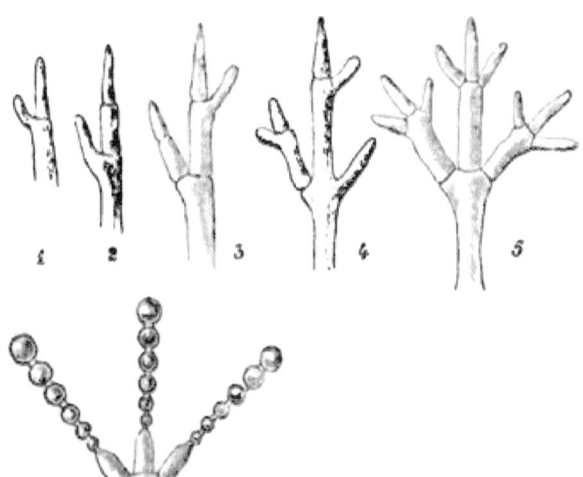

FIG. 27.—SPORE BEARING FILAMENTS OF *Penicillium glaucum*.

1-6. Stages in the formation of the branched ends of the filaments.

closely interwoven threads (**hyphæ**) which branch and twist in all directions. Each thread is composed of a variable number of elongated cells placed end to end. Each cell consists of a cellulose cell-wall, containing colourless granular protoplasm. The threads branch and form a loose cellular tissue, which may be termed a thallus, as being comparable in all respects to the thallus of the *Fucus*. In *Penicillium* the thallus is entirely composed of elongated cells loosely connected, and showing large intercellular spaces ; in *Fucus* only the medullary portion of its mass is so constituted.

The thallus does not long retain its white appearance, it soon begins to show greenish patches at intervals over its

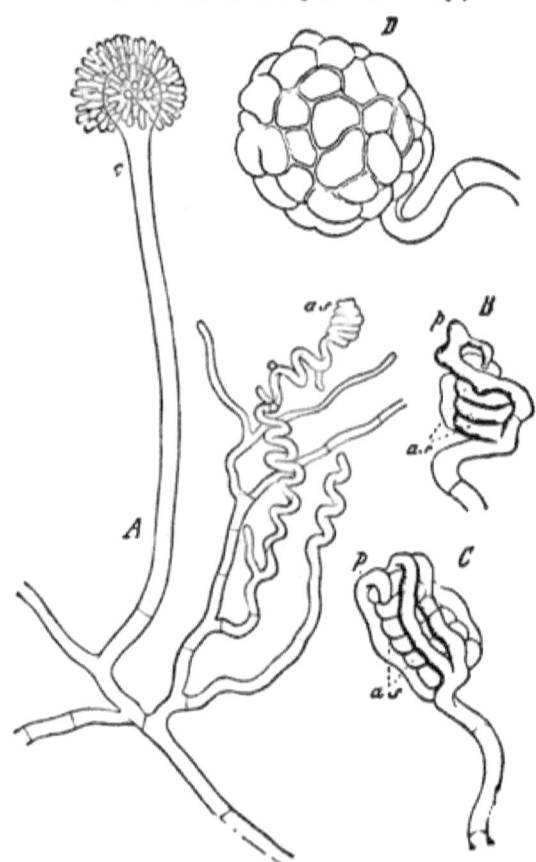

FIG. 28.—*Eurotium repens.* (De Bary.)

A, portion of thallus with erect spore-bearing filament (*c*); young ovarium (*as*). *B*, young ovarium (*as*) and spermarium (*p*). *C*, same beginning to be surrounded by sterile filaments, two shown in the front. *D*, ' fructification.'

surface. We must now endeavour to throw some light on this phenomenon. Microscopic examination of a portion of the thallus which shows this alteration in colour demonstrates at once a series of threads or elongated cells springing vertically from the thallus into the air and bearing at their free ends many strings or chains of minute rounded greenish bodies, commonly known as **spores**. More careful examination shows that these **spore-bearing filaments** are simply modified cells or threads of the thallus (fig. 27). Apparently any cell, may give rise to a filament, which, when it reaches a certain size, begins to branch at its free termination. The successive stages in that division will be best understood by a study of the figure (fig. 27). The terminal cells, after the branching has sufficiently progressed, bud off parts of themselves, the youngest buds being those nearest to the parent cell. This budding is a purely vegetative process, and, though the buds at first remain attached, they are very soon set free and blown about in great numbers. Each bud or spore consists of a very faintly yellowish-green cell-wall and colourless protoplasm. A nucleus is said to be present, but it is not easily seen without the assistance of reagents.

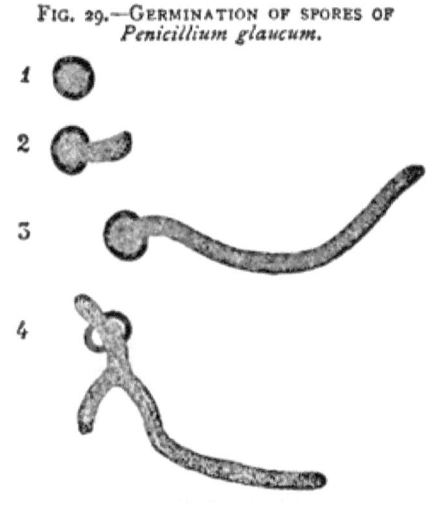

FIG. 29.—GERMINATION OF SPORES OF *Penicillium glaucum*.

If sown in or on a suitable medium, the spore begins to **germinate**. At one or more places on the spore wall a bud appears, which develops into a much elongated thread not unlike one of the threads of the parent thallus (fig. 29). The filament afterwards divides, and, alone, or in company with filaments formed by other spores, forms a felt-like thallus, like that which originally produced the spores.

So far, it would seem that we have to deal with a plant very different in life, history from such a form as *Fucus*. In the above account we have nothing comparable to the spermaria and ovaria and their contents; the two plants have only a thallus in common. More careful observation, however, discovers that we have by no means exhausted the life-history of *Penicillium*.

If the mycelium be placed under such conditions that oxygen is partially excluded, whilst the cultivation goes on in darkness, spore-bearing filaments after a time are not formed so plentifully, and the budding off of spores comes consequently to an end. In place of these, minute yellowish bodies make their appearance—the so-called 'fructifications.' It will conduce to clearness if we trace the development of these *ab initio*.

The first stage in the formation of a 'fructification' is the spiral coiling of the terminal cell of one of the threads of the thallus (fig. 28, A); the spiral coil so formed is a close one, and the cell becomes by transverse partitions divided into as many cells as there are turns in the spiral. At the same time a small branch from the same terminal cell grows up in a spiral manner round the other spiral and closely intertwines itself with it. Ultimately fusion of the two spirals takes place and the protoplasmic contents mingle with each other. After fusion of the two spirals, a series of filaments spring out from the parent filaments from which the spirals arose, which enclose and protect them. In some forms of mould very elaborate capsules are so formed. In *Penicillium* the surrounding envelope closely embraces the spirals and is of a spongy texture, owing to the continuous growth and division of the enveloping filaments. The chief or primary spiral, however, after fusion with the secondary spiral develops branches (*asci*) which push their way in amongst the enveloping filaments. At this stage the mass (already referred to above as the 'fructification') becomes detached from its thallus and may undergo further development either at an early date or after a long period of rest. If the conditions be favourable, a few weeks are required for the development of the asci (fig. 30), in the interior of each of which by a process of segregation, or free-cell formation, a number of cells are formed. As a general rule, eight cells appear in each ascus, each of which cells is in all essential points extremely like the spore formed from the thallus by ordinary vegetative division. They must not, however, be confounded with them, and the commonly accepted term of 'ascospore' given to these cells is misleading in that respect. Each of these spore-like bodies may, if suitably nourished, develop into a thallus exactly like that formed by the true spore, and in a precisely similar manner.

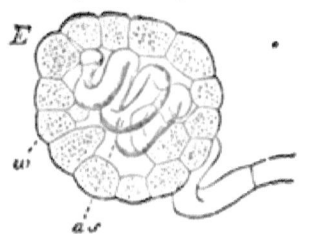
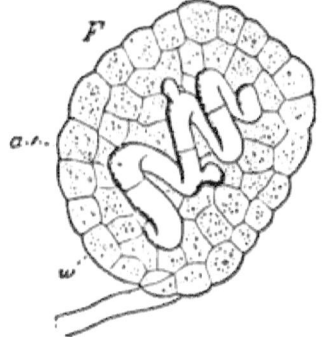
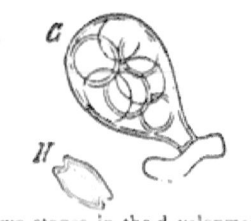

FIG. 30.—*Eurotium repens.* (De Bary.)

It will be necessary for us now to endeavour to obtain some clear conception of the relationship of these different series of phenomena to each other, and to trace the homologies between the various stages of the life-history of *Fucus* and those of the life-history of the mould we have just been considering. It will conduce to clearness if we repeat briefly what has been already said on these points.

E, F, two stages in the development of the fructification; *as*, primary spiral; *w*, wall of the fructification; G, ascus; H, 'ascospore.'

First, what corresponds in *Penicillium* to the thallus of *Fucus?* Obviously what we have named the thallus—viz. the felt-like tissue. The thallus of *Fucus* produced male and

H

female cells, which we termed respectively sperms and ova. These we found were produced in spermaria and ovaria. Have we anything comparable to this in *Penicillium*? Certainly, the primary spiral filament in the so-called 'fructification' is undoubtedly an ovarium, while the secondary spiral is as undoubtedly a spermarium.[1] At this point, however, a certain amount of divergence is observable. The whole contents of the spermarium fuse with or fertilise the contents of the ovarium. Again we notice that the spermarial or male filament is the active or kinetic filament coiling up to meet the terminal portion of the ovarium.

The phenomena taking place subsequently to fertilisation are also considerably modified. In *Fucus* the embryo at once developed into the adult plant, in *Penicillium* that development is postponed; in fact, the stimulus of the male fertilising matter seems needed for bringing about the formation of ova (fertilised, however) from the protoplasm of the ovarium and its branches ('asci'). The so-called 'ascospores' are, therefore, the delayed products of sexual union, and for that reason ought to be called embryos, just as the products of sexual union in *Fucus* were called embryos.

How shall we explain, then, the occurrence of an asexual method of multiplication?

It has been seen that *Penicillium* is dependent for its life on the obtaining of complex organic food matter, and is unable to decompose carbonic acid and build up organic compounds out of inorganic constituents. Manifestly, therefore, the food supply of *Penicillium* is considerably more limited than that of green plants in consequence of its parasitic habits. Moreover, it has been seen that its sexual method of reproduction is one of considerable complexity,

---

[1] Brefeld, who first made out the stages in the formation of ascospores in *Penicillium*, now believes that the process is vegetative and not sexual. De Bary's researches establish beyond doubt that Brefeld's first conclusion is the correct one.

and requiring a long time for its proper development. The chances of the ultimate formation of embryos in this manner are obviously much fewer than if the plant were not a parasite, and if its embryos were rapidly formed as in *Fucus*. There might be a possibility under these circumstances of the plant being entirely destroyed off the face of the earth were it not that the very efficient asexual mode of multiplication comes, so to speak, to the rescue, so that, by means of the simple vegetative budding above described, a plentiful supply of new plants may be formed with a large margin for waste. The spore stage is not represented in *Fucus*, where the, in that case, very efficient sexual method is amply sufficient to replenish loss of individuals and spread the seaweed wherever the salt-water flows.

By way of summary, then, we may say that while the thallus of *Fucus* produces male and female cells, the latter of which, after fertilisation by the former, develop into thalli similar to that from which we started, the thallus of *Penicillium* produces male and female cells, similarly capable after fusion of reproducing a thallus, but is able also to separate off certain asexual cells, conveniently termed spores, which may develop into thalli capable of forming either another and yet another generation of spores, or true sexual organs and a series of embryos.

If we agree to term the thallus of *Fucus* the **sexual generation**, as being the generation which produces sexual cells, then we would write its life-history thus :—

$$S\,T \longrightarrow \male + \female \longrightarrow S\,T \longrightarrow \male + \female$$

and so on, where S T stands for the sexual thallus and $\male$ and $\female$ for the male and female sexual cells respectively. If we agree, in like manner, to call the spore-bearing thallus an **asexual generation**, and to denominate it by the letters A S T and the spore by the symbol o, we might write the history of *Penicillium* thus :—

$$\text{S T}\text{---}\delta + \female \text{---AST}\text{---}\text{o}\text{---AST}\text{---}\text{o} \ldots$$
$$\text{S T}\text{---}\delta + \female \ \&c.^{1}$$

Amongst *Fungi*, then, for the first time we meet with what is known as **alternation of generations** between an asexual and a sexual condition—a phenomenon which we shall find lies at the base of all knowledge of the life-histories of the higher plants.

It will be seen that the asexual method of multiplication is much the more efficient of the two, inasmuch as it is infinitely simpler, waste of reproductive cells is not of so much moment, their formation takes up a very short space of time, and they are, at least for many generations, quite as fertile as the true products of sexual union. It is conceivable that under these circumstances the sexual method of multiplication might in the *Fungi* fall into disuse and ultimately disappear altogether. Hence arises the phenomenon of **apogamy** in *Fungi*, i.e. the absence of sexual reproductive powers. We have all stages in the degeneration exemplified by different forms. We have instances, for example, of male and female organs being formed which never unite, of dwarf male organs which perform apparently no function, and of forms like the common mushroom (*Agaricus*), where, so far as we know, no sexual organs are formed at all. Apogamy is especially interesting when viewed in relation to the life-history and habits of these plants.

A physiological classification of *Fungi* into two groups may be formulated, based on their habits. Some live on dead or decaying organic matter; such are termed **saprophytes**; others live parasitically on living plants and animals usually causing a more or less serious disease in the host; such forms may be termed **parasites**. As a general rule, it may be laid down that the more pronounced

---

[1] The colonial habit of the moulds accounts for the co-existence of the two generations on the same plant. A thallus may bear in one place sexual reproductive organs, in another spore-producing filaments.

the degree of parasitism in any fungus, the more degenerate are the reproductive organs. The impulse given to the plant causing it to produce reproductive cells probably comes from the protoplasm of the host instead of from the protoplasm of a male sexual cell (Marshall Ward). When surrounding conditions are such that extraneous impulse cannot be obtained, then true sexual reproduction supervenes and saves the parasite from extinction.

SECTION IV.—MUSCI—*POLYTRICHUM*.

We began our study of *Penicillium* by emphasising the salient features in its structure and life-history as popularly known. Similarly, in the case of the moss, we will begin our discussion of the type by noting certain general points which at once strike the eye (fig. 31).

First we note that the thallus, which in *Fucus* was a flattened branched brown expansion, and in *Penicillium* a colourless loose filamentous mass without definite form, is here distinctly more in accordance with what we are commonly disposed to associate the term plant. We note the existence of a distinct stem, from which leaves arise, and the continuation of the stem below ground as a root. We note, moreover, that the thallus has chlorophyll present in its cells. Further, at certain seasons of the year we find small cylindrical urns or boxes surmounted by pointed caps which spring from the free termination of the thallus and are separated from it by a long stalk. So far for the popular knowledge of the life-history of the moss. We must now deal more in detail with these various parts, and endeavour to trace a relationship between the stages in the life-history of the moss and those of the two immediately preceding types.

Treating first of the **thallus**, we may for convenience of description separate it into **stem, root**, and **leaves**.

Stem.—The stem of the moss presents us with an example

of differentiation, for we find in it still further developed the different systems of tissues foreshadowed in the stem of *Fucus* (fig. 32). Superficially, the cells have their walls thickened, and of a darker colour (yellow or brown). The cells forming the cortical tissue have also thickened cell-walls, but becoming thin-walled as they approach the centre. Such cells of tolerably uniform diameter and undifferentiated character receive the name of **parenchyma**, or **parenchymatous tissue**. The central cells of the stem differ in character in different species of moss. In the type chosen for consideration the cells are elongated and thick walled, forming a tolerably firm axis or support, to which the name of **sclerenchyma** or **sclerenchymatous tissue** is given. In higher plants there is found running through the stem, branches, roots, and leaves, a very perfect system of strands of sclerenchyma accompanied by vessels and variously modified cells, of which we shall have to speak afterwards more in detail. That system has been called the **fibro-vascular system**. One is at first inclined to look upon this axial strand in the moss stem as a rudimentary fibro-vascular strand. It is scarcely correct, however, to adopt that view, seeing that the moss plant and the ordinary flowering plant are not comparable organisms—in fact, as we shall afterwards see, do not belong to the same generation. Even the terms stem, leaf, root, are used to indicate structures, at the most, only analogous to the corresponding parts in higher plants. Only a few species of moss

FIG. 31.—*Polytrichum commune*, TERMINATION OF THE FEMALE PLANT. (Maout and Decaisne.)

show this amount of differentiation. Whilst a few possess a strand of elongated thick-walled cells in the axis of the stem, many have only thin-walled medullary parenchyma.

The stem of the moss may branch, whilst not infrequently a shoot or **stolon**, which may run along underground, or just on the surface, may be given off. The stolon usually takes root at some little distance from the parent plant, and forming an upright stem begins life independently.

The roots of the moss are more correctly termed **rhizoids**, as being the organs by which the thallus fixes itself to, and absorbs nourishment from, the ground. The rhizoids spring in a tuft from the base of the stem, differing, therefore, markedly from the continuation of the stem below ground, to which the term root is applied in most of the higher plants. When examined microscopically the rhizoids are found to be merely cellular outgrowths from the epidermis, and do not contain any of the subjacent tissues. They correspond to the epidermal hairs which are found so abundantly springing from the various organs, more especially of flowering plants. The rhizoids, unlike the stem, branch very freely, and usually form a very dense matting below ground, or just on the surface. The cells forming the rhizoids are elongated, and contain granular protoplasm, oil globules, &c. enclosed in an orange-coloured or brown cell-wall, the outer surface of which becomes gradually clothed with particles of the soil.

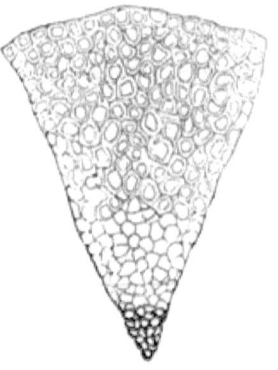

FIG. 32.—*Polytrichum commune*, TRANSVERSE SECTION OF THE STEM.

The **leaves** are also merely cellular outgrowths of the stem, and are composed of almost undifferentiated parenchyma, the cells of which, however, contain chlorophyll in addition to the ordinary constituents of such cells. In form the leaf is broad at its base and pointed at its free end. It is **sessile**, i.e. has no stalk, and is attached directly to the stem. In those species which possess an axial bundle of elongated cells, the leaf shows a central nerve, or **midrib**, of similar cells, continuous with those of the axial strand. The margin of the leaf commonly bears minute spines. The leaves are arranged in a definite order round the stem, approaching to a more or less perfect spiral.

It has been already remarked that the thallus had the power of throwing out from itself a stolon or shoot, which, after creeping along the ground for some distance, could take root, and develop into an independent plant. This method of multiplication is a form of **vegetative reproduction**, and it is a method especially common amongst mosses, and is by no means confined to the production of stolons. The first stage in the formation of a new plant, by vegetative multiplication from the root, is the production of a small branched green intermediate thallus known as a **protonema**, from which springs the erect stem of the thallus proper.

Reproductive organs.—The essential organs of reproduction are borne at the free termination of the stem surrounded by an **involucre** of leaves. The male organs may be borne on the same stem as the female organs, or on different plants. If on the same thallus, the spermaria and ovaria may be intermingled or may be arranged so that the ovaria are central whilst the spermaria surround them. The involucres differ slightly in the character of their leaves according to the sex. In *Polytrichum* the sexual organs are borne on different stems on distinct plants.

The **spermarium** is an elongated sac, the wall of which is composed of many cells arranged in a single layer deep. The cells contain chlorophyll bodies imbedded in the granular protoplasm. The sac is filled with cellular tissue, the mother cells of the sperms. The contents of each cell become gradually transformed into a sperm, round which, when mature, the cell-wall remains as an envelope. Each **sperm** consists of an elongated spirally twisted body, which terminates in two delicate flagella, by means of which it is

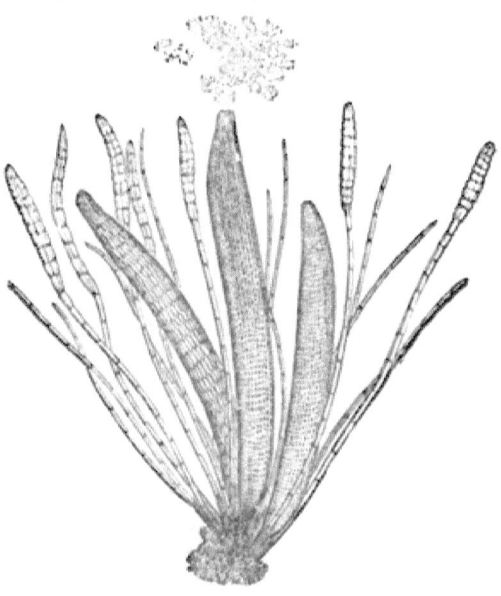

FIG. 33.—*Polytrichum commune*, TERMINATION OF A MALE PLANT. (Maout and Decaisne.)

FIG. 34. —*Polytrichum commune.*—PARAPHYSES AND SPERMARIA, ONE OF WHICH EMITS SPERMS. (Maout and Decaisne.)

FIG. 35.—*Polytrichum commune.*—SPERMS. (Maout and Decaisne.)

able to move in a fluid medium. When they first escape, the sperms with their enclosing cysts lie in a mucilaginous matrix, which, however, ere long becomes dissolved and disappears. In addition to the spermaria there are numerous sterile hairs, or **paraphyses**, which are slightly different in form, being more club-shaped and with a narrower stalk. They carry chlorophyll grains and resemble in other respects ordinary epidermal hairs, or the paraphyses of *Fucus*, with which they are homologous.

The female sexual organ or **ovarium** consists of a swollen basal portion, commonly called the **venter**, and a long terminal tube or **neck** (fig. 37). Both venter and neck are made of cells, two layers thick in the venter, and one layer thick in the neck. The venter when mature contains one large central cell, the **ovum**, whilst the canal in the neck is filled by

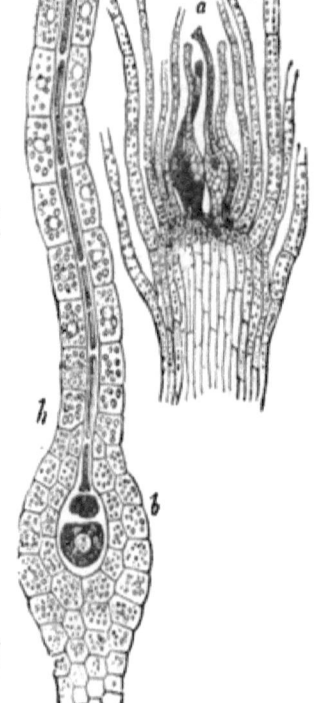

FIG. 37.—*Funaria hygrometrica.* (Sachs.)

A, apex of stem of a female thallus (× 100); *a*, female reproductive organs; *b*, leaves. B, female reproductive organ; *b*, venter with ovum; *h*, neck with seven canal cells.

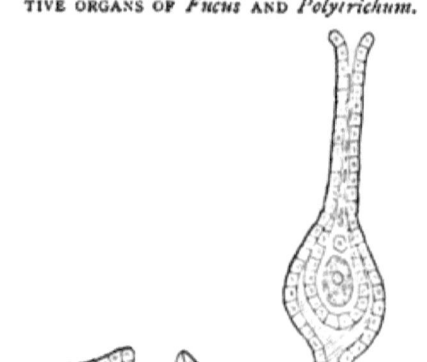

FIG. 36.— DIAGRAMMATIC REPRESENTATION OF THE HOMOLOGIES OF THE FEMALE REPRODUCTIVE ORGANS OF *Fucus* AND *Polytrichum*.

the mucilaginous remains of half-a-dozen long narrow cells, whose duty it is before fertilisation to swell and force open the neck to permit of the entrance of the sperms. The ovum, by transverse division, adds one more to the row of **canal cells**.

Notwithstanding the great apparent dissimilarity of the various organs to those of *Fucus*, it is possible to see in the venter the very much reduced cavity of a female 'conceptacle.' The comparison of the two cases will best be understood by reference to fig. 36, where a diagrammatic repre-

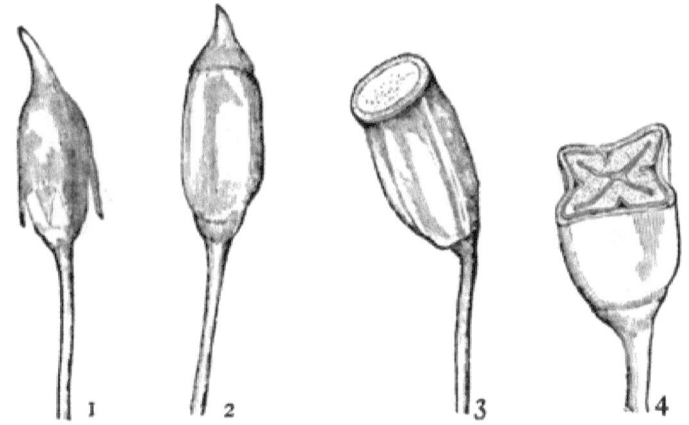

FIG. 38.—*Polytrichum commune*. (Maout and Decaisne.)

1. Theca with calyptra. 2, Calyptra removed to show operculum. 3, Operculum removed. 4, Transverse section of theca.

sentation of the two 'conceptacles' is given showing them, as it were, originating from the same thallus. It will be seen that the conceptacle of the moss is simply an upraised and free conceptacle of *Fucus*. In *Fucus* the contents of the ovarium broke up into eight cells, all of which became ova. Here seven of these cells perform a very subsidiary function, namely, that of forcing the mouth of the 'conceptacle' open for the entrance of the sperm. Naturally the close-fitting and protecting venter and neck do away with the necessity of a special protecting cell-wall or capsule for the ovum and the seven modified ova, or canal cells.

It is subsequent to fertilisation that the difficulty of

explaining the homologies of the various parts begins. On fertilisation the ovum becomes an **embryo**. The canal cells are now completely disorganised and disappear. The embryo rapidly divides and forms a mass of cells which soon differentiates into a stalk, or **seta**, and a capsule, or **theca**. As the development of this organism takes place in the venter, naturally the venter very soon becomes too large to contain it, and its walls give

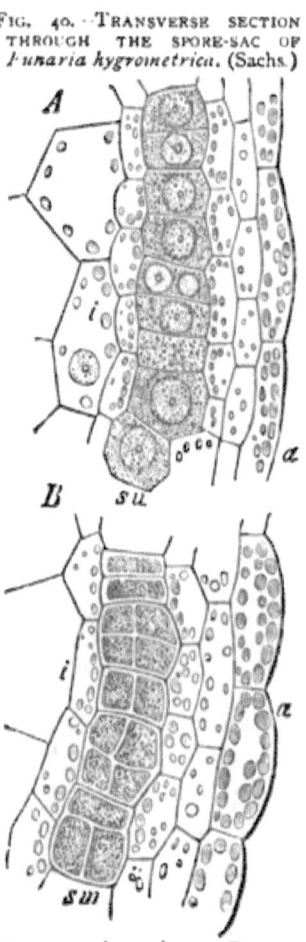

FIG. 40.—TRANSVERSE SECTION THROUGH THE SPORE-SAC OF *Funaria hygrometrica*. (Sachs.)

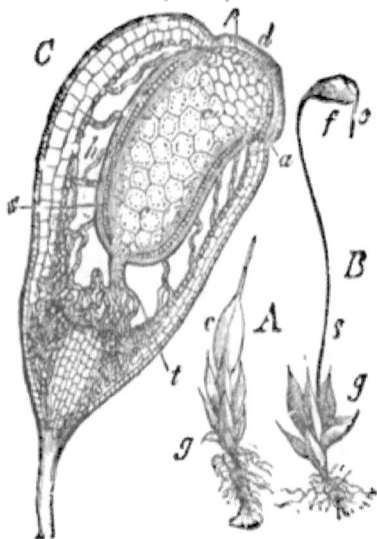

FIG. 39.—*Funaria hygrometrica*. (Sachs.)

A, female plant, with root hairs, and young theca enclosed in the calyptra, *c*. *B*, asexual generation nearly mature ; *s*, seta ; *f*, theca. *C*. longitudinal section of theca (magnified) ; *t c c*, columella ; *d*, operculum ; *p*, peristome ; *s*. archesporium ; *h*, air-spaces.

A, *s u*, archesporium. *B*, *s m*, mother spore-cells ; *a*, outer, *i*, inner side of the spore-sac.

way at the base, whilst the embryo bears on its head, or theca, the upper portion of the venter and its neck as a cap, or **calyptra**. The calyptra remains attached to the embryo for a time, and then drops off. It will now be necessary to study this product of sexual union, an organism, it is to be noted, quite different from the thallus which produced the sexual cells and which now bears the embryonic new generation as a parasite on itself.

As already stated, the new generation consists of a stalk, or seta, surmounted by a capsule, or theca. The seta is fixed firmly in the basal portion of the venter, and consists of a core of slightly elongated cells covered by a thickened epidermis. The seta swells slightly below the theca forming the **apophysis**. The seta is continued up through the theca as the **columella**. Surrounding the columella is an annular space traversed by thread-like cells, which stretch from the columella to the outer wall of the theca. The wall of the theca is several layers of cells deep, and has its epidermal layer strongly thickened. Closely surrounding the columella, but separated from the annular air-space, by two or more layers of cells containing chlorophyll, forming the **spore-sac** or **sporangium**, lies a layer of cells which are highly protoplasmic and are capable of active division This forms what is known as the **archesporium** (fig. 40). These cells do not become spores directly, but give rise to what are known as **mother spore-cells** lying in the interior of the now much enlarged sporangium. The walls of the mother spore-cells deliquesce, or become watery, forming a fluid medium in which float the rapidly developing spores, formed by subdivision into four of each of the mother spore-cells. The upper part of the columella is much enlarged, and forms a disc covering the sporangium and its contained spores. The margin of the disc-like head of the columella becomes continuous with the outer wall of the theca, which is itself in this region greatly modified. The terminal pointed portion of the theca separates as a lid or **operculum**. At the point of junction between the operculum and the theca, there is developed a series of multicellular hairs, the cell-walls of which are thickened and

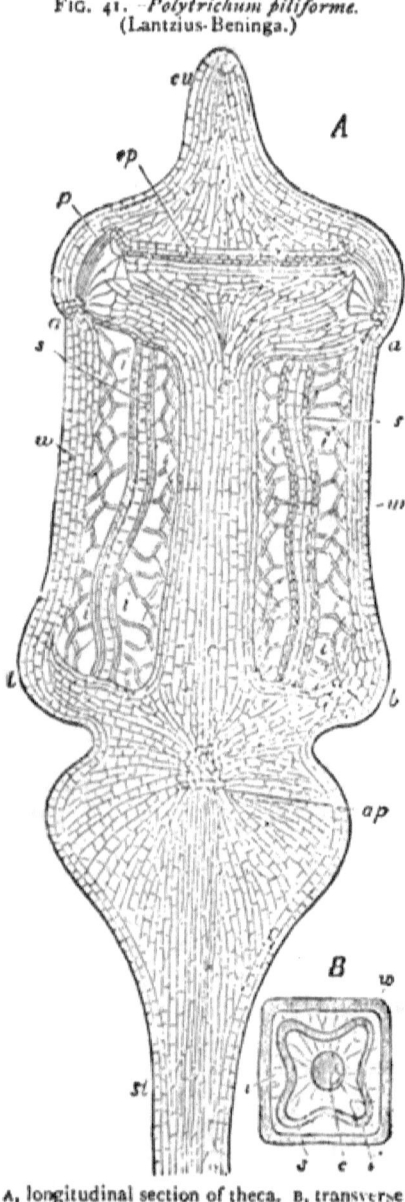

Fig. 41.—*Polytrichum piliforme.*
(Lantzius-Beninga.)

A, longitudinal section of theca. B, transverse section: *w*, wall of theca; *c u*, operculum; *c, c*, columella; *p*, peristomium; *e p*, epiphragm; *i, i*, air spaces; *s*, spore-sac; *s t*, seta; *a p*, apophysis; *a, a*, attachment of peristomium.

deep brown in colour. This fringe of hairs forms the **peristomium**. The hairs are broad at their bases and taper inwards, where they are attached to a thin plate or **epiphragm**, which forms a temporary lid to the theca after the removal of the operculum.

When the spores are ripe the operculum is forced off by the expansion of the peristomium, and the spores are shaken out by the swaying of the long seta in the wind. Each spore is a cell covered by an outer brown cell-wall or **exosporium** and an inner colourless cell-wall or **endosporium**, and contains protoplasm, oil globules, and chlorophyll. The time required for the development of the asexual parasitic generation varies in different species, but an average period is three or four months. The spore germinates rapidly when sown on moist soil, and forms a protonema. The general character of the protonema has already been described (p. 104).

From this intermediate thallus the true thallus springs as a lateral outgrowth. The mode of development and the varieties of form observable among protonemata cannot be dealt with in the present volume. The thallus originates from the subdivision of a single cell of the protonema, which may be termed an **apical cell** since it, or a descendant of it, retains its apical position, and by its subdivision increases the length of the shoot.

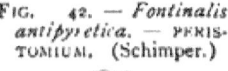

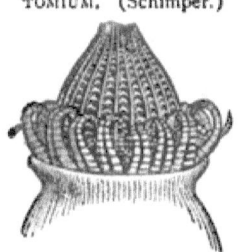

FIG. 42. — *Fontinalis antipyretica.* — PERISTOMIUM. (Schimper.)

Having gone over briefly the structure and life-history of a typical moss, it may be well by way of summary to follow the plan adopted at the end of

FIG. 43. — *Funaria hygrometrica.* (Sachs.)

A, germinating spores (×550); *s*, exosporium; *w*, root hair; *v*, vacuole. B, part of protonema three weeks after germination (×90); *h*, main branch; *b*, side branch; *k*, formation of a bud from which the stem of the moss arises.

the preceding sections, and give a short comparison of the stages in the life-history of the moss with those of the lower types already discussed.

We have to note in the first place the comparative importance of the thallus or sexual generation, which in *Polytrichum* assumes the external appearance of, and simulates in internal structure, an ordinary flowering plant. We note further the existence of an asexual generation which is parasitic on the sexual generation, although the succession of asexual generations in *Penicillium* is here represented by the power on the part of the sexual thalli to separate off portions of themselves in the form of protonemata, which are capable of producing again a sexual thallus by ordinary vegetative division. We note, moreover, that the spore-producing generation is a highly organised structure, and that it carries distinctively a sporangium, some of the contained cells of which form an archesporium, i.e. a group or layer of cells capable indirectly of producing spores or asexual cells, which, without union with any other cell, are able to form protonemata and new sexual plants. The seta and theca of the moss correspond, therefore, to the stalk and spore-bearing head of the fungus, together with that part of the mycelium which bears the sporangium. We have in the moss, in short, a plant which has made the most possible of its sexual stage, while the asexual plant, by being parasitic on the sexual, has arrested that development, and laid the foundation of a new type of plant altogether, viz. the asexual spore-bearing generation foreshadowed in *Penicillium*.

CHAPTER VIII.

METAPHYTA—VASCULARIA.

Section I.—Filices—*PTERIS*.

In discussing the morphology and life-history of the fern we are upon more familiar ground; the various parts of the adult plant, and its habit of producing much simpler intermediate plants capable again of giving rise to the plant from which it was itself developed, are all matters of common knowledge. It may be well, however, to summarise that knowledge in technical terminology.

Starting from the fern, commonly so called, we are able to distinguish an underground stem or **rhizome** from which **roots** are given off. We can, moreover, differentiate **shoots** springing from this rhizome and **fronds** or leaves, usually of large size, which appear above ground, and constitute the visible part of the plant. On the under surface of these fronds at certain seasons, and covered over and protected by an inturning of the leaf, or a scale-like projection of it, are to be found collections of brown granular-like bodies, known as **sporangia**, from which can be shaken a fine dust, composed of what are popularly and scientifically known as **spores**. These spores, if sown in a suitable soil, germinate and form small flattened green plants, anchored to the ground by minute **rootlets**, and not exhibiting any differentiation into the stem, root, leaves, &c. which characterised the true fern. To this organism the term 'prothallus' has been applied. It will be known throughout this chapter as the **thallus**. Upon this thallus **male** and **female reproductive** organs are developed, and from the female organ after it has been fertilised the new fern springs.

Following the course we adopted in the description of the moss, we ought to begin our study of the life-history of the fern by an account of the thallus; it will be more convenient, however, to commence with the product of sexual reproduction, i.e. the fern so called. As already stated, we distinguish in the adult fern, rhizome, roots, shoots, and fronds. It will be necessary to describe these successively in detail.

Rhizome.—The rhizome of *Pteris aquilina* consists of an elongated, brown, scaly body, irregularly thickened at intervals where the fronds are given off. To these thickened portions the term **node** is given, whilst the space between any two nodes is naturally termed an **internode**. The rhizome itself is covered by a scaly integument, dark brown in colour save along either side, where there is a lighter strip termed the **lateral line**. The rhizome shows as a whole a difference in age from one end to the other. One extremity is pointed—the growing point—whilst the other end is thicker, darker, and apparently withering away. The nodes also give rise to shoots which are successively older from the pointed to the withered end of the rhizome. It is worthy of note that the growing point is not bud-like whilst the shoots are so. It is the second youngest shoot that shows fronds above ground, the older shoots having done so in past seasons, and the youngest shoot being that which will take the place of the present bunch of fronds in the following year. Over the outside of the rhizome the **leaf-scales, ramenta**, or **paleæ** have already been alluded to. They must not be mistaken for the true leaves whose origin they surround.

The minute structure of the rhizome is of considerable importance, as in it we come face to face for the first time with that great differentiation of tissues so characteristic of the higher plants. If a transverse section be microscopically

FIG. 44.—*Asplenium adiantum nigrum.*—RHIZOME AND PINNÆ. (Maout and Decaisne.)

examined it will be found that externally the rhizome is covered by a single layer of tabular cells, the **epidermis**, the cell-walls of which are very thick and of a deep brown colour (fig. 46). From this layer may be given off uni- or multicellular hairs, technically called **trichomes**. These may be simple and hair-like, but frequently take on the appearance of sessile leaves (ramenta).

Enclosed by the epidermal layer on all sides lies the **fundamental tissue**, which composes the main mass of the stem, and which is modified differently in different parts of the section. Immediately beneath the epidermis lies the **subepidermis**, consisting of several layers of thick-walled cells, or **sclerenchyma**, gradually shading off into the general thin-walled **parenchyma** of the fundamental tissue. The epidermal and subepidermal cells are filled only with water or granular débris; the parenchyma of the fundamental tissue, on the other hand, contains nucleated granular protoplasm and starch grains closely applied to the cell-wall. Here and there in the fundamental tissue are to be seen groups of sclerenchymatous cells, with thickened cell-walls. Such sclerenchyma not infrequently takes on a horse-shoe or other characteristic shape. Most important of all, however, are the **fibro-vascular strands**, which are plunged irregularly in the fundamental tissue, and are variable in size. In transverse section one of these strands shows externally, and next the fundamental tissue a layer of cells known as the **endodermis** (fig. 47). These cells are formed from the fundamental tissue and are dead in the sense of containing no protoplasm; their cell-walls have been modified and form a definite boundary for the fibro-vascular strand. Immediately within the en-

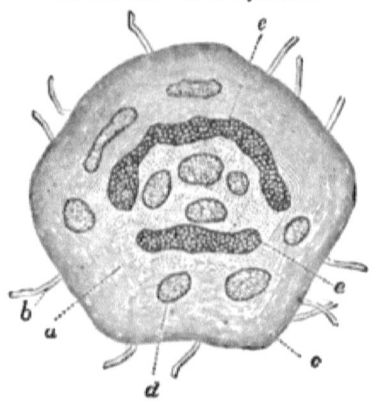

FIG. 45.—TRANSVERSE SECTION OF THE RHIZOME OF *Pteris aquilina*.

a, fundamental parenchyma; *b*, epidermal hair; *c*, cortex; *d*, fibro-vascular strand; *e*, sclerenchymatous strands.

FIG. 46.—TRANSVERSE SECTION RHIZOME OF *Pteris aquilina*. (Thomé.)
II.

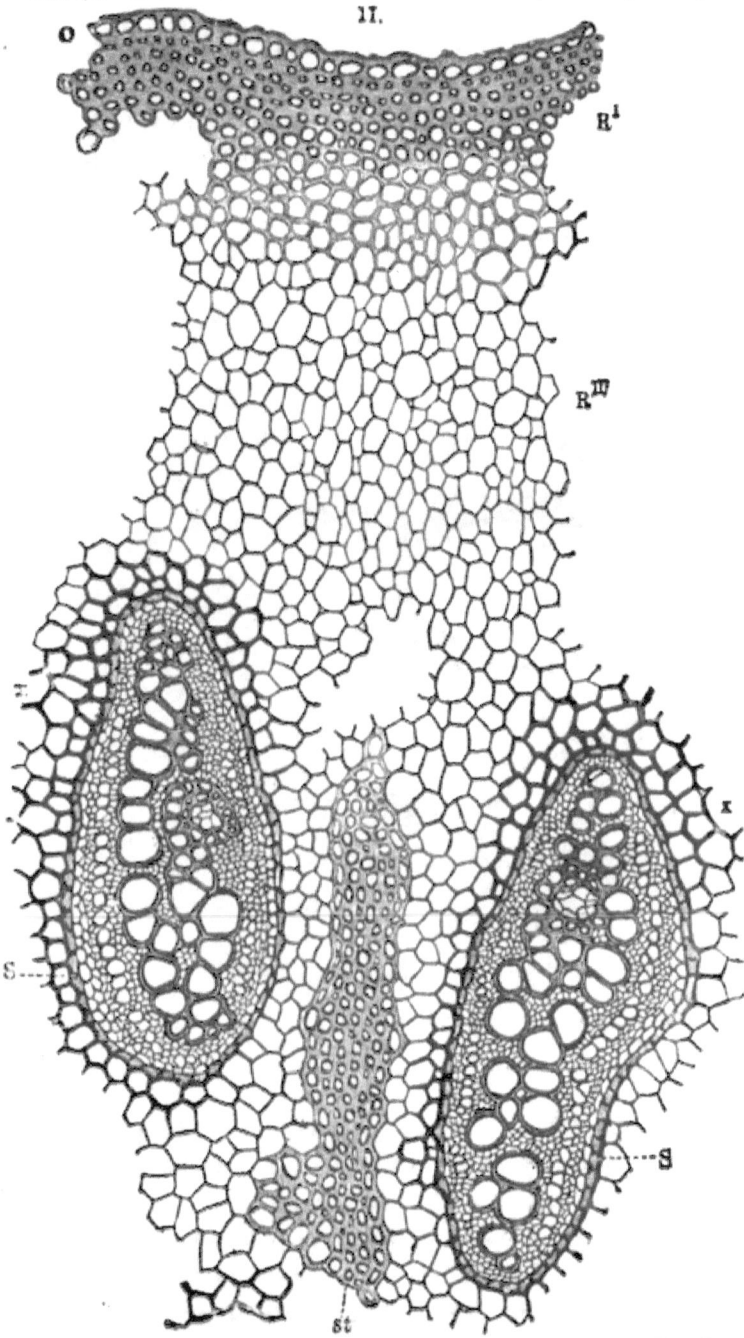

o, epidermis; R', thick-walled, R" thin-walled cortical cell; s, endodermis; st, sclerenchyma; x, fundamental parenchyma.

dodermis lies another layer of cells, also derived from the fundamental tissue, but differing from the endodermis in that the cells contain starch-granules in considerable abundance. Forming a zone of irregular thickness within this

FIG. 47.—PART OF A TRANSVERSE SECTION OF FIBRO-VASCULAR STRAND OF *Pteris aquilina*. (Sachs.)

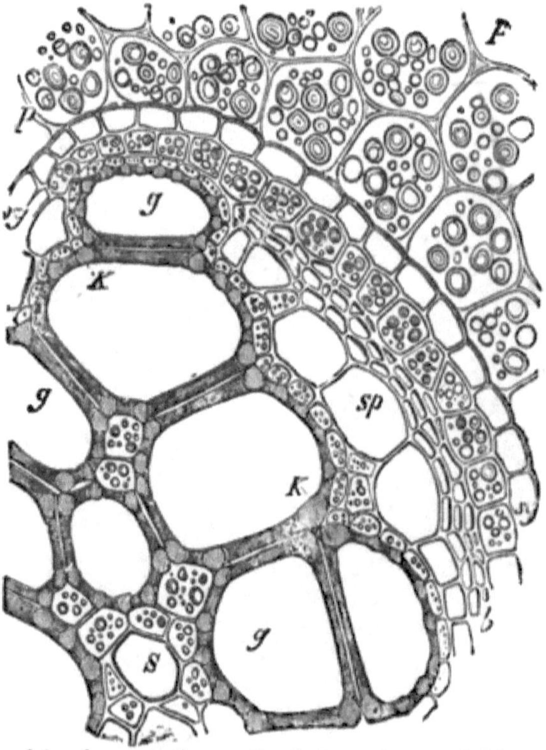

P, starch-bearing parenchyma; *S*, spiral vessel surrounded by prosenchyma; *g g*, scalariform vessels; *s p*, sieve tubes; *b*, bast; *s₁*, endodermis outside the phloëm sheath.

inner sheath (sometimes known as the **phloëm-** or **bast-sheath**) lies the **phloëm, or bast**, one of the two essential constituents of the fibro-vascular strand. The phloëm consists chiefly of vessels, along with a small amount of starch-bearing parenchyma. The cells are known as **bast parenchyma**; they are closely packed, elongated, and much crushed, the walls being considerably thickened. The vessels are of peculiar form and deserve special notice. In section they appear as large apertures lying internal to the bast fibres, and often surrounded by the starch-bearing parenchyma above referred to. Each vessel is an elongated tube whose walls are riddled with minute apertures. These apertures are not uniformly distributed, but are collected in areas, the so-called **sieve plates** (see fig. 68). From their possession of these curious discs the vessels of the phloem are known as **sieve tubes**. Enclosed by the phloëm lies a mass of parenchymatous tissue surrounding the vessels, and collectively known as the **xylem** or **wood**. The parenchyma does not differ from specimens of that tissue already described. The vessels are complicated in structure, and are known as **tracheæ**. The wall of each has laid down upon it internally a layer of secondary deposit, and that not uniformly, but in the shape of transverse bars. These bars are joined together at their ends ; hence a series of slit-like spaces are left where the primary cell-wall can be seen. The appearance of such a vessel reminds one forcibly of a ladder, the thickenings corresponding to rungs : hence the name given to these vessels, viz. **scalariform** (fig. 48). Associated with the tracheæ are found long, narrow vessels in which a spiral thickening has been laid down : these are characteristic of the xylem and are called **spiral vessels**. They are central in position (fig. 47). The structure of these several elements and their relationship to each other may be best made out by comparing a transverse and a longitudinal section of a strand.

A fibro-vascular strand, then, consists of two kinds of vessels surrounded by certain fibres and cells which strengthen, protect, or act as padding to the vessels, viz. the vessels of the xylem and the vessels of the phlöem—the tracheæ and sieve tubes respectively. These two important elements are differently arranged with reference to each other in different plants. In *Pteris* the arrangement is said to be concentric, seeing that the xylem is internal, and that the phloëm encloses it.

It will be necessary at this point to investigate the structure of the growing point of the rhizome in order to gain some idea as to the mode of origin of these various tissues.

FIG. 48.—*Pteris aquilina.* SCALARIFORM VESSEL. (Thomé.)

The growing point of the stem consists of one **apical cell**, full of protoplasm, the parent of innumerable cells surrounding it, and together with them forming the growing point of the rhizome These growing cells go collectively by the name of **meristem**. The growing apex is carefully protected by a series of loosely arranged ramenta, but possesses no distinct cap, such as we shall find true roots have. No differentiation of the cells into fibres, vessels, sclerenchyma, &c. is observable near the apex. At some distance from the growing point the cells will be seen to become elongated, thickened, and otherwise metamorphosed to form those modified cells described as composing the fibro-vascular strand.

It is possible, by prolonged maceration in water, or very dilute potash, to obtain a skeleton of the fibro-vascular system of the fern rhizome. The skeleton forms a very perfect network, or **netted cylinder**, from which smaller strands pass off into the leaves.

Roots.—Passing now to the roots we find that they are given off from the rhizome behind the growing point, and consist primarily of a group of actively dividing cells. The root is covered terminally by a **root-cap**, which originates by the subdivision of a cell segmented off from the apical cell, whilst other cells, likewise formed from the apical cell, become epidermis, fundamental tissue, and fibro-vascular strands (fig. 49). The parent roots give off lateral **rootlets**, which spring from cells of the fundamental tissue of the parent root near its apex, and before it has become differentiated into the elements of the fibro-vascular bundles. These again give origin to **root-hairs** like those of the moss. A transverse section of a true root exhibits an appearance not unlike that described for the stem, i.e. externally an epidermis, which as the root grows older may be replaced by sub-

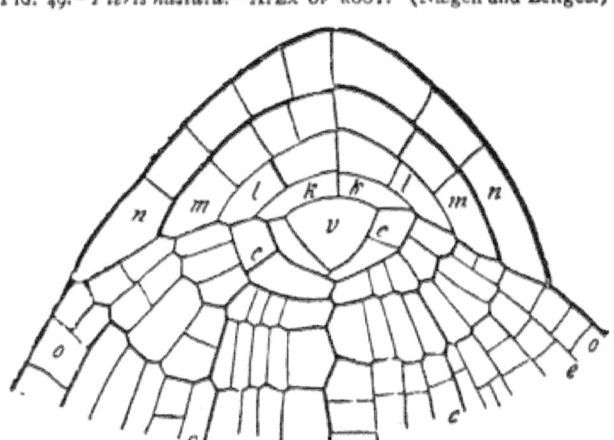

FIG. 49.—*Pteris hastata.*—APEX OF ROOT. (Nægeli and Leitgeb.)

v, apical cell ; c, o, e, tissues of the root ; k, l, m, n, tissue of the root cap.

epidermal tissue, fundamental tissue traversed by fibro-vascular bundles, and with portions of it metamorphosed into sclerenchyma.

Shoots.—The **leaves** appear on the rhizome as small buds, gradually elongating until they reach the surface of the ground. They are covered by ramenta which protect the young fronds from injury. Each leaf when in the bud has its several parts rolled up in crozier form (fig. 44). The arrangement of leaves in the bud is termed **vernation** or **præfoliation**. The leaves of all plants are not arranged in the same manner. Those of the ferns are said to have **circinate** vernation.

Frond.—The leaf or frond is usually a much branched structure of considerable size. It consists of a stout **rachis, leaf-stalk,** or **petiole,** and in *Pteris* of considerable length. From the petiole are given off **veins,** and from these again **veinlets.** These strands support the flattened green **lamina,** which is thus subdivided into **pinnæ** and **pinnules,** corresponding to the veins and veinlets respectively. The entire lamina is covered on both sides by an epidermis of flat green cells, bounding and enclosing loose parenchyma plentifully supplied with chlorophyll, starch, &c. The epidermal cells are prolonged into epidermal hairs, but have no intercellular spaces, with the exception of the **stomata.** A **stoma** is a minute aperture in the epidermis bounded by two chlorophyll-bearing guard cells, capable of altering the size of the stoma by their contraction or expansion under different hygroscopic conditions of the atmosphere, and according as the frond is or is not exposed to sunlight. The stomata are as a rule more abundant on the under surface of the leaf (fig. 71). Since the histological structure of a fern leaf is fundamentally the same as that of the angiosperm leaf a detailed description of that organ is postponed (page 152).

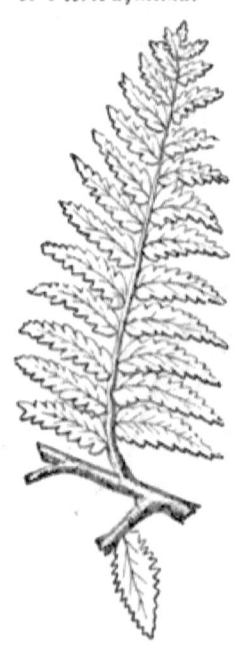

FIG. 50.— PINNA AND PINNULES OF A FROND OF *Pteris aquilina*.

One important structure developed on the leaf remains to be described, viz. the **asexual reproductive organ** or **sporangium.** At certain seasons of the year the edges of the laminæ will be found to be curled in towards the under surface, and will be found to enclose a number of small dark brown stalked bodies. These are the sporangia. In many ferns, where the sporangia are produced on the under surface of the leaf more towards its centre, there are developed scale-like outgrowths from the epidermis of the leaf, which have for their function the protection of the sporangia before they are mature. The epidermal covering is known as an **indusium**, and a group of sporangia enclosed by an indusium is termed a **sorus**. In *Pteris*, however, the edge of the leaf forms a false indusium, whilst the term sorus must be applied to the entire infolded margin and its contents. All the leaves of the fern do not carry sporangia—a point of some

FIG. 51.—*Pteris aquilina.*—SORUS AND INDUSIUM. (Maout and Decaisne.)

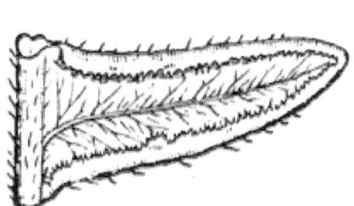

Pinnule with incurved edge.

Sporangia exposed by rupture of indusium.

importance, as we shall see subsequently. Those leaves which do carry sori, i.e. the fertile leaves, are termed **sporophylla**.

It will be necessary now to examine a sorus in greater detail.

If a section of the margin of a sporophyllum be made the sporangia will be found to be stalked capsules springing from the under surface of the leaf (fig. 51). Each sporangium is multicellular, and continuous with the epidermis of the leaf, the point of origin of a sporangium being termed the **placenta**.

The stalk of the sporangium, or **funicle**, is itself multicellular, but does not contain any fibro-vascular or fundamental tissue. In its mature state it usually consists of two or more rows of cells, although very young sporangia have only a single linear series. The capsule consists of a single layer of thin squames enclosing a space, filled in the mature sporangium by a large number of **spores**. The cells of the wall of

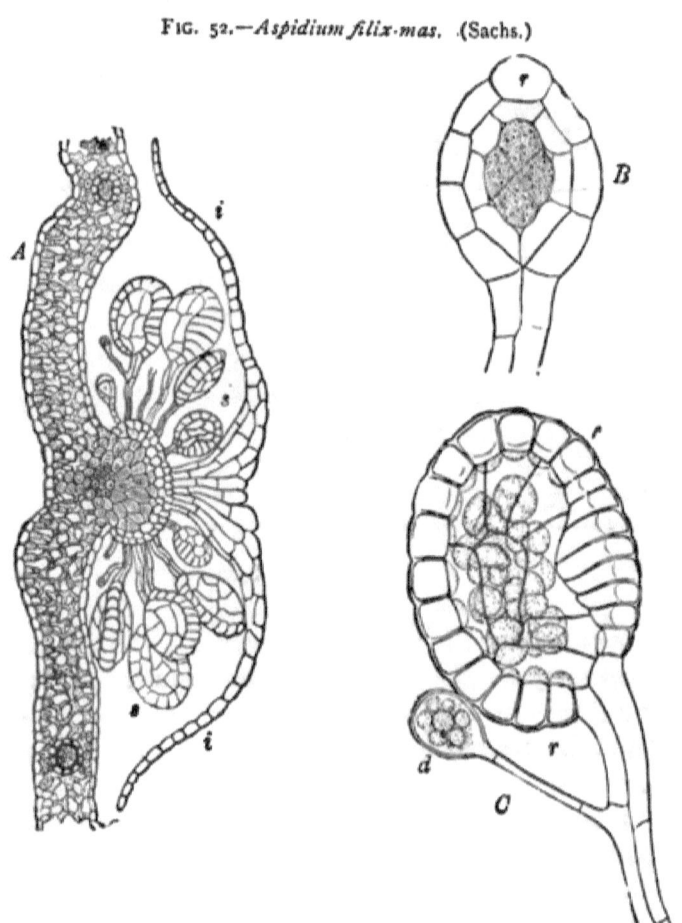

FIG. 52.—*Aspidium filix-mas.* (Sachs.)

A, section of leaf with sorus; *s*, sporangia; *i*, indusium. B, young sporangium; *r*, annulus. C, mature sporangium containing spores; *d*, glandular hair.

the sporangium are modified in one region, so as to form what is known as the **annulus**. The row of cells composing it have their walls greatly thickened and are of a dark brown colour. Rupture of the thin parietal cells is brought about by drying of the annular cells. The contents of the sporangium are thus ejected. If one of the spores be examined under a high power of the microscope it will be found to consist of a minute sac filled with granular protoplasm, with a nucleus. The wall is differentiated into a thin inner layer or **endosporium**, and a thick outer layer or **exosporium**.

FIG 53.—*Pteris aquilina.*—SPORE.

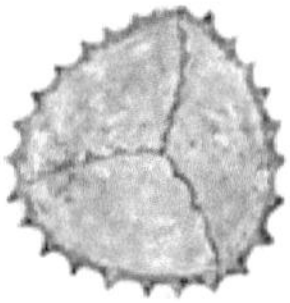

Among the fertile sporangia are occasionally to be seen barren sporangia, multicellular club-shaped hairs which have been termed **paraphyses**; in other words, sporangia which have not come to maturity, which have been crowded out in fact, and have not had room to develop, owing to the more vigorous growth of their neighbours.

As already stated, the sporangium and its contents are formed from the epidermal layer of the sporophyll. Its mode of origin is of importance and demands a brief description in passing. The sporangium first appears as a bud from an epidermal cell on that region of the leaf to which the name placenta has been given. The bud becomes segmented off from the epidermal cell by a transverse partition, just as is the case with multicellular or unicellular epidermal hairs. Indeed, a sporangium in the primary stages of its development is morphologically a hair or **trichome**. The unicellular trichome segments transversely into a proximal cell, which gives origin to the funicle, and a distal cell which gives origin to the capsule. The proximal cell segments repeatedly both transversely and longitudinally to form the funicle; the distal cell also repeatedly segments, but the details of segmentation are in that case of more importance. In the first place four cells are cut off tangentially, leaving the central cell to form what is known as the **archesporium**. These tangentially formed cells become the sporangial wall by repeated subdivision perpendicular to the surface of the sporangium. The archesporium next segments off again tangentially a layer of cells which may by subsequent division become a double layer, to which the name of **tapetum** is given. The remainder of the archesporium gives rise by subdivision to what are known as the **mother spore-cells**, usually sixteen in number. The tapetal cells do not remain long in existence as distinct cells, but deliquesce and form a sort of watery jelly in which the sixteen mother spore-cells float. Thereafter each mother spore-cell divides into four **spores**, each of which in the process of growth assumes the characters described above as possessed by the adult spore.

The various changes which take place in the development of a sporangium must be carefully borne in mind when the mode of origin of the sporangia of the higher plants comes to be considered. The main features in their development will be found to be the same, and homologies at present obscured by an old-fashioned terminology will, in the light of the life-history of the fern, become at once evident.

We have now considered at sufficient length the morphology of the vegetative and asexual reproductive organs of *Pteris*; we must now follow the spore through the changes which it undergoes when sown on moist, warm soil.

The first appearance of the future plant is the protrusion of a minute protoplasmic bud through the exosporium. This bud by growth and division becomes an elongated thread, which by future division becomes a flat expansion, the cells of which contain chlorophyll. Growth takes place chiefly at the distal end of the thallus, and in such a manner that the thallus becomes heart-shaped. Though at first composed of only one layer of cells, two or more layers soon make their appearance. The thallus is especially thick at some distance behind the growing point, and rises in a mound-like elevation on the under surface. From this mound root-hairs, or **rhizoids**, are given off which penetrate the soil and perform the same function that true root-hairs perform in the spore-producing plant. From the same mound are developed the **female sexual organs**, whilst the

male sexual organs originate in the immediate vicinity or generally over the thallus. The true sexual organs of reproduction are constructed on precisely the same pattern as those of the moss.

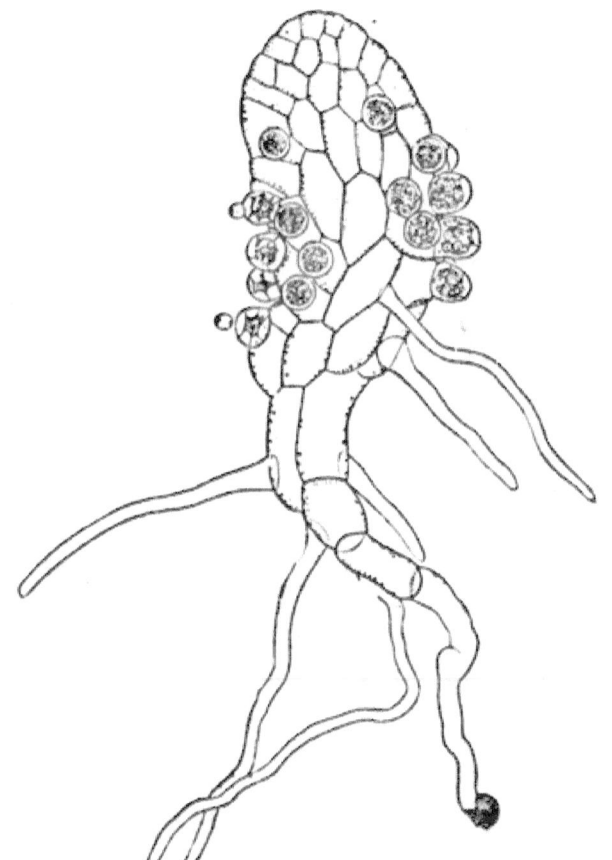

FIG. 54.—*Pteris aquilina.*—DEVELOPING THALLUS. (Maout and Decaisne.)

The male organs, or **spermaria** (antheridia), consist of extremely short multicellular hairs, composed of one central cell and a covering of chlorophyll-bearing cells, originating after the manner of the sporangia of the sporophyllum. The contents of the central cell become transformed into **sperms** of peculiar form. Each sperm originates from, and, until shed, is enclosed by, the cell-wall of the cell which arises by division of the central cell. The sperm is a spirally coiled body bearing a tuft of cilia at one end, and having attached to the other a delicate sac containing cell-sap and granules. The sperms according to recent researches are produced almost entirely from the nuclei of the daughter cells into which the central cell of the spermarium divides. This discovery is quite in harmony with the

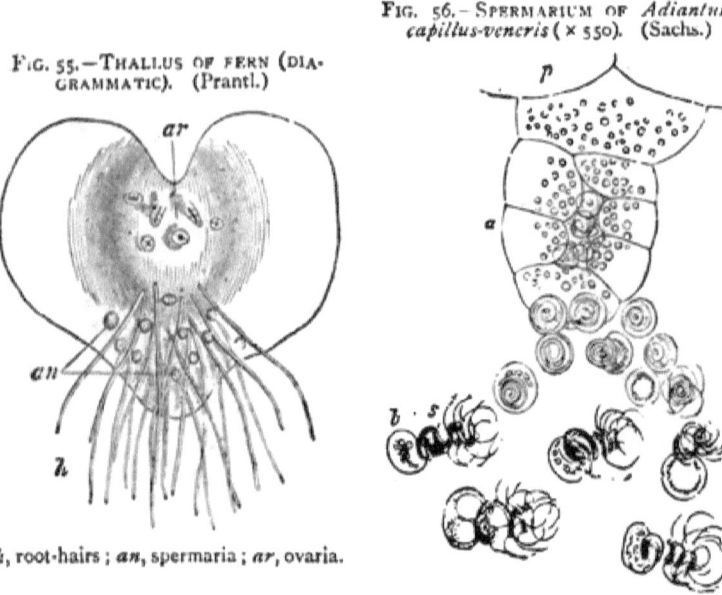

FIG. 55.—THALLUS OF FERN (DIAGRAMMATIC). (Prantl.)

h, root-hairs; *an*, spermaria; *ar*, ovaria.

FIG. 56.—SPERMARIUM OF *Adiantum capillus-veneris* (× 550). (Sachs.)

p, tissue of thallus; *a*, wall of spermarium; *s*, sperm with attached sac, *b*.

conclusions of many workers in the development of the sperms of animals.

The **ovarium** (archegonium) is not unlike the spermarium in general appearance. Like the spermarium also, it is formed from a bud of an epidermal cell, and is morphologically a trichome. As in the moss, it consists of a **venter** and a **neck**, but differs from the ovarium of that type in having the venter sunk in and continuous with the general

tissue of the thallus. It thus approaches more closely to
the ovarium of a unisexual *Fucus*. The neck consists of four
vertical rows of cells each from four to six in number. The
enclosed canal contains two or more canal cells, while the
venter contains the large naked **ovum**. As in the moss, the
canal cells, before maturation of the ovum, become mucilaginous, and act in the first place as a wedge to force open
the canal mouth, and secondly, when expelled, as a trap to

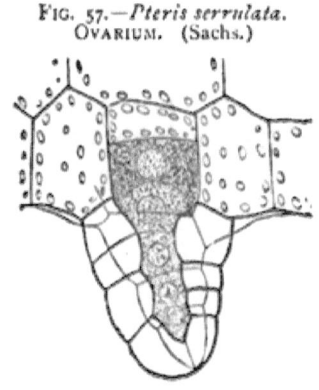

FIG. 57.—*Pteris serrulata*.
OVARIUM. (Sachs.)

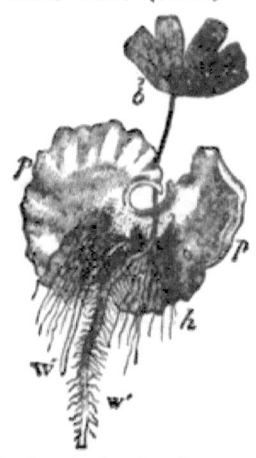

FIG. 58.—*Adiantum capillus-
veneris*.—THALLUS AND
YOUNG FERN. (Sachs.)

b, first leaf; *w'*, *w''*, roots;
h, root-hairs of thallus, *p*, *p*.

catch the sperms and conduct them to the mouth of the
ovarium. One or more sperms touch and fuse with the
ovum, thus fertilising it. The fertilised ovum, or **embryo**,
soon begins to segment into a number of cells, which early
in their history show indications of the respective parts of
the mature plant to which they are to give rise. That portion of the embryo next the bottom of the venter becomes
the apex of the young stem, and a peculiar organ known as
the **foot**; the part of the embryo pointing towards the neck
becomes the root and first leaf. The foot acts as an organ
for the transference of the nourishment from the nurse-like

thallus to the rapidly growing embryo, and corresponds to that which was so largely developed in the embryo of the moss, namely, the seta. The primary root appears first and penetrates the ground, taking on its proper nutritive function; subsequently the first leaf and the apex of the stem emerge, and, bending round, pass to the upper surface of the thallus. The thallus, or sexual generation, having now fulfilled its function, withers away, whilst the young fern develops gradually by division and differentiation of cells into the organism already fully described above.

It may prove by no means unprofitable if we pause at this point and briefly review the phenomena of the life-history of the fern, and draw attention to some of the more important features viewed comparatively.

In the first place, we have to observe **the growing importance of the asexual generation and the waning of the sexual thallus.** In the moss, it is true, we have this condition reversed, the thallus being the important organism, whilst the asexual plant was a mere parasite on it. In the fern the asexual plant is by far the more important of the two.

Again, we have in the fern a perfect example of **alternation of generations**, unlike that of the fungus in being a regular alternation, and differing from that of the moss in that the two generations are for the greater part of their lives totally independent of each other.

Once more we have to observe the **gradual simplification and degeneration of the sexual organs.** The ovarium is having its canal cells reduced in number, and the venter is becoming merely a hollow in the thallus, with which, indeed, its tissue is continuous. The spermarium is also simpler in structure, and gives rise to fewer sperms.

It is also worth observing that the **embryo fern is for some time contained in the thallus which thus acts as a nurse,** and from which the embryo obtains nourishment by means of a special organ, the so-called 'foot.' The embryo, moreover, has its parts arranged so that the primary root points towards the mouth of the canal, and consequently is able to reach the exterior with the minimum amount of difficulty, whilst one primary leaf is developed by which the embryo first obtains nourishment from the atmosphere on its own account. These various peculiarities will be referred to later on when we come to examine the much more complicated embryology of the 'flowering plant.'

There is a large variety of ferns, most of which are familiar objects to many whose tastes do not lie exactly in the way of morphological and etiological research. *Osmunda, Polypodium, Asplenium, Scolopendrium, Aspidium, Adiantum,* are all familiar names to fern collectors. There are, however, very many extremely interesting allied forms, amongst which botanists must look for the explanation of the mode of origin of those anomalies in structure and development which yet await elucidation. Such forms as *Marsilea, Salvinia, Marattia,* and *Ophioglossum,* especially claim attention, but the extent of the present volume forbids more than the mention of their names.

Section II.—Ligulatæ—*SELAGINELLA*.

In the preceding section we saw that the fern illustrated very well the principle of alternation of generations in plant life-history, i.e. the intervention of an asexual plant between two sexual thalli. In the moss we found that this alternation of generations was present, but masked by the parasitism of the asexual on the sexual plant. In the type we have now to consider we shall find that the converse holds good, namely, that the sexual thallus is parasitic, for a considerable time at least, on the asexual plant. *Selaginella,* the plant commonly known as a *Lycopodium* or clubmoss in hot-houses, i.e. the asexual plant, produces spores, which in their turn produce sexual thalli, only the sexual thalli never leave their parent asexual plant, and, indeed, develop inside the wall of the spore itself; another and still more striking example of one of the generalisations emphasised at the end of the preceding section, viz. that in the progress from lower to higher forms of plant life the importance of the sexual thallus gradually diminishes as that of the asexual plant gradually increases. Botanists are accustomed to give names to these two generations. That bearing the ovum is known as the **oophyte,** that bearing the spore as the **sporophyte.** The oophyte and the sporophyte therefore correspond to our thallus and asexual plant respectively. The term **gamophyte** will be employed throughout in preference to oophyte, as taking into account both the male and the female sexual organs. In the life-history of the moss, therefore, the oophyte bears the sporophyte parasitic on it, while in the fern, the oophyte (thallus) and sporophyte (fern proper) are distinct plants. In *Selaginella,* the sporophyte carries the oophyte for some time upon itself, and a considerable part of its development is gone through in that condition.

Sporophyte.—Let us now examine the sporophyte in detail, and, taking the vegetative organs first, as in the last type, we will consider it under the headings of stem, root, and leaf, dealing subsequently with the asexual reproductive organs, or sporangia.

Stem.—There are several striking differences between the stem of *Selaginella* and that of *Pteris.* In the first place, it is almost entirely aerial and not underground. It is cylindrical, long, and thin, and branches repeatedly in what is known as the **monopodial system,** i.e. where the branch is a lateral outgrowth from the principal axis, and not the result of dichotomous division of the same (p. 84). The arrangement of the branches, however, resembles that of *Fucus* in that they are all on the same plane. The stem is very slender, and consequently a considerable part of it rests on the ground; the primary part, indeed, may simulate the fern rhizome in being underground. Moreover, its relationship

Metaphyta—Selaginella.

to the rhizome is further hinted at by the habit it has of giving origin to rhizophores, which spring from the origin of

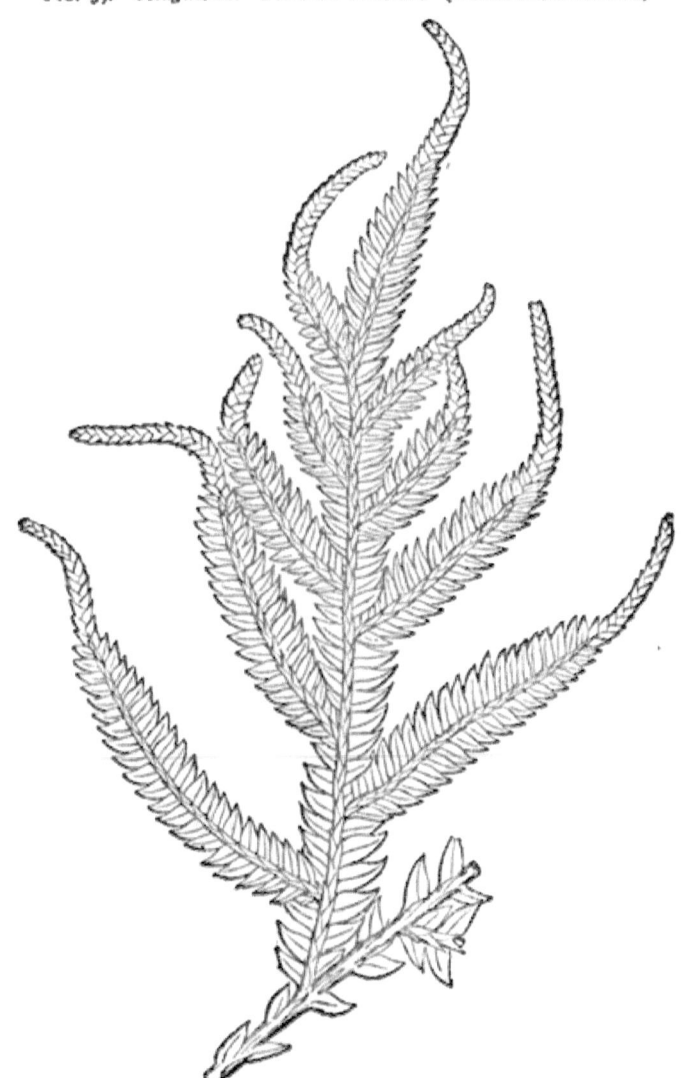

FIG. 59.—*Selaginella.*—FERTILE BRANCH. (Maout and Decaisne.)

secondary branches and descend to the earth. The stem is green, and no doubt takes part in the function of nutrition

(p. 197), in that respect assisting the leaves, which are small and inconspicuous.

The microscopic structure of the stem also shows a likeness to that of the fern. Externally the stem is covered by **epidermis**, the cells composing which are elongated and contain chlorophyll grains. Beneath the epidermis are several layers of closely packed **cortical cells** whose walls are much thickened. Inside this stratum and gradually merging into it lies the general fundamental **parenchyma**, the cells of which are larger and thinner walled. Plunged in the fundamental tissue are the **fibro-vascular strands**. These differ from the strands in the rhizome of the fern in that they are surrounded by a large **annular air-space**, in the centre of which the fibro-vascular strand is slung by means of anchoring strands composed of small parenchymatous cells. The fibro-vascular strand itself is very similar in structure to that of the fern, viz. a broad band of scalariform vessels with a few spiral vessels at either end of the band to represent the xylem, and an enclosing layer of phloëm consisting of small parenchymatous cells, the whole enclosed by one or more layers of phloëm sheath.

Leaf.—The leaves in *Selaginella* are of two kinds, small and large. These leaves are arranged one series on one side of the stem, the other series on the other. The ventral leaves, those lying next the ground, are the larger. The leaves of both types are sessile and very simple in structure. They are heart-shape, the broad base being next the stem. In microscopic structure they are covered by an **epidermis**, the cells of which contain chlorophyll granules, with stomata on the under surface only. The cells composing the epidermis are very similar to the general **fundamental tissue** of the leaf, which is composed of loosely arranged parenchyma with large and irregular intercellular spaces. Each leaf has one fibro-vascular bundle in the form of a **midrib**, consisting of the same elements as those constituting the fibro-vascular strands of the stem, only not so plentiful in amount. The fibro-vascular strand of the leaf is an offset from that of the stem.

Root.—The roots do not require detailed mention, being fundamentally the same in structure as the stem, though the arrangement of the tissues of the fibro-vascular strand is somewhat different. Numerous **root-hairs** are given off from the rootlets as they enter the soil. Structures known as **rhizophores** are developed, as already mentioned, from certain parts of the stem, near the bases of branches. These find their way to the ground and there give origin to true roots. The rhizophores have no root-caps, but are not therefore necessarily branches; for we have in botanical morphology numerous instances of true roots which have, while still aerial, no root-cap, afterwards obtaining one when they touch the soil.

It was stated in the last section that the apex of the stem in the lower plants consisted usually of a single cell, known as the apical cell, whilst the terminal growing points of the higher plants usually consisted of a group of cells known as primary meristem. In *Selaginella* and its allies we have numerous transitional stages between the single apical cell and the multicellular state. We will take an instance where the unicellular state is retained. Even in the very terminal portion of the stem, and not far from the apex itself, we find the young leaves mapped out in primary parenchyma. The **meristem** is formed by successive segmentations from either side of the **apical cell**, each segment producing by subdivision a group of cells forming the rudiment of a leaf.

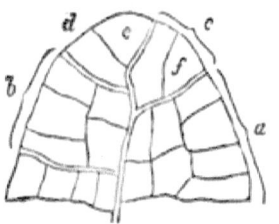

FIG. 60.—*Selaginella.*—APEX OF THE STEM.

Asexual reproductive organs.—The **sporangia** are not developed on all leaves of the sporophyte, but on certain leaves towards the ends of certain branches. The fertile branches have their terminal leaves modified (*a*) in form, and (*b*) in arrangement. The leaves are all the same size, and are arranged so as to form a four-sided spike, or **cone**, not unlike a fir cone pulled out. As we shall find later on, this simile is a strictly correct one, for the cone of *Selaginella* is morphologically comparable to the cone of a fir, since both bear sporangia or asexual organs of multiplication, although terms which are associated with the true sexual organs have become by long usage attached to the sporangia of the fir cone.

FIG. 61.—*Selaginella inæqualifolia.*
(Sachs.)

A, fertile branch with cone. *B*, section of cone (enlarged), showing sporangia, containing spermospores on the left hand, and ovospores on the right.

The **sporophyll** of *Selaginella* is hollow and spoonlike, broad at its base, and rapidly narrowing to a sharp point. It bears in its axil the **sporangium**, while between the leaf and the sporangium, and arising from the base of the leaf, is the so-called **ligule**, a structure which, since it encloses the sporangium and is epidermal in origin, is morphologically an **indusium**. Each sporangium is composed of a short stout funicle and a bivalved capsule, composed of one or more layers of chlorophyll-bearing cells. The sporangium appears in *Selaginella* to originate from the stem, but that fact need not prevent us from comparing its origin with that of the fern sporangium, since the leaf in *Selaginella* is extremely small, whilst the sporangium is relatively large. Moreover in many allies of the type we are considering the sporangia are borne by the leaf itself. As already stated, the sporangium is, when ripe, a bivalved capsule, although when young the wall of the capsule is complete. On examining the sporangia in more detail, we find that their contents differ from each other and also from the contents of the sporangia of the fern.

Before discussing the sporangia of *Selaginella*, it may conduce to clearness if we glance briefly at the sporangia of an allied type, *Lycopodium*. The sporangia in that type are developed in the axils of the sporophylla, and spring from their bases. The **spores** are small and rounded in form and all of the same size. They are comparable to the spores of the fern, and, by one unaccustomed to the microscopic study of plants, might be readily mistaken for them. Each spore is composed of a mass of **protoplasm** surrounded by firstly an **endosporium**, and secondly by an **exosporium**, which (as is usually the case) is raised into spines and prominences. This spore when sown is capable of producing a thallus bearing spermaria and ovaria. An examination of *Selaginella* at once exhibits to us a great advance in differentiation, for although the sporangia appear all perfectly alike, yet some contain what appear to be numerous small spores, like those of *Lycopodium*, whilst others contain a few very large spores, totally different in appearance. These have been known as microspores and macrospores respectively. These terms are by no means satisfactory, as we shall presently see. A ripe microspore, when artificially clarified and examined under a high power, shows externally a thick **exosporium** and thinner clear **endosporium**, but contains, instead of granular protoplasm, a considerable number of cells, one of which is segmented off by a distinct cellulose cell-wall. The rest of the cellular mass consists of small naked cells, which are

138 *Elementary Biology.*

apparently in process of transformation into sperms. Similarly when the so-called ripe macrospore is examined it is found to consist of a very considerable collection of cells enclosed in an **endo-** and **exosporium**, which latter has three very well marked ridges on one surface. The cellular tissue shows more or less distinct demarcation into two areas ; the

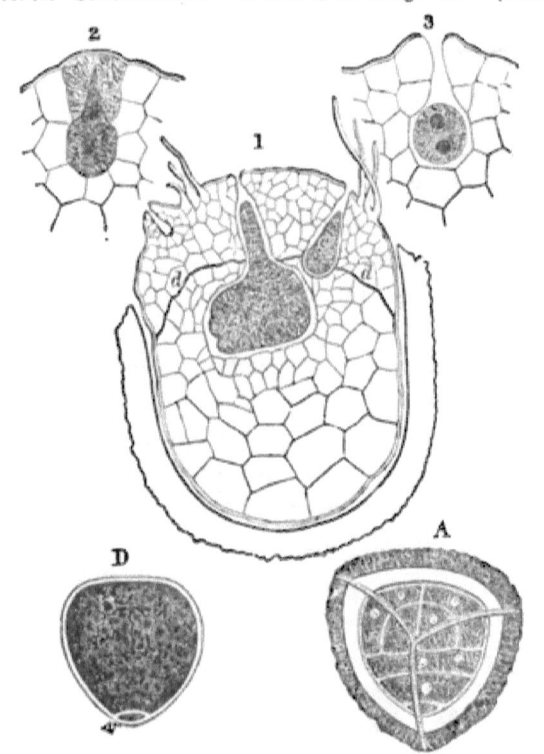

FIG. 62.—STRUCTURE OF THE SPORES IN *Selaginella.* (Pfeffer.)

1, 2, 3, ovospore of *S. martensii.* A, D, spermospore of *S. caulescens.*

upper of which, that is to say the part nearest the point of union of the three ridges, is termed the **thallus**, whilst the lower part has been termed the **endosperm**. In the thallus are found three or four funnel-shaped depressions, leading into minute cavities, which contain naked protoplasmic cells. These cells are on further examination found to be comparable to the cells found in the cavity of the ovarium of the fern thallus. There are in each cavity one large basal cell, or **ovum**, and one or more cells filling up the neck, i.e. **canal cells**. We have no option, then, but to consider this so-called macrospore as a thallus which is developing its **ovaria** within the spore-wall. The entire second or sexual generation has remained hidden in and protected by the spore-wall. What shall we say then of the microspore viewed in the light of this discovery? Simply that here, too, the thallus has never left the spore-wall, but has first of all divided into a **vegetative cell**, probably of no service save to guide us towards an explanation of this anomaly, and a number of **reproductive cells** which at once proceed to form **sperms** without forming spermaria at all.

It appears, therefore, that we have in the spores of *Selaginella* a great advance on the condition of affairs in the fern. In the first place we find **two kinds of thalli** instead of one, and these thalli are **unisexual** instead of hermaphrodite. How is this to be explained? Probably in terms of a law which we shall find of supreme importance in higher plants, namely, the **law of cross-fertilisation**. It is an advantage for a plant to be fertilised by male elements derived from another plant than itself. In the fern, because the thallus was a comparatively large organism and because it obtained its nourishment from the environment, probably the protoplasm of the thallus was sufficiently differentiated in the region of the ovaria from the protoplasm in the region of the spermaria to allow of the invigorating effect of inter-crossing being thus obtained. Possibly future experiments may show that true cross-fertilisation is as helpful to the Algæ and the Non-vascularia as it is in the case of the flowering plants; indeed there are numerous observations on record pointing to this conclusion. In *Selaginella*, since the thalli are not independent living plants, we have male and female elements produced in different thalli, which are produced from different spores, instead of being developed, as they might well be, on the same thallus inside the same spore-wall.

Again, how must we account for the disappearance of the thallus which ought to have been formed by the microspore, and the retaining of the thallus formed by the macrospore? Obviously when the cells which will produce sperms have been formed there can be no further use for a thallus bearing them only; whilst not only has the thallus producing ovaria to give origin to sexual cells, but it has also to nourish for a time the embryo that results from the fertilisation of the ovum. The thallus, in short, has to act as nurse to the fertilised ovum it has itself given birth to. Hence its persistence for a variable period dependent on the time taken by the embryo to develop. Moreover, we saw that the tissue in the interior of the macrospore is divisible into what has been termed thallus and endosperm. This latter would apparently correspond to the purely vegetative portion of the thallus of a fern, whilst the thallus proper is that portion which gives rise to the ovaria. It is possible, however, that the endosperm is an altogether new formation which has arisen during the gradual assumption of parasitism by the sexual generation, and for the special purpose of affording nourishment to the embryo during its development whilst inside the spore-wall.[1]

---

[1] Although speculations without detailed proofs are in many cases looked on with suspicion (and rightly so), yet they do so much towards relieving detailed description from the charge of dulness that no further apology is given for their introduction here. In the present instance, when one considers the fact that the unisexual thallus, whether formed from a microspore or a macrospore, must have, at one time in phylogenetic history, been a hermaphrodite structure, and that the spermaria are developed on a different part of the thallus from the ovaria; that, moreover, the presence of root-hairs on the exposed ovaria-bearing portion of the enclosed thallus of *Selaginella* clearly points to that being the morphologically ventral surface of the thallus, one cannot but suspect that the endosperm really corresponds to the spermaria-bearing portion of the hermaphrodite thallus. The division of the nucleus of

We have yet to describe briefly the mode of development of the sporangia and their contents, and to follow the development of the embryo into the young *Selaginella*. A word on the relation of *Selaginella* to the pine group of plants will complete the section.

It is needless to describe in detail the development of the sporangium, since it is, broadly speaking, similar to that of the fern. A **tapetal layer** is formed, which subsequently becomes absorbed. The **archesporium** also forms **mother spore-cells**, capable of developing microspores or macrospores. It would be preferable to distinguish these spores by terms indicative rather of their sex than of their size. The microspore is a spore capable of forming a male thallus, hence it might be termed a **spermospore**, whilst the macrospore might be termed an **ovospore**, an unavoidable hybrid, since the word oospore has already been given to the fertilised ovum or embryo.[1]

The development of the spores up to this stage is alike for both sexes, but here their development diverges. The mother cells of the spermospores are numerous, and each subdivides into four daughter cells which become the spermospores in question; the mother cells of the ovospores are also numerous, but only one of these subdivides into four daughter cells which become the four ovospores of the mature sporangium, the other mother cells remaining undeveloped.

After fertilisation of the ovum by a sperm the ovum rapidly segments, forming a **pro-embryo**, which differentiates

the embryo-sac of the angiosperm (p. 167), and the subsequent union of a portion of one daughter nucleus with a portion of the other, might on this view be looked upon as a species of cross-fertilisation (resulting in the more vigorous formation of endosperm) of a female nucleus by a male nucleus, rather than a union of two female nuclei as suggested by Marshall Ward.

[1] The term macrospore is even etymologically incorrect, since μακρὸς means 'long,' not 'large.' Megaspore would be more correct if we must use these terms.

into a portion known as the **suspensor** and the **embryo** proper. The suspensor forms the upper portion of the pro-embryo, that is, the part next the canal cells. The suspensor by increase in length pushes the embryo proper deep into the endosperm or vegetative part of the thallus. There the mapping out of the embryo into cotyledon (or seed-leaf), stem, and root takes place before its independent existence outside the spore-wall is established. During the embryonic period, as already explained, the thallus acts as nourishment to the young plant.

There are many points of resemblance between the structure and life-history of *Selaginella* and the *Gymnospermæ* (pine group), which point to their being transition forms between the *Selaginellidæ* and the *Angiospermæ*. There is no difficulty in tracing the relationship between *Selaginella* and such a type as *Pinus*, notwithstanding the tremendous difference in size; for in past ages of the earth's history closely allied forms have flourished which were even more gigantic than the largest pines, the spores of which form no small part of the coal of ordinary use. We have already drawn attention to the likeness between the cones of the two forms, and the structure of the sporangia also shows no great morphological differences. The anatomy of the stem, however, is much closer in its nature to that of the flowering plant than to that of *Selaginella*; but beyond this general statement further exposition of their agreements and differences must be omitted here.

Lastly, and by way of summary, we must emphasise the fact that we have in *Selaginella* true alternation of generations just as in the fern, only here the sexual generation is parasitic on, or at least commensal with, the asexual. If we were to attempt to represent this relationship diagrammatically we might do so thus :—

$$AST\begin{cases} ST\ \delta \\ + \\ ST\ \female \end{cases} \longrightarrow AST\begin{cases} ST\ \delta \\ + \\ ST\ \female \end{cases}$$

where A S T stands for asexual generation, and S T for sexual thallus.

SECTION III.—MONOCOTYLEDONES—*LILIUM*.

We now reach that point in our examination of the morphology of plants when it is necessary to consider what are popularly known as the flowering plants. For that purpose we shall devote our attention to two forms which illustrate well the characters of that group. A thorough grasp of the preceding section, where we examined *Selaginella* in detail, will help us considerably towards understanding the at first sight very different organisation of the types now before us.

In the first place we meet with what appears to be a perfectly new development in the morphology of plants, namely, the **flower**. That structure, however, turns out on closer examination to be simply a cone the constituent leaves of which have become variously modified, some coloured, some remaining green, and others, i.e. those bearing the sporangia, which are themselves considerably modified, very much altered in shape and microscopic structure. We find in the second place that certain of the sporangia—those which produce ovospores—do not shed their contents, but, covered over by the leaf on which they were produced, form with the sporophyll itself what is commonly known as the **fruit**. Indeed, we might briefly state the case thus : while the fern and *Selaginella* shed their spores, a flowering plant sheds its sporangia and their contents, and very often the sporophylla also.

Again, we find that there are many points of difference, or, rather, advance in the structure of the fibro-vascular strands, and in their mode of arrangement both in the stem and in the root. The leaves also are found to possess, what we may term, higher organisation, in virtue of there being greater differentiation of parts and more division of labour.

The *Angiospermæ*, as the plants we are now considering

are termed, are divided into two large groups, the *Monocotyledones* and the *Dicotyledones*. As an example of the first group we may take the lily or hyacinth; as an example of the second, the buttercup. The former we shall discuss in this, the latter in the following, section.

First of all, it may be well to point out several obvious points of distinction between these two plants, which are easily observed and appreciated on the basis of the knowledge of plant structure we have already gained.

A section of a stem of *Lilium* shows what we know now as fibro-vascular strands scattered apparently irregularly through the fundamental tissue, whilst a similar section through the stem of *Ranunculus* (buttercup) shows the strands arranged concentrically round the centre, which is either hollow or occupied by a mass of fundamental tissue known as pith. Again, the strands in *Lilium* are crowded towards the surface, whilst in *Ranunculus* there is a tolerably thick layer of cortex between the outer edge of the strands and the epidermis. Further, when we examine the ordinary foliage leaves the veins in *Lilium* are found to run parallel to one another, whilst those in *Ranunculus* start at various angles from a central midrib, and the veinlets branch and anastomose, or form a network over the entire lamina. Lastly, when we look at the cone or flower, we discover that although the leaves composing it are very different in colour, shape, and microscopic structure from the leaves which go to form a fir cone or a *Selaginella* cone, yet they are, broadly speaking, the same in general character in *Lilium* and *Ranunculus*, but differ in their arrangement on the cone-axis in these two types. In the lily they are obviously arranged in circles of three each, whilst the outer leaves at least in the buttercup are arranged in circles of five. These flowers are therefore said to belong to the **trimerous** and **pentamerous** types respectively. There are other points of distinction between the two forms we have selected, but these will be referred to later on.

Still continuing our general survey, we may observe that in the flower or cone of these angiosperms we have far fewer sporophylla than in the cone of *Selaginella*, but this distinction is bridged over by the flowers of such examples as the water-lily, a plant which, despite its name, is a far nearer relation to the buttercup than to the true lily. Again we have to note that some of the sporophylla are barren, namely, those which are coloured and lower down in the cone.

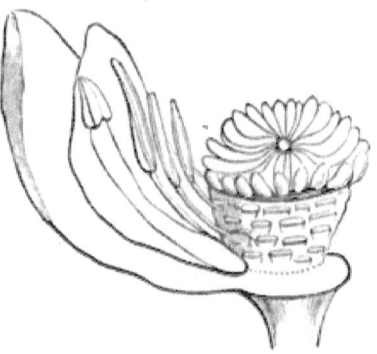

FIG. 63.—*Nymphæa alba.*—TRANSITION FROM PETALS TO STAMENS. (Maout and Decaisne.)

Were space a matter of no object, numerous intermediate conditions might be referred to which would help to convince us, if that were necessary, that in the lily and buttercup we have to deal with plants in no respect distinct in nature and life-history from those we have already considered in the preceding sections.

Stem.—The stem of *Lilium*, like that of the fern, is underground, but from its peculiar shape it receives the name of **bulb**. It is difficult at first sight to see exactly where the stem proper is. If a section be made of the bulb (e.g. of an onion or hyacinth) it will be seen to consist of two parts—a disc shaped lower portion, from the under-surface of which the roots spring, and an upper portion which is discovered to be composed of the thickened bases of the closely-packed leaves. The typical stem we have already seen consists of nodes, from which the leaves spring, and of internodes between the nodes. In the bulb the internodes are absent, and the nodes are closely crushed together, so that the stem is exceedingly short and reduced to a mere disc-shaped mass, from which the leaves spring. The only part of the stem remaining of tolerable length is the terminal shoot, which is elongated into a long axis on which the flower is borne. Between the bases of the leaves we may find **buds** or branch shoots about to give forth another floral axis in the next season. The likeness to the underground rhizome of the fern is thus again brought up.

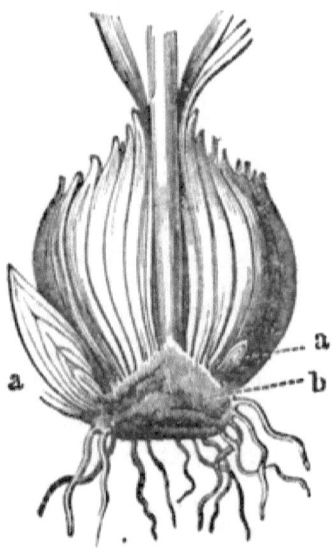

FIG. 64.—*Allium cepa.*—BULB. (Edmonds.)

a, a, buds; b, stem proper, from which roots originate.

The **floral axis** presents a more suitable subject for examining the structure of the monocotyledonous stem than the modified underground bulb. If a section be made across it it will show externally a colourless **epidermis**, enclosing a large soft **fundamental parenchyma** in which run the **fibro-vascular strands** (fig. 65). The mode of origin of these we shall notice later on; meantime it will be sufficient to draw attention to the fact that the smallest strands are placed close to the epidermis, while they increase regularly in size as the centre is approached. There cannot be said to be any distinct **pith**, that is, fundamental tissue left unmodified in the centre of the stem, for there is no clear line of demarcation between the fundamental tissue of the centre and that between the several strands. The course of the fibro-vascular strands in the stem may be best studied in a longitudinal section, such as that represented at fig. 65 B. There it will be seen (in an allied type) that the strands pursue a wavy course, arising close to the outside of the stem, curving inwards, and, after recurving outwards again and crossing the strands higher up, pass out entirely into the base of a leaf. These fibro-vascular strands when further examined are found to contain elements similar in general structure to those described in the stem of the fern, but differing in certain points of detail The tissue of the strand is confluent with the fundamental parenchyma, but the cells bounding the strand are much smaller and thicker walled: these cells are elongated and form a **prosenchymatous sheath** to the strand. Towards the outer side of the strand, i.e. that next the surface of the stem, immediately

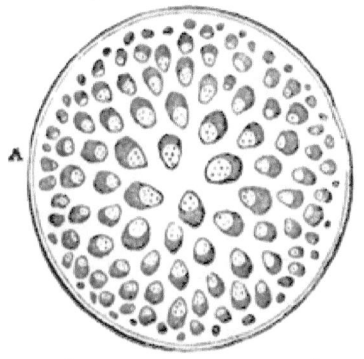
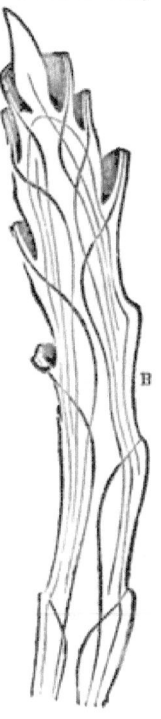

Fig. 65.—Monocotyledonous stem. (Maout and Decaisne.)

A. Diagrammatic transverse section.
B. Diagrammatic longitudinal section.

inside the prosenchymatous sheath, is found a mass of tissue which corresponds to the **phloëm** or bast of the fern strand, and goes by that name. It consists of **sieve-tubes**, long, thick-walled **prosenchyma** and thin-walled **parenchyma**. Next the inner side of the strand lies the **xylem**, or wood, which also consists of three elements, **tracheides**, or vessels with dotted walls, one or more **spiral** and **annular vessels**, a quantity of **prosenchyma**, and a little **parenchyma**. We have already briefly glanced at the general structure of the cells composing these several types of tissue. As we shall, however, require to use these terms constantly in the remainder of this and in the succeeding sections it may be well to give at this point a few more details regarding them.

148   *Elementary Biology.*

Parenchyma.—The parenchyma of the xylem and phloëm is mainly important as presenting us with the re-

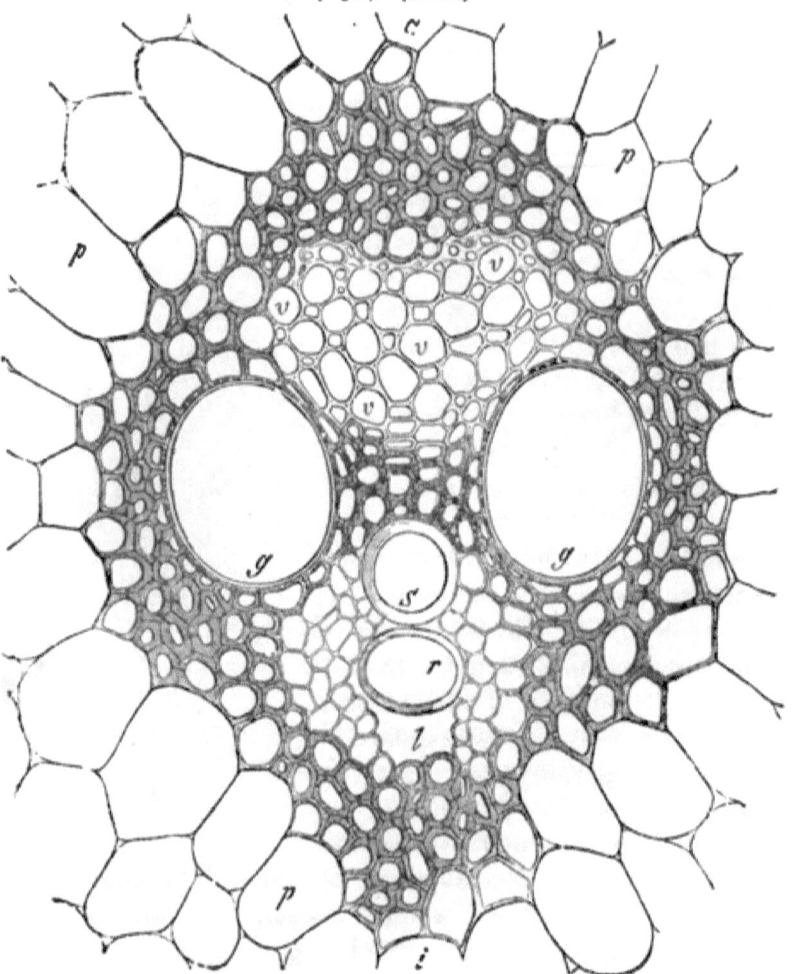

Fig. 66.—Transverse section of fibro-vascular strand of *Zea mais* (×500). (Sachs.)

p, fundamental parenchyma of *a*, outer and *i*, inner part of the stem, enclosing prosenchyma; *g*, *g*, pitted ducts; *s*, spiral vessel; *r*, annular vessel; *l*, air cavity; *v*, *v*, phloëm.

mains of the primitive cambium or growing tissue from which the entire strand was originally formed.

Metaphyta—Lilium.

Prosenchyma.—The prosenchyma represents parenchymatous cells which have been elongated in a fusiform manner (usually) in one direction (fig. 67). Their walls may become thickened either by **apposition**, i.e. the deposition of new particles of **cellulose** on the inner surface of the cell-wall, or by **intussusception**, i.e. the intercalation of similar particles between those of the primary cell-wall. Possibly both methods of cell-wall thickening may take place simultaneously. Chemical changes usually take place in the wall at the same time. Secondary thickening may take place regularly; in that case we have a **uniformly thickened** prosenchymatous cell of the type represented at fig. 66. In other cases we may have parts of the primary cell-wall left uncovered, when a **pit**-like depression results (fig. 67). In other cases still we may find that the secondary thickening has been laid down (in this case by apposition) in the form of a **spiral band** or **annular rings** upon the primary cell-wall. These varieties of cell-wall thickenings are commonest amongst the next type of tissue.

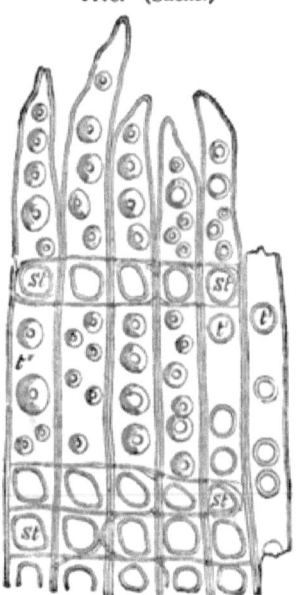

FIG. 67.—*Pinus sylvestris*. PROSENCHYMA WITH BORDERED PITS. (Sachs.)

Cell-fusions, vessels.—Vessels result from the fusion of two or more elongated cells arranged end to end. The adjacent walls have become completely broken down, or the walls may become perforated by a series of minute apertures through which the contents of the one cell may communicate with the contents of the other: good examples of this type of vessel are found in the **sieve-tubes** of the phloëm (fig. 68). It is probable, according to recent researches, that this intercellular communication occurs in a great number of tissues besides the sieve-tubes. Among the vessels of the wood, as already stated, a great variety of types exist, known as **spiral, annular, reticulated, scalariform**, and other vessels.

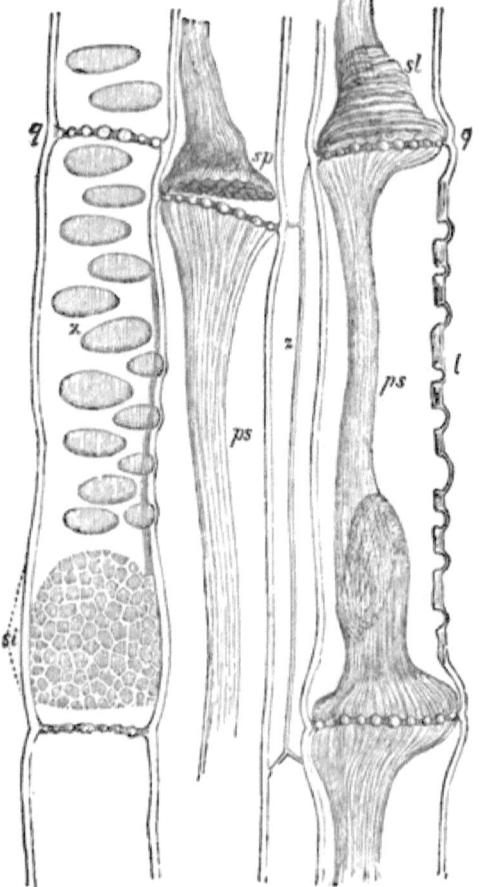

FIG. 68.—SIEVE-TUBES FROM PHLOËM OF *Cucurbita pepo* (×550). (Sachs.)

q, transverse section of a sieve; *si.* sieve on side wall; *x*, pits on face and *l*, on side view; *ps*, protoplasm contracted from the cell-wall; *z*, intermediate prosenchyma.

It is important to notice, in regard to the fibro-vascular strand of a monocotyledon, that there is no growing tissue present—it has all become **permanent tissue**. The strand is incapable, therefore, of growing larger when once formed; the strand is therefore said to be **closed**. We shall find this an important point of distinction between the monocotyledonous and the dicotyledonous type of stem, in which latter growing tissue or **cambium** is present, and where the fibro-vascular strands are therefore known as **open** strands, i.e. capable of further growth.

Root.—Passing next to the root, we find that the structure differs considerably from that of the stem, not in the character of the tissues present, but in their arrangement. It is easy to make out the **fibro-vascular strands** grouped together and forming a perfect **cylinder** in the centre, and surrounded by the **vascular sheath** or layer of fundamental tissue next to the cylinder. Outside the fibro-vascular cylinder is a very thick **cortex** (fig. 69). The **epidermis** soon disappears, and its place is taken by the outer layers

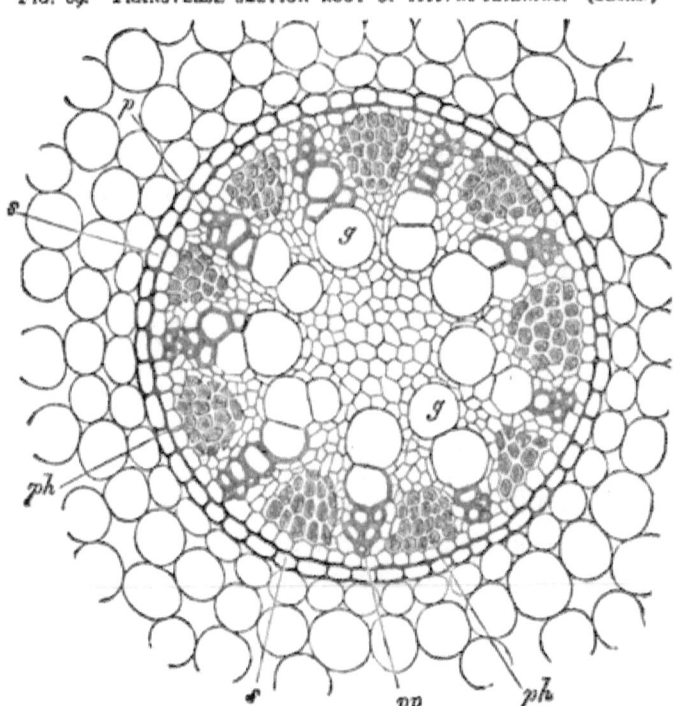

Fig. 69.—Transverse section root of *Acorus calamus*. (Sachs.)

s, fibro-vascular sheath, surrounded by cortical parenchyma and external to the pericambium ; *pp*, xylem ; *ph*, phloëm ; *g, g, p, p*, vessels of xylem.

of the cortex. Within the sheath, we again find points of difference from the stem in the arrangement of the various parts of the strands themselves. Immediately internal to the vascular sheath is a layer of cells known as the **pericambium**, or **phloëm-sheath**, which encloses the strands. The **bast** and **wood** of the strand, however, are not arranged so that the bast is outside and the wood inside, but so that the two portions lie alternating with each other. Such an arrangement is known as a **radial** strand.

The roots, as a whole, originate from the base of the flattened stem in the form of long branched or unbranched filaments, each terminated by **a root-cap.** The cap may be very well studied in the aquatic roots of the duckweed, an aberrant monocotyledon which exhibits a root-cap not differing essentially in this respect from that of the monocotyledon. The roots give origin to **rootlets** and **root-hairs** by which the absorption of food from the soil is carried on.

Leaf.—The leaves of the lily are peculiar in being **sessile**; their bases are generally the widest parts, and, in the case of the outer leaves of the bulb, enclose the entire stem.

FIG. 70.—ROOT-CAP OF *Lemna minor*.

a, root-cap ; *c*, epidermis of the root ; *b*, growing cells.

The **fibro-vascular strands**, as already stated, are arranged in a **parallel** manner, the veins running without branching from end to end of the leaf or merging into a vein which runs round the margin of the leaf. The microscopic structure of the leaf must now occupy our attention for a moment. Superficially the leaf is covered by an **epidermis** composed of flat tabular cells. The upper epidermis has numerous **stomata**; these are, however, much more numerous on the under epidermis (especially of dicotyledonous leaves). The guard-cells are, as a rule, smaller than the general epidermal cells, and are concavo-convex in outline, the space between being the stoma. The **guard-cells** contain chlorophyll, which is absent from the other epidermal cells. The stoma leads into a large **intercellular** space in the fundamental tissue of the leaf. This **fundamental tissue** is composed of chlorophyll-bearing cells, which are, next the epidermis, arranged in one or more regular layers and termed **palisade** parenchyma, whilst towards the middle of the leaf the cells form what is known as the **mesophyll**, or **spongy parenchyma**. Through the mesophyll run the **fibro-vascular strands**, which are similar in structure to those of the stem. The xylem lies next the upper surface of the leaf, since that is morphologically the side next the centre of stem. From either epidermis (though not in that of the type we are considering) arise **epidermal hairs**, which are prolongations of epidermal cells (fig. 72). Such hairs are termed **unicellular** when their cavities are continuous with those of the cells of which they are prolongations. Frequently, however, these hairs become **multicellular** by the subdivision of their cavities into chambers. A number of

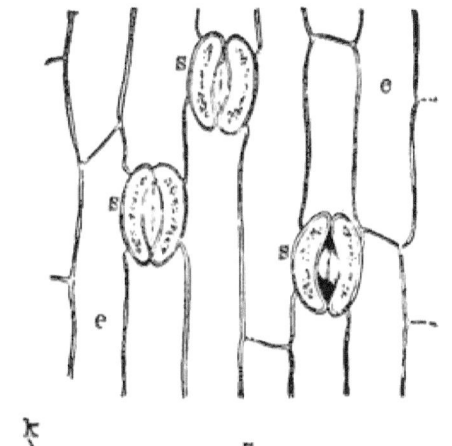

FIG. 71.—*A*. EPIDERMIS OF *Leucojum vernum*.
B. TRANSVERSE SECTION OF EPIDERMIS OF *Agapanthus umbellatus*. (Behrens.)

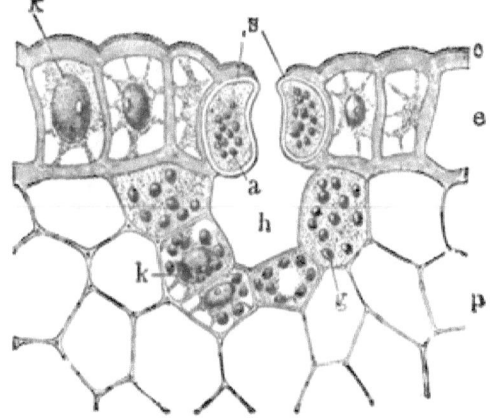

s, guard-cells containing chlorophyll grains, *a*; *c*, cuticle; *e*, epidermal cells; *k*, nuclei; *h*, air-space; *p*, general parenchyma.

FIG. 72.—FORMS OF HAIRS. (Thomé.)

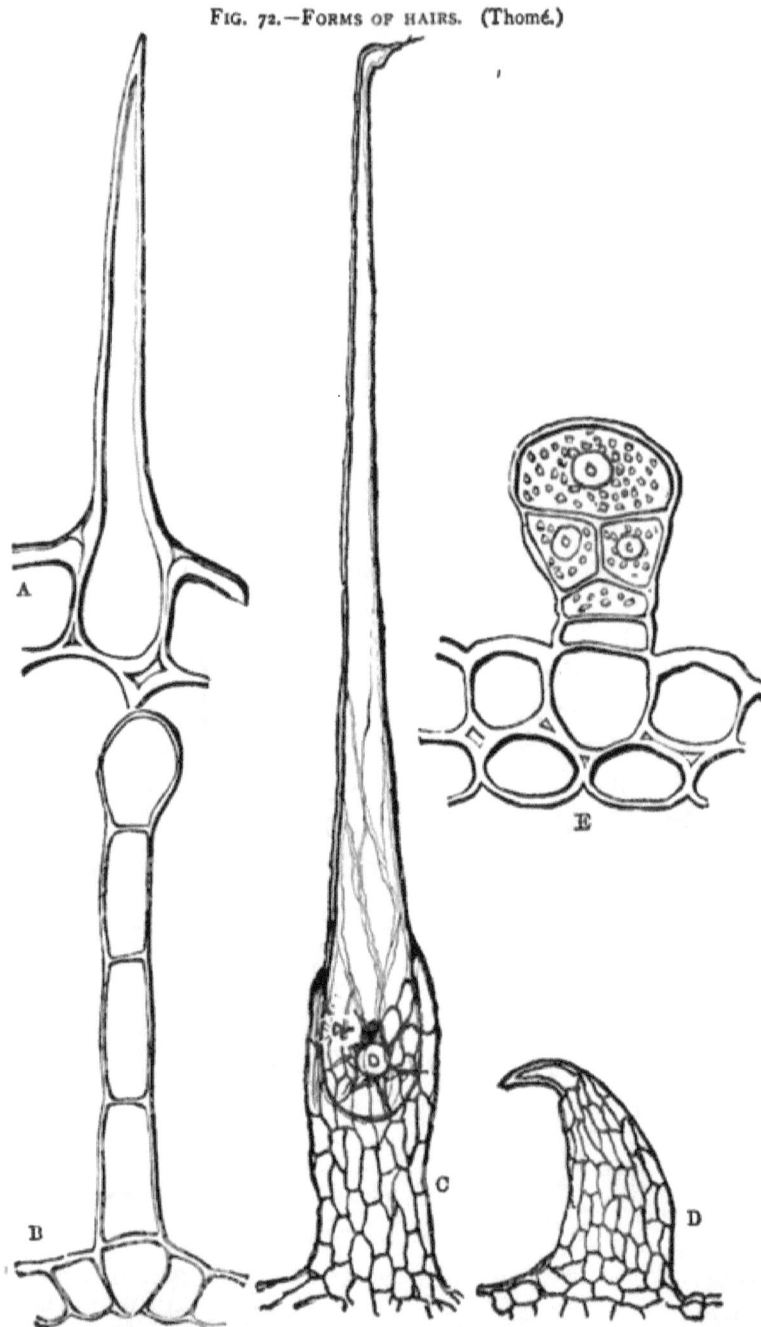

A, unicellular hair of *Pelargonium*; B, multicellular hair of *Geranium*; C, glandular hair of nettle; D, prickle of hop; E, glandular hair of *Lamium*.

hairs may become matted together, giving origin to a **prickle**, as in the hop, whilst in the nettle the leaf is covered with multicellular hairs, with the contents of the terminal cells modified into a substance capable of producing considerable irritation should its end be broken off in the skin. These may be termed **glandular hairs.**

Before passing to the consideration of the sporophylla, we must glance at the nature and mode of origin of certain substances which we have had occasion frequently to mention in reference to many points in our past survey, and which may conveniently be discussed at this point. They are substances found in the cells of plants, such as starch, inulin, aleurone, crystalloids, crystals, and such-like; chlorophyll we have already discussed (p. 38).

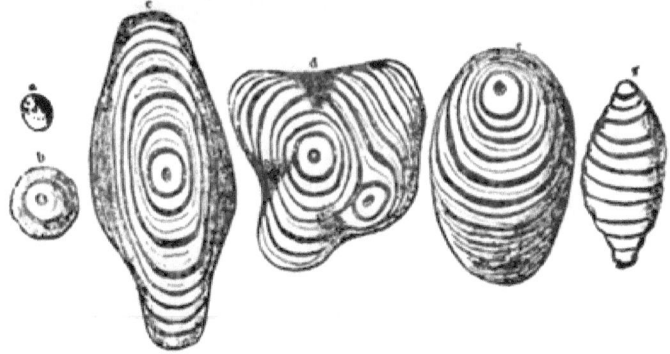

FIG. 73.—STARCH GRANULES OF *Solanum tuberosum*. (Thomé.)

Starch.—Starch is one of the most important of the derivatives of plant protoplasm. It is a compound of extreme abundance, some parts of plants, such as the potato tuber, consisting almost entirely of starch. Starch occurs in the form of granules, which possess a characteristic form for different plants. We may take those of the potato as a type. Each granule is ovoid in shape, and presents a usually eccentrically placed point known as the **hilum** round which the starch is arranged in a number of layers, alternating with thin films of water. The hilum is the most watery part of the granule. Starch has the same composition as cellulose ($C_6H_{10}O_5$), but a different constitution. The granule is believed to consist of a skeleton of **cellulose,**

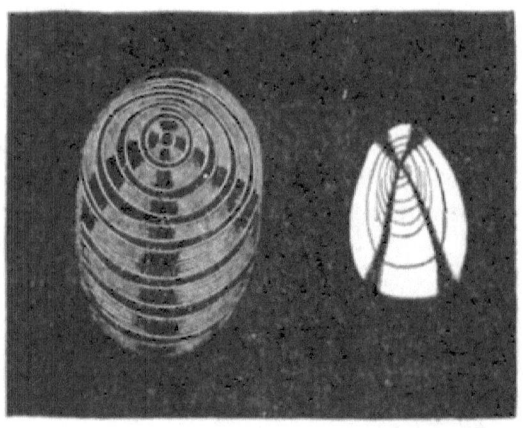

FIG. 73A.—STARCH GRAINS UNDER THE POLARISCOPE. (Vines and Dippel.)

the interstices of which contain the starch proper, or **granulose.** The physiological importance of starch, and of the other differentiation products of protoplasm about to be mentioned, will be referred to in the next chapter, where a general sketch will be given of the more important phenomena in the physiology of plants.

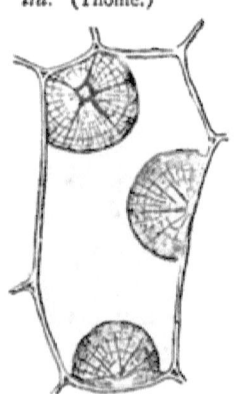

FIG. 74.—INULIN SPHERE CRYSTALS FROM *Dahlia.* (Thomé.)

Inulin, a chemical ally of starch, is found abundantly in the roots of many plants (e.g. the daisy tribe). It however differs from starch in that it exists in solution in the cell-sap, from which it may be precipitated by the action of alcohol, in the form of crystalline spheres, usually adhering to the cell-wall (fig. 74).

Aleurone is to be considered as a proteid reserve material (fig. 75). It is usually found in the form of grains which lie embedded in an oily matrix. It also occurs in a semi-crystalline form with which are associated minute rounded masses of a double salt of magnesium and calcium termed **globoids**. All these bodies have a nutritive value, to which reference will afterwards be made.

True **crystals** are also of common occurrence, especially in the cell-sap. They are most commonly composed of oxalate of lime, appearing in the form of short prisms or

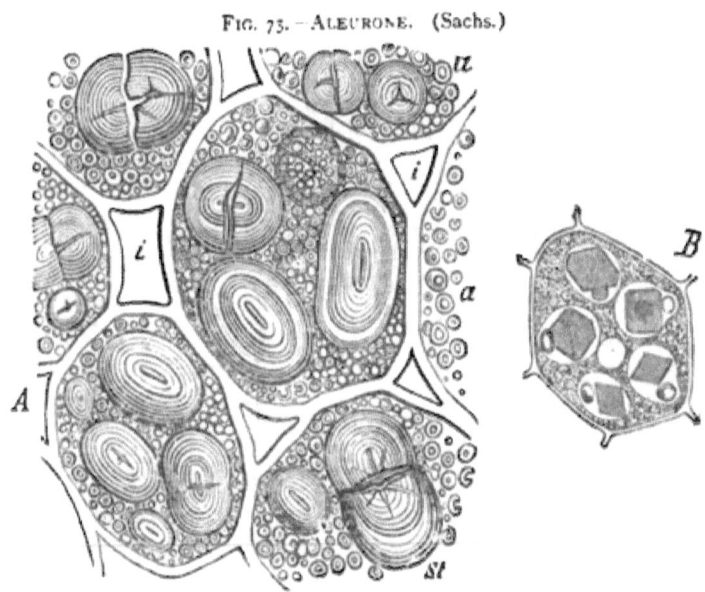

Fig. 73.—Aleurone. (Sachs.)

A, seed of *Pisum sativum* ; a, granular form of aleurone ; i, intercellular space; st, starch grains ; B, seed of *Ricinus communis*, crystalline form.

long and slender needles known as **raphides**. Calcic carbonate also occurs, but more rarely, and only, at least to any extent, in a few groups of plants. Club-shaped masses of calcic carbonate, pendent in certain cells of the leaf (e.g. of *Ficus elastica*), have been called **cystoliths** (fig. 77).

The reproductive organs.—We have already likened the flower of the lily to a fir cone, and emphasised the morphological identity of these two structures. We notice however, that the flower is much **depressed**, the diameter (short axis) of the cone being as great if not greater than the length (long axis). The examination of the flower of the water-lily, or of *Myosurus*, close allies of the buttercup, exhibits to us a condition of things where even the external likeness between the flower and the fir cone is unmistakable. The **sporophylla** are much reduced in number in *Lilium*; and further examination proves to us that that number is **definite** and **constant** for the whole group to which the lily belongs. We find that there are **nine fertile sporophylla** in all, six of which are male and three female. Surrounding the fertile sporophylla are six barren leaves, which differ from the ordinary foliage leaves in being coloured yellow, blue, red, or some other hue. These leaves form together what is known as the **perianth**. They are arranged in two **whorls**, the outer being termed the **calyx**, the inner the **corolla**. The leaves composing the calyx and corolla go by the name of **sepals** and **petals** respectively. The sepaline and petaline leaves differ in several points from the ordinary foliage leaves. In the first place they are **coloured**, but not green. An exception to this occurs in the sepaline whorl, where the outer surface

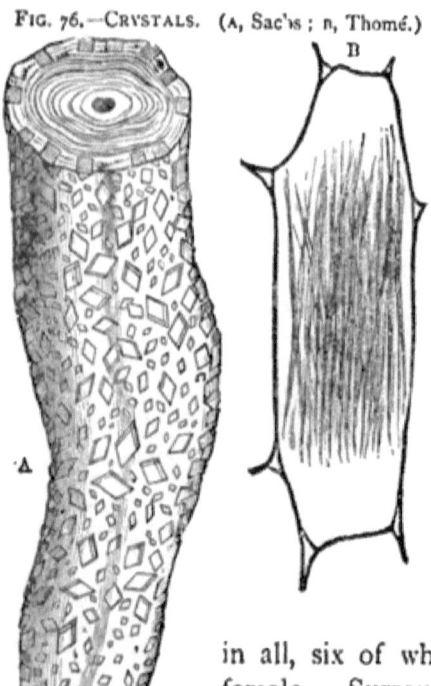

FIG. 76.—CRYSTALS. (A, Sac's; B, Thomé.)

A crystals of calcic oxalate from *Welwitschia mirabilis*; B, raphides from *Aloë retusa*.

of the sepals is frequently green. Amongst the dicotyledons the calyx is generally green, although endless variations

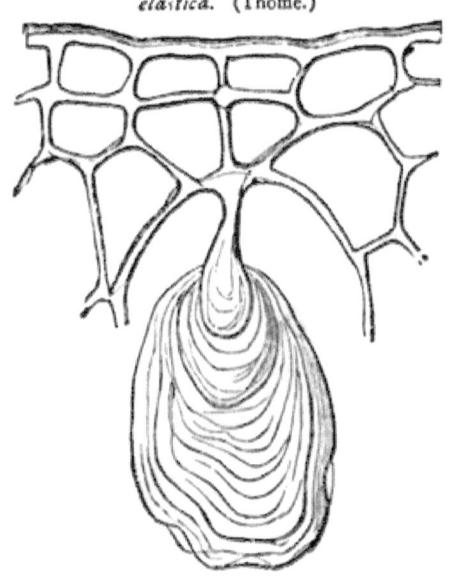

FIG. 77.—CYSTOLITH FROM THE LEAF OF *Ficus elastica*. (Thomé.)

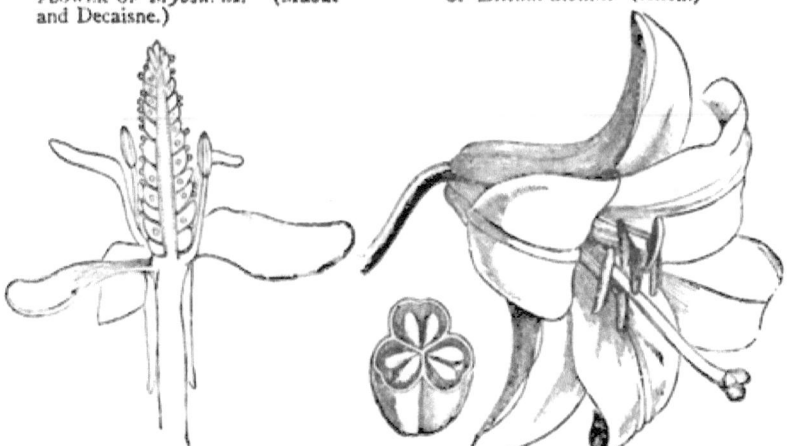

FIG. 78.—VERTICAL SECTION OF FLOWER OF *Myosurus*. (Maout and Decaisne.)

FIG. 79.—FLOWER AND OVARY (IN SECTION) OF *Lilium album*. (Allen.)

occur. The colouring matter is found to be in the form of crystals or granules, or simply diffused in the epidermal cells. In the second place the **shape** of the perianth leaves differs markedly from that of the ordinary leaf type. We cannot go into the discussion of the variation in the morphology of the perianth leaves, but must content ourselves with saying that their form is as various as their hue. In the lily they do not present shapes differing much from the tapering form assumed by the foliage leaves.

The **arrangement of leaves on the stem** has been considered of some importance by botanists, and its value cannot be exaggerated. There can be no doubt that primitively the mode of arrangement of the perianth leaves and sporophylla on the floral axis must have shown some likeness to the mode of arrangement of leaves on the ordinary branch, just as the arrangement of the sporophylla in *Selaginella* resembles that of the foliage leaves in the same type. Owing, however, to the great shortening and condensation which the flower axis has undergone (compare the bulb), the likeness has become in most cases completely obliterated. We are compelled, therefore, to discuss the arrangement of the floral leaves (**anthotaxis**) separately from that of the foliage leaves (**phyllotaxis**). The methods of arrangement in both cases may be very well studied in the foliage or floral bud.

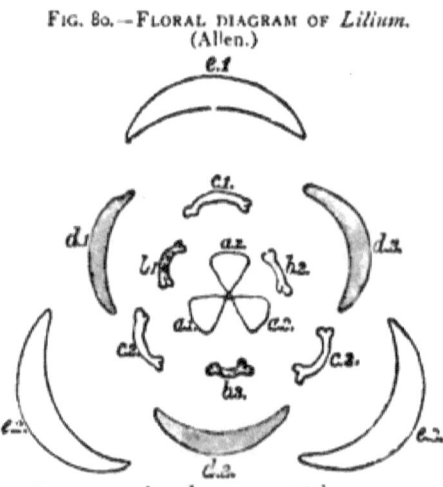

FIG. 80.—FLORAL DIAGRAM OF *Lilium*. (Allen.)

e, 1, 2, 3, sepals; d, 1, 2, 3, petals; c, 1, 2, 3, outer stamens; b, 1, 2, 3, inner stamens; a, 1, 2, 3, carpels.

The study of the relationships between flowers is greatly aided by the use of what are known as **floral diagrams**. In such a diagram the various perianth leaves and sporophylla

Metaphyta—Lilium.

are represented in ground plan. The floral diagram of a lily is represented at fig. 80. There the sepals are shown as forming an outer whorl of three parts, the petals as forming an inner whorl alternating with the parts of the calyx. Within these two whorls we find the nine sporophylla in three whorls, all alternating with each other and with the members of the perianth whorl. Notwithstanding the extreme dissimilarity of structure between the sporophylla and the perianth leaves we have no difficulty in deciding that both belong to the phyllon type, not only from this

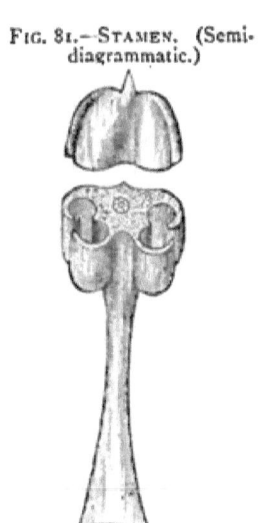

FIG. 81.—STAMEN. (Semi-diagrammatic.)

The anther has been sectionised to show the loculi.

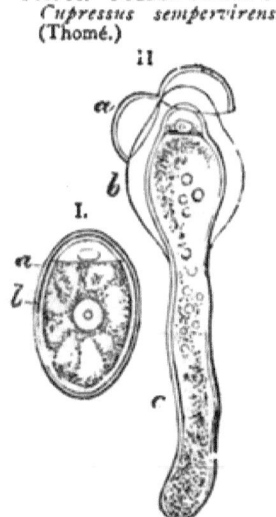

FIG. 82.— POLLEN GRAINS OF *Cupressus sempervirens.* (Thomé.)

I, *a*, entin ; *b*, intin ; II, formation of the pollen tube, *c*.

arrangement, but also from the study of such flowers as those of the water-lily, where we find a gradual transition from the sepals to the petals, and from the petals to the sporophylla (fig. 63).

The sporophylla, as we have already seen, are of two kinds, male and female. The male sporophylla form the two outer whorls of three each, and are known as **stamens**; the three central female sporophylla are known as **carpels**.

Each **stamen** consists of a petiole, or **filament**, and a club-shaped head, the **anther** (fig. 81). The anther itself consists of a centrally placed continuation of the filament known as the **connective**, which is, however, nothing more nor less than the midrib of the sporophyll, and four elongated bodies, two on either side of the midrib, all of them pointing towards the centre of the flower (**introrse**). These bodies are the **sporangia** which are sessile in the great majority of angiosperms. The sporangia are therefore, in the lily, developed not in the axilla, but on the edge of the sporophyll, towards its upper surface. The **spermospores** fill the interior, or **loculus**, of the sporangium, and are known when ripe as **pollen grains**.

Passing now to the central sporophylla, or **carpels**, we find that, in addition to still further modifications in form the three carpels have become united to form one mass known as the **ovary**, which is in this case described as compound (fig. 79). If a section be made across the ovary the three separate chambers which are then exposed demonstrate its compound nature. In each cavity we observe the **sporangia**, here known as **ovules**. The sporangia are stalked, are numerous, and are arranged in six rows, two rows in each chamber.

The ovary is continued upwards as the **style**, and ends in a bulb-like furrowed head, the **stigma** (fig. 79). The style, on a transverse section being made, is found to be hollow, and the stigma, if microscopically examined, is seen to be covered by a number of short hairs.

On what part of the sporophyll are the sporangia borne? A careful study of the development of the carpel shows us that the sporangia are really developed, as in the case of the male sporophylla, from the edge of the carpellary leaf. The edges are, however, during development turned inwards upon themselves, and ultimately unite so as to form a cavity, with, consequently, the upper surface of the carpellary leaf in the interior (fig. 83). The sporangia are thus completely enclosed in their sporophyll; and since sporangia are developed on both edges, the double row is thus accounted for. When the three carpels are fused together to form one ovary, manifestly the ovules (sporangia) will appear to originate from a central axis, in the formation of which the floral axis, or central part of the cone, may participate. The style, then, is simply the upper part of the sporophylla, the edges of which have not united in the centre, and the trilobed stigma is composed of the terminal points of the same, swollen up and covered with epidermal hairs for a purpose we shall discover presently.

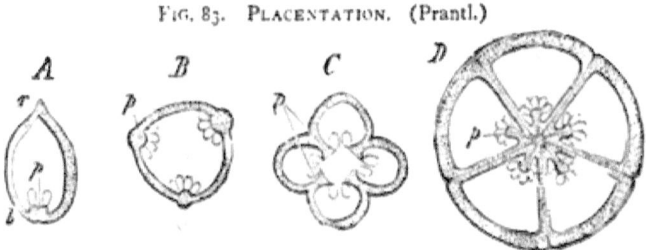

FIG. 83. PLACENTATION. (Prantl.)

A, one carpel, one loculus; B, three carpels, one loculus; C, four carpels, four loculi by upgrowth of thalamus; D, five carpels, five loculi; *p*, placenta.

Turning now to the **sporangium** itself we meet with still further differentiation from the type we described in the fern. The sporangium is stalked, but the capsule is doubled down on the **funicle**, and is adherent to it for a considerable distance. The portion of the funicle which is attached to the sporangium is termed the **raphe**. A sporangium turned upside down thus is said to be **anatropal** (fig. 84). The sporangium is pear-shaped, its pointed end being directed downwards towards the **placenta** or point of origin from the sporophyll. The wall of the sporangium is incomplete at this point, and the aperture left is termed the **micropyle**. The sporangia are not always anatropal. In many plants the sporangium is perfectly straight, with the micropyle pointing upwards (**orthotropal**); in other cases a half-way condition is maintained between the anatropal and the orthotropal, known as **campylotropal.** The sporangium has usually two cellular coverings, the outer coat being known as the 'primine,' the inner as the 'secundine.' It is preferable to discard these terms altogether and talk of them simply as the **outer** and **inner coats of the ovule.** The central tissue of the ovule is known as the 'nucellus, sunk in the interior of which is found one **ovospore,** which goes by the name of the 'embryo-sac.' If we study the development of the sporangia (male and female), we shall be able to distinguish clearly the homologies of the several parts.[1]

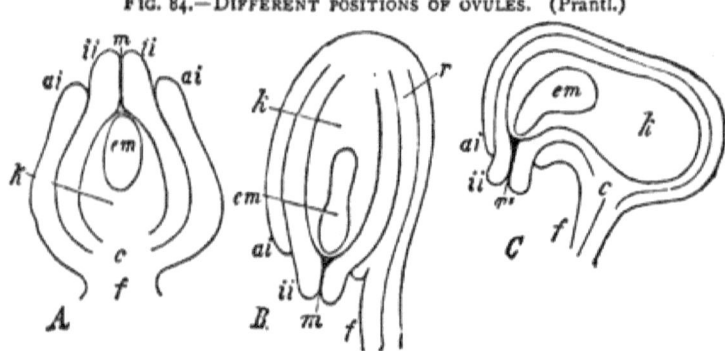

FIG. 84.—DIFFERENT POSITIONS OF OVULES. (Prantl.)

A, orthotropal ; B, anatropal ; C, campylotropal ; *a i*, *i i*, coats of the ovule ; *k*, nucellus ; *m*, micropyle ; *e m*, embryo-sac ; *f*, funicle ; *r*, raphe.

The development of the stamen.—The stamen appears first as a small prominence on the floral axis (or **thalamus,** as it is sometimes called). Very early a division of the prominence takes place, indicating the primary divisions into two pairs of **spermo-sporangia.** The tissue between the

---

[1] It is very unfortunate that the terminology of the reproductive organs of the Angiospermæ is so different from that of the lower plants. The terms ovule, anther, ovary, and such like, have, however, become by long usage so firmly associated with these structures that it is almost impossible now to get rid of them. It is necessary, however, that the student should in all cases know not only the terms in ordinary use, but also the terms which are morphologically correct. In order to familiarise the reader with either terminology, use will be made of both series of names.

two lobes becomes the future connective; the filament is an after-formation. The lobes are covered by **epidermis** and the layer immediately beneath it divides into two layers, the inner of which becomes the **archesporium**, whilst the outer layer subdivides into three layers, the inner two of

FIG. 85. - DEVELOPMENT OF THE STAMEN.

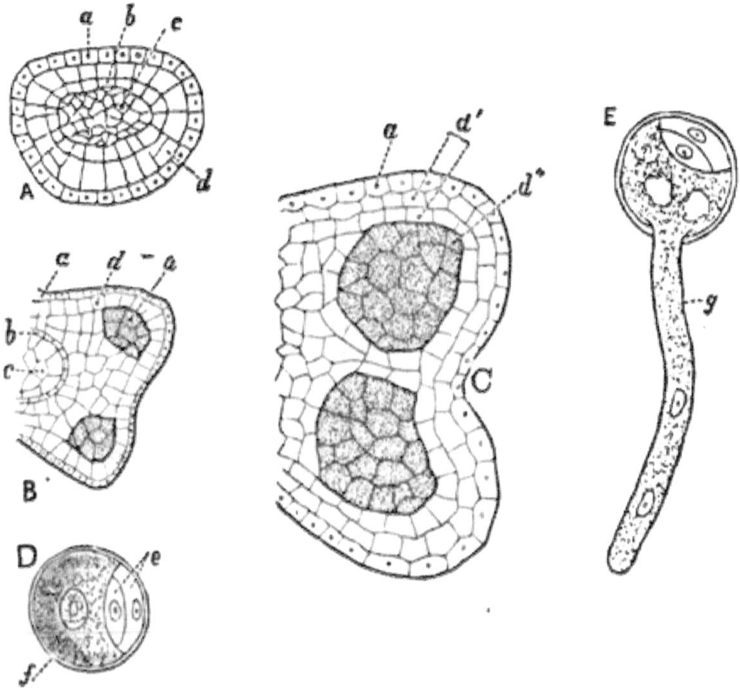

A, transverse section of young stamen; B, C, stages in the development of the anther; D, pollen grain; E, pollen tube developing from the reproductive cell: a, epidermis; b, bundle sheath; c, fibro-vascular bundle; d, layer which will become the tapetal layers, d', d''; e, vegetative cells; f, reproductive cell; g, intin.

which become disorganised and form **tapetal tissue**; the outer becomes, with the epidermis, the wall of the sporangium. The cells composing this inner layer have their walls irregularly thickened, and form what is known as the **endothecium**, while the term **exothecium** is sometimes given to the epidermis. The archesporium forms **mother spore-cells**, each of which subdivides into four daughter spore-cells, which in turn become, after the development of exo- and endo-sporium, the **spermospores**. As in the case of the spores of the fern, the exosporium (or **extin**) is ridged or elevated into spines, or otherwise variously sculptured. There are numerous apertures in the exosporium through which the endosporium (or **intin**) may be seen. Careful examination of the spermospore when fully developed reveals a structure highly suggestive of that of the spermospore of *Selaginella*, namely, the division of its contents into two portions, a **vegetative cell** or **cells** and a **reproductive cell**. The reproductive cell, however, does not undergo further division, and forms no sperms. Both cells are nucleated, and the much smaller vegetative cell is separated off from the other by a cellulose cell-wall. The ultimate fate of these cells we shall see later on, after we have studied the ovosporangium and its contents.

The development of the carpel.—The carpel, like the stamen, originates as a prominence of the thalamus, and after developing into a leaf-like structure forms on its inturned edges minute projections—the future **ovosporangia**

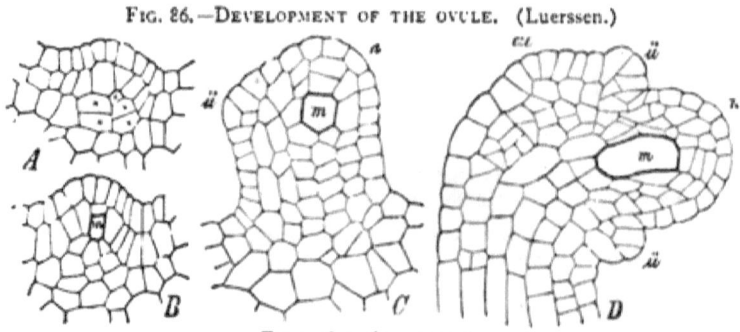

FIG. 86.—DEVELOPMENT OF THE OVULE. (Luerssen.)

For explanation see text.

(fig. 86, A, B). The projection becomes multicellular, and is covered over by the epidermis of the placenta. The projection gradually increases in size until it becomes differentiated into a head and stalk. The head forms the **nucellus**

(C, n^1, the stalk becomes the **funicle**. The cells immediately beneath the nucellus multiply tangentially and form the rudiments of the coverings of the ovule, the inner coat first, and the outer from beneath the origin of, and subsequently to, the inner coat (D, $i\,i$, $a\,i$). The ovule, though anatropal when ripe, is orthotropal at first, gradually becoming anatropal as it increases in size. These coverings to the sporangium are obviously new developments not present at all in the sporangia of the lower plants. The nucellus alone is the morphological sporangium comparable to that of the fern. The cell in the terminal portion of the nucellus immediately beneath the epidermis divides into two—an upper and a lower. The former becomes the **tapetum**, which in the ovosporangium is composed of one, or a very few, cells, whilst the latter becomes the **archesporium** (B, m). The archesporium whilst sunk in the nucellus next divides into four cells, of which one only becomes an **ovospore** (macrospore, embryo-sac). The other three cells, which are thus to be considered as **barren ovospores**, remain in a semi-disorganised condition on the summit of the fertile ovospore. This latter increases in size and very soon shows signs of division. The nucleus divides into two, each daughter nucleus retreating to opposite ends of the ovospore. Each of the two new nuclei again subdivides into four, and round three of either set protoplasm collects, thus forming three cells at either end of the ovospore. The two remaining nuclei reapproach the centre of the ovospore and there fuse, forming a new **secondary nucleus** for the ovospore. We have thus the contents of the ovospore subdivided into three small cells at the end nearest to the tapetum, and three small cells at the opposite end, with a large secondary nucleus between them (fig. 88). The cells of the upper of these two sets are arranged so that two cells are above and one beneath, the odd one having for its nucleus the sister of that nucleus which helped to form the new secondary nucleus of the ovospore. This lower cell is the **ovum** proper, whilst the two upper cells form the sole remnant left of the **canal walls** of the primitive ovarium. The three cells formed at the opposite pole may similarly be looked on as the rudiment of the **thallus**, probably that portion of it which would give rise, if completely developed, to spermaria, just as the vegetative cell of the spermospore, no doubt, contains chemical compounds necessary to the development of an ovarium.

Fertilisation. — In the life-history of vascular plants we have hitherto found that the male elements have been motile cells termed sperms, which in virtue of their movement have been able to migrate from the thallus bearing them to the female organs carried in other thalli. The pollen grain of a lily is itself, however, a non-motile structure, and no sperms are formed. How, then, is the male protoplasm to be carried to the ovum, and what in this case takes the place of the sperm in fertilisation?

Notwithstanding the fact that the majority of flowers are **hermaphrodite**, i.e. bear both male and female elements, it has been experimentally proved that, if an ovum be fertilised by the pollen of the same flower, the result, if there be any, is a weak and diminutive embryo, often incapable of developing into a perfect plant; whilst, on the other hand, if the ovum be fertilised by pollen taken from another flower, a healthy and vigorous embryo is produced. Thus **cross-fertilisation** tends to the maintenance of healthy tribal life, whilst **self-fertilisation** tends to produce a dwarf and weakly progeny, and ultimately extinction of the race unless cross-fertilisation intervenes and saves it. This law has a number of exceptions, but holds good in the great majority of cases. Granted, then, that foreign pollen (of course from a plant of the same kind) must be employed in fertilisation, how is the pollen to be conveyed from the male sporophyll of one flower to the female sporophyll of another, since the pollen grains, or spermospores, are themselves non-motile, and do not produce any motile sperms?

We have noticed already that the perianth leaves of the lily are **brightly coloured**. We may now notice further that they have a distinct odour, or **scent**. Lastly, an examination of the bases of the petals reveals the presence of small disc-shaped glands, to which the name of **nectaries** are applied, and which secrete a copious supply of nectar, a sweet, sticky fluid, not unlike honey, and containing a large amount of sugar in its composition. Everyone is familiar with the fact that insects of various kinds, especially bees, butterflies, and moths, visit flowers for the sake of this nectar, which they use as food. Further, it has been proved that they are attracted to the flower both by the scent (produced by the evaporation of volatile oils) and by the colour of the perianth. The insect in its movements in the interior of the flower, whilst sucking the nectar, rubs itself over with pollen, which when ripe tumbles out of the open sporangia. The pollen grains are viscid and sticky through having lain amongst the gelatinous tapetal cells. The insect's back and legs are covered with hairs, to which the viscid grains adhere. In this way the pollen grains are conveyed to another flower, where they fall, or are rubbed off by the insect, on the stigma. It is needless to say the action of the insect in this matter is a quite unconscious one. The stigma, it is to be remembered, is covered with hairs, also viscid and sticky, and to these some of the pollen grains adhere. They are nourished there by the secretion in which they are caught, and in some way or another are stimulated to further development.

The development of a pollen grain consists in the extrusion of part of its contents through the exosporium. The protuberance gradually assumes the form of a long thread or tube, the **pollen tube**, covered by the endosporium. The pollen tube lengthens and bores its way through the tissue of the style, and enters the micropyle of the ovule. There the termination of the pollen tube swells, and its wall becomes apparently more porous and suitable for the passage through it of the male protoplasm. The pollen tube fixes itself to the two upper cells of the rudimentary ovarium, and seems to become continuous with their substance. The nucleus of the male reproductive cell, which has meanwhile migrated down the pollen tube, becomes dissolved in the general protoplasm, and apparently in that form penetrates the endosporium and enters into the two upper cells, which

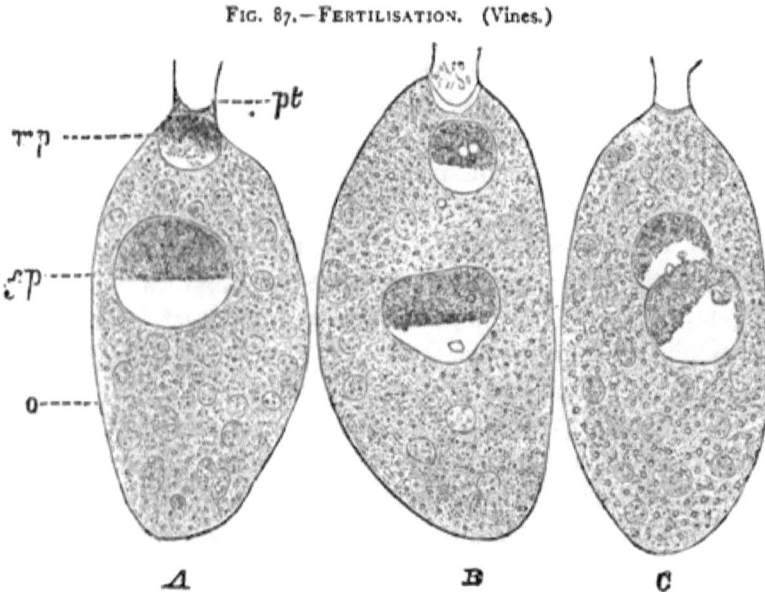

Fig. 87.—Fertilisation. (Vines.)

A, *B*, and *C*, successive stages in the fusion of the male and female pronuclei ; *p t*, pollen tube ; *m p*, male pronucleus ; *f p*, female pronucleus ; *o*, ovum.

are frequently spoken of as the **synergidæ**. These in turn fuse with the ovum, which thus has transferred to it some of the male fertilising matter. The nucleus (of the reproductive cell of the pollen grain) reaggregates and appears in the ovum, with the nucleus of which it fuses, completing the act of fertilisation. The pollen tube now withers away and the synergidæ disappear.

Results of fertilisation.—The first result of fertilisation is the assumption by the fertilised ovum or **embryo** of a

FIG. 88.—VERTICAL SECTION OF THE CARPEL. (Luerssen.)

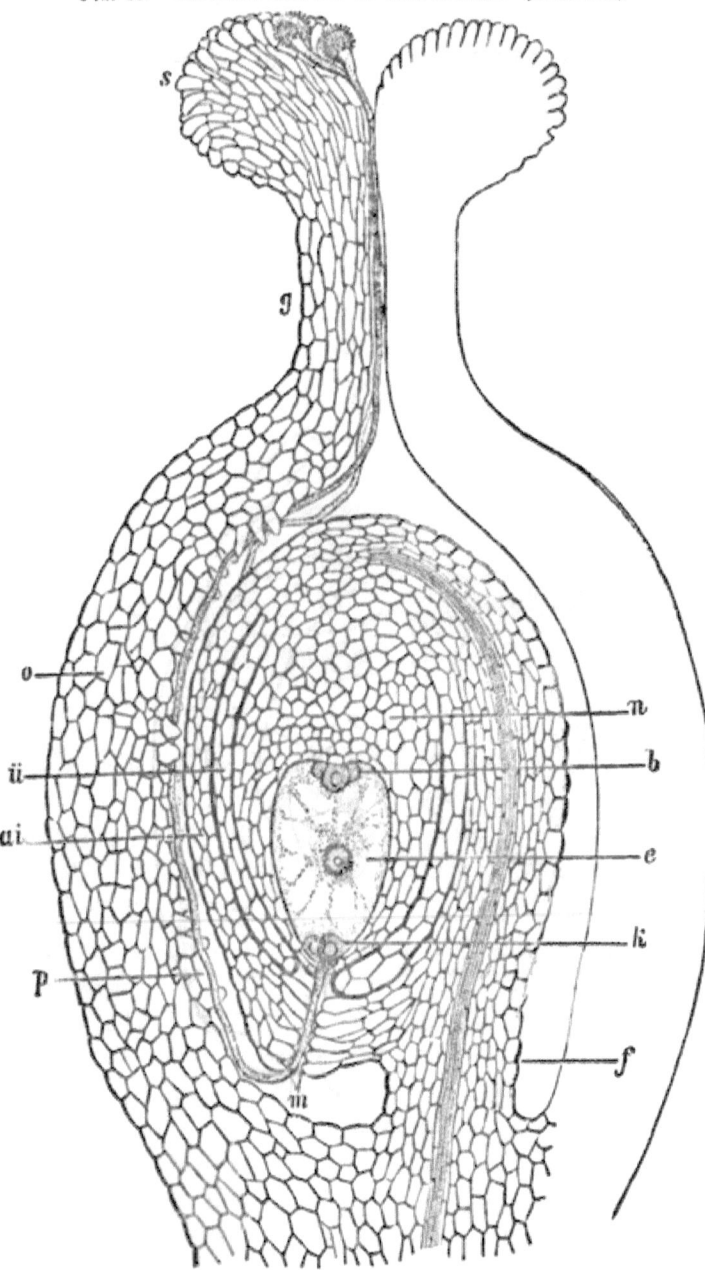

a i, outer ovular integument; *i i*, inner ovular integument; *o*, wall of ovary; *g*, style; *s*, stigma; *f*, funicle; *p*, pollen tube; *n*, nucellus; *b*, antipodal cells; *k*, ovum; *e*, embryo-sac; *m*, micropyle.

cell wall (compare the period of rest after sexual union in *Spirogyra* and other types). Meanwhile rapid subdivision of the secondary nucleus of the ovospore (embryo-sac) takes place, accompanied by the aggregation of protoplasm round the new nuclei to form cells. The result is a mass of cellular tissue, the **endosperm**, whose function it is to provide nourishment for the embryo about to be developed. In relation to the development of the embryo and the formation of a store of nourishment, it may be well to note

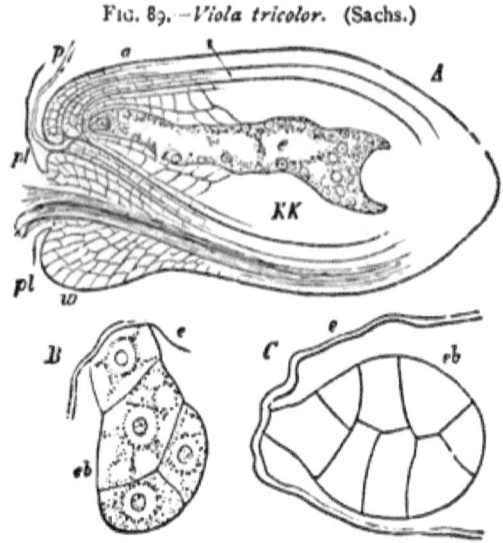

FIG. 89.—*Viola tricolor*. (Sachs.)

A, longitudinal section of anatropous ovule after fertilisation. *pl*, placenta; *w*, swelling on the raphe; *a*, outer integument; *i*, inner integument; *p*, pollen-tube entering micropyle; *e*, embryo-sac, with the fertilised ovum at the micropyle end, and numerous endosperm cells at the other. *B*, apex of embryo-sac, *e*, with young embryo, *eb*, of three cells, and one cell forming the suspensor. *C*, same, further advanced.

the existence in the funicle of a fibro-vascular strand, a feature absent from the funiculi of the lower types, as being unnecessary owing to the simplicity and short life of the sporangium (*Selaginella*), or to the fact that the embryo is not developed in the sporangium at all (*Pteris*). The ovospore now increases greatly in size and becomes completely filled with the endosperm, which appears first round the spore-wall and later in the centre. The cellular tissue (nucellus) surrounding the ovospore meantime disappears, becoming absorbed by the endosperm,[1] which takes its place morphologically and physiologically.

The development of the embryo.—The fertilised ovum soon segments into a short string of cells, one extremity being fixed to the end of the ovospore next the micropyle, the other end of the string lying free in the endosperm. This row of cells forms the **pro-embryo**. The proximal cells of the row, i.e. those next the micropyle, become the **suspensor**, and the single distal cell becomes the **embryo** proper.

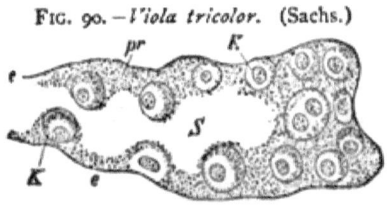

FIG. 90.—*Viola tricolor.* (Sachs.) Posterior end of embryo-sac: *e*, wall ; *S*, cavity of the embryo-sac; *K'*, *K'* young endosperm cells; *pr*, protoplasm of the embryo-sac.

The development of this distal cell into the embryo is of some importance, and it is at this stage that we meet with the first great difference between monocotyledons and dicotyledons. The account here given is true for both types up to a certain stage, when the points of difference will be emphasised.

The distal cell first undergoes subdivision, so that eight daughter cells are formed, which form a **blastoderm** (to use a convenient zoological term). These eight cells next become tangentially divided into eight concavo-convex cells externally and eight small tetrahedral cells internally (fig. 91). The external concavo-convex cells become **dermatogen**, or the layer destined to give rise to the epidermis ; the internal tetrahedral cells form the embryonic **periblem**, or fundamental tissue, and **plerome**, or fibro-vascular tissue. In the dicotyledons the embryo becomes flattened and heart-shaped, and shows a differentiation into two lobes, the **cotyledons**, or primary leaves, between the bases of which

---

[1] In some few plants it remains, and is then known as perisperm.

lies an actively growing mass of cells, the future **stem**, and a body known as the **hypocotyledonary axis**, the tip of which is covered by the terminal cell of the suspensor. This suspensorial cell divides transversely into two cells, the cell next the embryo (the **hypophysis**) giving origin by subdivision to a number of layers, the distal forming the terminal portion of the root, while the proximal cells form the embryonic root-cap, or **calyptrogen**.

The embryology of the monocotyledon does not differ from that just described, save that only one cotyledon is formed, consequently the young stem seems to spring from the side of the cotyledon rather than from the terminal part of the embryo. The manner of arrangement of the cells of the embryo is also somewhat different.

While these various changes have been taking place in the interior of the ovospore, concomitant changes have been occurring in the surrounding tissues of the ovule and ovary. After fertilisation the ovule becomes the **seed**, and the ovary, with its contained seed, the **fruit**. The outer covering of the ovule (now of the seed), is termed the **testa**, the inner the **tegmen**. Similarly, the ovarial wall, when it forms the wall of the fruit, receives the name of the **pericarp**, not infrequently differentiated into three layers, the **epi- meso-** and **endo-carp**. In some fruits the floral axis swells up round the ovary, and, becoming succulent, forms what is known as a false fruit, or **pseudocarp**. This does not, however, take place in the type which we are considering.

We have already seen how the various tissues of the adult plant are differentiated from meristem. The plant so formed may, like the lily, live only one year; it is then termed an **annual**, and its individual life, as a rule, ceases after it has matured its fruit. Plants which thus flower only once are termed **monocarpic**; others, again, flower after they are two years old and then die (**biennial monocarpic**); others only after they have lived for a number of years (**perennial monocarpic**). The majority (especially of dicotyledons) flower again and again year after year. These may therefore be termed **perennial polycarpic** plants.

When ripe the fruit falls off, and by withering or de-

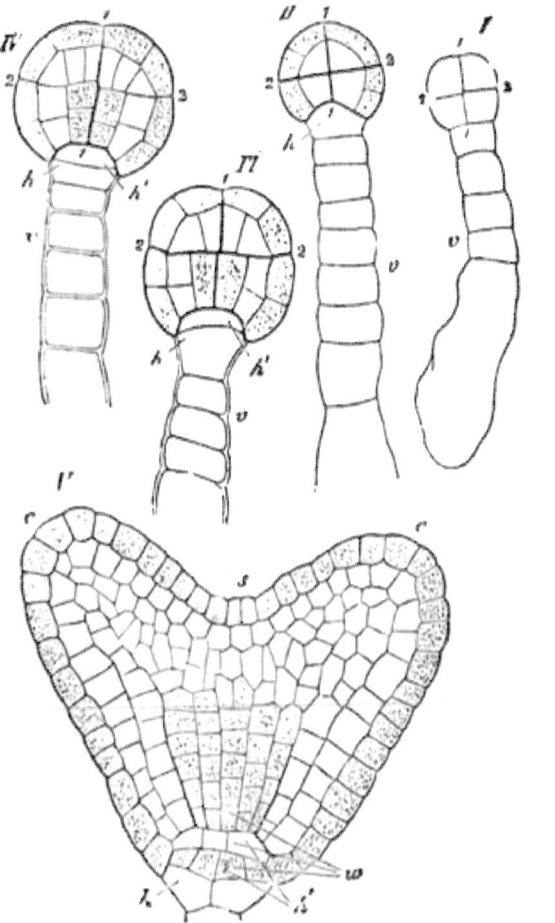

FIG. 91.—DEVELOPMENT OF EMBRYO OF DICOTYLEDON. (Sachs.)

The numbers indicate planes of division; v, suspensor; h, hypophysis; h', cell formed from the hypophysis; w, tissues of the embryonic root; s, stem; c, c, cotyledons.

hiscing allows the seeds to escape, or the fruit may dehisce while still attached to the stem. The seeds germinate when sown on a suitable soil under the proper conditions of heat

FIG. 92.—DEVELOPMENT OF THE EMBRYO. (Maout and Decaisne.)

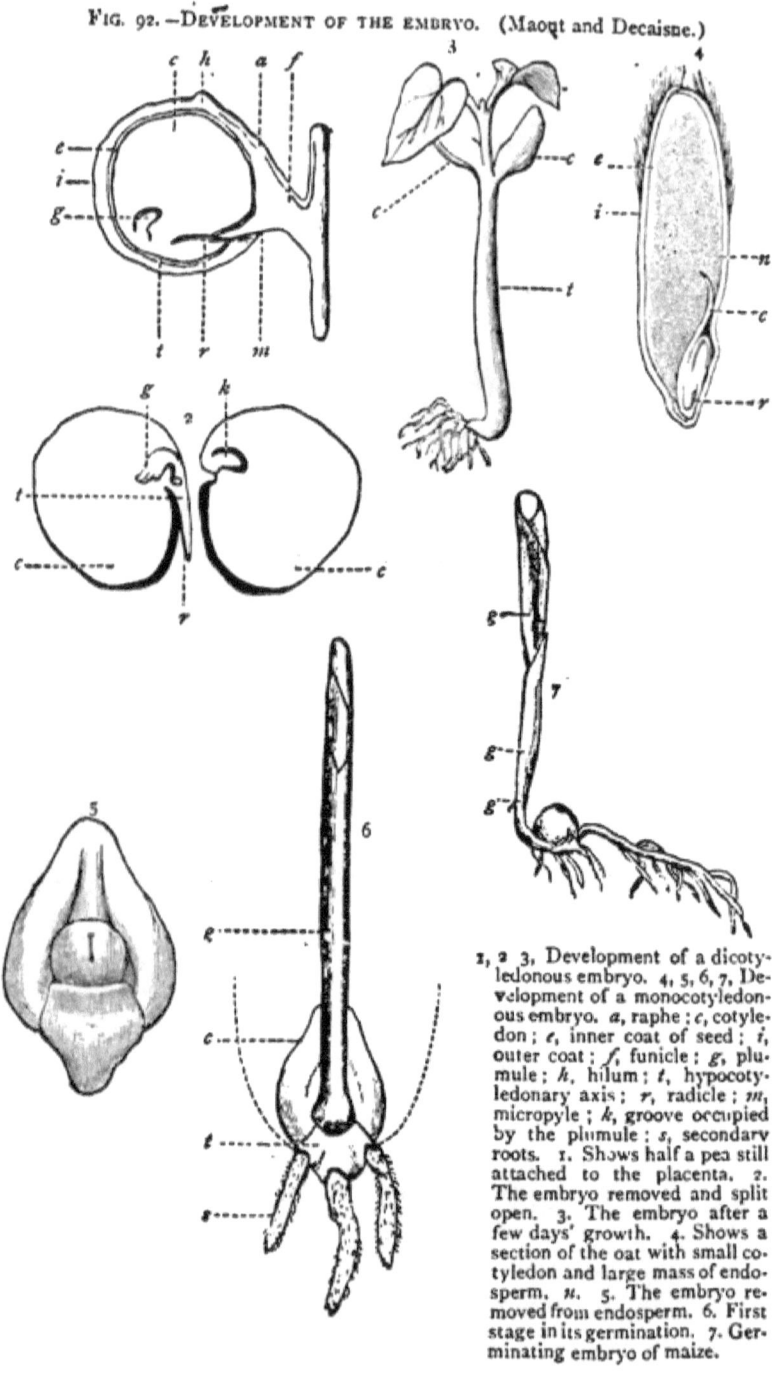

1, 2, 3, Development of a dicotyledonous embryo. 4, 5, 6, 7, Development of a monocotyledonous embryo. *a*, raphe; *c*, cotyledon; *e*, inner coat of seed; *i*, outer coat; *f*, funicle; *g*, plumule; *h*, hilum; *t*, hypocotyledonary axis; *r*, radicle; *m*, micropyle; *k*, groove occupied by the plumule; *s*, secondary roots. 1. Shows half a pea still attached to the placenta. 2. The embryo removed and split open. 3. The embryo after a few days' growth. 4. Shows a section of the oat with small cotyledon and large mass of endosperm. *n*. 5. The embryo removed from endosperm. 6. First stage in its germination. 7. Germinating embryo of maize.

and moisture. The root is the first part of the embryo to make its way through the micropyle and elongate. The plumule or young stem remains hidden for some time in the seed. When the primary root has taken fast hold of the soil the **secondary roots** begin to make their appearance to take its place functionally, and the primary root soon ceases to elongate. The plumule next emerges and increases in size. The stems of plants of the lily type increase in thickness very rapidly, but do not add secondary wood in future years if perennial. There are a number of arborescent lilies—such as the *Yucca, Dracæna*, and such like—which, however, form interesting transition links to the dicotyledonous type which we shall discuss in the following section. One point of some importance remains to be noticed with regard to the mode of origin of lateral branches of the stem and of the root axis. Lateral roots always originate from what was described at p. 150 as the pericambium layer, especially that portion of it which lies opposite to the xylem of the fibro-vascular strands, whilst branches of the stem axis originate from superficial layers of cells of the cortex into which the fibro-vascular strands afterwards become developed. The root method of development is termed **endogenous**, whilst the shoot method is termed **exogenous**. One result of the endogenous mode of origin is that the roots have to push their way through the cortex of the root; hence, where each root appears on the surface, it is surrounded by a collar of tissue which it has pushed aside, the **coleorhiza**.

FIG. 93.—ORIGIN OF SECONDARY ROOTS. (Prantl.)

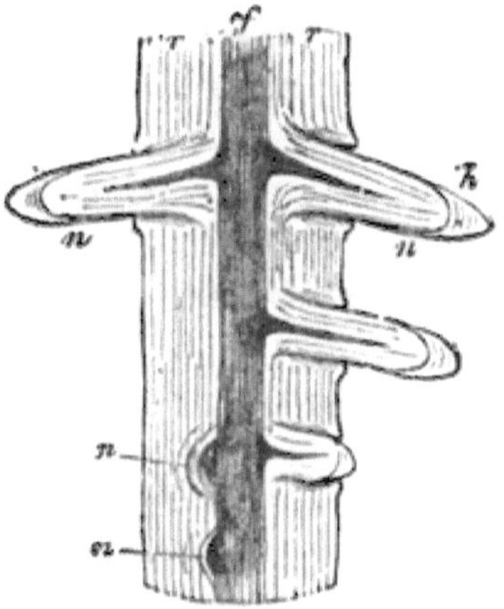

n, n, secondary roots in various stages of growth: *h,* root-cap; *r,* cortex; *f,* fibro-vascular core.

We have now completed our examination of the lily, and pass on in the next section to a survey of the points of difference and agreement between it and the buttercup. As already stated, the points of difference are chiefly in external configuration and arrangement of parts, in the arrangement of the tissues of the fibro-vascular strand, and in their mode of secondary growth ; and, lastly, in the structure of the embryo. We will devote special attention to these points. It will have been noticed that very little has been said hitherto of the physiology of plants ; that subject is postponed until our consideration of the morphology is completed, since the function of the several structures and the phenomena of nutrition, &c. will be thus more easily understood. The physiology of the several types, moreover, agrees in most essential points, hence by thus postponing our treatment of that subject until we have surveyed all the types we shall escape constant repetition.

SECTION IV.—DICOTYLEDONES—*RANUNCULUS*.

In selecting a type of the dicotyledonous flowering plants it is advisable to choose one where the various parts are as nearly as possible in a primitive or simple condition, where no parts of the flower are wanting (a **complete** flower) and where none have been specially modified for purposes connected with cross-fertilisation (a **regular** flower). The buttercup is a particularly favourable subject for investigation, for it is a complete and regular flower of the pentamerous type.

Stem.—The most important point of difference between the stem of the buttercup and that of the lily is in the arrangement of the fibro-vascular strands. As already seen, they are in the lily arranged irregularly in the fundamental tissue ; in the buttercup they are arranged **concentrically.** They therefore subdivide the fundamental tissue into a centrally placed **medulla** or **pith**, and a peripherally placed cortex, whilst joining these two tissues and running between the fibro-vascular strands lie plates of fundamental tissue to which the name of **medullary rays** has been given. The tissues of the strand are, moreover, also arranged **concentrically**. It is easily possible to differentiate three layers in the strand: internally and next the pith, the **xylem**, consisting of prosenchyma, parenchyma, and vessels. These latter are partly distributed through the wood (dotted ducts) and partly collected at the tips of the wood next the pith (spiral vessels), where the latter form what is known as the **medullary sheath.** Next we meet with a layer of actively growing tissue, the **cambium**, composed of parenchyma rich in protoplasm; and externally the bast, or **phloëm**, which is composed on its inner side of parenchyma, prosenchyma, and sieve-tubes, on its outer aspect of thick-walled prosenchyma.

As the stem grows older the strands increase in size, and approach one another so that the medullary rays are diminished. Moreover, a layer of cambium appears, uniting the cambium regions of the various strands together. The cambium of the strands and the cambium between the strands are known as **fascicular** and **interfascicular** cambium respectively. The interfascicular cambium has the power of forming xylem on its inner and phloëm on its outer side. Thus are formed new or **secondary strands**, which become wedged in between the primary strands, squeezing and crushing the medullary rays, of which nothing is ultimately left save a few thin plates or isolated patches of cells. The cambium of both kinds has, however, another duty to perform, namely, to add **new wood** and (to a less extent) **new bast** to the wood and bast already formed. Towards the end of the year when the vitality of the plant is ebbing, the cambium cells divide less rapidly and the cells are much smaller. Again, on the return of spring, when vitality is in full flow, the cells become much larger and divide rapidly. This cessation and renewal of growth form what are popularly known as **annual rings**. These rings are not so distinct in the bast, for there is not so much of it formed, nor is it formed so regularly. This formation of new layers of wood and bast may go on for an indefinite number of years, hence

FIG. 94.—DEVELOPMENT OF THE DICOTYLEDONOUS STEM. (Sachs.)

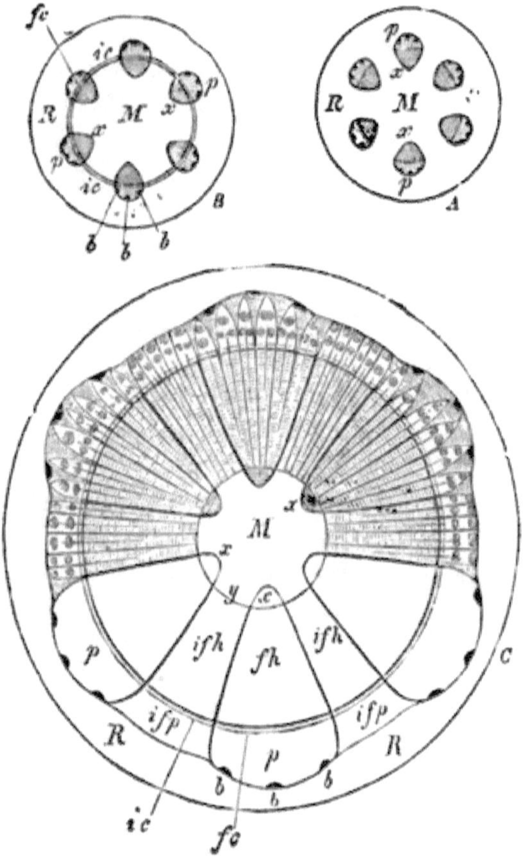

R, cortex: M, pith; *ic*, interfascicular cambium; *fc*, fascicular cambium; *p*, primary phloëm; *x*, primary xylem; *b*, hard bast; *fh*, *ifh*, fascicular and interfascicular wood.

the term **open**, or capable of continuous growth, as applied to strands of the dicotyledonous stem. Manifestly as the stem thus increases in size, some arrangement must be made whereby the cortex may increase concomitantly. Such an arrangement is found in the **cork cambium**, a layer of growing cells lying outside the bast. This layer is capable of growth in two directions—outwards and inwards. Outwards

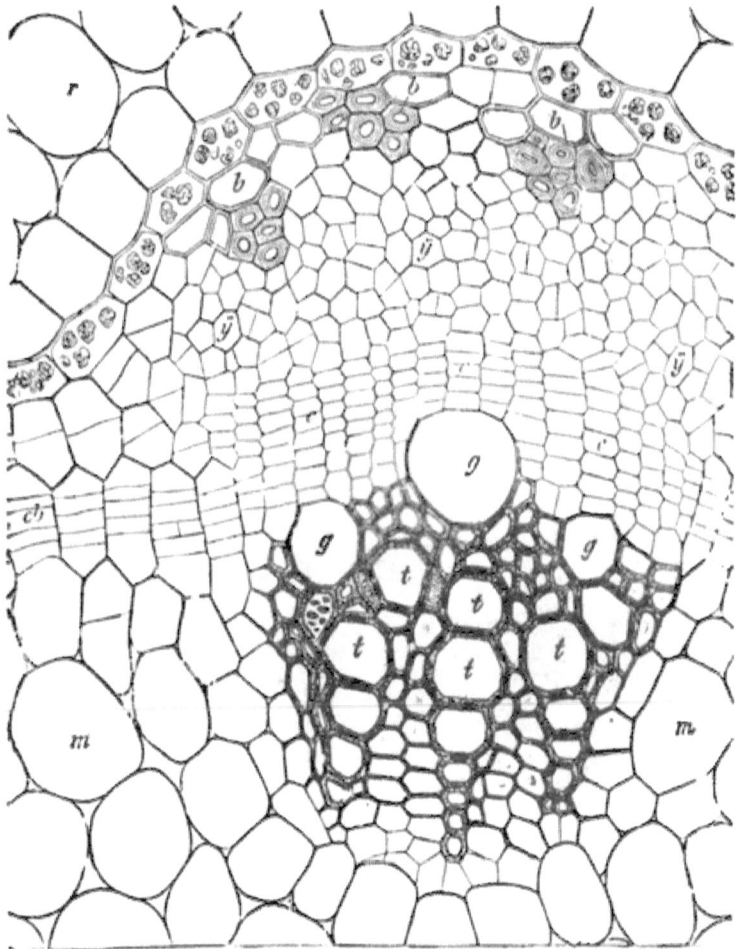

FIG. 95.—DICOTYLEDONOUS FIBRO-VASCULAR STRAND. (Sachs.)

b, hard bast ; *c*, fascicular cambium ; *c b*, interfascicular cambium ; *y*, sieve-tubes in soft bast ; *m*, fundamental tissue ; *g*, dotted ducts ; *t*, pitted vessels.

it forms a layer of **periderm**, or **cork**, the cells of which are dead and filled with air, and have their walls rendered almost impermeable to water ; and inwards a layer of **phelloderm**, or green cortex. The cork cambium itself is often known as **phellogen**. These successive layers of cork form the **bark**; even in young twigs little patches of cork form below the epidermis (usually beneath a stoma) and bulge it outwards, forming what are known as **lenticels**.

In the cortex, and frequently amongst the other tissues as well, are found vessels of an entirely different character

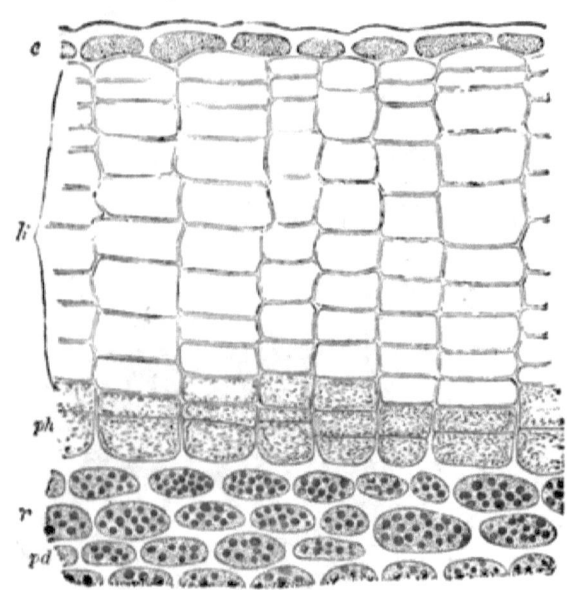

FIG. 96.—ORIGIN OF CORK. (Sachs.)

e, epidermis; *k*, cork or periderm; *ph*, phellogen, or cork cambium; *pd*, phelloderm.

from those already described. Two forms will be here described, the laticiferous vessels and the resin canals. **Laticiferous vessels** usually run in an irregular manner through the tissue in which they are found. They branch and anastomose. They contain a watery fluid known as **latex**, seen very well exuding from the cut stem of a dandelion. The latex is not always white, however. It may be red, blue, or yellow. Some varieties of latex are of great commercial value, such as, for instance, india-rubber, gutta-percha, and opium. Whilst laticiferous vessels are formed of straight or irregular cells, placed end to end and having

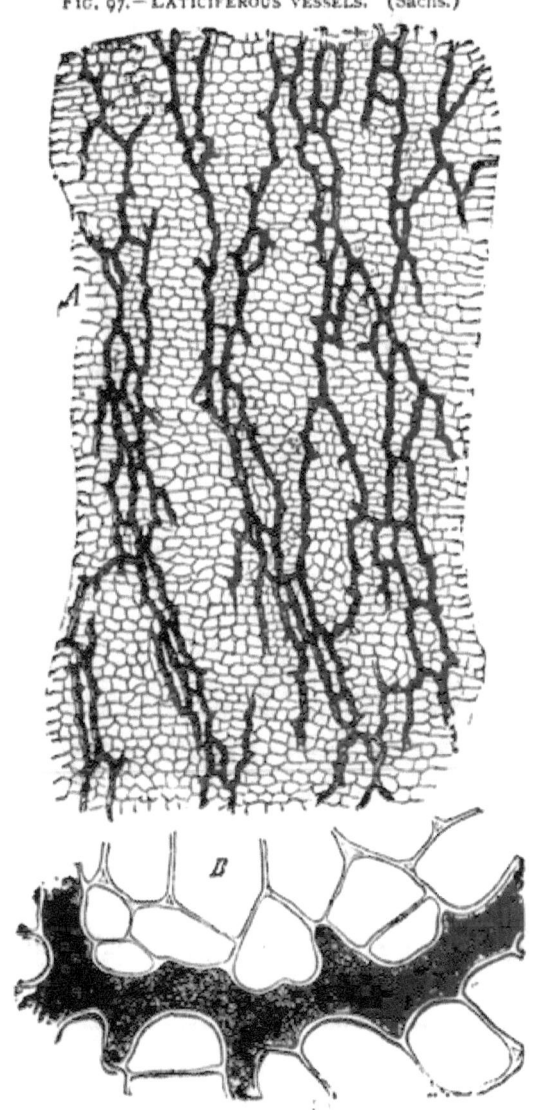

Fig. 97.—Laticiferous vessels. (Sachs.)

A, slightly, B, highly magnified.

their common walls absorbed, **resin canals** are formed by a number of cells enclosing a cavity, which is thus an intercellular space. They also contain substances of economic value, as turpentine, resin, &c.

Numerous other varieties of vessels, ducts, and glands might be mentioned, such as **oil glands, nectar glands,** cavities containing **volatile oils,** and such like. The peculiar glands of insectivorous plants will be described in sect. vi.

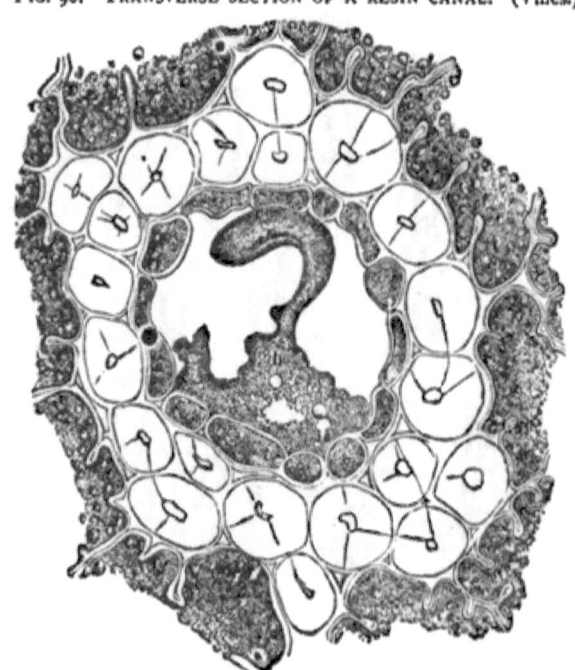

Fig. 98.—Transverse Section of a Resin Canal. (Vines.)

Root.—The chief point of importance in the dicotyledonous root in which it differs from that of the monocotyledon is its power of **increasing in thickness** by growth of secondary wood. It will be remembered that while the primary root of the monocotyledon soon ceases to grow, and has its place taken by adventitious roots, the primary root of the dicotyledon goes on growing, and increases in thickness by the addition of new wood and new bast to that already formed. The secondary layers of wood and bast arise from a fascicular and interfascicular cambium, which lies internal to the pericambium, and, owing to the position of the two parts of the primary strands, winds in a sinuous manner out and in between the primary masses of bast and the primary masses of wood. The cambium first makes its appearance opposite the bast portions of the strands.

Leaf.—The arrangement of the fibro-vascular strands in the dicotyledonous leaf differs from that of the monocotyledon in being netted or **reticulated**, the strands starting from one or more chief ribs, and gradually becoming smaller towards the leaf edge, branching and anastomosing as they go.

The shape of the leaf as a whole is most varied. We may distinguish, however, between **simple** and **compound** leaves, and reduce each leaf or leaflet (if compound) to one or other of the three types, **circular, elliptical**, and **ovate**. The shape of the leaf is always related to the arrangement of the leaves on the stem (**phyllotaxis**). It must be remembered that the main object of phyllotaxis is to enable the leaves to get a maximum of light and air. We will first consider one or two of the chief phenomena of phyllotaxis and then it will at once become apparent that the shape of the leaf and the phyllotaxis are closely correlated (Lubbock).

There are two chief methods of leaf arrangement, namely, where the leaves are arranged in pairs **opposite** to each other or in circles or whorls of more than two, and they are arranged in an **alternate** or spiral manner round the stem. These two methods may be termed the **verticillate** and the **spiral** respectively. The verticillate is often mimicked by the spiral when the internodes of the latter are very closely approximated, as, for instance, on the floral axis. There are many varieties of the spiral arrangement, but all are found to obey a definite law, viz. that if the numerator of a vulgar fraction indicate the number of times it is necessary to go round the stem before coming to the leaf directly above that from which the start is made (following the bases of successive leaves on the branch in regular order), and if the denominator represent the number of leaves passed, then the numerators of two successive fractions added together give the numerator, and the denominators added together the denominator of the succeeding fraction. Thus the

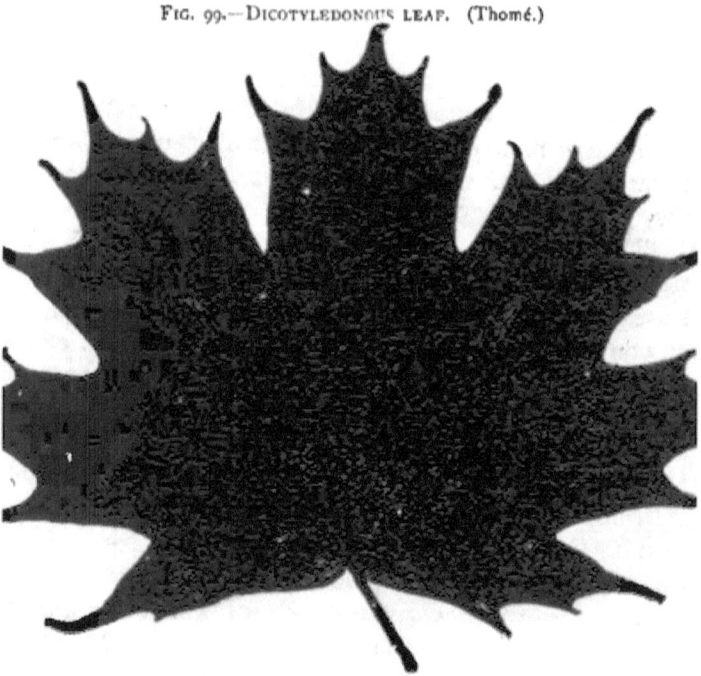

FIG. 99.—DICOTYLEDONOUS LEAF. (Thomé.)

simplest spiral phyllotaxis must be that where the leaves are **alternate**, one on one side and the other on the other side of the stem. Manifestly, under such circumstances, we must pass two leaves and go once round the stem to reach the leaf directly above that from which we started. Hence we have here a $\frac{1}{2}$ spiral. Again, still circling the stem once, every fourth leaf might be that directly above the starting point. The fraction then would be $\frac{1}{3}$. According to the law, the succeeding spirals must be $\frac{2}{3}, \frac{3}{8}, \frac{5}{13}, \frac{8}{21}$, and so on. The law, however, does not always hold good amongst the higher fractions, and seldom among the sporophylla and perianth leaves, where various modifying influences come into play. Now if a plant has large broad leaves, manifestly

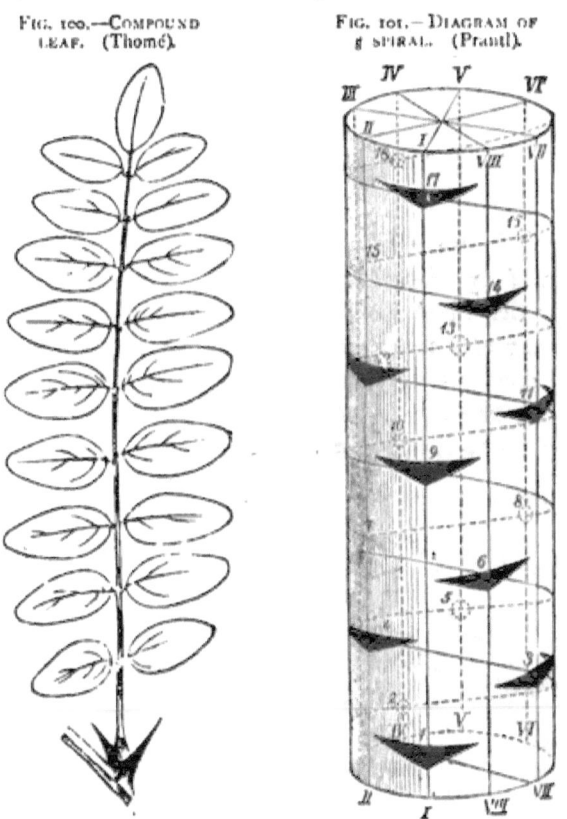

FIG. 100.—COMPOUND LEAF. (Thomé).

FIG. 101.—DIAGRAM OF $\frac{8}{21}$ SPIRAL. (Prantl).

if they are to obtain a maximum of light and air, they must be arranged on a wide spiral, and not in a whorl, else they will cover each other. So, also, if the leaves are small and narrow, they might well be arranged in whorls or close spirals, and still be sufficiently exposed to the air and light.

The flower.—It has already been pointed out that the flower of the buttercup conforms to what is known as the **pentamerous** type, that is to say, has its parts arranged in whorls of five each. This may be best seen by comparing the floral diagram (fig. 103) with the vertical section of the flower (fig. 102). The

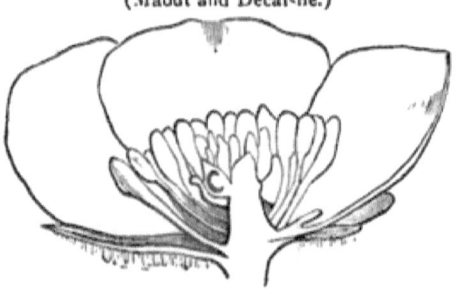

FIG. 102.—VERTICAL SECTION OF RANUNCULUS. (Maout and Decaisne.)

sporophylla are more numerous than in the lily, and are spoken of as **indefinite**. The **stamens** conform to the type already described for the lily. The **carpels** are, however, in *Ranunculus* free as well as numerous. Moreover, each carpel contains only one **anatropal sporangium** (ovule). After the ovum in its interior has been fertilised the carpel is then a **one-celled one-seeded fruit**. The carpels in the lily formed a **three-celled many-seeded fruit**. All the sporophylla, as well as the perianth leaves, spring from a convex **thalamus** or floral axis, and the stamens rise free from each other and the perianth, and at a lower level than the carpels. The stamens (**androecium**) are therefore said to be **hypogynous**, or beneath the carpels (**gynoecium**). The account of the structure of the sporophylla and the essential

FIG. 103.—FLORAL DIAGRAM OF RANUNCULUS. (Allen.)

a a, carpels; *b b*, stamens; *c c*, petals; *d d*, sepals.

elements of reproduction already given for the lily will, with very slight modification, do also for the type now before us. Repetition, therefore, is unnecessary. We have also directed attention to the chief points in the embryology in connection with that of the lily. We proceed now to give a brief account of the general physiology of the plant in application (with exceptions which will be pointed out) to all the types considered in the preceding sections.

Section V.—General Physiology of Plants.

As was pointed out in sect. i. of Chap. III. every organ in the plant body has a special duty or function to perform, a duty directly subservient to the welfare of the individual as a whole. Just as we may consider the plant body as a whole from a morphological point of view, so also we may discuss the **general physiology** of the vegetal organism as a whole. These two aspects may be denominated the **statical** and the **dynamical** aspects respectively. Previously, however, to entering upon the detailed examination of the dynamical or physiological aspect of plant life, it will be found of great assistance if we devote a short time to the survey of the special chemical elements which enter into the composition of the plant, and the conditions under which they occur there.

The easiest method of ascertaining the elements which compose the food of plants is by subjecting the entire plant to **destructive analysis** (footnote, page 25). The plant organism contains a very large percentage of **water** (uncombined) which can be dried off by application of a gentle heat (**desiccation**). Many of the volatile oils and aromatic substances are also got rid of by this means; we will not, however, consider them at present. The amount of the water present varies with the season of the year at which the examination is conducted, and the plant and part of the plant examined. Aquatic plants, such as the Algæ, contain a much larger percentage of water than terrestrial or aerial plants, though there are numerous exceptions to this rule. In spring, when active growth is commencing, the proportion of water rapidly increases. The younger parts of the plant also contain more water than older parts.

The dried or desiccated plant may further be subjected to **calcination**, or red heat, when the greater proportion of the solid residue is removed in the form of simple compounds, such as carbonic acid, water of combination, and ammonia. The elements found to be present by an examination of the products of calcination are carbon, hydrogen, oxygen, and nitrogen; whilst the **ash** left over contains, as a general rule, sulphur, phosphorus, chlorine, silicon, potassium, calcium, magnesium, sodium, and iron, all in the form of simple salts, or even as bases or oxides. Many other substances are found in particular plants, those, that is to say, growing in certain districts where such substances occur in the soil, or where the plant has peculiar facilities for the absorption of such substances. These **accidental constituents** are iodine and bromine, which are found in many marine plants, lithium, zinc, copper, aluminium, manganese, cobalt, nickel, strontium, and barium.

It will be convenient to classify these elements in the order of their relative importance, thus :—

I. Essential elements present in the plant organism in large amount. (C, H, O, and N.)

II. Essential elements present in small amount. (S, P, K, Ca, Mg, Fe.)

III. Non-essential elements present in variable amount, and not in all plants. (I, Br, Zu, Cu, Al, Mn, Co, Ni, Sr, Li, Ba, Si, Na, Cl.)

I. Essential elements in the plant organism, present in large amount.

CARBON.

Origin.—The carbon is obtained from the carbonic acid

of the atmosphere (p. 42). Parasites and saprophytes (p. 100) and carnivorous plants (p. 213), however, obtain their supply of carbon from organic compounds present in living or dead animals and plants.

Importance.—Carbon forms fully half the dry weight of the plant, and forms an essential constituent of proteids, carbohydrates, fats, and many transition substances (p. 26).

HYDROGEN.

Origin.—From the water obtained from the soil and from the air ; also from ammonia and its compounds present in the soil.

Importance.—As in the case of the carbon, hydrogen is an essential constituent of proteids, carbohydrates, fats, and many transition substances. It also, of course, forms an essential constituent of the omnipresent water.

OXYGEN.

Origin.—Most of the oxygen used in the formation of organic compounds in the plant is obtained from water and salts containing oxygen. The oxygen, on the other hand, required in the oxidising of protoplasm in the liberation of energy, is obtained from the boundless supply of free oxygen in the air.

Importance.—Again an essential constituent of the substances mentioned under hydrogen, as well as forming a necessary condition of plant life in its free form for purposes of oxidation (respiration, p. 35).

NITROGEN.

Origin.—The nitrogen found in combination in the plant body is entirely obtained from nitrogen in combination in the soil, as nitrates, nitrites, &c. Notwithstanding the enormous quantity of free nitrogen in the air, none of it seems to be used directly by the plant as food.

Importance.—Like carbon, hydrogen, and oxygen, an essential constituent of the same organic and inorganic compounds already shown to enter into the formation of protoplasm.

Not only carbon, but also hydrogen, nitrogen, and oxygen are, in the case of the saprophytes, parasites, and carnivorous plants, obtained from the organic compounds contained in the media in or on which they live.

II. Essential elements in the plant organism, present in small amount.

SULPHUR.

Origin.—The sulphur is obtained by the decomposition of salts of sulphur present in the soil. Undoubtedly the chief salt from which the sulphur is procured is sulphate of lime. This salt is probably decomposed by some organic acid in the plant, such as oxalic acid, crystals of calcic-oxalate being formed, the nascent sulphur combining with higher compounds. Many other sulphates, such as those of potassium, magnesium, and ammonium, are probably used in this way.

Importance.—Although sulphur is itself volatile, it is not burnt off during calcination, but is found in the form of sulphuric acid united with bases present in the ash to form sulphates. It forms an essential constituent of proteids and many transition substances.

PHOSPHORUS.

Origin.—Phosphorus, like sulphur, is obtained from its salts present in the soil. These salts are mainly those of lime, potash, and magnesia.

Importance.—Phosphorus, though present in very small amount, nevertheless seems to be in some way essential to the vitality of the organism. In addition to forming a constituent of the substance nuclein, of which the cell-nucleus is mainly composed, and of various proteids or derivatives of them, it also plays an important part in the metabolism of protoplasm; for no albuminoids can be formed if it be absent. It also enters into the composition of chlorophyll (p. 40).

POTASSIUM.

Origin.—Potassium is obtained from a variety of salts in the soil, of which the chief are the sulphate, phosphate, and chloride.

Importance.—Potassium, like phosphorus, is necessary for the metabolic processes in the plant. While phosphorus assists in the formation of proteids, potassium exerts a like influence in the formation of carbohydrates.

CALCIUM.

Origin.—Salts of lime in the soil, such as the sulphate, phosphate, nitrate, and carbonate.

Importance.—The use of calcium in the plant economy is still a matter of some doubt. Probably one of its uses is to form a medium whereby the excess of organic acids may be got rid of (see under sulphur).

MAGNESIUM.

Origin.—From the same salts as those of calcium. The chlorides of magnesium and of calcium are, however, unfavourable to the growth of the plant.

Importance.—The value of magnesium to the plant is involved in even greater doubt than is that of calcium. It has been found to be a constituent of the globoid associated with grains of aleurone where these occur (p. 157).

IRON.

Origin.—Many compounds of iron are employed to give the very small amount of that metal required by the plant.

Importance.—Iron is associated in some way with the formation of chlorophyll. Without it no chlorophyll is formed, and yet if more than a minute trace be present it acts as a poison on the plant. It does not, however, form a constituent of chlorophyll. It must, therefore, act simply as an essential agent in its production.

III. Non-essential elements in the plant organism, present in variable amount.

All these substances are not found in the same plant, nor at the same time. Some, indeed, are invariable constituents though they do not seem essential to life, e.g. sodium.

Sodium.—This metal might be said to be ubiquitous, and yet it cannot be said to be of essential service to the plant. It is obtained from salts in the soil, and is taken up chiefly in the form of sodium chloride.

Chlorine.—Chlorine, as has been mentioned above, is necessarily taken into the plant in the process of the absorption of potassium and sodium, but it does not seem to be necessary to the life of the plant.

Silicon, however, enters in considerable quantity into the composition of many plants of the grass tribe; whilst many of the lower plants have large deposits of silica (SiO_2) in the cells of the thallus. The silicious covering of the Diatoms and allied forms are composed almost entirely of this compound (p. 72).

Iodine and **bromine** are found in tolerably large quantities in certain of the marine Algæ, whence, indeed, a large proportion of the iodine and bromine of commerce is obtained.

With regard to the **other elements** mentioned under this head, we need only say that they are found rather as **accidental constituents** than as essentials in the plant organism. They are probably not peculiar to plant life at all.

The forms in which these various elements appear in the

plant will form a subject of study when we consider the dynamical aspect of plant physiology.

It is worth pointing out here that this analysis of plants yields us most important results when we consider their life-histories from an **agricultural** point of view. The whole question of **manuring** is founded on a knowledge of the chemical composition of plants. By the **rotation of crops**, the farmer is able to grow a plant on a soil impoverished by the preceding crop of many substances which its successor, however, does not require. Meantime, by rainfall and the natural disintegration of the soil, the land is becoming replenished with exactly those substances in which it has become deficient, enabling it, therefore, to supply food-stuffs for another crop of the former kind in a succeeding year. A comparison of the chemical composition of a few typical crops, as, for example, those in the subjoined table, will make this fact clearer.

1,000 PARTS OF DRY SOLID MATTER CONTAIN (Prantl):—

Plant	Ash	Potash	Soda	Lime	Magnesia	Ferric Oxide	Phosphoric Acid	Sulphuric Acid	Silica	Chlorine
Clover in bloom	68·3	21·96	1·39	24·06	7·44	0·72	6·74	2·06	1·62	2·66
Wheat (grain)	19·7	6·14	0·44	0·66	2·36	0·26	9·26	0·07	0·42	0·04
,, (straw)	53·7	7·3	0·74	3·09	1·33	0·33	2·58	1·32	36·25	0·90
Potato tubers	37·7	22·76	0·99	0·97	1·77	0·45	6·53	2·45	0·80	1·17
Apples	14·4	5·14	3·76	0·59	1·26	0·20	1·96	0·88	0·62	—
Peas (seed)	27·3	11·41	0·26	1·36	2·17	0·16	9·95	0·95	0·24	0·42

We have seen, then, that the food of plants is **solid, liquid, and gaseous**, and that it is obtained (in the case of green plants) from the **soil** and the **atmosphere**. We have already considered the composition of the atmosphere (p. 41); we have now to glance for a moment at the composition of the soil.

Composition of the soil.—The composition of the soil is as varied as that of the rocks by the disintegration of which it is in the main produced. The animals and plants living on it, however, add a considerable quantity of matter to the soil by their excrement while living, as well as by the products arising from the decomposition of their dead bodies. The character of the soil is dependent in the first instance on the nature of the subsoil and rock beneath, i.e. on the nature of the geological formation of the district in question. The character of the vegetation, as a rule, alters very considerably according as the soil is clayey, loamy, sandy, gravelly, chalky, or peaty. Not only so, but the presence or absence of various constituents determines whether the soil will be wet or dry, cold or warm, rich or poor. Particular crops are adapted to some soils rather than to others—a fact very familiar to all agriculturists. Indeed, the occurrence and distribution of many wild plants within their area of habitat depends entirely on the presence or absence of the suitable soil and the requisite amount of moisture.

General physiology of the plant.—It has already been pointed out in the early chapters of this book how necessary it is that the great law of the conservation of energy should be continually borne in mind when the physiology of protoplasm is being discussed, and it will be found most advisable if we adopt this law for our guide in discussing the physiology of the plant in general. Protoplasm is a highly complex store of potential energy, in virtue of the possession of which the plant is able to perform certain duties, related to the maintenance, partly of tribal, partly of individual life. Without protoplasm, so far as we know, no protoplasm is formed. Since, then, this store must be built up ere it can be broken down and used, it follows that we must discuss the physiology of the plants first from the **anabolic**, and secondly from the **katabolic** point of view. (Compare sec. ii. Chap. I., secs. ii. and vi. Chap. II., and secs. i. and ii. Chap.

III. in this relation). Under the head of **anabolism** we will discuss the **absorption** and **assimilation** of food-stuffs, both of which processes may be summed up under the one term **nutrition.** We will also consider the **circulation** of the various food-stuffs, both in their prepared and unprepared states, through the plant-body, and the **storage** of the excess. Under the head of **katabolism**, on the other hand, we will discuss the breaking down of protoplasm, and the formation in consequence of **degradation products**, or **katastates**, which may be again subdivided into **secretions**, or katastates still useful in the plant economy, and **excretions**, or katastates which must be got rid of. Lastly we will deal with the **results of katabolism**, or the various ways in which the energy liberated by the decomposition of protoplasm manifests itself in the plant. These results will be found to group themselves under the following headings: first, **growth and movement**; secondly, **irritability** or **sensitivity**; thirdly, **heat, light**, and **electricity**; and lastly, phenomena connected with the **formation of reproductive cells.**

I. Anabolism.

A. Nutrition.—All the food of the plant must necessarily be absorbed in the fluid form, i.e. in the form of a **liquid** or a **gas. Solids** absorbed are taken up in solution in water, those which are naturally insoluble in water being made so by some substance (acid) produced by the plant.

We must first consider the laws which govern the absorption of liquids and gases. All food material must pass through the cell-walls of the leaf and root-hairs, which, we have already seen, are the organs of absorption. Let us examine first the passage of liquids, i.e. water with salts in solution, through the cell-walls of the root-hairs; and it may be well to illustrate this subject by a simple physical experiment, before taking up the special case before us.

A glass vessel is taken containing distilled water, and in it is suspended a smaller glass vessel, which, however, has a bottom made of parchment or bladder instead of glass. In the smaller vessel is put a solution of common salt (NaCl). If the apparatus be left for some time, and the two liquids be then examined, it will be found that, although none of the salt solution would have passed through the membrane had the smaller vessel been suspended in air instead of in water, under the latter circumstances some of the salt solution has permeated the membrane, and can be detected in the surrounding water of the larger vessel by adding a small quantity of a solution of nitrate of silver, which gives with sodium chloride a white precipitate not obtainable from the distilled water before the experiment was begun. Moreover, if the contents of the inner vessel be examined, it will be found to contain a much weaker percentage of salt than at the beginning of the experiment, showing that the solution has been diluted by the addition of water. The quantity of the solution is, moreover, greater absolutely, showing that the passage of the salt alone, without water, will not account for the weakening of the solution (fig. 104). Both water and sodium chloride are crystalline substances, the former at a temperature of $0°$ C., the latter at all ordinary temperatures. Now if for the sodium chloride a solution of gum, or of white of egg, or other non-crystallisable substance, be substituted, it will be found that very little, if any, of the gum will pass through into the outer solution, though the density of the gum solution will become less in consequence of the passage of water into the inner vessel. Further, if sodium chloride solutions of different density be placed on either side of the membrane, a current is established between the two solutions, which continues until the density of both is identical. Lastly, if the membrane separate two solutions, both uncrystallisable, neither substance will pass over into the other, though the water of the solution may, until the density of the two fluids be the same.

From these experiments we may formulate a law to the effect that if a vegetal or animal membrane separate two solutions, both of which are crystallisable, a current will be set up through the membrane between them. This passage is known as **osmosis**. The current from the outer to the inner vessel in the experiment is known as an **endosmotic** current; that from the inner to the outer is termed an **exosmotic** current. Almost all crystallisable substances, which can wet the membrane, are capable of undergoing osmosis; non-crystallisable substances, as a rule, are not. Further, many substances pass much more rapidly through organic membranes than others, so that there may be a very rapid endosmosis accompanied by a very slow exosmosis, or *vice versa*. Moreover, the rate is also modified by the chemical nature of the substances inside or outside the membrane.

A root-hair is a vessel, a very small one it is true, containing in its cell-sap certain crystallisable and certain non-crystallisable substances. These are separated from the soil by two vegetal membranes, the cell-wall and the protoplasm. The soil contains various crystallisable salts in solution in water, or capable of being made so by the action of various acids &c. Here, then, we have all the conditions for osmosis. There will be a considerable endosmosis and little exosmosis, for the substances in the cell being in great part protoplasmic in their nature, and therefore non-crystallisable, will have little tendency to pass outwards into the soil, whilst the crystallisable solutions in the soil will tend to pass inwards through the cell-wall and protoplasm into the cell. It must be remembered, however, that the protoplasm itself acts in many cases

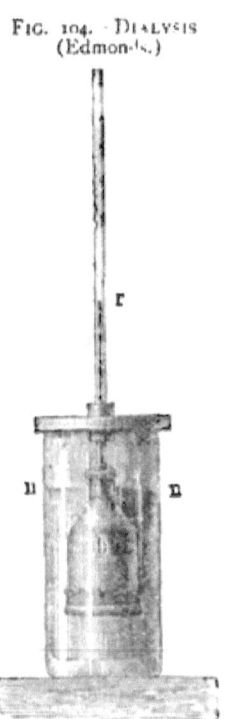

FIG. 104. — DIALYSIS (Edmonds.)

n, level of water in outer vessel; *h*, inner vessel containing salt solution; *r*, level of salt solution after experiment.

differently from the cell-wall, and hinders many substances from passing inwards which the cell-wall would allow to pass through.

The chemical nature of the cell-contents influences to a very great extent the nature and rapidity of the endosmotic flow. It is believed that the organic acids and their salts, always present in living cells, exert an attractive influence on the water, although probably other substances as well have a like, though not so great an, affinity for water. After exosmosis of the water of the cell-sap, the protoplasm contracts, leaving a space between it and the cell-wall. This phenomenon is known as **plasmolysis**, and takes place when the cells are treated with a solution of a substance having a strong affinity for water.

We have now to examine the laws governing the absorption of gases by plants.

From the composition of the atmosphere given at p. 41 it will be seen that it is a mixture of several gases, the principal of which, from a biological point of view, are oxygen and carbonic acid. It must be remembered that these gases are in no way chemically united, but are simply mixed completely and equally, in obedience to the law of diffusion, viz. that gases mix equally and in all proportions. The method by which these gases are absorbed by the plant cell is the same as that by which solids are absorbed. No gas can be assimilated unless it be first of all in solution in water or in cell-sap. The solubility of gases in water is, therefore, a subject of extreme importance in a discussion of the nutrition not only of aquatic, but also of terrestrial plants (p. 42).

(a.) **Absorption of water and dissolved salts.**—As already seen (p. 196), the soil consists of a mixture of a great many chemical compounds obtained from the disintegration of rock masses, and also from the ultimate decay and disintegration of animal and vegetal matter. The particles of which the soil is made up are surrounded by thin films of water, and it is this water (**hygroscopic water**) which is believed to be the medium for the transference of the salts from the soil to the cell. The water thus absorbed is replaced by more water drawn by capillary attraction from the more distant soil. It has been found that a dilute solution of a salt is more easily absorbed than a strong solution, and that the power of roots to absorb is greater when the temperature is high than when it is low.

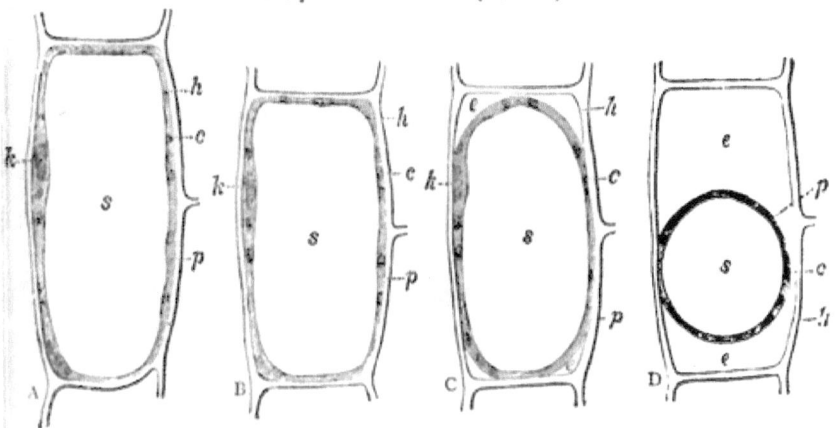

FIG. 105.—PLASMOLYSIS, illustrated on parenchyma from the peduncle of *Cephalaria leucantha*. (De Vries.)

A, turgid cell; B, the same cell in 4 p.c. nitre solution; C, in 6 p.c. solution; D, in 10 p.c. solution, showing complete plasmolysis; h, cell-wall; p, protoplasm; k, nucleus; c, chlorophyll corpuscles; s, cell-sap; e, nitre solution.

This latter fact is to be explained by the increased evaporation of water from the leaves under a high temperature.

Different plants, as we have already seen, require different salts in varying proportions. What, then, governs the absorption of a salt? Apparently the need of it by the plant, that is to say, a vital (for want of a more scientific term) and not a physical necessity. The extent to which any plant absorbs a particular salt is termed its **specific absorbent capacity** for that salt. The salt absorbed is assimilated, undergoes, that is to say, the preliminary changes of anabolism. The supply outside the root is greater than that inside, hence more is absorbed, anabolism constantly removing what osmosis is constantly supplying. We are here, of course, considering only such substances as are soluble in water, and which can penetrate through cell-wall and protoplasm into the cell-sap. What of those substances which are insoluble in water? How, for instance, can calcic carbonate be absorbed by the root when that substance is insoluble in water? It has been already shown that all living cells, in virtue of the katabolism which they are undergoing, are constantly giving off, or respiring, carbonic acid (p. 40). This carbonic acid, in the case of the cells of the roots, does not readily escape, but, becoming dissolved in the water surrounding the root cells, acts on the calcic carbonate, changing it into the bicarbonate, which is soluble in water. In this form calcium is taken into the plant. No doubt many organic acids are also employed by the plant in the work of rendering insoluble substances soluble.

The amount, then, of the various compounds in the soil which are found in the individual plant depends on the specific absorbent capacity of the plant, and on the composition of the soil. Several examples of the composition of the ash of plants have been already given at p. 195.

Leaves, stems, and even flowers are able under certain circumstances to absorb water and salts in solution, a fact familiarly known to all lovers of floral decoration.

(b.) **Absorption of gases.**—Since, as mentioned above (p. 191), free nitrogen is not used by the plant, we need not consider its absorption at all. Indeed, the plant is always bathed in free nitrogen, though no direct assimilation of the gas takes place. The two gases whose absorption we have specially to study are oxygen and carbonic acid.

Absorption of oxygen.—Oxygen is absorbed by the plant for two purposes, to assist in the formation of organic compounds and also to oxidise these same compounds in order to liberate the potential energy stored up in them. Oxygen then takes part both in anabolism and katabolism ; that employed in the former process is obtained from the compounds of oxygen in the soil (water and oxy-salts), that employed in the latter process is obtained from the atmosphere in solution in water. In the one case it performs a nutritive, in the other a respiratory function.

The absorption of carbonic acid is a purely nutritive process, taking place in sunlight and in the presence of chlorophyll (p. 40).

What becomes of the various food-stuffs absorbed by the plant? They become transformed into organic compounds under certain conditions. This transformation takes place in two stages—primarily the formation of certain comparatively simple organic compounds, which may be termed primary products of assimilation, which are afterwards built up into higher organic compounds.

Assimilation.—The process known as assimilation consists in the decomposition of the carbonic acid and water absorbed by chlorophyll-bearing cells and the building up of the products of decomposition into some comparatively simple anastate. This process is accompanied by the liberation of oxygen. Probably the anastate so formed is **formic aldehyde.** In that case the primary change might be represented thus :—

$$CO_2 + H_2O = CH_2O(\text{formic aldehyde}) + O_2$$

by the abstraction of one atom of oxygen from water and one from carbonic acid. The carbonic oxide and hydrogen are then said to be in a nascent condition, and would readily unite to form formic aldehyde with the liberation of a molecule of oxygen. These changes take place in the chlorophyll-bearing parts and in sunlight only. By the formation of such anastates the dry weight of the plant is increased considerably. The **conditions of assimilation** have already been discussed in sections v. and vi. of Chap. II.

The **construction of nitrogenous compounds** out of such primary products of assimilation and the nitrogen salts absorbed by the roots forms the second stage in the process of anabolism. At this point, however, the nature of the chemical changes involved becomes difficult to follow, and the results of experiment and even of observation are anything but beyond doubt. It is probable, however, that the compounds of nitrogen unite with such compounds as formic aldehyde, to form substances known as **amides**, the chief of which in the plant is **asparagin**. These amides are then transformed into **proteids**, and then into **protoplasm**, or into protoplasm directly, by the action of already formed protoplasm. These changes take place quite independently of sunlight and chlorophyll, which are necessary only for the primary stages of anabolism.

Circulation.—We have already had frequent occasion to assume the transference of substances from one part of the plant to another. We must now glance at the methods by which the food-stuffs in the plant are distributed through the organism.

Water is of course the great solvent in the plant, so that the question of the circulation of food-stuffs really resolves itself into a discussion of the **movements of water**. The manner of entrance of water with salts in solution through the root-hairs has already been considered under the head of **osmosis**. The same principle holds good in the passage of water with food-stuffs in solution from cell to cell. We have to consider two types of plants, however, in dealing with this question, viz. the vascular and the non-vascular. In the latter the entire circulation is one of osmosis from cell to cell, the cause of the movement being the disturbance of the equilibrium between different cells by the removal, by anabolic changes, of many of the substances undergoing osmosis, the object of the movement being the re-establishment of the equilibrium. Naturally this movement is a very **inconstant** and **irregular** one. It also takes place in vascular plants in those parts where there are no vessels, as, for example, in the cortex of the root, the parenchyma of growing parts, &c. The turgid cells near the vessels, however, give up some of their contents, which become squeezed into the latter, more especially when the quantity of liquid in plant is at a maximum, e.g. in spring.

The extent of surface exposed by a plant by means of its leaves is enormous, and from this **evaporation of water** is constantly taking place. Since, however, the cells of the leaves and neighbouring parts remain turgid, it follows that the supply of water must be constantly renewed; that, in fact, the amount of water got rid of by **transpiration** must be balanced by the amount absorbed; and that in consequence there must be a constant flow, at least during the time when the leaves are out, from root to leaf. What is the course of this **regular** circulation? Numerous experiments have proved that the water travels by the **young wood** of the fibro-vascular strand, and by the **substance of the cell-walls**, and not through the cavities of the vessels save under the conditions mentioned above. The **amount** of water transpired by the leaves varies of course with the nature of the plant and of the atmospheric conditions, according to laws which may easily be deduced. The stomata have an important influence also on the amount transpired. The **rate of circulation** of water in the stem is very considerable, in some cases from 100 cm. to 150 cm. per hour.

It has already been stated that the primary stages in anabolism take place in the leaf, the result being the formation of, in the first instance, some comparatively simple anastate such as formic aldehyde and then of some proteid. Starch, the great reserve store compound, is also employed as an anastate, though probably it is a product of the katabolism of protoplasm in the first instance. In order that the plant may be nourished a circulation of these substances must take place. Since, however, starch and proteids are practically insoluble it follows that they must be **digested**, or turned into soluble substances, before they can be circulated. This alteration of substances so as to make them soluble is known as **metastasis**, and is brought about by means of compounds produced by the plant itself which are known as **ferments**. There are four chief kinds of ferments known : the first is termed the **diastatic** ferment, its function being to render starch soluble ; this it does by transforming it into sugar. The second, the **proteolytic** ferment, has for its function the transformation of proteids into **peptones** (soluble proteids) in the presence of an acid. The other two ferments are less important : one has for its function the decomposing of substances known as glucosides (compounds of sugar with some aromatic principle), the other the converting of cane into grape sugar. All four perform their function in the same way, viz. by **hydration** (p. 23), the ferment itself not being altered in the process.

The paths by which these various products of fermentation move may be summarised thus :—

(*a*) By **osmosis**, from cell to cell in the parenchyma.

(*b*) By **intercellular communication of protoplasm** in sieve tubes (and doubtless many other tissues).

(*c*) By **laticiferous vessels**.

The object of this circulation is twofold, viz. **to supply plastic material wherewith to build up new protoplasm, and to carry material to storehouses** in the stem, or root, or other parts of the plants. In these stores the food-stuffs are modified again into insoluble forms, such as starch, oil, aleurone and various amides. They are again transformed into soluble carbohydrates and proteids as they are wanted, and transferred up the stem to the seat of anabolic activity. This storage of plastic material in an insoluble form is the visible expression of the transformation of kinetic into potential energy ; while the reconversion of the insoluble store into soluble plastic material is the first step in the transformation of the potential energy of the stored food into kinetic energy. **Both transformations are accom-**

panied by a manifestation of heat, a very noticeable instance being the heat developed during the germination of the embryo.

In order that the various gases used in the metabolism of plants may be supplied as directly as possible to the cells where that metabolism is going on, it is necessary that they should permeate every part of the plant. This they do by

FIG. 106.—INTERCELLULAR COMMUNICATION OF PROTOPLASM. (Vines.)

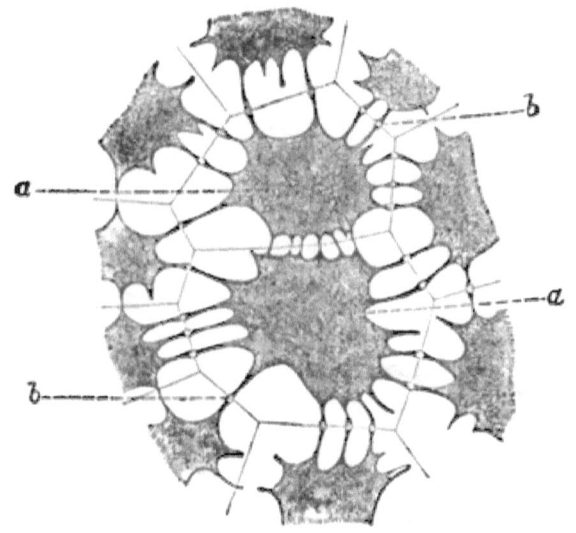

a, protoplasm of cell ; *b*, protoplasmic threads connecting adjacent cells.

way of the **intercellular spaces** and in obedience to the ordinary laws of gaseous diffusion. The stomata aid greatly of course in the entrance of the gases into the interior of the plant, although much of the gas passes directly through the cuticle into the subjacent tissues. Where stomata do not occur as in the Algæ, the latter is the only method.

Having briefly glanced at the various stages in the anabolism of protoplasm, we may now consider its katabolism, which must take place before the energy stored up in the complex compounds of which we have found protoplasm to be composed becomes available.

Katabolism.—The chief agent in the decomposition of protoplasm is oxygen. The oxidation of carbon compounds and the liberation of carbonic acid we have already termed respiration, so that we may conveniently consider that subject first.

The inhalation of oxygen and exhalation of carbonic acid must be most carefully distinguished from the absorption of carbonic acid and liberation of oxygen. In the case of the animal, the determination of the ratio between the gas inhaled and the gas exhaled is a comparatively easy process; in the plant it is complicated by the **reabsorption of the carbonic acid** so produced in the anabolism which goes on during sunlight. In the dark, however, in the great majority of green plants, and also in colourless plants both at night and in daylight, it is easy to prove the exhalation of carbonic acid in respiration. In the animal the oxygen which is inhaled is almost immediately employed in the oxidation of organic compounds; in the plant, on the other hand, the oxygen may be absorbed and stored up as **intramolecular oxygen**, and used as an oxidising agent long afterwards. The **chief products of respiration** are the same in both plant and animal, viz. water-vapour and carbonic acid. It has been found, however, that in some plants carbonic acid is replaced as a product of respiration by other so-called **organic acids**, such as oxalic and malic acid. No doubt also much of the carbonic acid and water is transformed into cellulose, as suggested at page 60, or excreted directly as such.

The other **products of katabolism** are some of them useful (**secretions**), some of them useless (**excretions**). It has already been seen that what are considered as waste products in the animal world, e.g. carbonic acid, water, and such like, are far from being so in the plant world. In addition to these substances, however, there is a large number of others secreted, or excreted by the plant, into the discussion of which, however, we cannot enter here. Many of these bodies, such as the **aromatic substances**, the **colouring matters** of flowers, the **vegetal alkaloids**, perform very important services in metabolism. **Nectar** (p. 169) and the **odorous substances** employed in cross-fertilisation in the manner already explained, are instances in point. For a complete discussion of the subject of waste products, reference must be made to Vines' *Lectures on Plant Physiology*, lect. xii.

Results of metabolism.—We have lastly to glance at the results of metabolism, which are chiefly expressible in terms of the law of the conservation of energy. We may consider these results under two headings: first, those connected with the evolution of heat, light, and electricity; and secondly, those which are related to growth and movement. Connected with the phenomena of movement may be considered those of sensitivity, or irritability.

Heat.—Heat, we have already seen, is the ultimate form into which all kinetic energy becomes transformed (p. 14). The energy evolved by the plant is very considerable, and all forms of it very rapidly undergo degradation into the final form of energy. The surface of a plant, however, exposed to the air is very great, so that the heat evolved is very speedily dissipated. Of course, where the greatest metabolism is going on, as, for instance, in the reproductive organs, in the growing shoots, and in germinating seeds, there the greatest amount of heat is evolved. Unless specially protected, however, the temperature of a plant seldom rises above that of the surrounding air, for the reason above stated. It is more frequently beneath the temperature of the air, owing to the cooling effect of evaporation from the exposed parts.

Light.—The manifestation of light by plants, often known as **phosphorescence**, is a phenomenon exhibited only by the lower plants, such as some of the Fungi and Algæ.

Like heat, light is a by-manifestation of kinetic energy, of course connected with the general metabolism of the plant. The origin and mode of development of the luminosity have not as yet been satisfactorily explained.

Electricity.—The existence of electrical currents has been much more carefully investigated, and numerous valuable results have been arrived at. The connection between the electrical phenomena displayed and the vital processes awaits, however, further elucidation. It is well known that certain chemical changes are always accompanied by an electrical disturbance, and probably similar chemical changes in the plant metabolism give rise likewise to similar electrical manifestations. The well-known carnivorous plant *Dionæa muscipula* has been very carefully investigated, with the result that a very distinct electrical current has been observed during the folding of the leaf; a movement which takes place when the leaf is irritated by a suitable stimulus. The results of many researches on this subject may be summed up in few words. During the life of a plant, normal electrical currents are constantly traversing its various parts, though considerable doubt prevails as to the true nature of these currents, and their connection with the expenditure of energy, which, we have seen, is so intimately related with the evolution of heat and light. In addition to these ordinary or normal currents, other special currents are developed in parts of plants, which, like the leaves of *Dionæa*, are capable of movement upon stimulation. In these cases the electrical disturbance is undoubtedly intimately connected with the chemical changes suddenly set up in the organ by the stimulus applied.

Among the directly visible results of the expenditure of energy are, however, the very marked ones of growth and movement.

Growth.—Without the expenditure of energy no growth can take place, for growth is an increase in the bulk of the plant, usually accompanied by a temporary or permanent change of form. Growth is, of course, the result of active constructive metabolism, and as such involves an increase in the dry weight of the plant. We shall glance first at the general conditions of growth, and then briefly summarise the phenomena of growth.

Conditions of growth.—Growth can take place only in the living plant, the growth of unorganised substances being merely the result of accretion. Growth is, in the first place, due to expenditure of energy taking place under certain conditions of temperature. Again, an adequate food supply in the form of the substances essential to the nutrition of plants is necessary. Water more especially is of importance. In addition, however, to these general conditions, growth is modified by the ability of the protoplasm itself to assimilate and respire, i.e. the anabolic and katabolic powers of each individual cell must be taken into account. Now it has been shown by Spencer that the mass of a cell increases as the cube of the dimensions, while the surface increases only as the square. The surface of the cell, however, is the area of nutrition, i.e. the larger the surface, other things being equal, the more nourishment can be absorbed. Again, the same surface is the area of excretion, so that the surface of the cell is at once alimentary and purificatory. In the early life of the cell the anabolism is in excess of katabolism. As, however, that excess gradually makes itself apparent in increase of bulk, Spencer's law comes into operation, and with the increase of size the possibility of the maintenance of the same equilibrium between the anabolic and katabolic process comes to an end. The relative excess of waste products may kill the cell, but much more frequently, as in young cells, restoration of the original conditions takes place by division of the cell into two or more parts. Thus growth of the individual cell brings about growth of the plant as a whole.

The **phenomena of growth** are too complex for any detailed treatment here. The most that we have space to notice are some of the general characters of growing parts, and their behaviour in response to certain changes in external conditions.

Growing parts, e.g. the tip of the shoot, root, &c., are remarkable for possessing an extreme **flexibility** though they have small power of **elastic recoil**. If a young shoot or branch be twisted it frequently remains so deformed during its entire life; a fact that is well known and even embodied in a proverb. Again, all growing parts are extremely **succulent**. This might be expected, since a great mass of the food supply comes to the growing parts in the form of a watery solution. The abundance of water indeed makes the cells turgid and **tense**; a condition in itself favourable to assimilation and growth. The growing parts are, moreover, very **extensible**. As the very tip (**punctum vegetationis**) is the region of most active cell division, so the region behind the tip is that of maximum growth.

The greatest amount of growth takes place during the night. In the dark, when assimilation is in abeyance, cell division is at a maximum. So in the same way the shaded side of a plant grows more than the illuminated side, with the result that the shaded side gradually bends round to the light. This phenomenon is known as **heliotropism**. Many parts of plants have, however, a tendency to bend away from the light. Such parts may be termed **apheliotropic**. The term **geotropism** has been applied to the tendency which roots have to bend towards the earth's centre. Although it is probable that gravitation has not a little influence in producing this movement, yet the fact that the shoot grows upwards, in opposition to the same force, seems to throw some doubt on the assertion that this is the only influence at work. In addition to these movements growing parts seem also to be subject to a movement termed **nutation**, due to unequal growth of different parts. Examples of this movement are universally found in the growing shoot and radicle, while modifications of the same type are exhibited by the twining of tendrils, climbing stems, twisting of elongated fruits, flower peduncles, &c.

There are many examples of movement exhibited by leaves (e.g. of sensitive plant), flowers (stamens), and other parts, which are not due to growth, but manifest themselves in response to external stimulus, or take place at certain periods of the day or of the life of the plant, as a result of certain chemical changes going on in the plant itself. An instance will be given in the concluding section of this

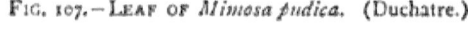

Fig. 107.—Leaf of *Mimosa pudica*. (Duchatre.)

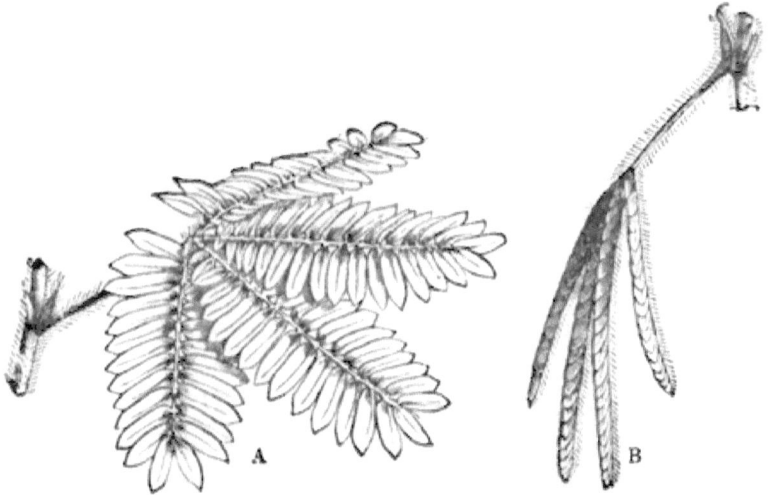

A, during the day.   B, during the night or after irritation.

chapter when we discuss the remarkable phenomena presented by carnivorous plants.

Section VI.—Carnivorous Plants.

Even an elementary text-book on biology would be incomplete without an account of the remarkable phenomena presented by the so-called carnivorous plants. Although these forms belong to a number of different tribes, they all agree in being able to absorb nitrogenous organic compounds from the dead bodies of insects which they are able to catch and kill by means of remarkable modification of their leaves. The number of species which possess this power is not great. They belong to widely separated families, and are found scattered all over the globe. They comprise some well-known forms, such as the famous pitcher-plant, *Nepenthes*, the familiar *Drosera* or sundew, and *Dionæa*, Venus's fly-trap. On examination we find that it is

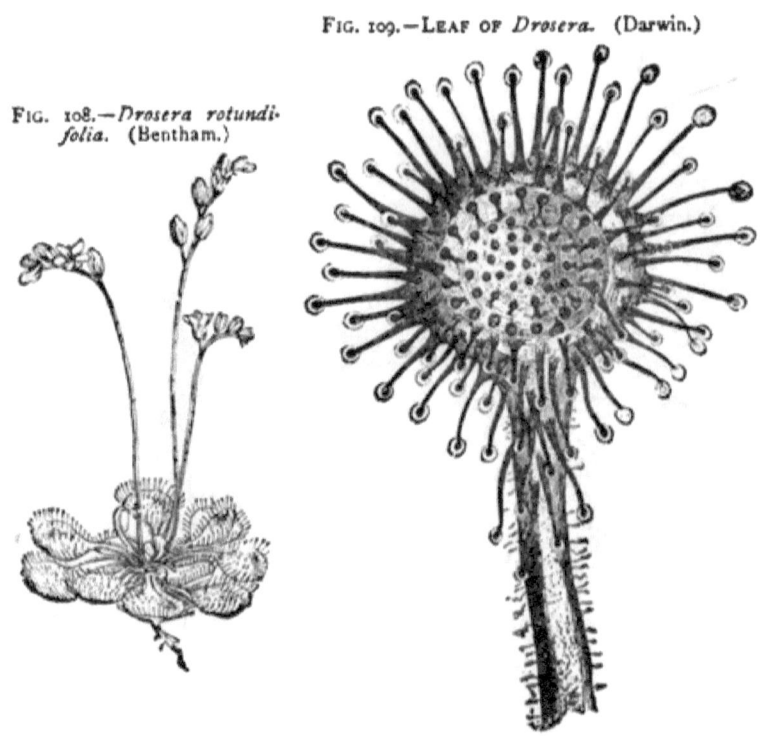

FIG. 108.—*Drosera rotundifolia.* (Bentham.)

FIG. 109.—LEAF OF *Drosera.* (Darwin.)

possible to make a physiological classification of carnivorous plants according to the way in which they treat the animals they catch. One group is represented by the sundew, which is able, not only to kill, but to digest the insects which it catches; the other, represented by *Sarracenia*, is unable to do more than absorb the gases which arise by decomposition of the dead bodies of the insects caught by the leaf. A short account of the structure and physiology of these two types will sufficiently explain the mode of operation of the mechanism employed in either case.

Drosera rotundifolia.—The sundew, found in quantities on our marshy hill-sides, is a small plant consisting of a few small roots, a rosette of peculiarly shaped leaves, and an upright flower-bearing stem. The leaves are the organs by

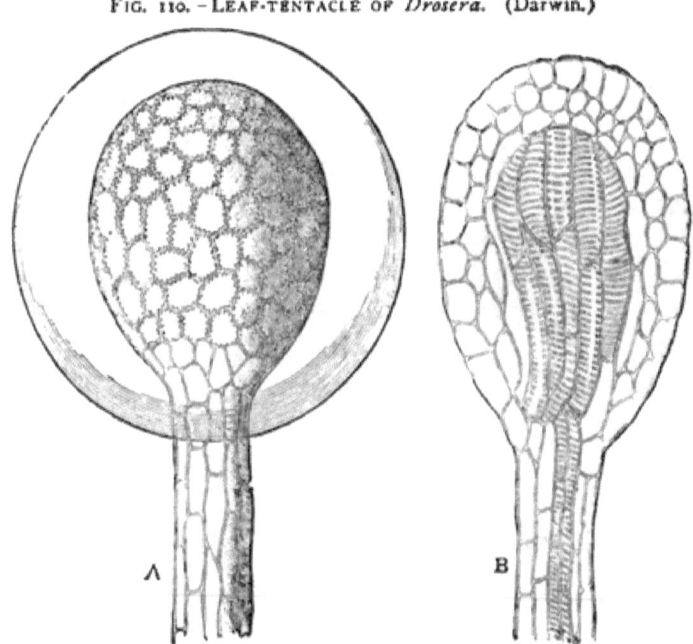

FIG. 110.—LEAF-TENTACLE OF *Drosera.* (Darwin.)

A, glandular head with droplet of the secretion. B, anatomy of the gland.

which the nutrition is carried out, and therefore merit fuller description. Each leaf consists of a long petiole with a flat spoon-shaped lamina, which is of a greenish purple or red colour, and beset with tentacles, which are morphologically soft thorns, from one to two hundred in number. Each tentacle is tipped by a bulb-like gland, surrounded by a minute drop of a viscid secretion, which gives to the plant its popular name of sundew. Microscopic examination shows the tentacle to be composed of a small fibro-vascular strand reduced to its simplest elements, surrounded by parenchyma, and covered by epidermis. Should a fly chance to alight on an uninjured leaf, it is immediately caught by the viscid secretion on the glands of the short central tentacles. Gradually, apparently in response to a stimulus conveyed from the centre of the leaf to the periphery, the much longer marginal tentacles begin slowly to curve over their victim. The fly soon becomes drowned in the secretion produced by the large number of tentacles which ere long will have folded over it. The entire movement takes about a quarter of an hour.

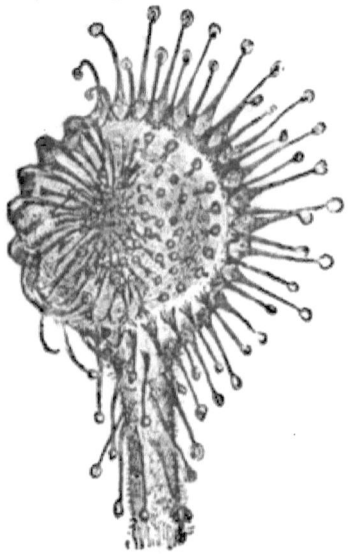

FIG. 111.— LEAF OF *Drosera* WITH TENTACLES PARTIALLY INFLEXED. (Darwin.)

The secretion, however, seems to have the power not only of killing the insect, but afterwards of digesting it — that is to say, of rendering the insoluble nitrogenous compounds composing its body soluble and easily absorbed. The ferment (proteolytic) in the secretion acts in presence of an acid also found in the secretion, and is therefore, as we shall see afterwards, quite comparable to the ferment found in the stomachs of animals.

The tentacles may be made to bend inward by a simple touch, but not by wind or rain. Contact with a solid or the absorption of the minutest trace of a nitrogenous fluid is, however, the most efficient stimulus.

Sarracenia purpurea.—The extraordinary leaves of this plant are particularly well adapted to fulfil the function of catching and destroying insects and such like, which may be unfortunate enough to tumble into their widely open trumpet-shaped mouths. The secretion, however, produced by the glands in the interior does not seem to have the power of digesting the dead bodies. The genus *Sarracenia* itself is

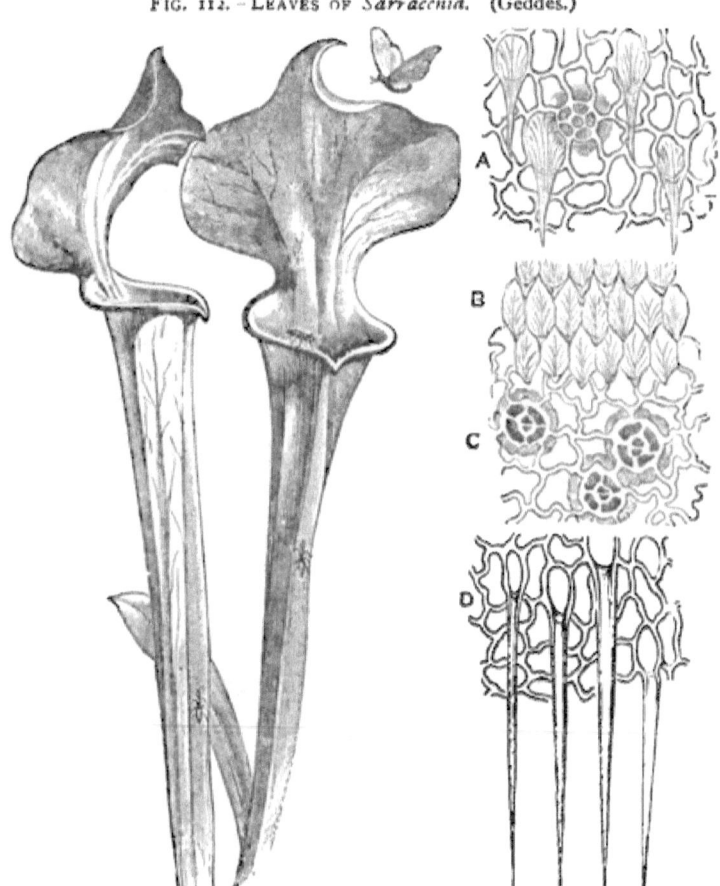

FIG. 112.—LEAVES OF *Sarracenia*. (Geddes.)

A, attracting and secreting surface. B, glassy epidermis. C, secreting surface. D, detentive surface.

distributed over the eastern States of North America, and is abundantly cultivated also in hothouses in this country.

The leaves, like those of *Drosera*, are radical. Each trumpet-like leaf is surrounded by a large gaudy nectar-secreting blade, serving as a protection from the rain, which would otherwise soon fill the hollow portion of the leaf and render it useless. The microscopic structure of the trumpet is of some importance. The lid and the mouth of the tube are covered by honey glands, and by small downwardly directed hairs. Some of these glands are also distributed on the outside of the trumpet on the ladder-like ledge which runs up one side. Following upon the gland-bearing area is a zone covered by slippery epidermal cells; after that a zone on which are numerous glands secreting the fluid with which the trumpet is partly filled. Lastly, there comes a zone where the epidermal cells are pulled out into long, stiff downwardly directed hairs or bristles. An insect, lured up the honey-strewn path on the outside of the pitcher in search of more honey, climbs into the mouth itself, and, gently goaded by the short hairs of that region, reaches the glassy epidermis over which it slides rapidly downwards amongst the secretory glands, only to be stranded on the long bristles, which, though they permit of a downward, effectually prevent an upward, movement. Indeed, the struggle of the hapless visitor only serves to stimulate the glands to more active secretion, washing it into the putrid fluid below.

Virgil's lines—

> Facilis descensus Averno;
> Sed revocare gradum superasque evadere ad auras,
> Hoc opus, hic labor est—

are not more applicable to the descent into Avernus than they are to trumpet-shaped leaves of *Sarracenia*.

The leaf seems to have the power only of absorbing the gases arising from the decomposition of the dead bodies and decaying animal matter lying in the pitcher.

The description of these two species must suffice to illustrate this subject. Full details of the marvellous adaptations for the absorption of nitrogenous organic compounds occurring in other species and genera will be found in the article on 'Insectivorous Plants' in the *Encyclopædia Britannica* or in Darwin's *Insectivorous Plants*.

CHAPTER IX.

METAZOA—INVERTEBRATA.

SECTION I.—HYDROZOA—*OBELIA*.

IT will be remembered that in Chap. IV. sect. iii. we divided plants into two great groups, Protophyta and Metaphyta. Amongst animals we similarly formed the two divisions of Protozoa and Metazoa. We have now completed our survey of the chief types of the Metaphyta, and are prepared to take up the thread dropped in Chap. VI., and follow out a few of the principal modifications exhibited by the various groups of the Metazoa.

As examples of the lower Metaphyta we selected *Spirogyra* and *Fucus*. Both these forms belong to the Algæ. Among the lower Metazoa a similar large group exists, the **Hydrozoa**, some of the members of which are, indeed, frequently mistaken for Algæ by the uninitiated. There are numerous points of superficial resemblance between the two groups, far apart as they really are in structure and physiology.

The type most frequently selected to illustrate the group of the Hydrozoa is *Hydra*, the fresh-water 'polype,' a selection, however, by no means in all respects fortunate, since its method of development is far from typical. We will employ it only in order to illustrate the minute structure of the Hydrozoa, and describe the mode of reproduction and life-history in a more generalised form, such as *Obelia geniculata*.

220 *Elementary Biology.*

Obelia is one of the salt-water Hydrozoa, variable in size, but seldom reaching a greater height than six inches. It is

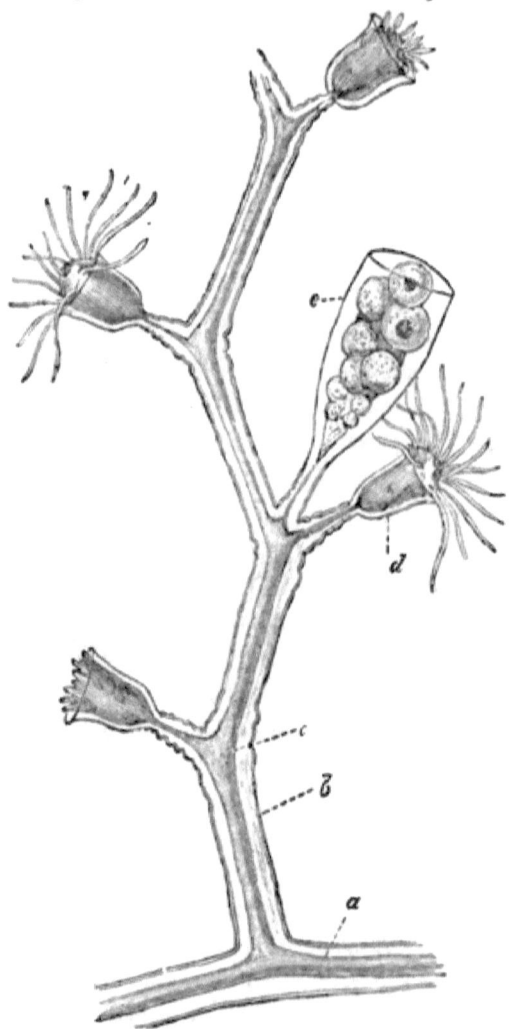

FIG. 113.—PORTION OF A COLONY OF *Obelia geniculata.*

a, c, cœnosarc ; *b,* perisarc ; *d,* zooid ; *e,* sexual zooid with rudimentary gonophores.

fixed to the rock by a network of root-like filaments, which, however, are only superficially comparable to roots. The upright stems spring from the rooted portion, each stem having smaller branches. There may be few or many upright stems, and the root-formation or **stolon** may show a corresponding variability in extent. Each branch is terminated by a **zooid**, and the entire structure is a colony, the persons of which are thus intimately connected with each other.

The **stolon** is a branching and anastomosing network of delicate tubes, the cavities of which are perfectly continuous with each other and with the upright stems which spring from them. The tubes of the stolon are covered externally by a horny, laminated cuticle, known as the **perisarc**, enclosing a cellular axis or **cœnosarc**. The outer layer of the cœnosarc shows no very clear division into cells, though nuclei are scattered at intervals through it, pointing to the fact that the layer is of cellular origin. The cavity of the tube is lined by a layer of cells bearing cilia. To the outer or protective layer the name of **ectoderm** is given; to the inner or digestive layer, that of **endoderm**. These two terms must on no account be confounded with the terms ecto- and endo-sarc used in describing the differentiated layers of protoplasm in the Protozoa (p. 56). The endoderm and ectoderm are layers of cells; the ectosarc and endosarc are layers of protoplasm of one cell. The structure of the upright branches is the same as that of the stolon, save that the central cavity becomes larger and more distinct as the ends of the various branches are reached.

It will be advantageous at this point to digress and examine another related Hydrozoon known as *Hydractinia*. A common species (*H. echinata*) is found covering the shells of many hermit-crabs. Like *Obelia* it consists of a rooted branched stolon and upright stems. But the stems are short, and each is terminated by a single zooid. Four distinct types of zooid can be identified. One known as the **alimentary zooid** consists of an upright stem or **body**, continuous with the stolon at its fixed extremity, and terminated at the other by a swollen head, bearing in the centre a mouth, and fringed with a circle of **tentacles**. The head is conical, and the tentacles spring from its broadest portion. The conical eminence over the origin of the tentacles is known as the **hypostome**. The hypostome bears the terminal mouth aperture leading into the interior of the zooid. The cavity into which the mouth leads we shall term the

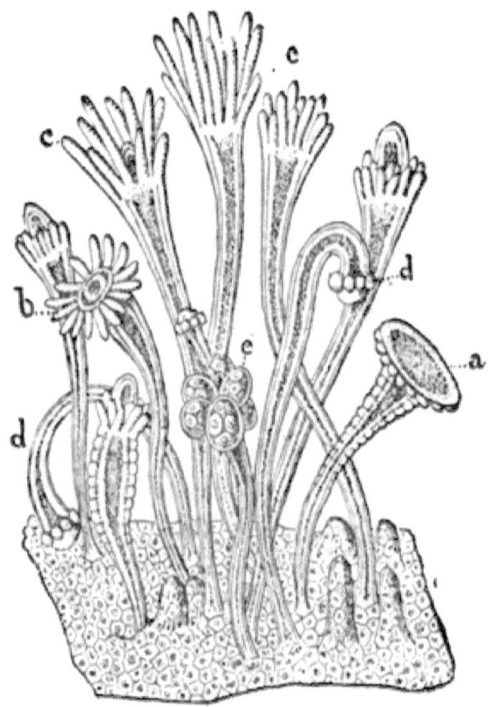

a, alimentary zooid ; *d*, tentacular zooid ; *e*, reproductive zooid

enteron, but defer the explanation of that term until we have completed our study of the general morphology. Another kind of zooid is seen near the alimentary zooid, possessing a body and swollen head ; but the head carries no tentacles, and there is no mouth. This degraded form we shall term a **tentacular zooid.** Yet another type is to be distinguished, like the tentacular zooid in general appearance, but bearing two-thirds of the way up a number of swellings. This is the **reproductive zooid**.[1] Lastly, there are to be found scattered here and there throughout the colony upright stiff branches, incapable of movement and tapering to a point. The perisarc in this type of zooid is largely developed. This we may term a **protective zooid**. Before proceeding to the comparison of *Hydractinia* and *Obelia* we must endeavour to explain this peculiar arrangement and modification of parts.

We have often had occasion to refer to division of labour as the key to the understanding of the evolution of highly developed from lowly developed types, briefly sketched out in Chapters II. and III. We must again employ this explanation in the present instance. Examining into the functions of the several zooids in the colony, we find that the alimentary zooid digests food not only for itself but for the whole colony; the tentacular zooid works towards the same end by catching and killing small animals floating in the water; the reproductive zooid, fed like the others through the stolon by the nourishment prepared by the alimentary zooid, confines its attention to the production of gonophores (p. 227) capable of forming sexual elements; whilst lastly, on the approach of danger, all three varieties of zooid rapidly contract under shelter of the strong pointed protecting zooids, which stand up firm and erect to shield the others from harm. The tentacular zooid no doubt also serves to warn off enemies by its active movements on the border of the colony. In other words, we have in a *Hydractinia* colony a number of persons all reducible to the same type but each modified in some peculiar way to perform one or other of the functions necessary to the maintenance of individual and tribal life. We have morphological differentiation accompanied by physiological specialisation or **division**

---

[1] Though termed the reproductive zooid, it is to be noted that it does not produce sexual cells (p. 227).

of labour. As in the plant we found leaves nutritive in their function and leaves reproductive (sporophylla), leaves protective (sepals) and leaves attractive (petals), so in the Hydrozoa we have zooids performing nutritive, protective, and reproductive functions; only in the case of the plant we had differentiations of organs, in the Hydrozoa differentiation of persons or zooids.

If we now return to the consideration of *Obelia*, we find that the various zooids are becoming more closely, i.e. organically, united, but physiologically less dependent on each other. All the zooids (the protective zooids are wanting) are, moreover, aggregated or gathered together on one branch; a manifest gain, for not only is a far smaller amount of stolon required, but the colony being closely packed can maintain itself in healthy life, with less expenditure of energy, and is moreover not so liable to injury in its compact form. If space permitted, we might instance Hydrozoa that showed still further aggregation. We must content ourselves by a reference to *Hydra* only. In this form we have not only the functions performed by one person, but we have degeneration and simplification taking place as well. *Hydra* does not form colonies, and the individual consists of one zooid similar to the alimentary zooid of the *Hydractinia*, but with the power of producing sexual organs, which latter are of a far simpler type than those possessed by *Obelia* or even *Hydractinia*.

We must now leave general questions and devote ourselves to the study of the social economy of the colony, and the life-history through which it passes.

As already mentioned, the alimentary zooid of a *Hydractinia* or an *Obelia* does not materially differ from a *Hydra*. It will, therefore, be convenient to describe the histological structure and mode of life of *Hydra* as an example of an alimentary zooid. One point of difference we must, however, note, viz. that the perisarc is absent in *Hydra*. The body and tentacles, eight in number, are eminently contractile, and are composed of two layers—an outer ectoderm and inner endoderm. The cavity, or enteron, opens to the exterior by the terminal mouth, and is continuous throughout the body and into the tentacles. The ectoderm is composed of large pyramidal cells, having the pointed ends, which are internal, pulled out into long processes; these processes from the ectoderm cells form a tolerably complete layer beneath the ectoderm termed the **neuro-muscular layer.** The ectoderm cells are nucleated and granular, and contain, in addition, pear-shaped bodies, known as **nematocysts.** The nematocysts are organs of offence and defence. Each consists of a small sac in the interior of which is coiled a very long barbed thread, lying bathed in what is no doubt a poisonous fluid. The animal can at will evert the thread with great rapidity, with the effect of stupefying or poisoning the prey it strikes. Nematocysts occur in the endoderm also. The tentacles of the alimentary and tentacular zooids of *Obelia* and other genera are plentifully supplied with nematocysts. Numerous young cells lie in nests round the pointed inner ends of the ectoderm cells (fig. 114), ready to take the place of the ectoderm cells when these are shed, as they frequently are when a nematocyst is fired.

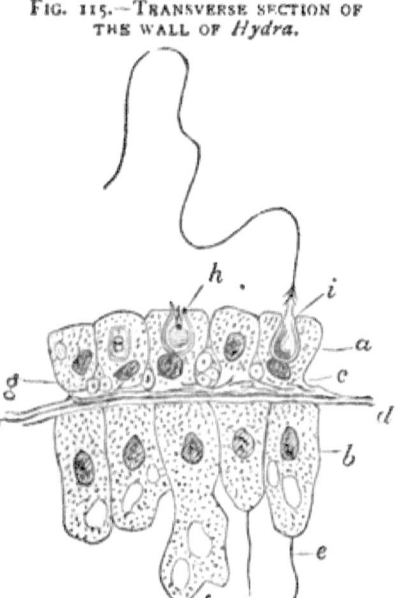

FIG. 115.—TRANSVERSE SECTION OF THE WALL OF *Hydra*.

a, ectoderm; *b*, endoderm; *c*, neuromuscular layer; *d*, basement membrane; *e*, cilium on an endoderm cell; *f*, amœboid endodermal cell; *g*, ectoderm cell with young cells at its base; *h*, *i*, nematocyst.

The endoderm differs considerably in character from

the ectoderm. The cells are large and irregular, and are at one time furnished with one or more cilia; at other times they are amœboid and throw out blunt pseudopodia. They rest on a fine **structureless lamina**, which again supports the neuro-muscular layer above mentioned. It is a point of considerable biological interest to find, as we do in *Hydra viridis*, **chlorophyll corpuscles**, more especially when we learn that these have the power of decomposing carbonic acid just as in the plant.

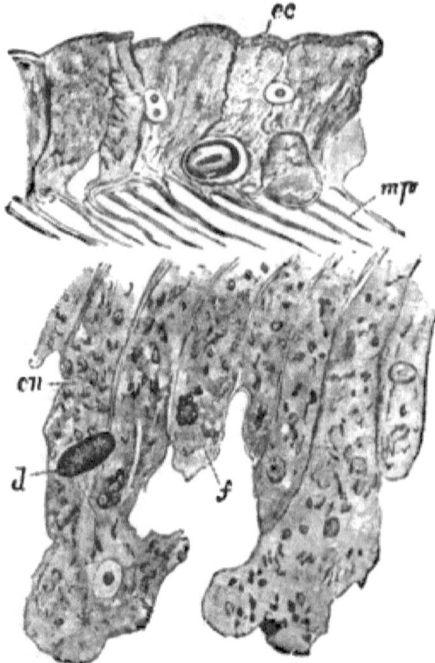

FIG. 116.—LONGITUDINAL SECTION OF THE BODY WALL OF *Hydra*, KILLED DURING DIGESTION. (T. J. Parker.)

ec, ectoderm; *en*, endoderm; *mp*, neuro-muscular fibres; *d, f*, food particles.

Food material taken into the mouth disintegrates in the enteron, and the food particles are taken into the interior of the endoderm cells, which lose their cilia and become amœboid for the purpose. In the interior of the endoderm cells the food particles gradually become transformed into soluble food-stuffs termed **peptones**. This process is known as **intracellular digestion**, and is of common occurrence in many of the lower animals. The other parts of the body are no doubt nourished by osmosis of the soluble peptones from cell to cell. The excreta and useless parts of the food are ejected by the mouth.

This account of the structure and physiology of *Hydra*

will serve also for that of the alimentary zooid in *Obelia* or *Hydractinia*.

Turning now to the reproductive zooids, we are at once brought face to face with the phenomenon of alternation of generations, which we found to be so important a feature in the life-history of plants. It is strange, however, that, whilst it is the higher plants that exhibit this phenomenon best, it is, on the other hand, most perfectly developed in the lower animals. The reproductive zooid in *Obelia* consists of a short branch over which, however, the perisarc is continuous. The modified zooid within the perisarc gives off buds, consisting of protrusions of both endoderm and ectoderm. The bud increases in size, and, at the same time, takes on a bell-shaped form with a projecting tongue pendant from the concavity. We need not follow all the stages in its development, but rather describe briefly the completed product. The bud when ripe drops off and swims away a free, independent organism, a **gonophore** or **medusoid**. These medusoids were long looked on as distinct animals, before their development from the fixed colony was clearly made out.

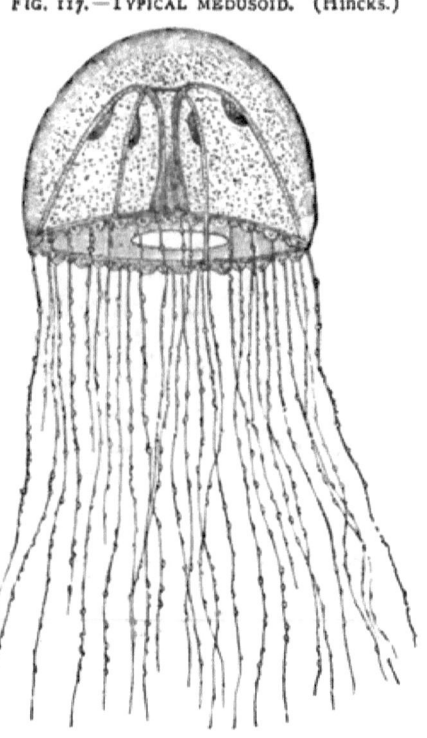

FIG. 117.—TYPICAL MEDUSOID. (Hincks.)

A **medusoid**, as already stated, is bell-shaped, the concavo-convex body being known as the **disc**, or **necto-calyx**.

The edge of the bell has an inwardly directed rim, or **velum**, and carries four or a multiple of four long tentacles (fig. 117). The tongue, or **manubrium**, is not unlike the head of an alimentary zooid turned upside down and denuded of tentacles. The cavity of the manubrium leads into a quadrangular space, or **enteron**, which again is prolonged into four radial canals, hollowed out of the tissue of the disc and united by a circular canal which runs round the rim. Prolongations of this canal occupy the axes of the tentacles. The cavity of the manubrium, enteric cavity, and

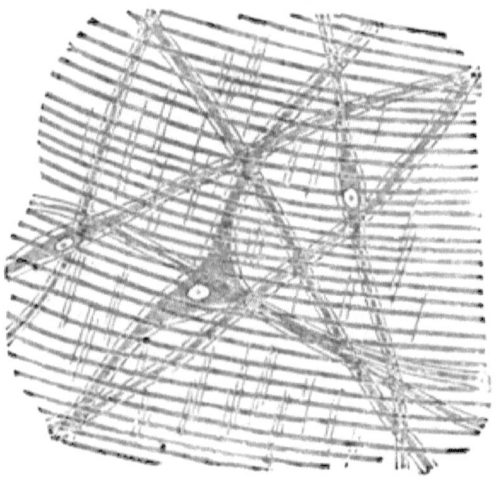

FIG. 118.—MUSCLE-FIBRES AND NERVE CELLS FROM THE NECTO-CALYX OF *Aurelia aurita.* (Schäfer.)

the entire series of canals are lined by endoderm. In fact, the medusoid is merely a greatly modified zooid (which has arisen as a bud from the reproductive zooid) turned upside down and free swimming. The medusoid, however, is a much more highly organised creature than its parent. In the first place, its tissues are more highly differentiated. In the hydroid form there were no cells specially set apart to contract; each cell retained that power. In the gonophore there are often distinct muscular fibres scattered through the nectocalyx, by the rhythmic contraction of which the umbrella is made to pulsate and the gonophore to move. The muscular fibres are cells which have become elongated in one direction, and though still nucleated they show a differentiation of the protoplasm which takes the shape of a very marked transverse striation. In *Hydra* every cell was sensitive to touch.[1] In the medusoid there are, scattered

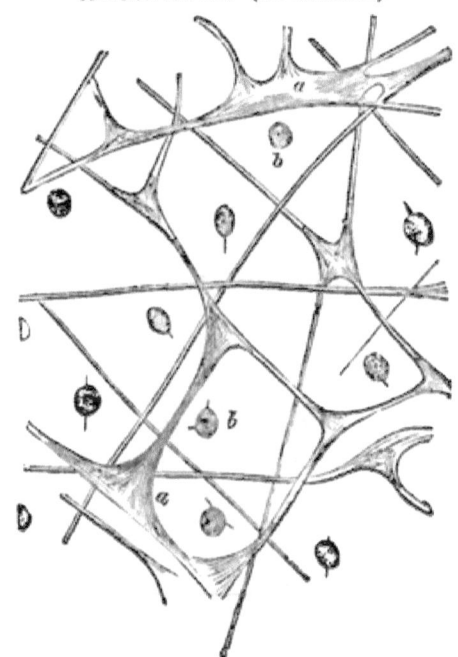

FIG. 119.—MESODERMAL TISSUE FROM THE NECTO-CALYX OF *Aurelia aurita*. (M. Schultze.)

through the necto-calyx, special branched cells, which have probably for their function the regulation of the muscular movements, and, therefore, termed **nerve-cells**. These cells and fibres are specially numerous near the edge of the bell. Sensitive cells, since they convey to the animal the impres-

[1] There is some ground for believing that the processes of the ecto-dermal cells of *Hydra* are nervous as well as muscular in function; hence the term 'neuromuscular' applied to them. Jickeli has, moreover, lately described true nerve-cells in *Hydra*.

sions made upon them by the external environment, might naturally be expected to be ectodermal in origin, and the nerve-cells of the medusoid have been found to originate from superficial cells which have become sunk in the more or less gelatinous tissue that fills the spaces between the ectoderm and endoderm. This gelatinous tissue, through which numerous cells are scattered, is looked upon as a middle layer, much more highly differentiated in the higher animals, and termed there the **mesoderm.**

Moreover in the free-swimming gonophore we meet for the first time with **sense-organs**, special nervous organs for the reception of impressions of the outside world, whether in the form of vibrations of light or of sound. In the neighbourhood of these organs the nervous elements are very fully developed; indeed, the cells which make up the sense-organ are in direct continuation with the terminations of the nerve-cells. The sense-organs are of four different kinds, **ocelli** or eyespots, **otocysts** and **tentaculocysts** or organs of hearing, and **olfactory pits** or nasal organs, all of which are found round the margin of the bell, and most of them near the bases of the marginal tentacles. Since, however, these organs are specialised in their character we need not enter into further detail with regard to them.

Just as the thallus of the fern was an independent generation for the dissemination of the type, producing sexual organs at a distance from the parent asexual plant, so the medusoid is a very effective means for the dispersal of the embryos of the Hydrozoa. After a certain period of free existence the gonophore develops ovaria or spermaria between the ectoderm and endoderm layers in the manubrium or on the course of the radial canals.[1] The sexual products escape by the mouth or by rupture of the wall of the canal, fertilisation taking place in the sea-water. The **ovum** is a

---

[1] Weisman has shown that the ova and sperms are really produced in the stem and afterwards migrate into the gonophore.

naked, often amœboid cell; the **sperm** has the typical head and flagellum which are so characteristic of the male sexual cell.

The fertilised ovum or **embryo** segments into a large number of cells, which arrange themselves into a hollow sphere. This is known as a **blastula**, and the central cavity as the **blastocœle** or **segmentation-cavity**. From the wall-cells, however, many cells are given off by budding until the wall has been made two layers thick. The embryo is now known as a **planula**, and the cavity left or afterwards formed in it is known as the **enteron** or primitive alimentary canal. The outer layer is that which will give rise to the ectoderm, and is called the **epiblast**; the inner layer gives rise to the endoderm, and is known as the **hypoblast**. The epiblast cells at this stage are ciliated.

The planula is a free swimming organism, using its cilia as organs of locomotion. After a time the cilia disappear and the embryo settles down on one end. It then forms an adherent disc and begins to branch over the rock or seaweed on which it has fixed itself, elongating and sending out buds, which develop into zooids like those already described in the adult fixed form with which we started. The perisarc meantime forms, and by a branching of the stolon in all directions a new colony is produced.

There are several points of great importance to be looked at before we pass on to the consideration of a higher type. In the first place we may emphasise the appearance of a differentiation of the cells formed by segmentation of the ovum, into two or, in the medusoid, possibly three layers, which give origin in process of development to entirely different series of organs. We may note especially the development of the nervous elements from the ectoderm and the lining of the alimentary canal from endoderm. Again, the occurrence of marked alternation of generations in both kingdoms is worthy of thought. The early differentiation of tissues in the animal and the appearance of the sensitive system are also points of great importance. With regard to the latter we must here briefly describe how the nervous system of the higher animals has probably arisen from the simple elements we find in the Hydrozoa.

Briefly stated, in the animal groups immediately above the Hydrozoa the tendency is first of all towards elongation of the body and concentration of the sense-organs at the anterior or head end. Naturally that would lead to aggregation of the nervous elements at the anterior end and along either side as being the points of most frequent contact. The head as containing the sense-organs, and therefore being the regulating centre for the entire body, would contain, naturally enough, the largest number of nerve-cells, which would form one or more clumps or **ganglia** at either side of the mouth, connected by **commissures** or connecting strands of nervous tissue for the sake of co-ordination ; and from these ganglia nerve impulses would be sent off along the nerve fibres collected in the form of **lateral cords** or bands along either side of the body. This is the actual arrangement in many of the lower worms, and intermediate stages are not wanting connecting such types with the diffused nerve plexus of the Hydrozoa.

We have thus seen that the hydrozoon begins its life-history as an amœboid cell ; that by segmentation and formation first of a one-layered and then of a two-layered sac or planula it passes on to the adult stage by subsequent differentiation. We may now examine a type of which the same is true, but which goes further, and where the embryo is itself segmented. Further, an aperture is opened at the posterior end of the enteron to permit of the more convenient escape of excreta, and special organs are developed out of mesoblast for the performance of duties which each individual cell of *Hydra* has to perform for itself. These organs are lodged in a space hollowed out of the mesoblast itself, the cœlom, or body-cavity, or in outgrowths from the primitive alimentary canal.

Section II.—Vermes—*LUMBRICUS.*

One of the largest of the natural groups into which the animal kingdom is divided is the **Vermes**; and this group is of special importance, not only on account of its size, but also because it is amongst the forms included within it that we must look for the type on which the majority of the lower animals are built. Moreover there is good reason to believe that even the higher animals are closely related genealogically to the worm group, for they undoubtedly still retain many vermian characteristics, if not in their adult state, yet in the embryonic phases of their life-history.

To illustrate the group of the Vermes, and at the same time to obtain a basis for the correct understanding of the morphology of the higher forms of animal life, we may take the common earthworm. Although *Lumbricus* is perhaps not a perfectly satisfactory type of vermian structure, yet that disadvantage is more than counterbalanced by the readiness with which it can be obtained, and the ease with which the principal features in its anatomy may be made out.

Lumbricus terrestris is familiarly known to everyone as the animal which burrows in soft, moist earth, appearing on the surface during rainy weather and sinking far down as drought comes on. Its habits and general physiology are also well known after their admirable expression in Darwin's work on *The Formation of Vegetable Mould by the Action of Worms.* That the earthworm swallows large quantities of mould from which it extracts the small quantity of food material it requires (in the form of decaying vegetable matter), and that it has the remarkable power of replacing lost parts of its body, and recovering from very serious injury, and that rapidly too, are facts very familiar to everyone who has handled a spade. The general appearance of the animal also, the long, tapering, many jointed body, without any distinction into head, neck, trunk, and appendages, the marked yellow band present nearer one end at certain seasons of the year, the serpentine motion, and perhaps even the existence of the rows of bristles on its under surface by which that movement is facilitated are likewise common knowledge.

It will be remembered that in Chap. III. sect. i. we discussed the differentiation of organs according to the duties which they severally had to perform; and we saw that it was possible to classify these organs according to the share they had in collecting, assimilating, and distributing the food (p. 51). It will be found most convenient if we adopt this classification in the discussion of the morphology of the animals with which we have yet to deal. In the types of plant life which we considered, and in the Hydrozoa, the examination of which we have just concluded, it was not possible nor advisable to treat of the various organs separately from each other according to that plan; for what particularly strikes us in these types is the want of that extreme differentiation of organs which we shall afterwards see is so characteristic of the higher animals. The leaves were the organs of respiration as well as of nutrition, in both of which functions the stem and branches, if green, participated. The branches, stem, and roots were the organs of circulation, but they were also organs of support, and frequently played an important part in nutrition, in addition to that already referred to. Indeed it might be said that the highest plant is far below an animal even so low as the worm, because of this want of differentiation, although the power the worm possesses of replacing lost parts also points to a lowness of organisation, expressed in the plant by the power it likewise possesses of reproducing itself by buds, shoots, and cuttings, and of giving origin to new leaves and branches when the former ones are removed. We have just seen that among the lowly organised Hydrozoa the same characters are prominent.

We may best commence our examination of *Lumbricus* by a survey of its **external characters**. The animal varies greatly in length, some giant earthworms being known to naturalists who have investigated specimens from tropical countries. A common length for the species so abundant in our own country is from three to nine inches. The body is of tolerably uniform diameter throughout, and is pointed at either end. Its length is subdivided into compartments by a series of rings from one to three hundred in number. The compartment between every two rings is known as a segment or **somite**. Although at first sight the distinction is not very apparent, yet if a careful examination be made it will be found that the earthworm possesses, if not a head, at least an **anterior** or **head end**, which may be recognised by its more pointed character and darker colour. The **posterior end**, though also tapering, ends more abruptly. The **dorsal aspect** is more darkly coloured than the **ventral aspect**, which latter is further distinguished by the presence of bristles, or **setæ**. The setæ may be readily felt if the forefinger and thumb be gently drawn from the tail to the head of the living worm. On the ventral surface of the anterior end will be found the **mouth** or anterior opening of the alimentary system. The projection of the body above and in front of the mouth is known as the **prostomium**. Similarly at the posterior end, but in this case at its very extremity, will be found the posterior opening of the ali-

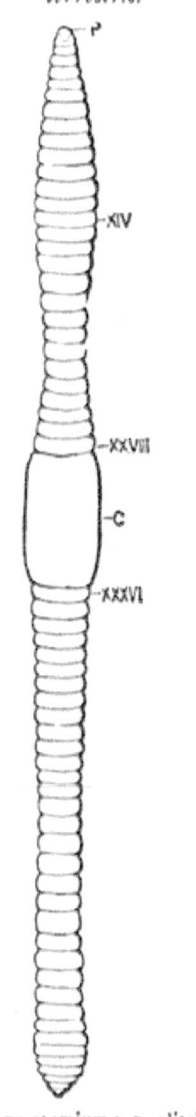

FIG. 120.—*Lumbricus terrestris*.

p, prostomium; c, clitellum. (The number of somites behind the clitellum should be greater.)

mentary system, the **anus**. Some distance from the anterior end there occurs a swelling on the body, usually of a yellowish colour, thus contrasting with the dark reddish brown of the general body surface. This swollen portion goes by the name of the **clitellum**. The clitellum usually occupies the position of the twelve somites after the twenty-eighth. The ventral aspects of the ninth to the fifteenth somites are also slightly tumid, marking the openings of the ducts from the **reproductive organs** and from certain organs accessory in function to the ovaria and spermaria. These are the chief features which strike the eye in an examination of the external surface of the worm. If, however, a hand lens be employed two minute apertures will be found on the ventral surface of each somite, which mark the openings of the purifactory or **renal organs**, known in the worm as **nephridia**.

We may now suppose the worm to be laid open by a median longitudinal incision along the dorsal surface. If this incision be carefully made, and if the skin be pinned back, the internal anatomy may be seen with very little supplementary dissection.

The alimentary system.—The alimentary system consists of a straight tube running from the mouth to the anus, with certain dilatations at intervals. The dilatations are of great importance as indicating morphological differentiations in the alimentary system into parts which have different functions to perform in the preparation of food. We may note first the cavity into which the food enters, the **buccal cavity**, which opens immediately into a part of the alimentary tube provided with exceedingly thick walls, known as the **pharynx**. The anterior part of the pharyngeal wall is composed of muscular tissue, and is connected with the wall of the body by a large number of **radiating muscle bands**. After the pharynx there follows the œsophagus, a narrow slightly sacculated tube, which opens at its posterior end into a large sacculation or **crop**. Attached to the wall of the œsophagus are three (or in some worms two) pairs of glands, known as **calciferous glands.** These glands contain crystals or granules of carbonate of lime. They appear to communicate with the œsophagus, but their function has not as yet been determined. The crop is, like the pharynx, an extensible muscular organ, and in it the food matter is no doubt stored before it passes into the drum-shaped **gizzard**, whose powerful muscular walls and thick horny lining crush

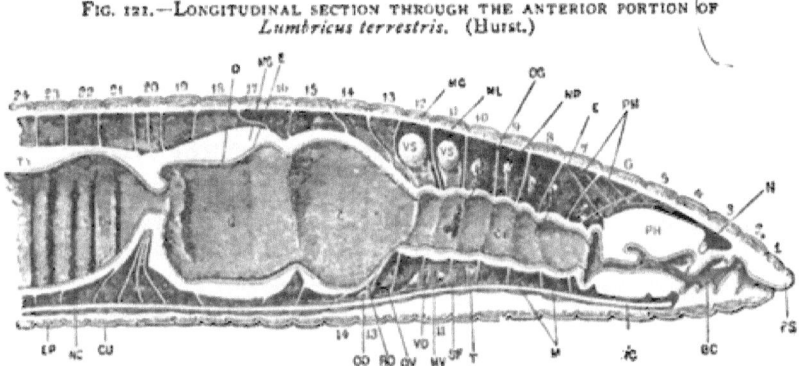

FIG. 121.—LONGITUDINAL SECTION THROUGH THE ANTERIOR PORTION OF *Lumbricus terrestris.* (Hurst.)

BC, buccal cavity; C, crop; CU, cuticle; D, thickened cuticle of the gizzard; E, epithelium of the alimentary canal; EP, epidermis; G, gizzard; IN, intestine; M, retractor muscles of the anterior part of the œsophagus; MC, circular muscles of the body-wall; MG, muscular wall of the gizzard; ML, longitudinal muscles of the body-wall; MV, posterior median vesicula seminalis; N, dorsal portion of the nerve collar cut across; NC, ventral nerve-chain; NP, nephridium; OD, oviduct; OE, œsophagus; OG, aperture of calciferous gland; OV, ovary; PH, pharynx; PM, retractor muscles of pharynx; PS, prostomium; SF, mouth of vas deferens; T, anterior testis; TY, typhlosole; VD, vas deferens.

any foodstuffs that require mastication or grinding. The posterior portion (third) of the gizzard has thinner walls, and leads into the long glandular and sacculated **intestine**. Down the dorsal surface of the intestine, and hanging free in its interior, runs a curious fold, the **typhlosole**, a structure which is found in a large number of animals. It no doubt serves to greatly increase the area over which absorption of the food takes place, for it is in the intestine that that process especially goes on. The numerous folds and sacculations of the intestinal walls over and above the typhlosole fold must also serve to greatly increase the area of absorption, an end of great importance when we bear in mind the relatively small quantity of food matter which must be present in a large amount of humus swallowed. The intestine is almost enveloped in a **yellowish granular tissue,** which is probably of use in rendering the food capable of absorption.[1] The intestine terminates at the **anus**, the external opening which we have already noted in the examination of the external characters.

When we examine microscopically the constituent tissues of the alimentary canal we find them to consist of a layer of **columnar cells** internally, surrounded by **connective tissue,** composed of delicate fibres and branched cells, in which are embedded numerous **blood-vessels** followed by an inner layer of circular, and an outer layer of longitudinal **muscular fibres.**

Nutrition.—The physiology of nutrition is extremely simple, for the worm, living as it does on decaying vegetable matter, takes into its alimentary canal food already partially digested, or at least rendered very easily digestible by the natural processes of decomposition taking place in the environment. No doubt the salivary and other secretions which the worm mixes with the food accelerates this process or has a similar decomposing effect on the vegetable matter which has not already undergone disintegration. The nitrogenous and other compounds are absorbed by the cells lining the alimentary canal, although the part played by the yellow cells, which, as has been already mentioned, line the outer surface of intestine, is still looked upon by some as doubtful. The excreta, consisting of the earth from which the food matters have been extracted, are ejected from the anus and accumulate often in large piles at the mouth of the worm's burrow. The nutritive substances having been

---

[1] By some biologists this tissue is considered as vasifactive, or blood-producing.

absorbed by the columnar cells lining the intestine find their way into the vessels which lie in the connective tissue beneath.

The circulatory system.—The vessels which lie in the wall of the intestine have extremely thin walls, often indeed only one cell thick, and are known as **capillaries**. These capillaries, however, lead into a very complete system of larger vessels, some of which run longitudinally, others circularly round the intestine and in the body-wall. The principal **longitudinal vessels** are three in number, one large vessel running dorsally along the top of the alimentary canal, and two ventrally placed, one immediately beneath the intestine (**subintestinal**), the other close to the ventral body-wall, and separated from the subintestinal vessel (as we shall afterwards find) by the nervous system. From its position it has been named the **subneural** vessel. From all of these vessels numerous smaller branches are given off, which run in a circular manner round the intestine or the body wall. The arrangement of these **circular vessels** is very complicated, and it will not be necessary for us to do more than glance at the more important branches. Moreover the manner in which they are arranged differs according to the part of the body examined. If we select a somite near the middle, we find that from the dorsal vessel a large vessel is given off on either side, which splits up into numerous smaller vessels, ultimately becoming continuous with the capillaries already mentioned as forming a network in the walls of the intestine. The dorsal vessel also gives off on either side a smaller branch, which, after giving off capillaries on its way, opens into the lowest of the two ventral vessels. The other longitudinal vessel also gives off branches to the wall of the intestine and the organs in its vicinity.

In the anterior region of the body the arrangement is somewhat different. In the first half dozen-somites the arrangement is quite irregular, all the longitudinal vessels breaking up into a close network of capillaries, spreading over the pharynx, body-wall, and buccal cavity. In the succeeding six somites the lateral hoops, instead of being delicate tubes and opening into the sub neural vessel, are large, swollen, tapering sacs which unite the dorsal to the sub-intestinal vessel. These vessels are known as 'hearts,' although, as we shall presently see, they are functionally not quite equivalent to the heart of higher animals.

The vessels contain a red coloured fluid, with a few corpuscles suspended in it. Although some uncertainty still exists as to the real nature of this **hæmal fluid**, there can be little doubt but that it is in most respects comparable to the blood of the higher animals. Some biologists are inclined however to consider another fluid found in the spaces between the intestine and the body-wall, and known as the **cœlomic fluid**, as equivalent to true blood. The cœlomic fluid is colourless and contains amœboid corpuscles, and is distinctly albuminous in its chemical composition. Probably both the hæmal and the cœlomic fluids together perform the functions ascribed to true blood.

Circulation. — There seems to be no very definite mechanism for distributing the food matters absorbed from the intestine through the body. It is true that the swollen circular vessels in the anterior part of the body exhibit tolerably definite and rhythmic contractions from above downwards, but the impetus so given to the hæmal fluid cannot be sufficient to send it through the complicated series of vessels described above. If the cœlomic fluid is to be considered as the true medium employed for the distribution of nourishment, then no mechanism exists at all for circulation beyond the continuous wriggling movements of the body, movements which, considering the spongy character of the tissues of the earthworm, may serve very effectually in lieu of the force-pump commonly called a heart.

The purificatory system.—For the removal of the products of decomposition two kinds of purificatory organs are necessary, viz. those which have for their duty the removal of gaseous products, and those whose function it is to get rid of the nitrogenous waste. We shall first of all consider the former.

The respiratory system and respiration.—No special organ exists in the earthworm for getting rid of the gaseous excreta, unless the hæmal fluid be looked upon as the agent in the process. Respiration is always a double process, and consists of **internal respiration**, a gaseous interchange between the tissues and the blood on the one hand, and **external respiration**, a gaseous interchange between the blood and the atmosphere on the other. Blood may in fact be defined from this point of view as the medium by which oxygen is conveyed to the tissues from the air, and by which carbonic acid is transferred from the tissues to the exterior. The hæmal fluid is very plentifully distributed to all parts of the body, and thus serves as an agent for the collection of gaseous waste, whilst at the same time it gives up to the tissues oxygen obtained from the external air. Again, the distribution of the fluid in the body-walls admits of its absorbing oxygen from the atmosphere, whilst at the same time it facilitates the excretion of carbonic acid. If this be the case then the two blood fluids of the earthworm would together correspond to the blood of the higher animals—the one being respiratory, the other nutritive. True blood performs both functions, an obvious economy when the animal type becomes more complicated, as it enables two operations to be performed by one agent, and avoids the necessity of a double pumping mechanism.

The renal system and excretion.—There is no doubt whatever as to the organs for the purification of the body from the nitrogenous excreta. The renal system consists of a large number of coiled tubes complicated in structure and distributed in pairs, one pair in each somite of the body (fig. 122). Each tube is known as a **nephridium** (νεφρός, a kidney), and consists of three distinct portions, a much convoluted thin portion terminated by a funnel-shaped opening, a thick walled but less convoluted glandular portion, and lastly a still thicker walled muscular portion which opens to the exterior by a minute aperture between the outer and inner rows of setæ on either side and close to the inner. The arrangement of the various portions of the nephridium in the somite is sufficiently important to merit description. Each somite, as has been already noted, is separated from the neighbouring somites on either side by an incomplete partition running from the body-wall inwards to the intestine, and known as a **septum** or **mesentery**. To this septum the nephridium is closely related, lying on it in a series of loops, the muscular parts of the tube being external, and the various other folds arranged on the septum in a definite order. The nephridium as a whole lies on the posterior side of the septum, but the funnel-shaped inner end pierces it and opens on the anterior surface, that is to say, into the cavity of the somite in front of that in which the main body of the nephridium lies. The cells lining the mouth of the funnel are ciliated. The septum is plentifully supplied with blood-vessels, many of which are intimately connected with the folds of the nephridium. Doubtless the nitrogenous waste is absorbed by the glandular portion of the tube, and ejected by the contractile part to the exterior.

We have now to glance at the **locomotory** and **protecting organs**, for a skeleton or supporting system is absent. We have already referred to the subdivision of the body into somites, separated from each other by incomplete septa. We have also noted the existence of large annular spaces surrounding the alimentary canal, spaces which we have seen contain a (probably) nutritive fluid. It will be seen that the several somitic cavities taken together really form one large broken-up cavity lying between the alimentary canal wall on the one hand, and the body-wall on the other;

whilst the septa are merely plates serving for the attachment and support of the nephridia and the alimentary system. This large space, or rather series of spaces, is known as the body cavity, or, better, cœlom. Glancing backwards at the

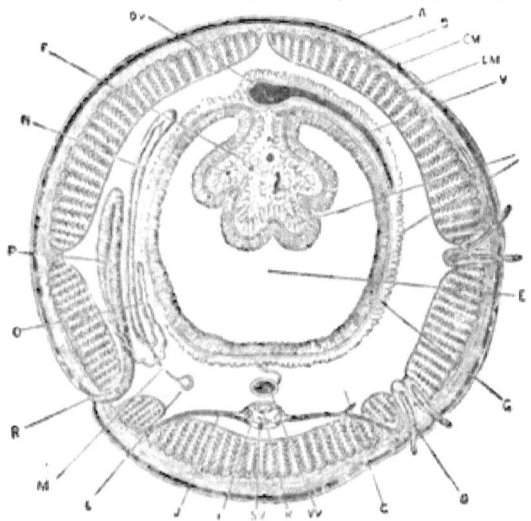

Fig. 122.—Diagrammatic transverse section through the middle of the body of *Lumbricus terrestris*. (Milnes Marshall.)

A, cuticle; B, epidermis; C, cœlom; CM, layer of circular muscles; D, seta; DV, dorsal vessel; E, cavity of intestine; F, cavity of typhlosole filled with hepatic cells; G, epithelium of intestine; H, hepatic cells clothing intestine; I, ventral nerve-cord; J, nerve; L, ciliated funnel of the nephridium; LM, layer of longitudinal muscles; M, point where nephridium perforates the septum; N, O, P, loops of the nephridium; R, external aperture of the nephridium; SV, subneural vessel; V, lateral vessel; VV, ventral vessel.

structure of the types of the Hydrozoa discussed in the last section we see that that space is entirely absent. The space in the interior of *Hydra* or *Obelia* is not a cœlom, but an alimentary canal, or enteron, although one without an anus and without differentiation into stomach and intestine.[1]

[1] It is of the utmost importance that students should, from the very commencement, guard against the misuse of the two terms cœlom, or body-cavity, and enteron, or alimentary cavity. If a clear distinction be not drawn between these two spaces, endless confusion is apt to be created in the minds of beginners in the subject. The enteron may be defined as a cavity always nutritive in function and enclosed by hypo-

Here, however, both cavities are present. The relation of the one to the other, and the structure of the body-walls, will be best understood by the examination of a transverse section of the middle of the body.

Externally covering the entire surface, save where the nephridial, alimentary, and reproductive apertures occur, lies a very thin and tough membrane, not formed of cells, but of a cuticular substance known as **chitin**, chemically related to keratin (p. 27). This membrane or **cuticle** is easily removed, and is probably secreted by the layer (ectoderm) immediately beneath it. That layer is cellular and corresponds to the outer or **ectoderm** layer of *Hydra*. The cells forming it are columnar, and have scattered amongst them many glandular cells, whose duty it is no doubt to secrete the cuticle. The ectoderm covers the double **muscular layer**. The outer circular muscles are arranged in the form of an almost continuous sheet from one end of the body to the other, but the inner longitudinal layer is broken up into bands which are separated from each other by the rows of bristles and the openings of the nephridia. The septa are thin, partly muscular, partly fibrous plates originating from and continuous with the body-wall.

On the ventral surface of each somite four pairs of minute pits occur, from each of which projects a long curved bristle, or **seta**, thicker towards the middle and tapering to either end. These bristles are chitinous in their nature, and are of cuticular origin. The ectoderm retreats into and lines each pit, whilst there are minute strands of muscle fibre springing from the body-wall and attached to the sunk end of the bristle, by means of which the seta can be projected and withdrawn at will.

The nervous system and nervation.—In connection

blastic, or endoderm cells; whilst the cœlom is a space between two layers of mesoblast, containing organs derived, it may be, from all three layers. In animals like *Hydra*, in which the mesoderm is wanting, manifestly no cœlom can occur.

with the maintenance of individual life we have yet to treat of the system which regulates the action of the various tissues and organs of the body, and maintains communication between the external world and the internal economy. In the worm the nervous system has arrived at a much higher stage of differentiation than that attained in the Hydrozoa. The nerve fibres are not irregularly diffused, but collected in definite strands or **nerves**, and the cells, in which, presumably, the nervous changes originate, are grouped together into **ganglia**. In the last section we saw that probably the first stage in the development of a definite nervous system consisted in the gathering of the nerve fibres into two lateral cords, with branches to the different organs, and the aggregation of the nerve cells on either side of the body into a mass at the anterior end of the cord of that side. This was followed by the approximation of the two ganglia to form a brain. Lastly the two cords also approached each other on the ventral side and united to form a ventral chain with lateral branches. When segmentation of the body ensued, ganglia were formed on the cords in each segment to serve as centres for local nerve impulses. Hence we find the nervous system of *Lumbricus* shows a pair of closely united ganglia above the œsophagus, and therefore named **supra-œsophageal**, from which spring two **circum-œsophageal commissures**, which surround the gullet and unite underneath it in two **sub-œsophageal ganglia**. From the sub-œsophageal ganglia the **double cord**, with its **pairs of ganglionic swellings**, passes backwards along the ventral surface, piercing each successive septum, and giving off a nerve to it on either side in its passage. The two united ganglia, which occupy the centre of the ventral wall of each somite, also give off nerves to the organs in the neighbourhood.

Sense organs and sensation.—The earthworm can scarcely be said to possess any sense organs, but it possesses a generalised sensitiveness, due to the plentiful distribution of nerve fibres through the body, and which, in many respects, takes the place of a series of specialised organs, corresponding to the senses of touch, taste, sight, hearing, and smell. Its sensitiveness to touch and its dislike to sunlight are well known; and, though not possessed of organs of sight or of smell, it is able easily to find its way to stores of food and to retreat from sources of danger into a burrow.

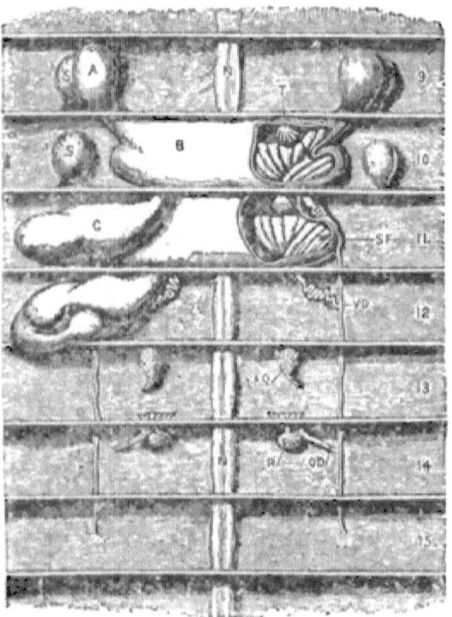

FIG. 123.—DIAGRAMMATIC REPRESENTATION OF THE ARRANGEMENT OF THE REPRODUCTIVE ORGANS OF *Lumbricus terrestris*. (Hurst.)

A, B, C, the vesiculæ seminales; N, nerve-cord; O, ovary; OD, oviduct; S, spermathecæ; SF, mouth of vas deferens, VD; T, testis.

The reproductive system.—The **ovaria** are two extremely minute organs situated in the thirteenth somite and attached to the ventral portion of the posterior side of the septum separating that somite from its predecessor. The **ova** are typical, nucleated cells, which, when ripe, are shed into the cœlom, and find their way, by some means not yet known, into the wide ciliated mouths of one or other of two tubes which open internally on the anterior face of the succeeding septum, and, after piercing it, open to the exterior by a small aperture on the ventral surface of the fourteenth somite, near the outer row of setæ. Each of these tubes is known as an **oviduct**.

The earthworm is hermaphrodite, but, as in the case of most of the hermaphrodite higher plants, it does not fertilise its own ova. The fertilising sperms are obtained from another worm, and stored in four small spherical sacs, or **spermathecæ**, which open one pair between the ninth and tenth, and the other pair between the tenth and eleventh somites.

Passing now to the male organs we find that the **spermaria** are, like the ovaria, microscopic bodies attached to the mesentery. There are two pairs of spermaria, and they lie on the posterior sides of the septa, separating the ninth and tenth, and the tenth and eleventh somites. The **sperms** are, however, not sexually mature when they leave the spermaria. They are known as **spermospores** from which sperms are afterwards formed by a process of budding. This further development takes place in large irregular organs known as **vesiculæ seminales**, or seminal reservoirs (fig. 123). The vesiculæ seminales are four in number, two on either side of the ventral middle line, and occupy the cavities of the tenth and eleventh somites, growing forwards and backwards when fully developed into the ninth and twelfth somitic spaces. The spermaria are found fully developed only in young worms, and the vesiculæ seminales, though present along with the spermaria, attain a large size only in the adults.

The fully developed sperms, each consisting of a long, rod-shaped head and flagellum, are conveyed to the exterior by four wide-mouthed delicate sperm-ducts, or **vasa deferentia**. The mouths of the vasa deferentia open on the anterior faces of the septa immediately behind those to which the spermaria are attached. The ducts in continuation with the funnels run backwards, the two vasa deferentia on either side fusing and opening by one aperture on the ventral wall of the fifteenth somite, the somite immediately behind that on which the oviducts open.

Fertilisation and development.—The ripe ova, on their escape from the oviducts, are fertilised by sperms (of another worm) squeezed out of the spermathecal openings. The fertilised **ovum**, or **embryo**, is then enclosed in a chitinous shell, formed by the glandular area of skin before mentioned as occurring, roughly speaking, between the twenty-fourth and thirty-sixth somites, and named the clitellum.

After a short period of rest, during which, no doubt, molecular rearrangements are taking place in the protoplasm of the embryo, **segmentation** commences. The result of segmentation is the formation of, what was termed in the

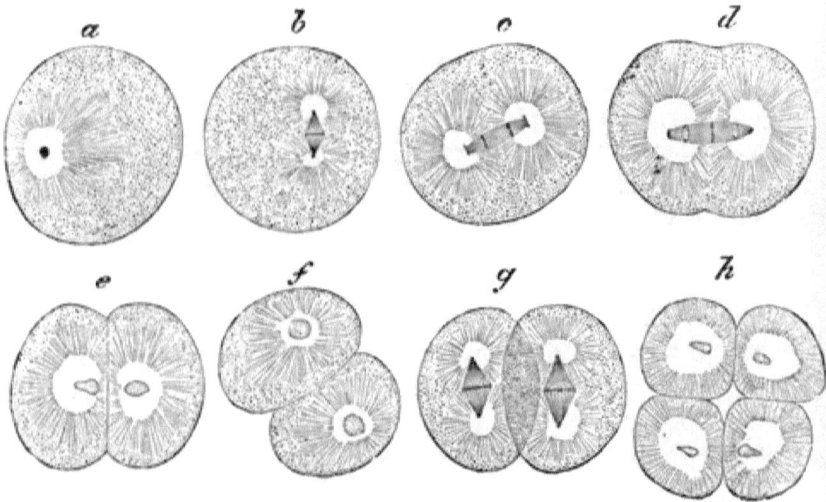

FIG. 124.— PRIMARY STAGES IN THE SEGMENTATION OF THE FERTILISED OVUM OF *Lumbricus*. (Schäfer.)

preceding section, a **blastosphere**, but in this case of a peculiar type. In the worm the blastosphere is flattened, and the cells forming the sac-wall are of unequal size, being on one side large and clear, on the other, small and more granular. Further there is nothing corresponding to a **segmentation-cavity** between the two layers. But owing to the more rapid growth of the smaller cells, the larger clear cells become enclosed, so that the embryo is composed at this stage of an outer epiblast and an inner hypoblast layer enclosing a small cavity. The worm is now in the **gastrula** stage of its development, and is comparable to the planula formed by *Hydra* and *Obelia*. The small cavity in the interior of the gastrula is the primitive alimentary canal, or **archenteron**; its slit-like mouth forms the **blastopore**, afterwards to become the true mouth.[1]

By this time the **mesoblast** has made its appearance by the multiplication of two large cells, covered over by epiblast and lying close to the blind end of the gastrula. It forms a plate of cells on either side of the body from end to end of the embryo. These plates become segmented into blocks, known as **mesoblastic somites**, each of which becomes hollowed, forming a layer of mesoblast surrounding the enteron and a layer applied to the epiblast. This is known as **metameric segmentation** to distinguish it from the segmentation of the egg. The two layers of mesoblast are of great importance in embryology, and are named the **splanchnopleure**, or visceral, and **somatopleure**, or body layers respectively. Between the two layers there lies a space, the **cœlom**, or body-cavity, subdivided into as many small chambers as there are mesoblastic somites, and bounded in front and behind by partitions formed by the fusing of the anterior wall of each mesoblastic somite with the posterior wall of that immediately in front. The anus is formed late in development by a tucking in of the posterior region of the body. The enteron is thus placed in communication with the exterior at both ends.

The several organs found in the cœlom are formed from the rapidly increasing mesoblast, save the nervous system, which is formed out of epiblast and sinks into the mesoblast in the course of subsequent development and growth of the embryo.

In concluding our survey of *Lumbricus* we may note for future reference the importance of the segmented condition,

---

[1] It will be afterwards seen that the mouth is usually formed in an entirely different manner (p. 262).

and especially the first appearance of that character in its embryology. As we shall afterwards find, segmentation and the formation of mesoblastic somites are features of the highest importance in the morphology and development of the higher types. Again, we may note the epiblastic origin of the nervous system, also almost invariably the rule in the animal kingdom. The origin of the cœlom, the formation of the enteron, and its differentiation into an alimentary canal are also worthy of attention if any generalised view is to be obtained of the mode of origin of the various morphological types of animal organisation.

CHAPTER X.

METAZOA—VERTEBRATA.

SECTION I.—*AMPHIOXUS.*

IT has been already seen that it is possible to subdivide the Animal Kingdom into the groups Protozoa and Metazoa, and that the Metazoa may be again divided into those with and those without a vertebral column—Invertebrata and Vertebrata, or more correctly Achordata and Chordata. Of the former group we have examined two representatives, *Obelia geniculata* and *Lumbricus terrestris*. These two forms may be taken to represent the great classes Hydrozoa and Vermes respectively. But between these and the Chordata there come an immense series of forms, represented by such animals as the sea-urchin and starfish (Echinodermata); snail, mussel, and cuttlefish (Mollusca); cockroach and bee (Insecta); lobster and crab (Crustacea); and many others less familiar. To enter into the discussion of these groups would necessitate the study of many different types, greatly exceeding the limits of this text-book.

We may pass, however, from the study of the earthworm to that of the Chordata the more easily and naturally inasmuch as zoologists believe that that group had in far past ages worm-like ancestors. In discussing the structure of the nervous system of *Lumbricus* it was noted that the generally diffused nervous system in the lower types, consisting of nerve-fibres and nerve-cells, had become aggregated, first, into two lateral cords, and then, by approximation,

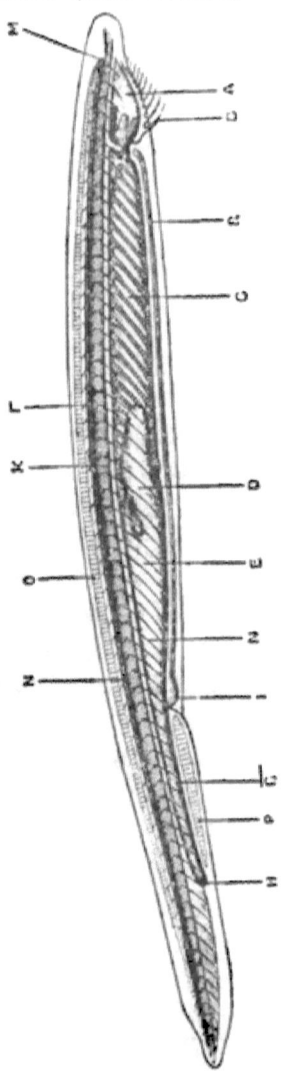

Fig. 125.—*Amphioxus lanceolatus.* (Milnes Marshall.)

A, buccal cavity; B, buccal tentacles; C, pharynx; D, liver; F, stomach; G, intestine; H, anus; I, atrial pore; K, notochord; L, spinal cord; M, eye; N, septa; O, dorsal fin; P, ventral fin; R, transverse muscles in floor of atrial cavity.

into the form of a nervous cord lying along the ventral surface of the body provided with a large ganglionic enlargement anteriorly and a series of smaller ganglia posteriorly on the cord, one in each somite. In the early Chordata these lateral cords seem to have become approximated on the dorsal side of the body, and formed what are known among the Vertebrata as the **spinal cord**. Further, the spinal cord became supported and strengthened by the formation underneath it of a bar known as the **notochord**.

It is indeed fortunate that we possess in *Amphioxus lanceolatus* a minute fish-like animal, found abundantly burrowing in sand in the Mediterranean and other regions, a survival of some ancient group of the Chordata, comparatively speaking not far removed from this primitive type. We shall give an account in the first place of this form, and then point out some of the conclusions which may be drawn from its study with regard to the various and important differences which we notice existing between the vertebrate and the invertebrate types.

External characters.—*Am-*

phioxus lanceolatus is from 1½ to 2 inches in length, and when living is delicate, translucent, and fish-like. Its body is compressed from side to side and pointed at both ends. No limbs are present. A series of small and delicate filaments may be seen protruding from the anterior end. A narrow ridge or fold of skin, known as the **dorsal fin**, runs along the back. At the tail end this ridge becomes broader and more distinct, and is there termed the **caudal fin**. On the ventral surface the caudal fin is continued forwards for a certain distance; finally, however, in the anterior two-thirds of the ventral surface it is replaced by two ridges separated by a groove.

The **mouth** is an oval slit on the ventral surface of the body, near the anterior end, from the margin of which spring the filaments already referred to. Two other apertures are to be found on the ventral surface: the **anus**, situated a little to the left of the middle line, just in front of the caudal fin, and an aperture known as the **atrial pore**, situated at the point where the ventral continuation of the caudal fin ends. The sides of the body are obliquely marked, the lines indicating the outlines of muscle bands or **myotomes**, and running dorsally and ventrally from the median line backwards. It is important to notice this point, as it exhibits to us one of the points of evidence of the origin of the Chordata from segmented worm-like ancestors.

The alimentary and respiratory systems.—As in the worm, the alimentary canal is straight and even simpler than it was in that type. The mouth opens into a **buccal cavity** lined by ciliated epithelium. The buccal cavity is separated posteriorly from the pharynx by a circular fold of membrane or diaphragm. This diaphragm is pierced by an aperture fringed by numerous ciliated lobes. The buccal cavity opens into the **pharynx**, or anterior portion of the alimentary canal, and it is here that we meet with a great point of difference between the worm and *Amphioxus*. Unlike that of the worm, the pharynx is not purely alimentary in function but is also the organ of respiration. It will be necessary for us, therefore, to study the alimentary system in connection with the respiratory system.

The pharynx is a wide tube or sac, and extends fully half the length of the body. Its lateral walls are pierced by a series of oblique slits, putting the cavity of the pharynx in communication with a space which lies round the alimentary canal known as the **atrial cavity**. These slits are lined by columnar ciliated cells, the cilia of which during life are constantly in motion. The slits are known as **branchial slits**, and the columns between them as **branchial arches**. Each arch is strengthened by having developed in its interior a chitinous rod. The long oblique bars are connected to each other by short crossbars, so that the slits rather resemble an open meshwork than anything else. Dorsally and ventrally the pharynx has developed on its wall a couple of ridges, the hollow between which is known as the **hyperbranchial groove** and **hypobranchial groove** respectively.

Posteriorly the pharynx rapidly narrows into a short straight **intestine**. The intestine is not of the same calibre throughout. Immediately after leaving the pharynx it is very narrow; it then widens considerably, giving off forwards a diverticulum or sac known as the **liver**, again narrowing gradually until it ends at the anus at the base of the caudal fin.

It will not be possible to understand the mechanism of alimentation and respiration until we have considered the chamber—the so-called **atrial cavity**—into which the branchial slits open. The relation of this cavity to the cavity of the pharynx on the one hand, and to the exterior on the other, may be best understood by studying their mode of origin. In the very young *Amphioxus* there is no atrial cavity, and the branchial slits open directly to the exterior as do the branchial slits of an ordinary fish. Late in the course of development two ridges appear along the sides of the body above the level of the branchial slits. These folds of skin grow downwards until they have met on the ventral surface of the body. They then fuse all along the middle line, save opposite the posterior end of the pharynx, where they leave a small aperture already mentioned—the atrial pore. In front these folds form the side-walls of the buccal cavity. The cavity thus enclosed—the atrial cavity—must not be confused with the body-cavity, or cœlom, afterwards to be mentioned.

Alimentation and respiration.—The primary stages in these two processes take place simultaneously, and by means of the same organ. The sea-water containing minute organisms enters the buccal cavity, being induced to do so by the incessant action of the cilia on the cells lining the cavity. The food particles are then collected from the water and enter the intestine. The water meantime escapes through the branchial slits, and in streaming over the branchial arches carries fresh oxygen to, and removes carbonic acid from, the blood circulating in spaces (**lacunæ**) in the branchial arches. The water escapes from the atrial chamber by the atrial pore. The food matter, after being mixed with the liver secretion and undergoing digestion in the wider portion of the alimentary canal, is absorbed into the circulation in the intestine proper.

The circulatory system.—Just beneath the floor of the hypobranchial groove of the pharynx there lies a large blood-vessel, the **cardiac aorta**, which gives off a series of lateral branches, which enter into the branchial arches, and there break up into smaller vessels. On each lateral branch, just before it enters the arch, there is a small dilatation, which has the power of contracting rhythmically, known as a **branchial heart**. The blood, which is colourless and contains very few corpuscles, is collected again from the branchial lacunæ into two vessels, one on either side, situated close to the sides of the ridges of the pharynx which form the walls of the hyperbranchial groove. These are the two **dorsal**

aortæ. Posteriorly to the pharynx the two aortæ unite into one dorsal aorta, which gives off secondary branches or **arteries** as it goes, each of these in turn breaking up into a series of lacunæ in the several organs of the body.

In the intestinal wall there are a number of vessels, known as **portal veins**, carrying impure blood and food material from the intestine to the saccular dilatation from the wide portion of the intestine—the so-called liver. In the liver the portal veins form a capillary network, and from it the blood is again collected and carried to the cardiac aorta to be distributed to the branchial arches. The cardiac aorta also receives impure blood from the muscles and other organs of the body.

Circulation.—We have seen that there is no distinct heart in *Amphioxus*, its place being taken by the cardiac aorta and the small branchial hearts at the origin of the branchial vessels.

The cardiac aorta contains impure blood—that is, blood laden with gaseous and liquid excreta from the various organs of the body. The impure blood passes into the branchial arches, there, as we have seen, coming in contact with fresh oxygen dissolved in sea-water, whilst at the same time the gaseous waste matters are got rid of. The blood collects in the two dorsal aortæ, which may be said now to contain so far pure blood, and is distributed to the body generally. The blood is again collected by **veins** from the intestine and is carried to the liver, and from the liver again and body generally to the cardiac aorta, thus completing the circuit.

The excretory system.—It is doubtful whether *Amphioxus* possesses any organs comparable to the nephridia of the earthworm. Two short secretory tubules, with pigmented walls which open into the atrial cavity, opposite the end of the pharynx, are looked upon by many as **renal organs**.

It will be remembered that in the earthworm the alimentary canal, nephridia, and reproductive organs lay in

Metazoa—Amphioxus.

a large cavity—the cœlom—which was further subdivided by the various mesenteries or transverse plates. In *Amphioxus* the **cœlom** is also present, although much more irregular in in its nature. In transverse section it can be seen in various places surrounding the alimentary canal, and anteriorly as a much reduced space above the pharynx. The

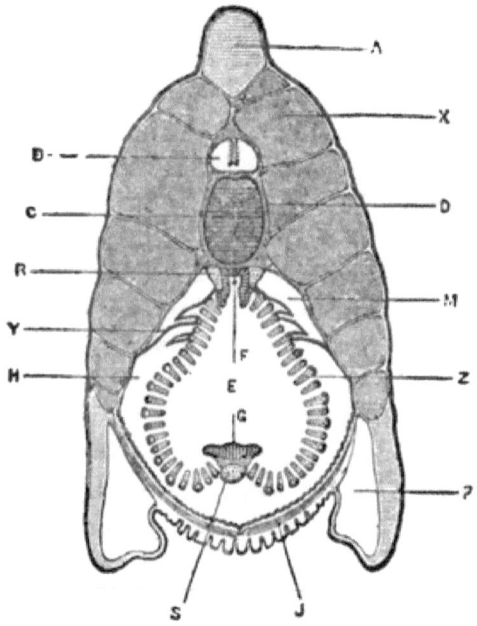

FIG. 126. — TRANSVERSE SECTION THROUGH ANTERIOR PHARYNGEAL REGION OF *Amphioxus lanceolatus*. (Milnes Marshall.)

A, dorsal fin ; B, spinal cord ; C, notochord ; D, connective-tissue sheath ; E, pharynx ; F, hyperbranchial groove ; G, hypobranchial groove ; H, atrial cavity ; J, transverse muscle-bands ; M, P, cœlom ; R, left dorsal aorta ; S, cardiac aorta ; X, myotome ; Y, fold of pharynx ; Z, branchial bar.

compressed character of the body and the addition of the atrial cavity, which it is, however, to be noted is really a part of the outer world, render the limits of the cœlom more difficult to define. If, however, the primary stages in the development of the atrial cavity be borne in mind, no difficulty will be experienced in understanding the relationships of the two cavities. We have now to glance at the

Locomotory, protective, and supporting systems.—Protection is afforded rather by the habits of the animal than by any hardened integument such as we find among fish or Crustacea. *Amphioxus* live, as a rule, buried in sand below water; a skin specially suited to perform a protective function is therefore unnecessary. The body is well provided with muscles. They are in the form of **myotomes,** or long thick plates, separated by fibrous septa. The muscle fibres themselves are arranged horizontally in the long axis of the body, so that the characteristic fish like motion is brought about by alternate contraction of the muscle bands, first on one side, then on the other. A sheet of transversely placed muscle fibres also stretches along the floor of the atrial cavity, the duty of which is to expel the water from the atrial cavity.

It is in *Amphioxus* that we first meet with rudiments of the **skeleton** in the interior of the body, which becomes so fully developed in the higher forms of animal life. It could not well be simpler than it is in *Amphioxus*, for it consists only of a delicate rod of clear thin-walled cells lying immediately above the pharynx and alimentary canal. It has been called the **notochord.** The notochord is enclosed by a sheath of fibrous tissue, and from its nature is highly elastic. The notochord, it is important to note, extends throughout the entire length of the body. In addition to this axial rod the lips of the buccal cavity are strengthened by delicate **bars,** from which arise yet finer bars to support the tentacular processes. The **branchial bars** may also be looked upon as part of the internal skeleton; whilst the entire body is strengthened by a considerable development of dense **fibrous tissue** which surrounds the notochord, the nervous system (immediately dorsal to the notochord), separates the muscle plates from each other, and strengthens the bases of the fins.

The nervous system.—The **nervous system** is dorsally placed, and supported beneath by the notochord. It consists of a hollow rod of nerve-fibres and cells surrounded by connective tissue.

The **spinal cord**, as the rod may be termed, is not so long as the notochord, ending a short distance behind its anterior termination. When we come to examine the frog in the next section we shall find that this relation of the spinal cord to the notochord is of great importance. From the spinal cord are given off many **nerves** in two series ; a dorsal series consisting of nerves which spring by only one root from the cord, and a ventral series, each of which has many roots. The nerves of the dorsal series alternate with those of the ventral series. The fibres are distributed to various organs and other parts of the body, and apparently differ in function, the dorsal nerves being concerned in carrying nervous impressions to the spinal cord from the exterior (**sensory nerves**), the ventral nerves corresponding to what are known as the **motor** and secretory **nerves** of higher animals—i.e. whose duty it is to convey nerve impulses to the muscles, glands, and other organs of the body (p. 318).

The **sense-organs** are very rudimentary. The sense of **touch** is, of course, fully developed, and the sensations are conveyed to the central nervous system by means of the sensory spinal nerves just referred to. A minute sac-like hollow in the skin, lined by ciliated epithelium, situated close to the anterior end of the spinal cord, is believed to represent the **olfactory organ**, whilst a pigment spot placed on the anterior extremity of the cord itself may do duty for an **eye**.

The details of the nervous system in the Chordata, and how it performs its functions, will be more fully dealt with in the two succeeding sections.

The reproductive system.—Lastly we have to discuss the **reproductive organs**, which, like most of the organs in *Amphioxus*, are very simple. The animals are male and female. In both sexes the reproductive glands are situated in the cœlomic space, which is continued down into the outer walls of the atrial cavity. There are no reproductive ducts nor openings. The **ova** and **sperms** are shed by the rupture of the inner wall of the atrial fold into the atrial cavity, the former probably escaping by the buccal cavity to the exterior after passing through the branchial slits, the latter probably by the atrial pore.

Fertilisation and development.—The ova are fertilised by the sperms after leaving the body of the female. The ovum is enclosed in a delicate cell-wall. The **embryo**, or fertilised ovum, immediately segments, and by successive division the originally unicellular ovum becomes a multicellular hollow sac or ball termed a **blastosphere**. When fully formed one side of the blastosphere becomes invaginated, or pushed inwards, so that a double-walled cup is formed, the shell membrane being meantime cast off. The cup elongates into a flask, and the originally wide open mouth, where the inner and outer walls were continuous, becomes narrowed to a small aperture—the **blastopore**. While in this condition the outer wall of the embryo is ciliated, and the body rotates freely in the water. The embryo is now a **gastrula**, composed externally of a layer of ciliated ectoderm, and internally of long columnar endoderm cells.

At this point there follow some very important changes. First, the embryo becomes flatter on one side. This flattened area, known as the **medullary plate**, becomes converted into a groove or valley, partly by the formation of two ridges, which rise up along the sides of the plate, and partly by the downward curving of the centre of the plate itself. The folds, or **dorsal laminæ**, gradually enclose the blastopore, and unite together behind it. The blastopore is thus made to open on what will become the dorsal surface. The laminæ unite above the medullary groove from behind (the blastopore end) forwards, roofing over a tubular cavity formed partly by the laminæ as a roof, and partly by the curved medullary plate as sides and floor. This

tube is still open in front, however, and is in communication
with the gastrular cavity, or **archenteron**, by the blastopore.
The narrow open limb will become the spinal cord of the
adult, and will become separated from what is destined to
be the enteron, or alimentary canal below.

Meantime from the walls of the archenteron there have

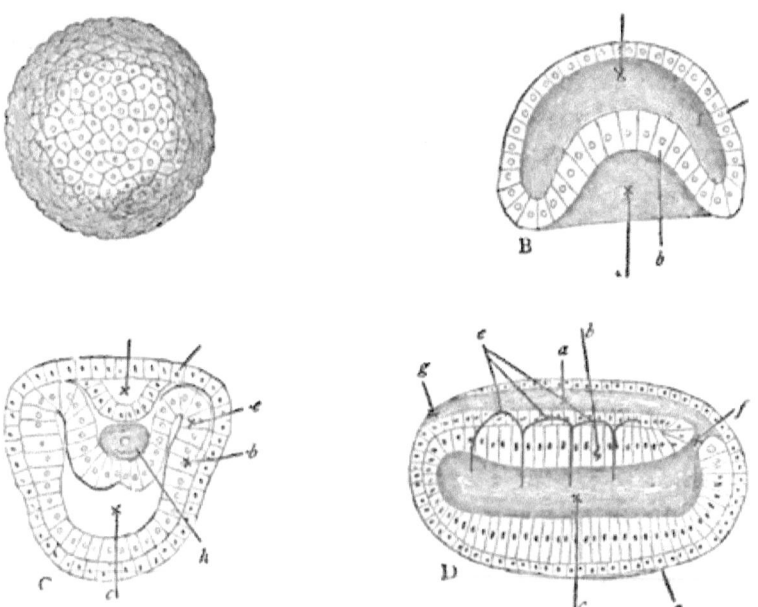

FIG. 127. DEVELOPMENT OF *Amphioxus lanceolatus*. (After B. Hatscheck.)

A, blastosphere ; B, gastrula ; C, transverse section of the embryo ; D, longitudinal section of the embryo ; *a*, ectoderm ; *b*, endoderm ; *c*, enteric cavity ; *d*, neural canal ; *e*, mesoblastic somites ; *f*, neurenteric canal ; *g*, anterior opening of the neural canal ; *h*, notochord.

been forming a series of saccular outgrowths, which ere long
become disconnected from the archenteron, and lie along
its sides as cubical bodies, known as the **mesoblastic
somites.** Each block becomes subdivided into a dorsal
and a ventral portion. The dorsal part becomes transformed
into the muscle plates, while the ventral portion splits into
two layers : the inner, or **splanchnic layer**, forming the

muscular and other layers of the alimentary canal (save the cell-layer lining the canal which is formed by endoderm); whilst the outer or **parietal layer** applies itself to the body-wall, and becomes transformed into a muscular layer. The space between these two layers is the **cœlom**.

The origin of one other important organ may be alluded to, namely, the **notochord**. That structure is formed by the folding off of a ridge from the dorsal wall of the enteron. This band afterwards becomes distinct and enveloped, as does also the nerve-cord, by cells developed from the mesoblastic somites, which become modified to form the fibrous sheath above alluded to. The embryo meanwhile becomes elongated, and the communication between the neural and enteric canals is interrupted, the notochord growing backwards between the two canals. The anterior end of the neural canal now becomes closed, and the walls of the canal thicken to form the spinal cord of the adult. It will be noted that at this time the alimentary canal is a tube closed at both ends. It is put in communication first anteriorly and, later on, posteriorly, by the wall of the tube and the wall of the body growing together, and by the subsequent absorption of the tissue at the point of union. In this way are formed an anterior depression, or **stomodæum**, and a posterior depression, or **proctodæum** (anus).

In a quite similar way the gill-slits are formed in the pharynx, or anterior portion of the enteron. We have already seen how the atrial folds arise along the sides of the body and enclose the atrial cavity. The further changes which take place need not be dealt with. They consist in the gradual moulding of the body of the embryo into the shape it ultimately assumes: the formation of a **liver** as a diverticulum from the **mesenteron**—as the alimentary canal between the proctodæum and stomodæum is termed—and of reproductive and circulatory organs from the mesoblastic somites.

It will have been seen, so far, that the great point of advance in organisation which *Amphioxus* shows over *Lumbricus* is the possession by the former of an endoskeleton supporting a dorsally placed nervous system. Further, as a consequence of the mode of formation of the nervous system, a transverse section of the body of *Amphioxus* exhibits two tubes—a large ventrally placed cœlom, and a small dorsally placed nervous canal. *Lumbricus*, on the other hand, in transverse section, exhibits only one tube— the alimentary canal—the nervous system lying free in the cœlom.

Finally, although the alimentary system of the worm is scarcely less complicated than that of *Amphioxus*, yet the respiratory system in the latter is greatly in advance of the simple dermal respiratory mechanism in *Lumbricus*.

We have now completed our study of this very simple chordate, and we have now to consider a more highly developed type of the class, so as to obtain some idea as to how the simple organs of *Amphioxus* become modified in these higher forms.

Section II.—Amphibia—*Rana*.

In the preceding section we noted that the great point of advance in the structure of the higher animals was the possession of a backbone, or vertebral column, above which (i.e. dorsally) lay the nervous system in the form of a tube developed from the outer layer of the body of the embryo, and beneath which (i.e. ventrally) was situated the body-cavity, a space containing the chief organs of alimentation, circulation, purification, and reproduction. In *Amphioxus* the vertebral column we found to be of very simple structure, being merely a rod of cellular tissue, or notochord, but enclosed by a tough membrane continuous with the septa separating the myotomes from each other, and present also as a sheath round the dorsally placed nerve-cord. In forms higher in the scale than *Amphioxus* this notochord becomes much modified. The originally cylindrical rod is encroached upon by the fibrous sheath which covers it, and the sheath itself becomes transformed into or replaced by cartilage, or 'gristle' (in the lower fishes, e.g. skate and shark), and by bone (in bony fishes, e.g. cod, and all the higher animals). Moreover the flexibility of the primitive axial rod, which would otherwise have been lost in the firm osseous cylinder, is still obtained by the segmentation of the osseous column into separate short cylinders, or **vertebræ**, capable of a limited amount of movement on each other.

In accordance with the plan adopted in the preceding sections, we may begin our study of one of the higher animal types by a brief summary of the external characters. In regard to the choice of a suitable type for the discussion of the structure and general physiology of the higher Chordata there is much to be said in favour of the newt or the salamander. The Amphibia, to which these examples belong, is a remarkably interesting group in many respects. Among them, for example, we find the first appearance of true lungs, the characteristic respiratory organs of the reptiles, birds, and mammalia, and the life-history of many members of the class presents us with stages where the transition from the fish-like condition—respiration by gills, or branchiæ—to the true air-breathing condition can be easily demonstrated. Again, the skeleton in the Amphibia, and especially in those members of the group cited above, is found in a very typical condition, and the modifications which have taken place in birds and mammals can be more easily understood after a careful study of the system in its relatively simple state.

The difficulty of obtaining specimens of the newt or salamander is a serious drawback, and we are accordingly compelled to fall back on the common frog (*Rana temporaria*) for dissecting purposes, although the skeleton of that form is so much specialised as to render it a less suitable subject for the preliminary study of that system. We will therefore adopt the frog as the subject for consideration, save in the case of the skeletal system, where the skeleton of the salamander will be taken as our type.

External characters.—A very cursory examination of the external characters of the frog enables us to distinguish a **head, neck, trunk,** and **fore** and **hind limbs** (fig. 128). The wide **mouth, nostrils, eyes** are easily seen on the head; and the **ears** may be identified as two small rounded patches a short distance behind the eyes. There is no external ear, but the drum, or tympanic membrane, is itself exposed. Posteriorly only one opening can be made out, the opening of the **cloaca**, a small chamber into which the ducts of the renal and reproductive glands open together with the alimentary canal.

The animal is covered externally by a soft, moist, pigmented **skin**, which is very loosely attached to the body proper. The underlying space is occupied by a colourless fluid, called **lymph**, which will call for a more detailed description presently.

The alimentary system.—We have already seen that the alimentary system in the animal consists essentially of a tube of variable length, running from mouth to anus, into which the food is introduced, and in which it is subjected to the action of certain fluids or secretions which render it capable of being absorbed through the walls of the alimentary canal, directly or indirectly into the terminal vessels (capillaries) of the circulatory system. In *Lumbricus* and in *Amphioxus* that canal is straight and simple, but in the frog it has become much modified. In the first place it is much longer than the body of the animal, and consequently is coiled up inside the body-cavity. In the second place, it has become differentiated into several distinct regions: a buccal cavity, where (though not in the frog) food is masticated; an œsophagus, or tube for the carriage of the food down to a stomach, or store-chamber, where the food is mixed with digestive secretions; an intestine, or narrow canal, where further digestive changes are effected, and where the nutritive part of the food is chiefly absorbed into the circulation; and lastly a rectum where the effete or useless portions are collected, and from which they are periodically got rid of through the cloaca.

FIG. 128.—RANA TEMPORARIA. (Milnes Marshall.)

Again, the secretions with which the food is mixed, and which render it capable of being absorbed, are produced in glands which are either minute and sunk in the wall of the alimentary canal itself, or are large and distinct from it, but opening into it by ducts at various points. These glands, as we shall afterwards see, are formed as outpushings from the alimentary canal itself. The two chief glands of this nature are the liver and pancreas.

It will be necessary now to describe the course of the alimentary canal and the structure of that organ and of the glands which open into it. It will be convenient to subdivide it into four regions, viz.—the buccal cavity, the œsophagus, the stomach, and the intestine—and to describe in connection with these several regions the glands which are specially related to them.

The buccal cavity.—The **mouth** is proportionally of large size, the gape being very wide. The upper jaw is fringed with a row of small **teeth**, and additional patches of teeth may be felt on the roof of the mouth behind the jaw-teeth. These are known as **maxillary, premaxillary,** and **vomerine** teeth respectively from the bones of the skull on which they are supported (p. 301). The lower jaw bears no teeth, but has attached immediately behind its most anterior portion the tongue, a flat bilobed organ of large size, free behind and capable during life of being everted with great rapidity. The large bulgings due to the eyeballs may also be noted on the roof of the mouth.

Six openings may be easily made out on the walls of the buccal cavity. Most noticeable of all of course is the wide **pharynx,** or upper part of the œsophagus, and close to it the small slit-like **glottis,** or aperture of the respiratory system. Two other apertures are visible in the hinder portion of the cavity. These are the **eustachian tubes** leading into the ears. Lastly, in front and on the outer side of the vomerine teeth are two small apertures, the **posterior nares,** or inner nostrils.

The entire buccal cavity is lined by a continuation of the outside skin termed a **mucous membrane,** since it contains many small glands whose function it is to secrete **mucus**— a sticky, more or less watery fluid mainly of service in keeping the membrane moist and facilitating the act of swallowing. The microscopic structure of skin proper and mucous membrane may be best considered together. The skin consists of a series of layers of cells, the superficial layers being composed of flat plates or squames and the deeper layers of more rounded or polygonal cells. To this portion of the skin is given the name of **epidermis**.

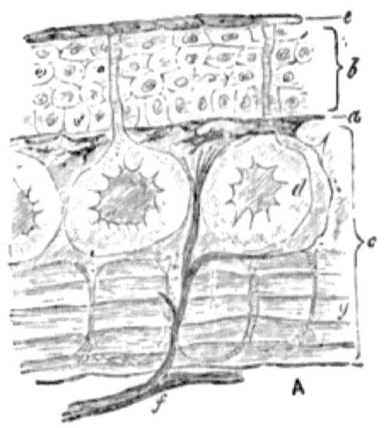

FIG. 129.—VERTICAL SECTION SKIN OF RANA. (Owen.)

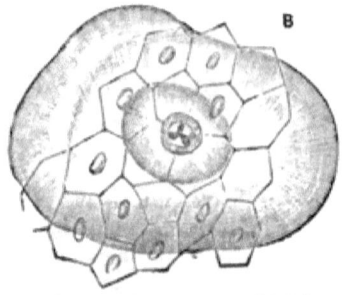

A, vertical section: *e*, superficial layer of epidermis; *b*, deep layers of epidermis; *a*, layer of pigment cells: *c*, dermis· *d*, mucus gland; *g*, connective tissue; *f*, blood-vessel. B, surface of mucus gland.

The epidermis rests on, and is organically connected with the **dermis**, which is composed chiefly of fibrous tissue, blood-vessels, and nerves, amongst which are imbedded, especially next the epidermis, a large number of irregular pigment cells. The dermis is elevated into a series of vascular papillæ which project into the epidermis. In the dermis, and with their ducts piercing and opening on the surface of the epidermis, are many subcutaneous or **mucous glands**, already referred to. The subcutaneous tissue is separated from the underlying muscles of the body-wall by a large lymph space.

The **mucous membrane** of the buccal cavity does not differ essentially from the skin in structure; the layers of cells are, however, fewer in number, the pigment cells are absent, and the vascular supply is more abundant. We shall find, later on, that the

FIG. 130.—VERTICAL SECTION OF A TOOTH. (Quain.)

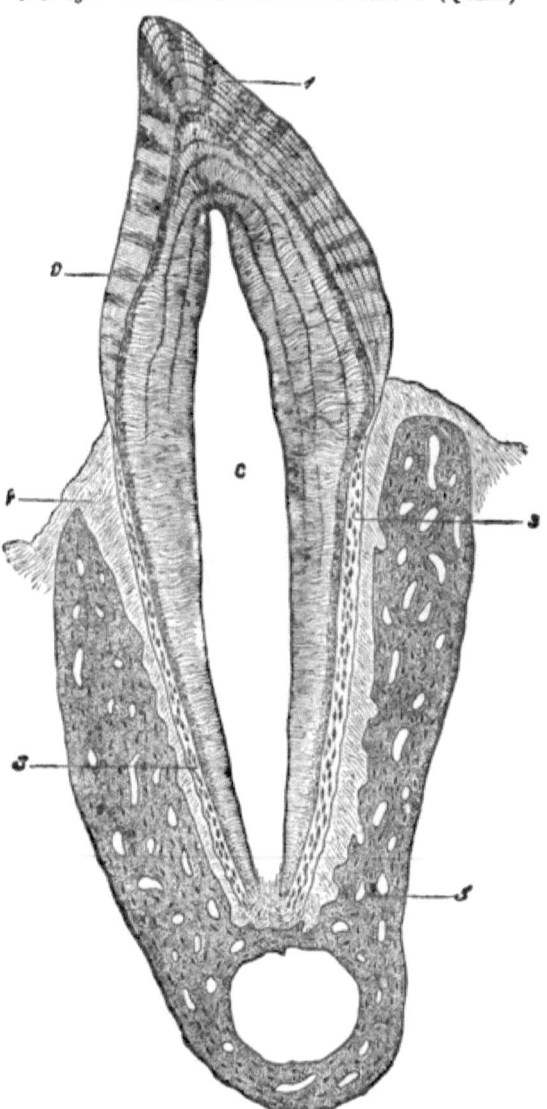

c, pulp cavity; 1, enamel, with radial and concentric markings; 2, dentine, showing tubules and concentric lines of growth; 3, cement (bone); 4, periosteum or bone-sheath; 5, bone of jaw.

character of the mucous membrane is considerably modified in other portions of the alimentary canal.

The teeth,[1] already described as present on the upper jaw and palate, next claim some attention. They are by no means so distinct and elaborate in structure as those of the higher animals, such as those of the rabbit or dog ; yet the several layers distinguishable in the teeth of those latter forms are to be seen even in the frog's teeth. Each tooth consists essentially of a papilla of the dermis, capped by epidermis, which has become considerably modified. In the frog these teeth are constantly being renewed as the older teeth become worn away. A typical tooth, say of a dog, consists of a crown and neck above the level of the jaw, and a fang sunk in a cavity, or alveolus, in the jaw itself. In the frog the tooth is simply united to a process of the bone beneath. The surface of the exposed portion is covered by an exceedingly hard dense substance termed enamel, covering a hard but sensitive core of dentine—a substance not unlike bone—which again contains in its interior a papilla of submucous tissues. The enamel consists of long closely packed prisms of phosphate of lime, while the dentine is partly organic, being composed of long branching tubules, imbedded,

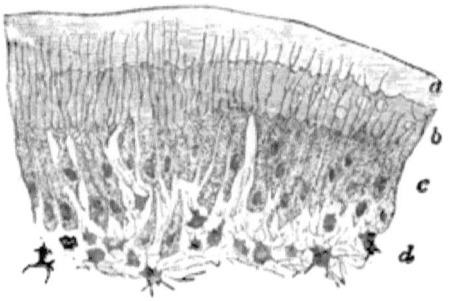

FIG. 131.—SECTION OF A PORTION OF DEVELOPING TOOTH. (Quain.)

a, outer layer of dentine, fully calcified ; *b*, uncalcified layer; *c*, dentine-forming cells; *d*, pulp.

---

[1] The student is recommended to study the figures of the histology of the frog in Howes' *Atlas of Biology*. The figures introduced in the text are mainly taken from *Quain's Anatomy*, and illustrate the histological structure of the mammal. Good woodcuts of the microscopic structure of the lower vertebrata are still a desideratum, but those employed in the text, as being in most points applicable, may serve the purpose in the present instance.

however, in a matrix consisting chiefly of phosphate of lime.

The cavity of the tooth (pulp cavity) is occupied, as has already been stated, by a papilla of submucous tissue. Over the surface of the papilla there lies a number of branched cells, from each of which proceeds an especially long branch which enters a dentinal tubule. When we come to speak of the minute structure of bone, the meaning and function of these fibres will become apparent.

The only other organ we need mention in the buccal cavity is the **tongue**. It has already been stated that, contrary to the usual rule, the frog's tongue is free behind and attached to the jaw in front. The organ is composed of bands of muscle separated and at the same time bound together by connective tissue. The surface of the tongue is covered by mucous membrane, which is, however, elevated to form papillæ. There are also special papillæ, which have to do with the sense of taste. These will be referred to later on when the senses come to be discussed.

We must now endeavour to gain some general idea of the nature of the alimentary canal and the modifications met with on its course. The **pharynx** opens into a wide dilatable tube, the **œsophagus**, opening in its turn into a thick-walled **stomach** (fig. 153). The stomach together with the lower part of the œsophagus is partly hidden by the **liver**, a large, brown lobed organ, lying ventral to the alimentary canal, and attached to its wall just anterior to the proximal or cardiac end of the stomach. On leaving the stomach the alimentary canal narrows, and forms a tube of uniform bore, the **small intestine**, which lies coiled on the right-hand side of the lower portion of the abdominal cavity. The small intestine bends forward along the wall of the stomach, and encloses in the fold a long whitish organ, the **pancreas**. Lying between the lobes of the liver is a small round sac, of greenish colour if full, the **gall-bladder**. From the gall-bladder a delicate tube, the **bile-duct**, passes away, traversing the substance of the pancreas and receiving in its course ducts from that organ. The bile-duct finally opens into the small intestine about midway along the recurrent fold. This first portion of the intestine is known as the **duodenum**. The intestine thereafter makes a series of coils and finally enlarges abruptly into a large short tube, the **rectum**, which opens into the chamber already referred to as the **cloaca**.

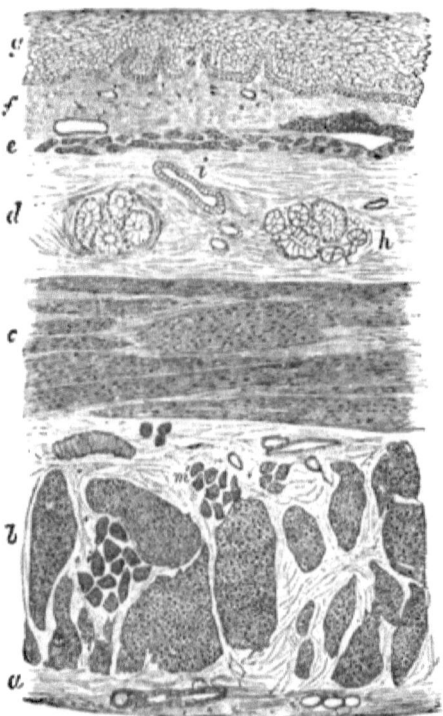

FIG. 132.—VERTICAL SECTION OF THE HUMAN ŒSOPHAGUS. (Quain.)

a, connective-tissue layer; *b*, longitudinal muscles, cut transversely; *c*, circular muscles, cut longitudinally; *d*, layer containing mucous glands; *e*, layer of muscle fibre; *f*, subepithelial tissue (dermis); *g*, epithelium layer (epidermis).

The entire outer surface of the alimentary canal and its glands is covered by a shining membrane continuous with a similar membrane covering the inner wall of the abdominal cavity, and known as the **peritoneum**. The peritoneum rises from the dorsal wall of the abdomen and becomes continuous with the layer reflected over the viscera, forming naturally a double layer, which attaches the alimentary canal and its glands to the abdominal wall, and forms the delicate membrane known as the **mesentery**. The mesentery, as we shall afterwards see, serves to support not only the alimentary canal but also blood-vessels, ducts, and nerves.

The alimentary canal, therefore, consists of a tube for conveying the food to a storing and digesting organ, from which it is passed into another tube, in which it is mixed with and further acted on by digestive fluids secreted by certain organs opening into the canal, through whose walls absorption of nutriment takes place. The refuse is collected in the rectum and ejected to the exterior periodically. The wall of the œsophagus is composed of three layers, internally—(1) mucous membrane with mucous glands (fig. 132, d, e, f, g) surrounded by (2) a layer of muscle fibres (b, c) and (3) of connective tissue (a). It will be most convenient to refer briefly at this point to the essential characters of the muscular and connective tissues, since we shall meet with them in almost every part of the body.

Muscle.—Like every tissue in the organism muscle is composed of cells. The cells are much elongated in one direction, and have the function of contractility specially developed. There are two varieties of muscle, **striped** and **non-striped**. The protoplasm of the cell or fibre of striped muscle is greatly modified, being transformed into a bundle of exceedingly delicate fibrillæ, each of which appears to consist of alternate dark and light segments. The cell-wall is exceedingly thin, and is known as the sarcolemma. Nuclei may be observed scattered here and there through the fibre, or immediately below the sarcolemma of the muscle-fibres of higher forms. The alternate light and dark segments of the individual fibrillæ give the fibre as a whole a transversely striped appearance, whence this variety of muscle derives its name. Striped muscle is also known as 'voluntary' because it is the variety met with in muscles under the direct command of the will. There are, however, exceptions to this rule, as, for instance, in the heart, where the fibres are striped, but where the muscles are independent of the influence of the will. The voluntary muscles of the frog are sometimes branched as in the tongue (fig. 135).

The other variety of muscle, termed non-striped or

involuntary from the fact of its occurring in situations where movement is outside the dominion of will, consists of cells less far removed from their typical condition. The protoplasm is longitudinally striated, suggesting the differentiation into fibrillæ which we have studied in the striped muscle-cell, and a delicate envelope is present correspond-

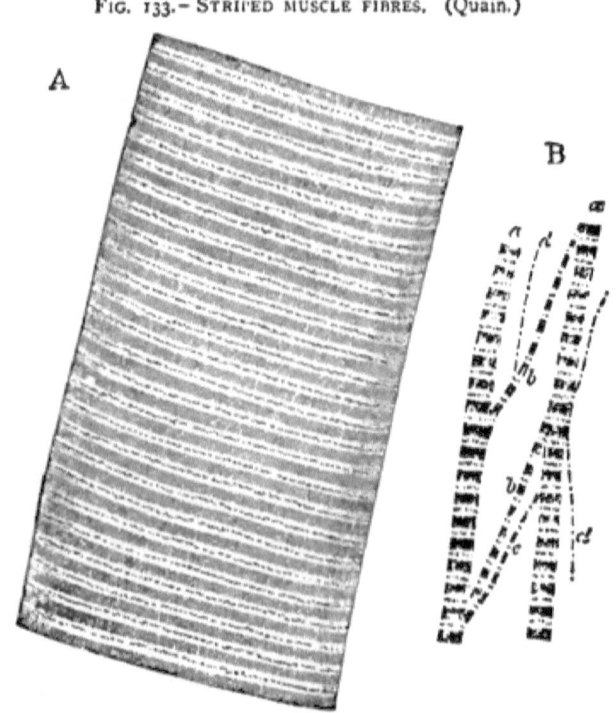

Fig. 133.—Striped muscle fibres. (Quain.)

A, portion of a muscle fibre; B, part of the same teased, showing groups of fibrils, a, b, c, and ultimate fibrillæ, d, d.

ing to the sarcolemma. The cell possesses an elongated nucleus lying centrally in the protoplasm.

In the case of both striped and non-striped muscle the cells are bound together by an intercellular cement into elementary bundles, or fasciculi, which are again collected into larger bundles. Both large and small bundles are held together by connective tissue, to which we may now briefly refer.

Connective tissue, which performs, as its name indicates, a purely mechanical function, namely, that of binding other tissues together or sheathing special organs, consists typically of three elements —white fibres, elastic fibres, and cells (figs. 137-9). The white fibres are pale, extremely fine and wavy, and unbranched; the elastic fibres, on the other hand, are

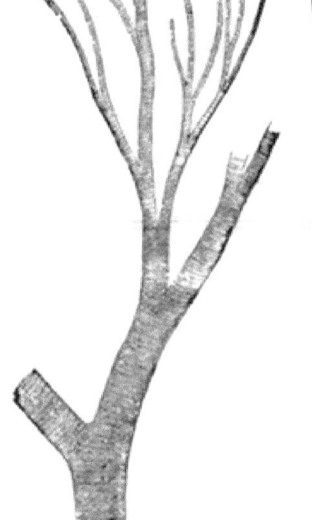

Fig. 136.—Fibres of non-striped muscle. (Quain.)

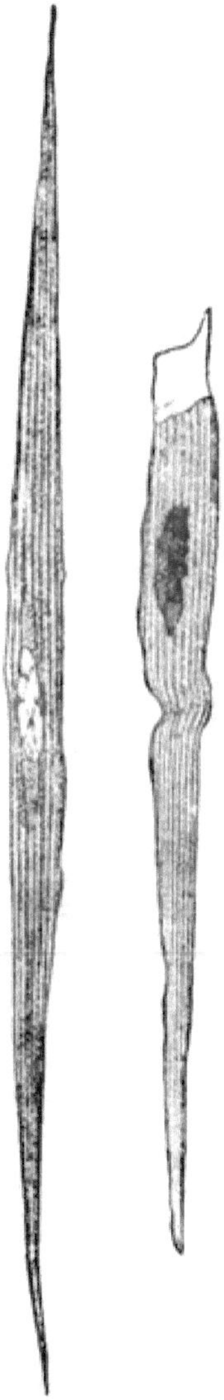

Fig. 135.—Branched muscle fibre from the tongue of the frog. (Quain.)

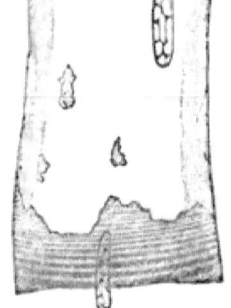

Fig. 134.—A muscle-fibre torn so as to show sarcolemma and nuclei. (Quain.)

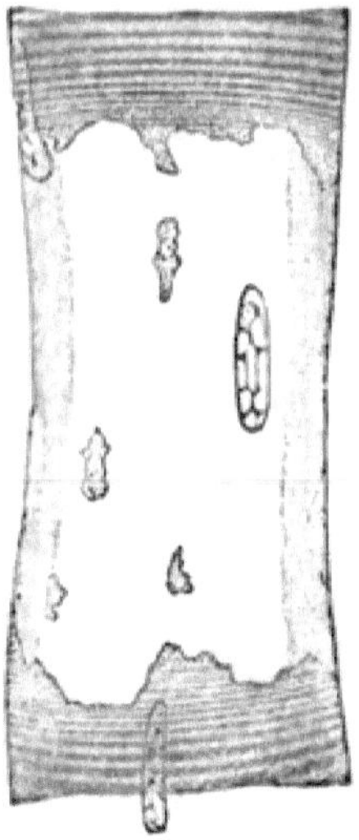

sharply defined, branched, and show a disposition to curl up at their free ends. The connective-tissue cells are typical branched nucleated cells, of quite irregular form and size. These three elements are present in variable amount in different varieties of connective tissue.

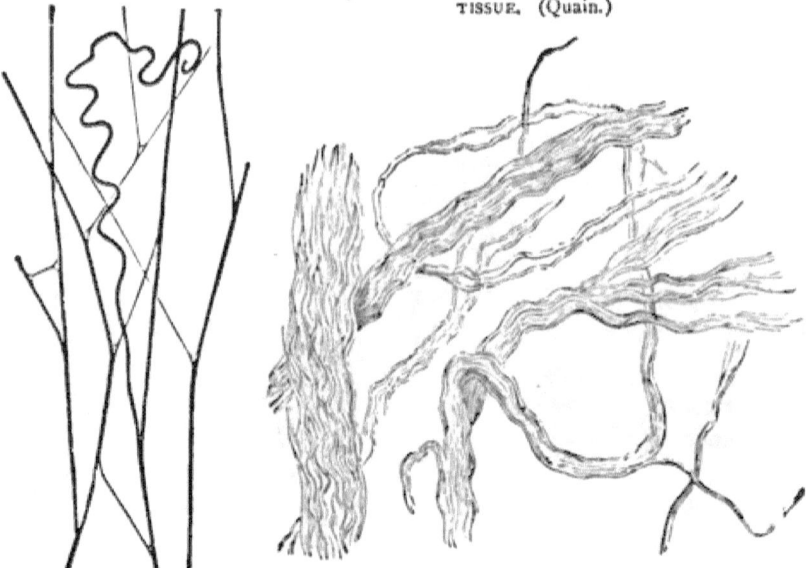

Fig. 137.—Elastic fibres of connective tissue. (Quain.)

Fig. 138.—White fibrous elements of connective tissue. (Quain.)

In the wall of the œsophagus the muscles are for the most part non-striped. In the upper portion only are the

Fig. 139.—Connective tissue corpuscles. (Quain.)

fibres striped. The fibres are arranged in two layers (fig. 132), an inner circular and an outer longitudinal. Their function is to assist by their contraction (and consequent narrowing of the œsophagus) in pushing the food down into the stomach. The wave of contraction that follows the food is known as **peristalsis**.

The **stomach** may be divided into a proximal or cardiac (nearest the heart) portion and a distal or pyloric end. Its wall from within outwards consists of (1) a mucous coat with special glands ; (2) a submucous layer of connective tissue, non-striped muscle, blood-vessels, nerves, and absorbing ducts known as lymphatics ; (3) a non-striped muscular coat, whose fibres are arranged in two layers similarly to those of the œsophagus ; and (4) a connective tissue coat formed by the peritoneum.

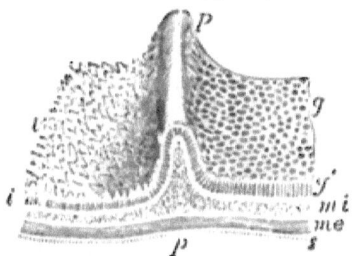

FIG. 140.—PORTION OF THE WALL OF THE ALIMENTARY CANAL AT THE JUNCTION OF THE STOMACH AND SMALL INTESTINE. (Quain.)

The **intestine** similarly consists of four layers— mucous, submucous, muscular, and fibrous (fig. 140).

A detailed study of the last three of these layers is unnecessary in the present instance, but the principal

s, peritoneum ; *me*, muscular layer ; *mi*, layer of submucous tissue ; *g, g* mucous layer ; *p, p*, pyloric valve ; *i*, villi of small intestine.

characters of the mucous layer merit more careful consideration. In the case of the stomach it is thick, relatively to the other layers, from the presence of closely packed tubular glands, not unlike the test-tubes used in chemical manipulations. The glands (**gastric glands**) are arranged vertically to the surface of the stomach, and consist of a wall formed of columnar or cubical cells capable of secreting into the cavity of the tubule a digestive fluid known as **gastric juice**, having for its function the rendering soluble of certain substances in the food chemically known as proteids (p. 26). The glands are surrounded by fine connective tissue, capillaries, and lacteals prolonged upwards from the submucous layer. It is from the blood circulating in the capillaries that the secretory cells lining the glands obtain the materials for the formation of gastric juice, the most important constituent of which is a ferment called **pepsin**. In the intestinal mucous membrane there are similar glands, known there by the name of **Lieberkühnian follicles**, and having a similar function to those in the gastric wall. In addition, however,

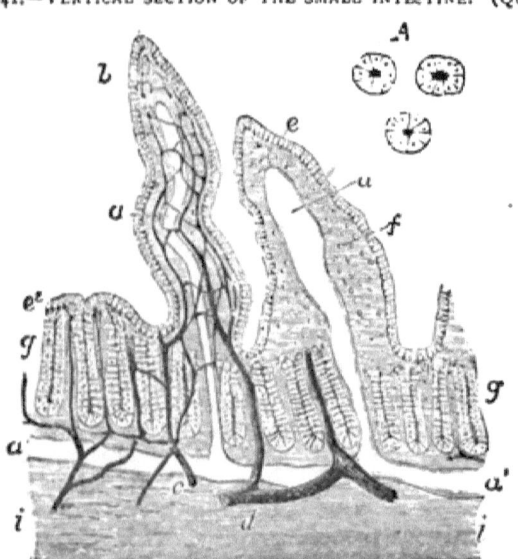

Fig. 141.—Vertical section of the small intestine. (Quain.)

i, i, submucous layer containing blood-vessels *d, c,* and large lacteal, *a, a'*; *g, g,* mucous layer with Lieberkühnian follicles ; *e, e',* epithelial layer; *a.* lacteal in the interior of a villus ; *b,* network of blood-capillaries in the subepithelial tissue (*f*) of the villus.

the mucous membrane is elevated between the mouths of the follicles into long papillæ, or **villi**, which are, structurally speaking, follicles turned inside out. Each villus is covered by columnar cells resting on a basement membrane, and covering a core of submucous tissue, consisting of lymphatics, or, as they are here termed, lacteals, nerves, blood-capillaries, and connective tissue. Among the columnar cells are found many wide-mouthed goblet-shaped cells, whose function it is to secrete mucin to keep the surface of the intestine moist, and to dilute the intestinal digestive juice as it flows from the follicles.

At the junction of the intestine and the stomach the circular muscular coat is very much thicker, and forms a **sphincter valve** (fig. 140). When it is contracted no food can pass from the stomach into the intestine; relaxation takes place only when the food in the stomach has been sufficiently acted on by the gastric juice.

In the **rectum** both follicles and villi are absent, and the mucous membrane consists simply of stratified squamous cells with a few mucous glands.

The **liver** is the largest organ in the body, and consists

FIG. 142.—GOBLET CELLS. (Quain.)

of a single right and a double left lobe. The two lobes are united by a transverse commissure of liver substance. The liver lobes are composed of an immense number of polygonal lobules of small diameter ($\frac{1}{15}$ to $\frac{1}{30}$ of an inch). Each lobule is composed of many liver-cells, also polygonal in form. The cells have extremely fine cell-walls, with protoplasmic contents and nucleus, in which intracellular and intranuclear networks can be readily made out. The intercellular spaces open into minute ducts, lined by cubical epithelium, which in turn communicate with the duct already referred to as the **bile duct**. The **gall-bladder**, already mentioned, is practically an enlargement on the course of the bile-duct, in which the surplus bile is stored.

In reality the duct from the liver opens into the gall-bladder, from which in turn the true bile-duct arises, opening into the alimentary canal in that region known as the duodenum.

Bile is, in the frog, a greenish-yellow viscid fluid, highly antiseptic in character, and for that reason of service in preventing putrefaction of the intestinal contents. It performs the additional function of serving to assist in rendering

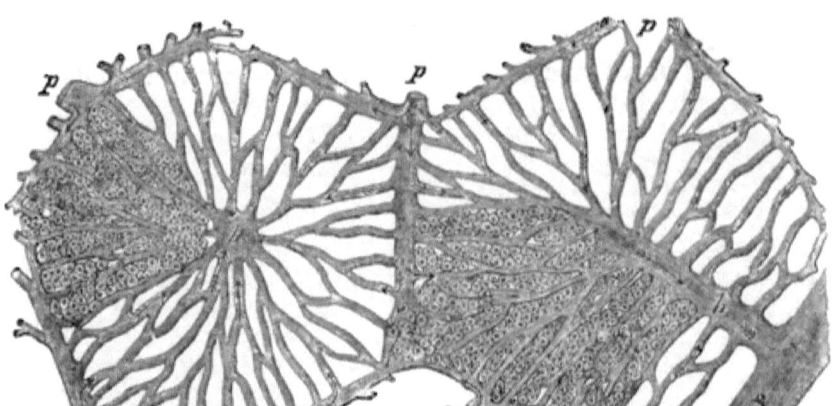

FIG. 143.—TWO LIVER LOBULES (SEMI-DIAGRAMMATIC). (Quain.)

h, h, intralobular vein; *p,* interlobular (portal) veins; *s,* sublobular (hepatic) vein. The arrows represent the course of the blood. Liver-cells are represented in one part of each lobule.

fatty substances in the intestine capable of being absorbed through the intestinal wall. The formation of bile is, however, by no means the only function which the liver has to perform. Probably its chief function is to act as a manufactory and storehouse for **glycogen**, or animal starch. The physiology of the so-called glycogenic function of the liver is, however, not yet fully understood.

The arrangement of blood-vessels in the liver is of the

highest importance, and will be described in connection with the circulatory system.

One other digestive gland may be referred to, viz. the **pancreas**. This organ lies in the fold of the duodenum, and is the agent in the formation of pancreatic juice. It consists of a series of closely packed tubules, lined by cubical glandular cells which have the power of abstracting the constituents of the pancreatic juice from the capillary blood-vessels distributed in large numbers through its tissue. The secretion differs from that of the stomach in being alkaline (that of the stomach is acid), but, like the gastric juice, it has the power of rendering proteid substances soluble which have escaped the action of the gastric secretion. It also assists in the absorption of fat, and, in addition, transforms starch into sugar—a function in the higher animals mainly performed by the secretion of the

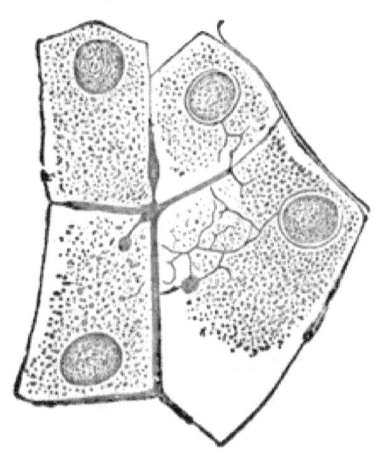

FIG. 144.—FOUR HEPATIC CELLS WITH COMMENCEMENTS OF A BILE-CAPILLARY. (Quain.)

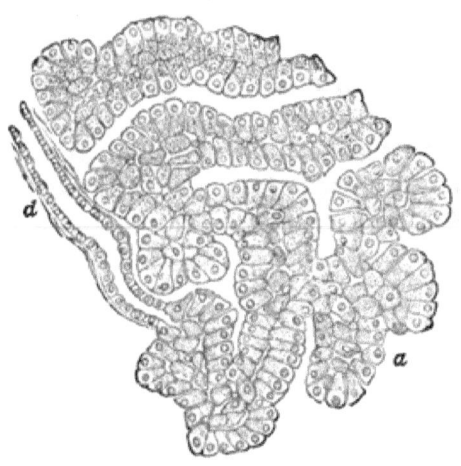

FIG. 145.—SECRETORY TUBULES OF THE PANCREAS. (Quain.)

a, secretory tubule; *d*, origin of a pancreatic duct.

salivary glands. These latter are absent, however, from the Amphibia.

By the action of these various secretions the contents of the alimentary canal are thus rendered capable of absorption. That process takes place through the walls of the small intestine chiefly, where there are very many special vessels known as lacteals and blood-capillaries in readiness to receive the soluble products. The **lacteals** are extremely delicate ducts, whose walls are composed of a single layer of thin plate-like cells (squames). They abound in the villi of the small intestine and in the wall of the alimentary canal generally. These lacteals communicate with larger trunks, which ultimately pour their contents into the general blood circulation. The food matters also enter the capillaries and so pass directly into the circulation.

The **circulatory organs** are in the frog, and, indeed, in all the Vertebrata, very highly differentiated. It will not be possible to give more than a brief outline of the plan of these organs. Further details must be obtained from zoological treatises.

Generally speaking, the circulatory system of any one of the higher animals, and of the frog in particular, consists fundamentally of a pumping organ or heart and two sets of vessels, one passing from the heart (arteries) and one passing to the heart (veins). **Blood,** the contents of these various organs, is, as we have previously seen, a fluid which has two all-important duties to perform, viz. (1) to convey to the various tissues of the body the nutriment absorbed from the alimentary canal, and (2) to act as the medium for the carriage of a supply of oxygen to the tissues whereby that disintegration of organic compounds may be effected which we have seen to be a *sine quâ non* in the manifestation of life, and incidentally to act as the medium for the conveyance of the products of disintegration from the tissues to the exterior.

The blood of the frog is a red, slightly viscid fluid, which on being examined under the microscope is found to consist of an almost colourless medium or plasma in which floats an immense number of blood-corpuscles of two kinds—the one irregular in shape, colourless, and not unlike *Amœbæ* in

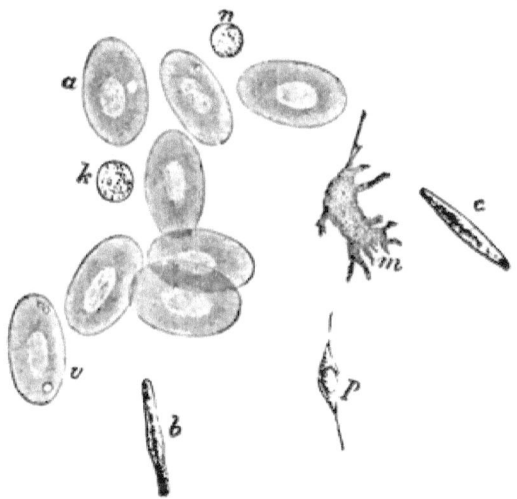

FIG. 146.—BLOOD-CORPUSCLES OF THE FROG. (Ranvier.)

a, red corpuscles seen on the flat ; *v*, vacuoles in a corpuscle ; *b*, *c*, red corpuscles seen in profile ; *n*, *k*, colourless corpuscles at rest ; *m*. colourless corpuscle showing pseudopodia ; *p*, coloured fusiform corpuscle.

general appearance, and exhibiting when living that indefinite motion which has already been described and termed amœboid ; the other definite and elliptical in shape and reddish yellow in colour. It is from these latter that the blood derives its red colour.

Blood after death, or if withdrawn from the living body, does not long remain liquid. In the plasma extremely delicate branched filaments (fibrin threads) make their appearance, in the meshes of which the corpuscles become entangled. The clot (coagulum) subsequently contracts, with the result that the watery element (serum) of

FIG. 147.—FIBRIN THREADS. (Schäfer.)

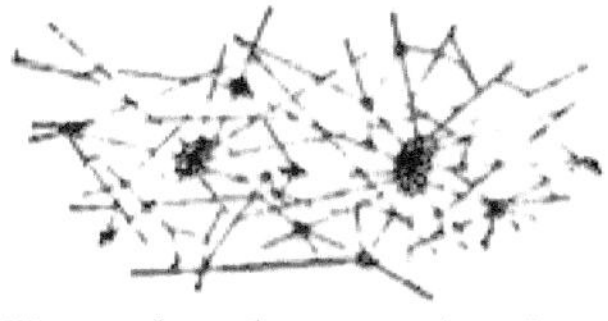

The coloured corpuscles have been removed by washing.

the plasma is expressed. We might therefore classify the various constituents of blood thus :—

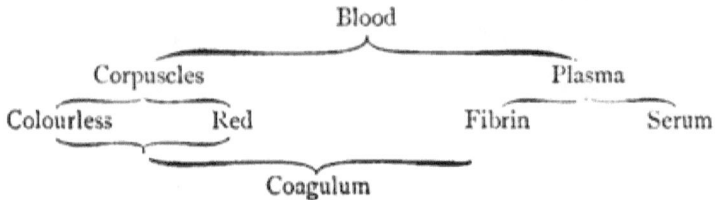

The two most important functions of blood have been mentioned above; it will be sufficient to add here that the plasma performs the double duty of carrying nutritive material to the various tissues, and of removing from them many of the waste products always being formed there during life, while on the colouring matter of the red corpuscles, hæmoglobin (p. 21), devolves the duty of carrying oxygen gas from the exterior to the tissues.

Naturally, therefore, a considerable difference exists between blood passing to the tissues from the heart (**arterial blood**) and blood passing from the tissues to the heart (**venous blood**). Arterial blood contains about 17 % of oxygen gas (by volume), while venous blood contains only 6 %. Similarly arterial blood contains about 30 % of carbonic acid gas (by volume), while venous blood may have as much as 40 % to 45 %. There are also other points of difference between arterial and venous blood, the most noticeable of which is the bright scarlet colour of arterial, contrasting in this respect with the dull red of venous blood.

The red corpuscles are derived from the white in a manner not yet accurately determined. The white in their turn are developed in a variety of situations in the body, chief amongst which are the so called **blood-glands**.

The **heart**, or pump which drives the blood through the vessels, is a hollow, muscular, pyramidal sac, lying in the anterior part of the body-cavity known in the higher animals as the **thorax**, where indeed it forms a distinct subdivision of the cœlom. The heart is enclosed in a double-walled sac, or **pericardium**, between the walls of which there is a space filled with a colourless nutritive fluid known as lymph.

From and to the heart a number of large blood-vessels pass, dividing afterwards into smaller branches. The heart itself is subdivided into three chambers, a **ventricle**, which composes the apex and a considerable portion of the body, and two **auricles**, which occupy the base of the pyramid. The heart lies close to the ventral body-wall in such a way that the apex points backwards and the large vessels arise from near the base and pass forwards. Above or behind the heart lies a large membranous sac known as the **sinus venosus**, into which all the impure blood is poured in the course of the circulation; below or in front of the heart and springing from the ventricle is a large muscular vessel known as the **truncus**

FIG. 148.—ARRANGEMENT OF THE CHIEF ARTERIES AND VEINS IN THE FROG. (Owen.)

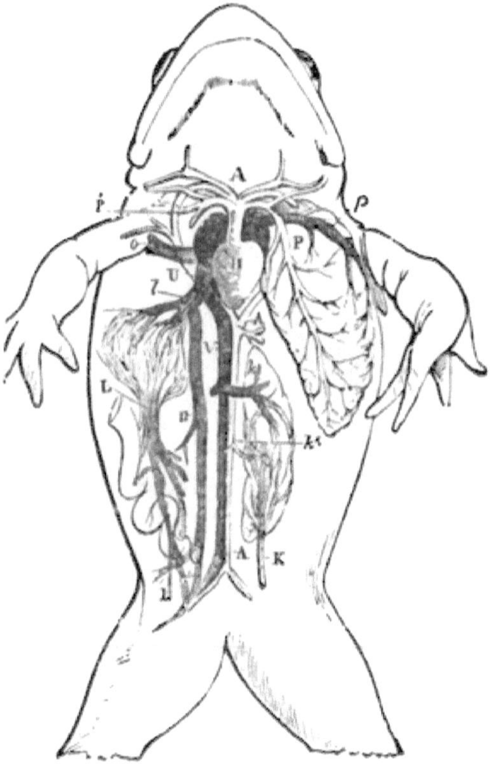

H, heart; A, above the origin of the common carotids; P, the left lung; p, pulmonary vein; P', pulmocutaneous artery; o, right precaval vein; l, hepatic vein; L, portal vein; V, postcaval vein; A, union of the two aortæ; U, right aortic arch; k, renal vein; k', renal artery; n, anterior abdominal vein; A', division of the aorta into two common iliac arteries going to the hind limbs. Compare this figure with fig. 53.

arteriosus, by which pure blood leaves the heart to pass to the tissues. It very soon branches into a number of large **arteries** afterwards to be specified. Lastly, one vessel opens directly into the left auricle, while the sinus venosus manifestly is connected with the right auricle.

Before entering into further details with regard to the circulatory system it will be necessary for us to understand clearly the nature of the three important sets of vessels concerned in the transport of the blood, namely, the arteries, veins, and capillaries.

Arteries and **veins** have fundamentally the same structure, but they differ in the relative amounts of the

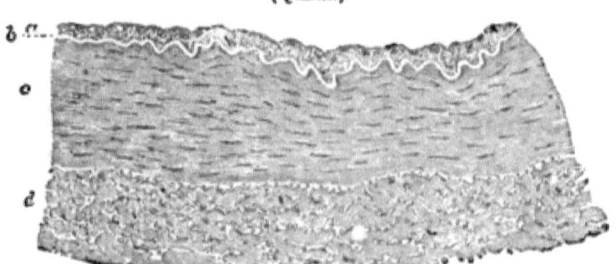

FIG. 149.—TRANSVERSE SECTION OF THE WALL OF A TYPICAL ARTERY. (Quain.)

a, epithelial layer; *b*, elastic membrane; *c*, tunica media; *d*, tunica adventitia.

separate elements entering into the composition of their walls. The wall consists of an internal epithelial lining of flat squames followed by a sub-epithelial membrane composed of elastic fibres: this is known as the tunica intima. The tunica media consists of a thick layer of circularly arranged muscle-fibres of the non-striped variety, plentifully mingled with delicate elastic fibres. The whole is strengthened and attached to adjacent parts by a tunica adventitia composed of connective tissue in which all three elements of that tissue—cellular, fibrous and elastic—are well represented. The veins differ from the arteries chiefly in two points; first, in that the various coats are thinner; and secondly, in the presence (in most veins) of valves or pocket-like flaps formed by the tunica intima and tunica media. These valves are so arranged that a current of blood flowing in the normal direction into the heart encounters no opposition,

FIG. 150.—TRANSVERSE SECTION OF WALL OF A TYPICAL VEIN. (Quain.)

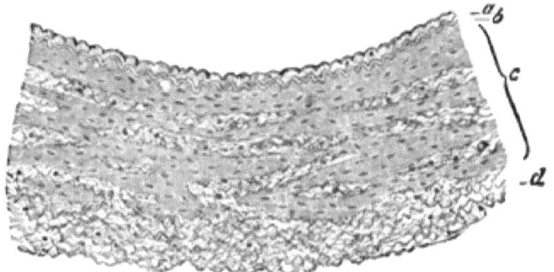

a, epithelial layer; *b*, elastic membrane; *c*, tunica media; *d*, tunica adventitia.

whilst a regurgitation from the heart causes the pockets to open and press against each other, and so prevent the backward passage of impure blood to the tissues (fig. 151).

FIG. 151.—VALVES IN A VEIN. (Quain.)

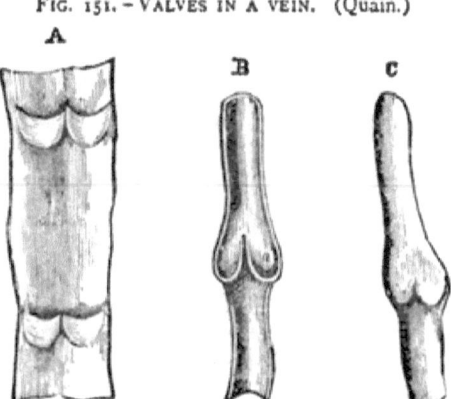

A, vein cut open; B, longitudinal section of vein showing the valve in action; C, the same seen from outside.

Capillaries are exceedingly delicate vessels, which form the connection between the artery and its corresponding vein, and whose walls have been reduced to a tunica intima of epithelial cells only. Every artery subdivides into capillaries; every vein is formed by the reunion of capillaries; the current of the circulation is from the artery to the vein through the capillary network so formed. Capillaries thus form the ultimate subdivisions of the circulatory system, and as such bring oxygen and nutritive fluid into close relation with the tissues, and at the same time extract the waste products produced in the tissues as a consequence of metabolic changes taking place there.

FIG. 152.—CAPILLARY NETWORK UNITING AN ARTERY AND A VEIN IN THE WEB OF THE FROG'S FOOT. (Quain.)

The arrows indicate the direction of the blood-flow.

Having now briefly noticed the general character of the constituents of the vascular system it will be necessary to sketch the course of the chief blood-streams through the body. A little consideration will show us that there must be three important currents, viz. (1) a blood-stream from the alimentary canal which passes through the liver to the heart, carrying the products of assimilation into the general circulation; (2) a blood-stream from the heart to and from the various organs of the body; and (3) a blood-stream to and from certain purificatory organs—the lung and the kidneys.

The first current is conveyed by a large vein, the **portal vein**, which on the one hand has its terminal capillaries diffused in the walls of the intestine, and on the other breaks up into a similar capillary network in the substance of the liver, in which organ the constituents of bile are abstracted from the blood, while at the same time glycogen is removed and stored in the liver-cells. This blood-stream is known as the **portal circulation**.

The second or **systemic circulation** is more elaborate.

Starting from the truncus artericsus the blood is pumped by the ventricle into a number of vessels springing from the truncus. These vessels are six in number, three on either side: nearest the origin of the truncus, a pair of vessels we may know as **pulmo-cutaneous**; next two **aortæ**; and lastly the two **common carotids**. We have already seen that the heart consists of three chambers, a ventricle and two auricles. The sinus venosus opens into the right auricle, while it has been noted that one vessel, to be known now as the **pulmonary vein,** opens into the left auricle. The auricles in turn open into the ventricles, and the auriculo-ventricular openings are guarded by valves which prevent regurgitation. Further it will be noted that the truncus arteriosus springs more from the right than the left side of the ventricle. When the ventricle contracts, therefore, the blood occupying the right side of the ventricle will be the first to enter the truncus. Now we have already learnt that the sinus venosus receives all the impure blood from the systemic veins; while the pulmonary vein, on the other hand, contains pure blood from the respiratory organ, the lung. Under these circumstances, when the auricles contract and pour their contents into the ventricle, the ventricle will contain pure blood on its left side, impure blood on its right side, and mixed blood in the middle. Therefore the ventricular contraction will drive into the truncus first of all impure blood, which will find its way into the first of the branches of the truncus, namely, the pulmo-cutaneous arteries, by which vessels the blood is conveyed to the lung and skin (the two great respiratory organs in the frog) to be purified. The blood immediately following will pass into the two aortæ, and the last and purest blood will enter the carotids. This process is greatly assisted by a special valve in the interior of the truncus, which closes the entrance to the pulmo-cutaneous arteries after they have been filled. By the aortæ (which afterwards unite) the blood (mixed) is carried to all the chief organs of the trunk, to the limbs, stomach, intestine, &c. supplying

Fig. 153.—Venous System of the Frog. (Milnes Marshall.)

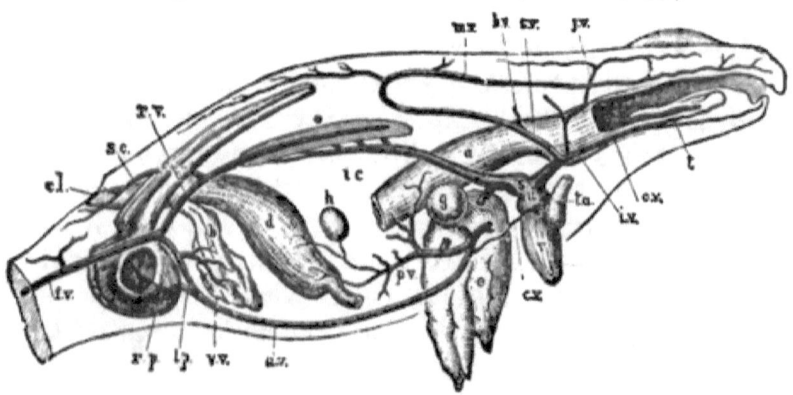

a, stomach; *a.v.*, anterior abdominal vein; *b.*, bladder; *b.v.*, brachial vein; *cl.*, cloaca; *c.v.*, cardiac vein; *d*, rectum; *e*, liver; *e.v.*, external jugular vein; *f.v.* femoral vein; *g.*, gall bladder; *h*, sp'een; *i.c.*, inferior vena cava; *i.v.*, innominate vein; *j.v*, internal jugular; *l.p.*, left pelvic vein; *m.v.*, musculo-cutaneous vein; *o*, kidney; *p.v.*, hepatic portal vein; *r.p.*, right pelvic vein; *r.v.*, right renal-portal; *s.*, sinus venosus; *sc.*, sciatic vein; *s v.*, subclavian vein; *t.*, tongue; *t.a.*, truncus arteriosus; *a.*, right auricle; *v.*, ventricle; *v.v.*, vesical veins.

Fig. 154.—Arterial System of the Frog. (Milnes Marshall.)

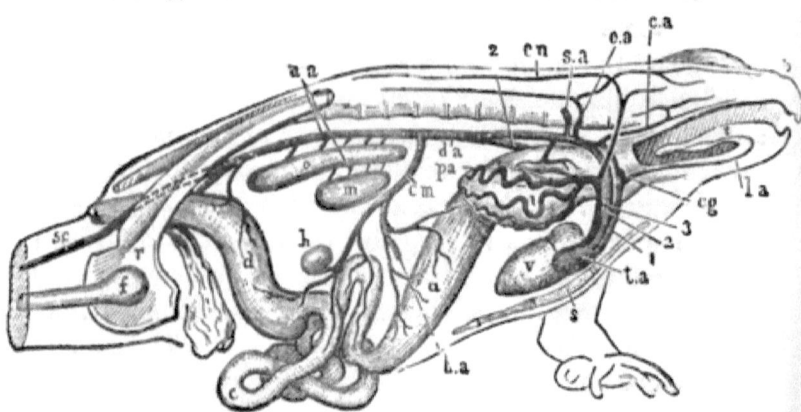

b, nostril; *c*, small intestine; *c.a.*, carotid artery; *c.g.*, carotid gland; *c.m.*, cœliaco-mesenteric artery; *cn*, cutaneous artery; *d.a.*, dorsal aorta; *f.*, femur; *h.a.*, hepatic artery; *i*, right lung; *l.a.*, lingual artery; *m*, spermarium, or testis; *o.a.*, occipito-vertebral artery; *p.a.*, pulmonary artery; *r*, pelvic girdle; *s.*, sternum; *s.a.*, subclavian artery; *s c.*, sciatic artery; *u.a.*, urino-genital arteries; 1, carotid arch; 2, systemic arch; 3, pulmo-cutaneous arch.

these viscera with nutriment and oxygen. The purest blood passes by the carotids to the head region, where naturally the purest blood is wanted.

Similarly the impure blood is returned to the heart by special veins from each organ, uniting ultimately into four large vessels, two anterior or **precaval veins** and one posterior or **postcaval vein** which run direct to the sinus venosus, and one **anterior abdominal**, which, after traversing the ventral body-wall goes to the liver.

The details of the arrangement and distribution of the smaller branches though of great importance cannot be dealt with here. Figs. 148, 153, and 154 will, however, show many of these details, which can be made out without difficulty in the animal itself. (The names of the various veins and arteries indicate sufficiently the origin and distribution.) One point must, however, be briefly noticed with regard to the renal circulation. The common aorta gives off a number of branches to each of the two kidneys lying in the dorsal portion of the cœlom, while the renal veins open into the postcaval: this is the normal arrangement of artery and vein. But in the frog an additional means of circulation is present in the shape of a large vessel known as the **renal-portal**, which carries venous blood from the hind-limb and lumbar region to the kidney. The renal-portal on either side gives off a branch to the anterior abdominal, so that blood coming from the hind-limbs may pass to the heart by two channels, through the liver by the anterior abdominal, or through the kidney by the renal-portal.

Respiratory system.—Before venous blood can be made use of again as a carrier of oxygen to the tissues it must be purified by the removal from it of the carbonic acid, water, and other waste products collected in its passage through the systemic capillaries. We shall consider first the removal of the carbonic acid. This duty is performed by the **lungs**, two semi-transparent sacs of large size situated ventrally to the œsophagus. At the posterior end of the buccal cavity, and immediately beneath the opening of the œsophagus, may be seen a slit-like aperture, already mentioned, known as the **glottis**, the walls of which are strengthened by cartilage. The glottis leads into a cylindrical chamber from which the two lung-sacs open. Each lung is a hollow tapering bag, externally covered by a layer of

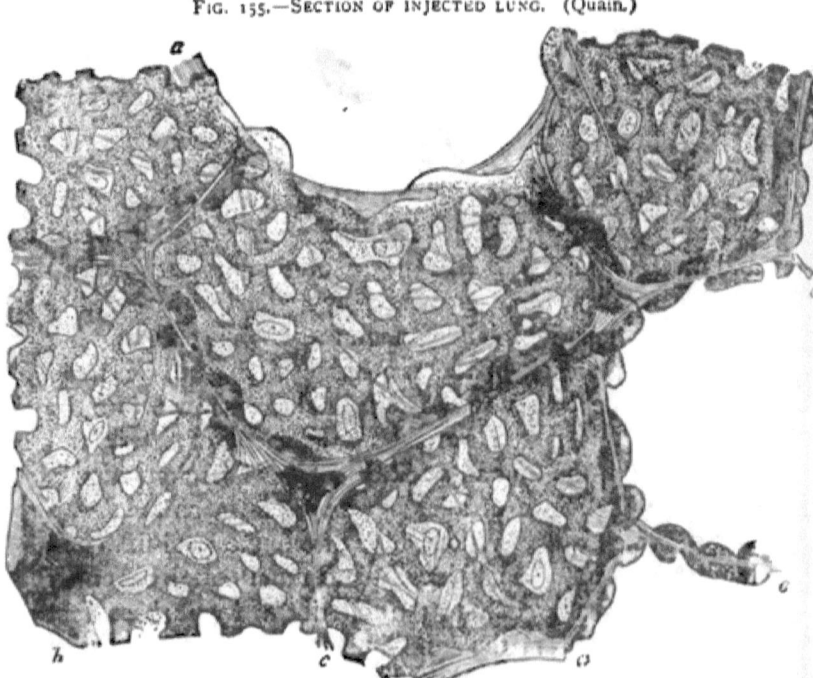

Fig. 155.—Section of injected lung. (Quain.)

a, a, free edges of the pulmonary sacs (alveoli); *c, c,* partitions between neighbouring alveoli in section; *b,* small artery giving off numerous capillaries which form network over the alveolar wall.

the same membrane which has already been described as covering the viscera generally, here, however, known under the special name of **pleuron**. The inner surface of the lung is thrown into folds and ridges, giving the wall the appearance of being honeycombed. Manifestly the superficies of the lung-wall is thus greatly increased. The pulmonary artery already mentioned in considering the branches of the truncus arteriosus here subdivides again and again, and its ultimate capillaries ramify in the lung-wall, separated from the air which normally fills the lung by a single layer of squamous epithelium. It is manifest that a gaseous exchange between the atmosphere and the blood circulating in the capillary terminations of the pulmonary artery is thus made possible. (It must be noted that the pulmonary artery, despite its name, contains venous blood.) The wall of the lung is exceedingly elastic, and readily collapses if the glottis be kept open or the wall be punctured.

In principle the lung of the frog does not differ from the gill of the fish, for in both the end to be gained is the exposure of a maximum amount of blood to the atmosphere. In the fish the blood is carried outside the body in capillaries, which ramify in processes supported by a connective tissue framework, and thus meets with the oxygen dissolved in the water, while in the frog the air is sucked into the interior of the body to the blood, a method by which risk of injury to so delicate and important a system is reduced to a minimum. If space permitted, it would be interesting to trace the manner in which the lungs have arisen as a modification of a curious organ—the swim-bladder—developed in many fish. By altering the quantity of air contained in the swim-bladder, fish are able to increase or decrease their buoyancy. In higher animals, such as the rabbit or the dog, the lung, instead of being a single hollow sac, is composed of an enormous number of extremely minute sacs closely packed together (fig. 155), and communicating with the external world by means of a series of branched tubes (**bronchi**), which ultimately unite to form one large tube (**trachea**), of which the sole representative in the frog is the small cylindrical chamber into which the glottis opens. The gain in the extent of respiratory surface in the mammalian lung by this arrangement must be at once evident, whilst at the same time every particle of air inhaled is made use of. In the frog, on the other hand, only the air nearest the wall of the lung can be employed for respiratory purposes; a loss, however, not of much importance, since pulmonary respiration is in the frog greatly assisted by secondary respiration through the skin. The mode of inspiration in the frog differs from that of the higher animals, since, instead of

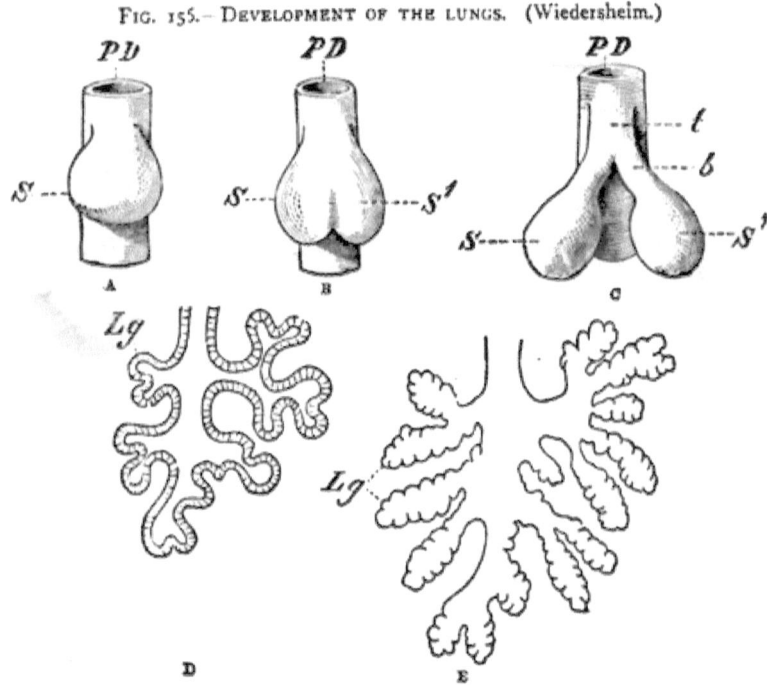

FIG. 155.—DEVELOPMENT OF THE LUNGS. (Wiedersheim.)

PD, primitive intestine; *S*, *S'*, lung-sacs; *t*, trachea; *b*, bronchus; *Lg*, seconda y pulmonary sacs.

employing the muscles of the lung and the abdominal wall, &c. to bring about the distension of the lung, the frog inhales by the nostrils, so filling the buccal cavity, then, shutting the œsophagus and nostrils by means of the muscles of the buccal wall, it forces the air into the lungs, from which it is expelled by the natural elasticity of the lung itself.

Renal system.—It will now be necessary to glance at the mechanism by which the water and soluble nitrogenous waste are removed from the blood and got rid of. That duty is performed by two organs, the **kidneys**, which have already been mentioned in connection with the circulatory system as lying dorsally one on either side of the dorsal aorta, and receiving branches from that vessel. The kidneys are closely attached to the dorsal body-wall, and are covered on the ventral aspect by a layer of peritoneum. Each kidney is a flat elongated body of a dull red colour. Entering the outer edge of each is the renal-portal vein, and leaving the same edge, a little more than half-way down, is a delicate tube known as the **ureter**, by which the renal excreta are got rid of. The ureters open into the common chamber, or cloaca, behind the opening of the rectum.

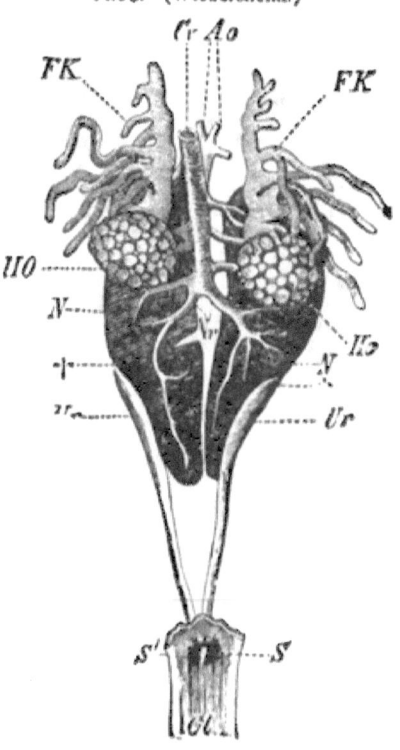

FIG. 157.—KIDNEYS AND SPERMARIA OF FROG. (Wiedersheim.)

N, N, kidneys; *Ur, Ur*, ureters; †, their point of origin; *S, S'*, their opening into the cloaca, *Cl*; *HO*, spermaria; *FK*, fat body; *Ao*, aorta; *Cv*, vena cava; *Vr*, efferent veins.

In structure the frog's kidney is essentially an immense number of nephridia closely packed together supported by connective tissue and permeated by the capillary endings of the renal artery and renal and renal-portal veins. Each nephridium consists essentially of a terminal double-walled sac, containing a tuft of capillaries communicating on the one hand with a small artery and on the other with a small vein. The tuft and its capsule together form a **glomerulus**. The space between the walls is continuous with the **tube** of the nephridium. The tube-wall is lined by secretory epithelium, which differs in character in different regions. It pursues a very convoluted course through the substance of the kidney, and is in intimate relation throughout with the renal capillaries. It ultimately unites with other tubules, and all finally open into the ureter above mentioned. In passing through the capillaries of the glomerulus, part of the water in the blood is squeezed out into the space between the two walls of the sac, whence it trickles down the tube, washing out in its course the soluble nitrogenous waste abstracted meanwhile by the secretory cells from the renal capillaries surrounding them. The water and the nitrogenous and other salts contained in solution in it go by the name of **urine**, the most important constituent of which is a complex nitrogenous compound known as **urea**.

FIG. 158.—TUFT OF CAPILLARIES IN A GLOMERULUS WITH RELATED BLOOD-VESSELS. (Quain.)

a, artery; *af*, afferent branch; *m*, capillary tuft; *ef*, efferent vein; *b*, capillaries of the efferent vein.

Urine does not escape directly from the ureter to the exterior. It is collected in a large bilobed and very extensible sac, the **urinary bladder**, which opens on the ventral surface of the cloaca, just in front of the rectal aperture. From the bladder the urine escapes to the exterior periodically.

So far we have followed the course of the blood only to and from special organs. A very large amount of the blood is devoted, however, to the nourishing and oxygenating of the muscular and skeletal or supporting system. At p. 273 we have glanced at the histological characters of muscle, so that we may now proceed to the consideration of the hard parts—or, in other words, the **skeleton**, or **skeletal system**.

The only representative of the skeletal system we have yet had to deal with was the notochord of *Amphioxus*, a structure, however, of supreme importance ; for, as indicated at p. 258, we find that this rod forms the basis on which the chief part of the skeleton of the frog and of higher animals as well is built.

The **skeleton** is composed of two substances, **bone** and **cartilage**. The histological character of these are of some importance.

Cartilage is, like most other tissues, composed of a matrix in which are embedded numerous cells. The matrix is relatively very abundant ; it consists of a homogeneous intercellular substance very elastic in its nature. The cells are spherical or polygonal, and frequently occur in small groups which result from the fissiparous division of a single cell. By studying the process of division it may be made out that the matrix is produced by modification of the old cell-walls, which are successively cast off as new walls are formed round the daughter-cells.

The matrix is not always homogeneous. In one variety of cartilage there may be formed in the matrix delicate elastic fibrils (**yellow fibro-cartilage**), in another wavy fibres of white fibrous tissue (**white fibro-cartilage**) (fig. 16). Cartilage whose matrix is free of either form of fibril is known as **hyaline cartilage** (fig. 159).

Bone similarly consists of a matrix and embedded cells, although here both cells and matrix undergo considerable modification. The cells are repeatedly branched, and lie in spaces (**lacunæ**), which are moulded to the form of the contained cell. The branched processes of the cells lie in delicate canals (**canaliculi**), and these again communicate with the canaliculi of neighbouring lacunæ. Moreover the

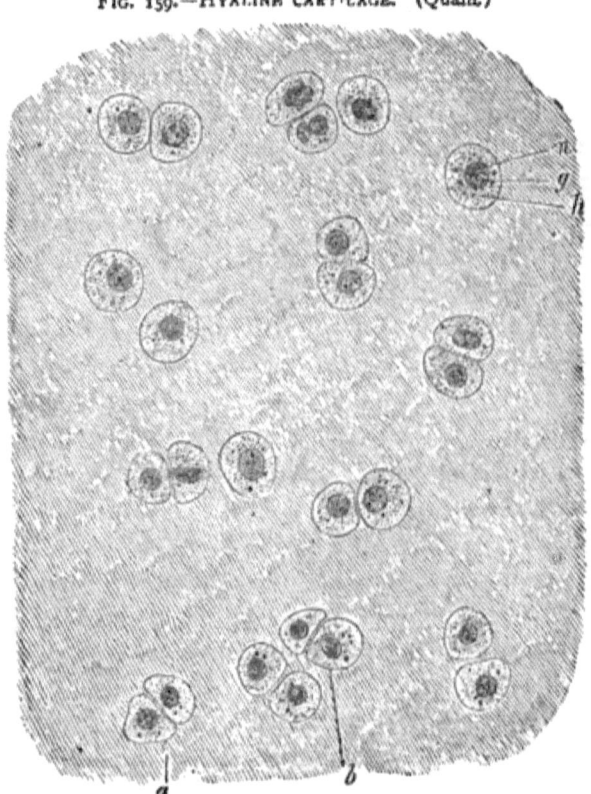

FIG. 159.—HYALINE CARTILAGE. (Quain.)

a, group of two cells; *b*, group of four cells; *h*, protoplasm of cell, with fat granules, *g*; *n*, nucleus.

lacunæ themselves are arranged in circles round larger spaces (**Haversian canals**) which contain one or more blood-vessels. The Haversian canals anastomose and form a complete network in the bone and act as the channels by which nutrient blood-vessels pass to every part of the bone.

The **skeleton**, looked at as a whole, consists of an axial vertebral column terminated anteriorly by the skull, and having attached to it two girdles, each bearing a pair of appendages, which constitute the appendicular skeleton. It will be advisable to compare the skeleton of the allied salamander with that of the frog, since the skeleton of the latter deviates considerably from the typical condition.

Fig. 160.—Transverse section of typical long bone (humerus) (Quain.)

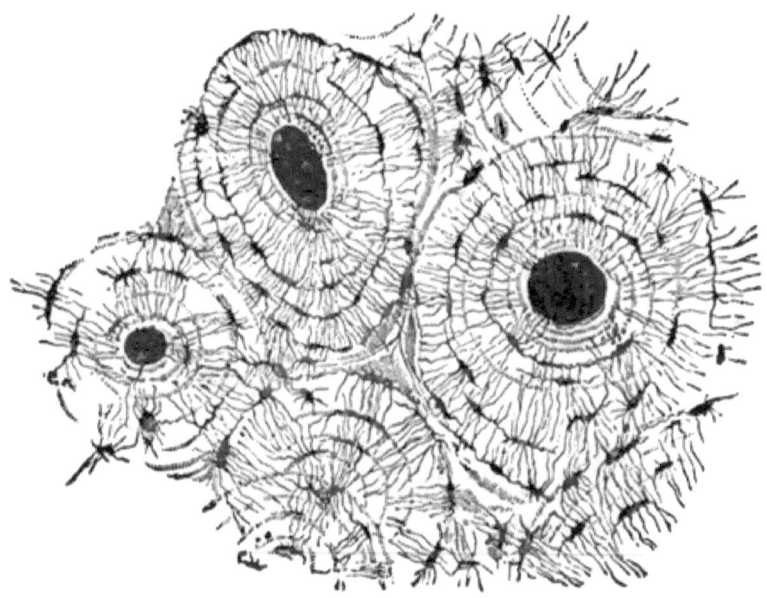

The section shows three Haversian canals, with three concentric rings of lacunæ, from each of which spring a number of canaliculi.

The axial **vertebral column** is composed of a series of vertebræ articulated to each other, and all more or less resembling each other. A typical **vertebra**, say from the middle of the back, consists of a short cylindrical body (**centrum**), from the dorsal side of which an **arch** arises, the apex of the arch being prolonged upwards as a **spinous process**. The arches of the successive vertebræ, when placed together, thus form a canal in which lies the spinal cord, and which therefore goes by the name of the spinal or **neural canal**. From either side of the arch there projects a longer or shorter process known as the **transverse process**. It is to this process and to the body of the vertebra that the **ribs** are articulated in those forms which possess ribs; here, however, ribs are absent. In addition we must note the existence of facets or the points of articulation of the successive vertebræ on each other. There are two **facets** in front and two behind, also borne on the sides of the arch. Vertebræ differ from each other in size, in the length and direction of the

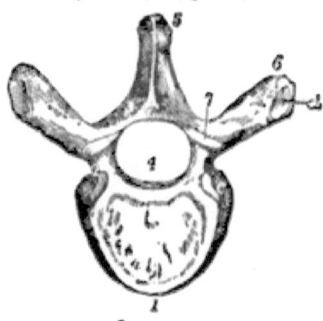

FIG. 162.— A TYPICAL VERTEBRA (HUMAN). (Quain.)

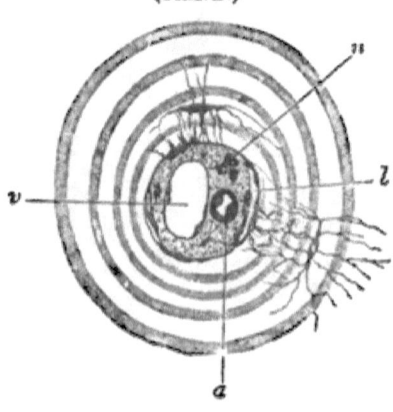

FIG. 161.— A HAVERSIAN SYSTEM. (Schäfer.)

v, vein; *a*, artery; *l*, lymphatic.

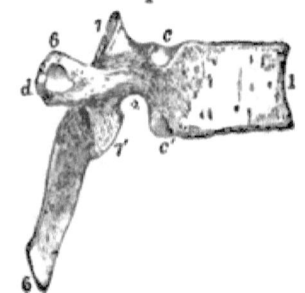

1, centrum; 2, arch; 4, neural canal; 5, spinous process; 6, transverse process bearing facets, *d*, 7, 7'; *c*, *c'*, facets on centrum. (The upper figure shows a vertebra seen from before backwards, the lower is a lateral view of the same.)

transverse processes, and in other less important points. A comparison of the vertebral column of the newt with that of the frog shows that in the latter the tail vertebræ are absent and that the last few vertebræ have coalesced into a long fluted bone, the **urostyle**, in which, however, evidence of the union can still be made out.

The several vertebræ are bound together by connective tissue, but in such a maner as to permit of a limited amount of movement.

The **skull** is too complicated a structure to allow of detailed treatment here, and therefore only the essential features will be referred to. It is to be noted that the neural canal communicates with the cavity of the skull by the **foramen magnum**, a large aperture in the posterior wall of the skull. The skull is hinged to the first vertebra by two **condyles**, or smooth processes between which a peg-like projection of the first, or atlas, vertebra fits.

The skull itself may be said to consist of three parts, a cylindrical box, the **cranium**, or skull proper, to which are attached two pairs of sense-organs, the olfactory and auditory capsules; a framework attached to the sides of the cylinder and forming the upper jaw, the **maxilla**; and a lower jaw, or **mandible**, articulating on either side with the posterior part of the upper framework. The cranium itself is composed partly of cartilage, partly of bone. Posteriorly, i.e. in the occipital region, it consists of a floor and two side walls of bone (the **basi-** and two **ex-occipitals**) and a roof of cartilage, the ring thus formed bounding the foramen magnum. The floor of the middle portion of the box is formed mainly of cartilage strengthened by a dagger-shaped bone,

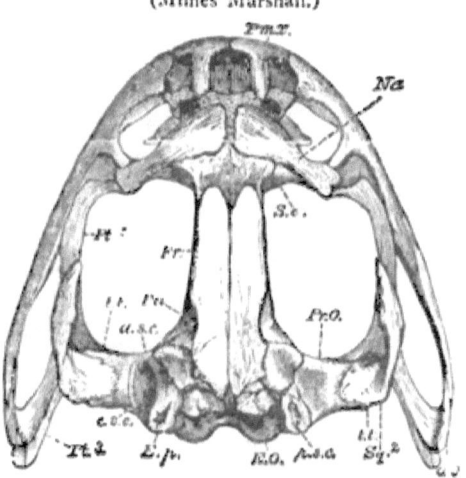

FIG. 163.—DORSAL VIEW OF THE FROG'S SKULL. (Milnes Marshall.)

Pmx., premaxilla; *Na.*, nasal; *S.e.*, sphenethmoid; *Fr.*, parieto-frontal; *Pr.O.*, prootic; *E.O.*, ex-occipital; *Q.J.*, quadrato-jugal; *Sq.*, squamosal; *Pt.*, pterygoid; *Pa.*, palatine.

the **para-sphenoid**; the walls are composed of cartilage and the roof of two narrow plates closely united, the **parieto-frontal** bones. Anteriorly the walls of the cylinder are composed of a bony girdle, the **sphenethmoid**, while above that bone and in front of the parieto-frontals, are two small bones known as the **nasals**. Attached to the occipital ring, one on either side, are the ear or **otic capsules**, composed partly of bone, partly of cartilage, while the nasal bones shelter the **nasal capsules**. The **eye** is not attached to the

FIG. 164. - LATERAL VIEW OF THE FROG'S SKULL. (Milnes Marshall.)

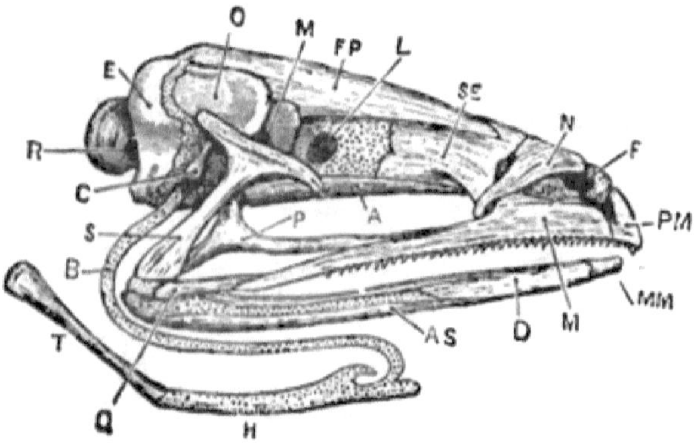

A, para-sphenoid; AS, angulo-sphenial; B, I, anterior and posterior horns of hyoid; H, body of hyoid; C, columella; D, dentary; E, exoccipital; F, nostril; FP, parieto-frontal; L, exit of optic nerve; M, maxilla; MM, mento-meckelian, or chin bone; M', exit for fifth and seventh nerves; N, nasal; O, prootic; P, pterygoid; PM, premaxilla; Q, quadrato-jugal; R, exit for ninth and tenth nerves; S, squamosal; SE, sphenethmoid.

skull, but lies free on either side, midway between the ear and nose.

The upper framework attached to this box consists of a number of narrow bones passing from the ear-capsule on the one hand to the nose-capsule on the other, and forming with the skull a bony ring round the eye. In front and on the under surface of the skull lie four small bones, two rod-like and stretching from the sphenethmoid outwards, the **palatines**, and two triangular bones lying in front of the palatines, the **vomers**, which have already been referred to as carrying teeth. In front of the two nasals are two small

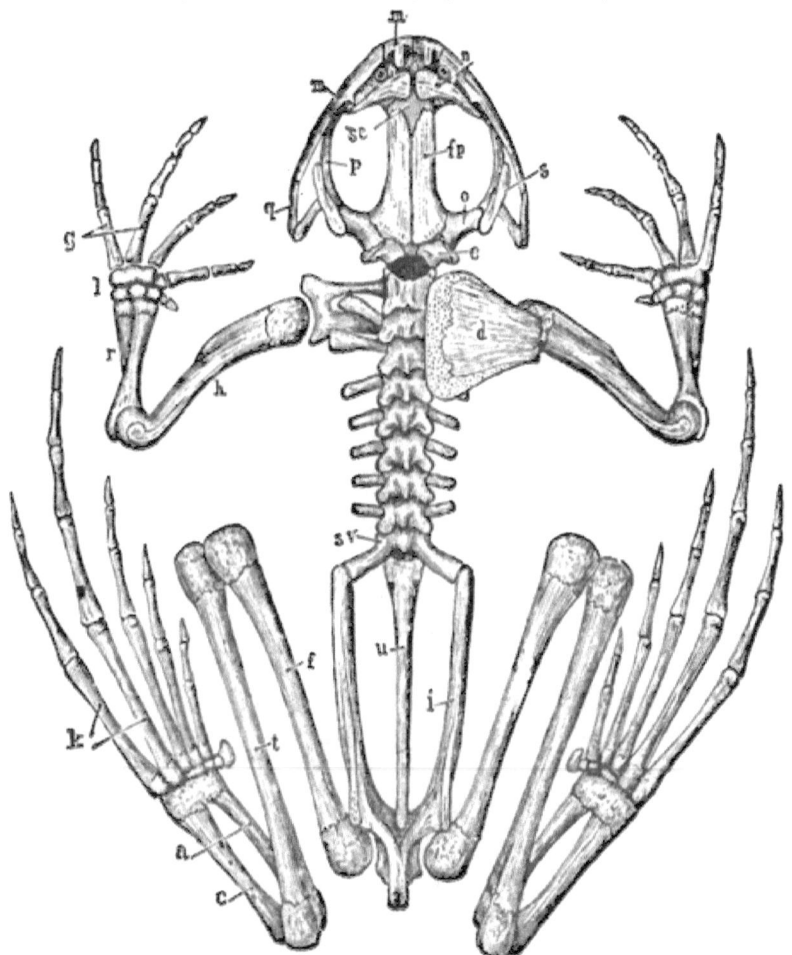

FIG. 165.—SKELETON OF FROG (DORSAL VIEW, WITH LEFT SCAPULA AND SUPRA-SCAPULA REMOVED). (Milnes Marshall.)

a, astragalus (tibiale); *c*, calcaneum (fibulare); *d*, suprascapula; *e*, ex-occipital; *f*, femur; *fp*, parieto-frontal; *g*, metacarpals; *h*, humerus; *i*, ilium; *k*, metatarsals; *l*, carpus; *m*, maxilla; *n*, nasal; *o*, prootic; *p*, pterygoid; *pm*, premaxilla; *q*, quadrato-jugal; *r*, radio-ulna; *s*, squamosal; *se*, sphenethmoid; *sv*, sacral vertebra; *t*, tibio-fibula; *u*, urostyle.

bones, the **premaxillæ**, which form the most anterior part of the upper jaw. The premaxillæ articulate with two bent rod-like bones, the **maxillæ**, which pass backwards along either side. Both maxillæ and premaxillæ carry teeth. The hoop is completed by a triradiate bone, the **pterygoid**, which, with the assistance of a small bone, the quadrato-jugal, unites the posterior end of the maxilla to the skull, the whole being steadied by a hammer-shaped bone, the **squamosal**, which passes from the point of junction of the quadrato-jugal and pterygoid to the upper portion of the ear-capsule.

The **mandible**, or lower jaw, consists of two halves or **rami**, each of which again is made up of four smaller bones. The rami articulate with the quadrato-jugal on either side.

There is also an arch (the **hyoid**), composed, partly of cartilage, partly of bone, supporting the tongue and throat.

The skull, and indeed the entire skeleton, of the embryo is at first composed of cartilage only, part of which afterwards becomes altered into bone, part remaining cartilaginous during life. Not only in the amphibian skull, but also in the skull of the higher animals, certain bones are developed from the skin, **membrane bones**, either over the parts which have remained cartilaginous or in addition to the cartilage bones already formed. Many of the bones forming the framework of the jaws are membrane bones.

Turning now to the **appendicular skeleton** we note first that it consists, as already stated, of two hoops or girdles to which are attached the fore and hind limbs respectively. These are known as the pectoral and pelvic girdles; both are composed essentially of six bones or their cartilaginous representatives. The fore and hind limbs are also built on the same type.

Pectoral girdle and fore-limb.—The pectoral girdle consists of a median ventral bar of bone, the **sternum**, terminated posteriorly by a plate of cartilage known as the **xiphi-sternum**. Springing on either side from the median line anteriorly to the sternum are a pair of strong bones, the **coracoids**, and anterior to these another pair of more delicate rod-like bones, the **clavicles**. Attached to the outer ends of the clavicle and coracoid of either side is a broad flat bone, the **scapula**, also tipped by a plate of cartilage known as the **supra-scapula**; while in the middle line and in front of the inner union of the clavicles there lies a small osseous rod, the **omo-sternum**, continued forward as a delicate cartilaginous plate. The six bones above referred to as forming the essential elements of the pectoral girdle are the two clavicles, two coracoids, and the two scapulæ, which form a half-circle with the cartilaginous supra-scapulæ arching over the back. At the junction of the coracoid and scapula there is a circular depression, or **glenoid** cavity, into which the upper end of the fore-limb fits.

A typical **fore-limb** consists of three parts: the **arm**, composed of one bone, the **humerus**; the **fore-arm**, of two bones jointed to the lower end of the humerus, the **ulna** externally, and the **radius** internally; and a **hand**, composed of many bones, forming proximally the **wrist** and distally the fingers, or **digits**. Typically, the wrist, or **carpus**, consists of an **ulnare** articulating with the distal end of the **ulna**, a **radiale** articulating with the distal end of the radius, and a small intermediate bone, the **intermedium**. In front of the intermedium is a larger nodule, the **centrale**, and beyond it five small bones, the **carpals**. To these five carpals are articulated the five jointed digits, each made up of a **metacarpal** and several **phalanges**. In the frog considerable modification has taken place. In the first instance the radius and ulna have fused to form one bone, though the distinction is still visible at the extremities, while the nine bones of the typical carpus has been reduced to six and the first digit is rudimentary.

Pelvic girdle and hind-limb.—In the pelvic girdle there is nothing corresponding to the sternum, though the other elements of the pectoral girdle are represented. The scapula is represented by a long curved bone on either side, the **ilium**, placed dorsally and having its free end attached to the transverse process of the last free vertebra. The ilium is fused posteriorly to the ilium of the other side, and the two ilia together with the representatives of the clavicles and coracoids of the pectoral girdle form a disc, the whole structure being not unlike the 'merrythought' of a fowl. The posterior part of the disc is composed of two fused **ischia**, the homologues of the coracoids, while the anterior and ventral portion is formed of the two **pubes**, or the homologues of the clavicles. A union such as this between two bones typically free by means of cartilage is known as a **symphysis**. As in the pectoral girdle, at the junction of the ilium and ischium there is a concavity into which the upper end of the hind-limb fits. Here, however, the pubes take part in the formation of the cavity, which is known as the **acetabulum**.

In the typical hind-limb the same arrangement of parts is maintained as in the fore-limb, though the bones are known by different names. The **leg** is formed by the **femur**, whose proximal end rotates in the acetabulum and whose distal end articulates with the proximal end of the **fore-leg**. The fore-leg like the fore-arm is formed of two long bones, the **fibula** externally and the **tibia** internally. These in turn articulate with a **fibulare** and a **tibiale**, between which lies an **intermedium**. A **centrale** and five **tarsals** complete the ankle, or **tarsus**. To the five tarsals are articulated five **metatarsals**, which with a number of **phalanges** form the five **digits** of the hind-limb. As in the case of the fore-limb, so also the hind-limb of the frog deviates considerably from the typical limb just described. The tibia and fibula are fused together, as were the radius and ulna ; the tibiale and fibulare are long bones and are fused at their extremities, their relatively great size accounting for the extent of the sole of the frog's foot. The other bones of the tarsus are only present in the form of two partly cartilaginous, partly osseous nodules. The five metatarsals and their phalanges are, however, well developed.

Metazoa—Rana.

Having briefly sketched the essential features in the structure of the skeleton we must now pass to the nervous system, which has been already described as lying in the brain-box and the canal formed by the apposition of the neural arches of the vertebræ.

The nervous system.—The nervous system of the frog shows a very great advance in differentiation upon that of

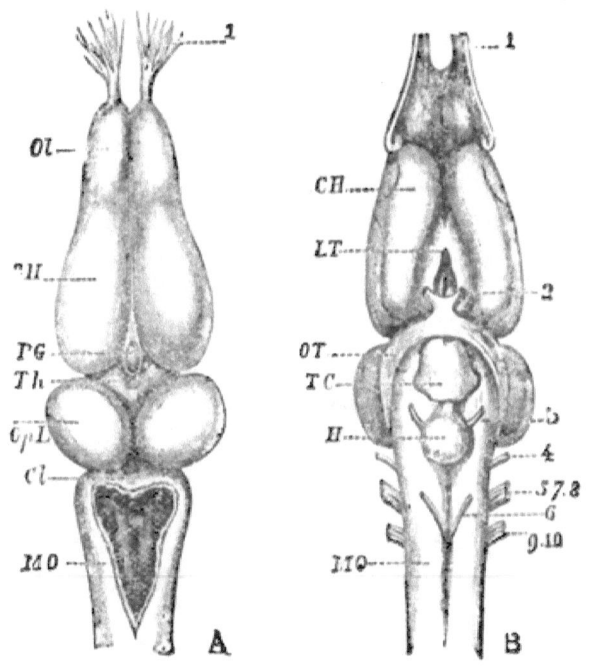

Fig. 166.—Brain of frog, A, from above; B, from below. (Ecker.)

1, olfactory nerves; Ol, olfactory lobes; CH, cerebral hemispheres; LT, lamina terminalis; Th, thalamencephalon; PG, pineal gland; OpL, optic lobes; Cl, cerebellum; MO, medulla oblongata; 2, optic nerves; OT, optic chiasma; H, pituitary body; 3–10, cerebral nerves.

Amphioxus. In the amphibian brain, indeed, we have represented all the most important parts of the brain of the mammal (dog, rabbit, &c.). The nervous system consists of a spinal cord enlarged anteriorly to form the brain, the former being lodged in the neural canal of the vertebral column, the latter in the cavity of the skull, or cranium. From both are given off many nerves, known as cranial and spinal nerves, according as they arise from the brain itself or from the spinal cord.

The brain.—The brain consists essentially of three portions—a fore-brain, a mid-brain, and a hind-brain.

The **fore-brain** is composed of two portions, the **prosencephalon** and the **thalamencephalon**. The former consists of two pear-shaped masses, narrowed anteriorly and known as the **cerebral hemispheres**. From these there project two smaller lobes, the **olfactory lobes**. The thalamencephalon is much smaller and consists dorsally of a thin plate uniting the two laterally placed **optic thalami**, from which in turn on the ventral surface spring two broad bands of nerve-tissue known as the **optic tracts**. The optic tracts cross each other and form what is known as the **optic chiasma**. Posteriorly from the dorsal surface of the thalamencephalon there springs a small vascular prominence known as the **pineal gland**. This structure has recently been shown to be in all probability the rudiment of an eye. Ventrally also a similar structure, the **infundibulum**, terminated by a small mass of tissue, the **pituitary body**, arises from the posterior portion of the thalamencephalon. The pituitary body is, however, of totally different origin from the pineal gland, and is indeed a bud from the roof of the mouth, which becomes separated off and united to the base of the brain in the course of development.

The **mid-brain** is composed dorsally of two large prominences—the **optic lobes**, connected ventrally by a broad belt of nerve-tissue. The mid-brain is also known as the **mesencephalon**.

The **hind-brain**, like the fore-brain, consists of two regions—the **metencephalon**, or **cerebellum**, and the **myelencephalon**, or **medulla oblongata**. These two parts cannot be easily distinguished from each other on the ventral aspect; but dorsally the metencephalon is coincident with a ridge of nerve-tissue, the cerebellum, which overlaps

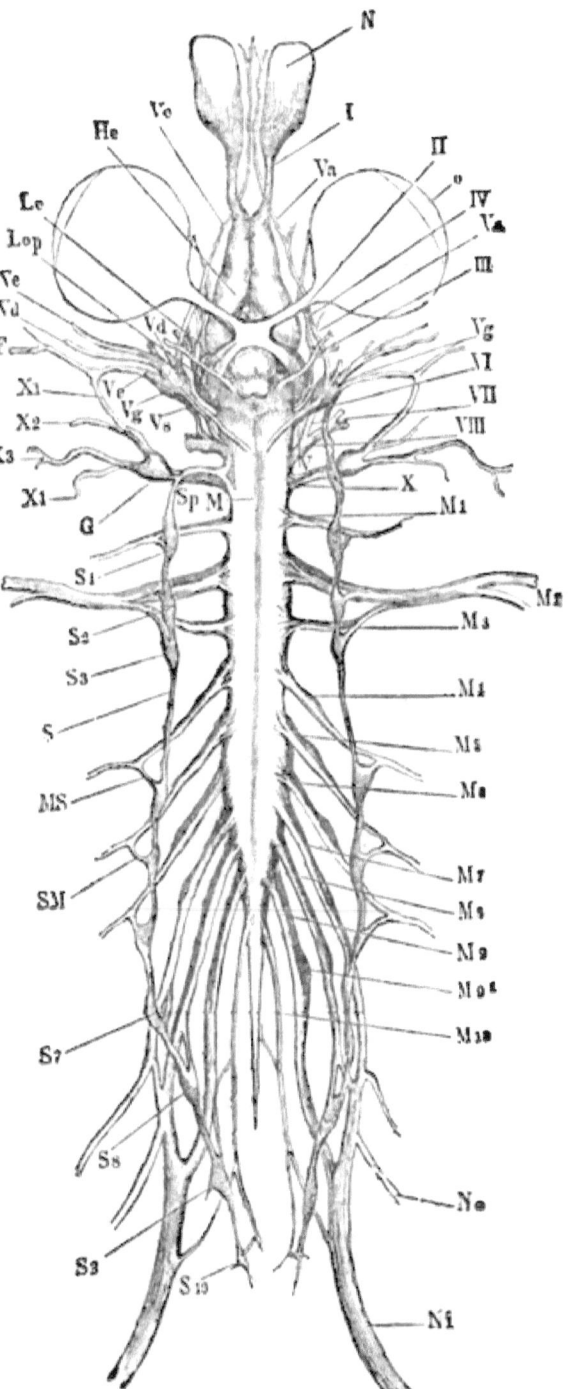

FIG. 167.—NERVOUS SYSTEM OF FROG (VENTRAL ASPECT). (Ecker.)

F, facial nerve; G, ganglion on X; He, cerebrum; Lo, optic tract; Lop, optic lobe; M, boundary between medulla and spinal cord; M 1-10, spinal nerves; Ms, connection between 4th spinal nerve and sympathetic chain; N, nasal sac; Ni, sciatic nerve; No, crural nerve; o, eyeball; S, sympathetic trunk; S 1-10, sympathetic ganglia; Sp, continuation of sympathetic into head. The numbers refer to the cranial nerves (see table on p. 310).

the broad triangular-like area of the myelencephalon, or medulla.

The medulla is continued directly into the **spinal cord, or myelon.** It is relatively of considerable size, and for the greater part of its length is a thick broad belt, with a well marked groove running down its upper or dorsal surface. Its latter third is much thinner and narrower than the rest and terminates in a delicate thread, the **filum terminale,** which lies within the anterior end of the urostyle.

The cranial nerves.—There are ten pairs of cranial nerves, all save the first springing from the ventral aspect of the brain, and, after escaping from the cranium, breaking up into finer branches and becoming distributed to the various organs which it is their duty to supply. They may be tabulated as follows :—

Nerve	Origin	Distribution
I. Olfactory	Olfactory lobes	Nasal sacs (sensory)
II. Optic	Optic chiasma	Eyes (sensory)
III. Oculi-motor	Floor of mesencephalon	Muscles of eye (motor)
IV. Pathetic	Floor of mesencephalon	Muscle of eye (motor)
V. Trigeminal	Floor of myelencephalon	Mandible and maxilla (sensory and motor)
VI. Abducens	Floor of myelencephalon	Muscle of eye (motor)
VII. Facial	Floor of myelencephalon	Palate and face (sensory and motor)
VIII. Auditory	Floor of myelencephalon	Ear (sensory)
IX. Glosso-pharyngeal	Floor of myelencephalon	Tongue (sensory and motor)
X. Vagus, or Pneumogastric	Floor of myelencephalon	Lungs, heart, stomach, and other viscera (sensory and motor)

From the spinal cord also ten pairs of **spinal nerves** are given off. Each nerve arises from the cord by two roots, one dorsal or posterior, the other ventral or anterior. The two roots unite before leaving the neural canal, and the nerve formed by their union passes through one of the **intervertebral foramina,** as the spaces between the several vertebræ are termed. The posterior root, which is known as the sensory root, for a reason to be afterwards explained

(p. 317), has a ganglionic swelling upon it. The first spinal nerve is known as the **hypoglossal**, from the fact that it is distributed to the muscles of the tongue; the next two (**brachial plexus**) supply the fore-limbs; the fourth, fifth, and sixth are distributed to the muscles of the body-wall; the next three go to the hind-limbs and parts in the vicinity;

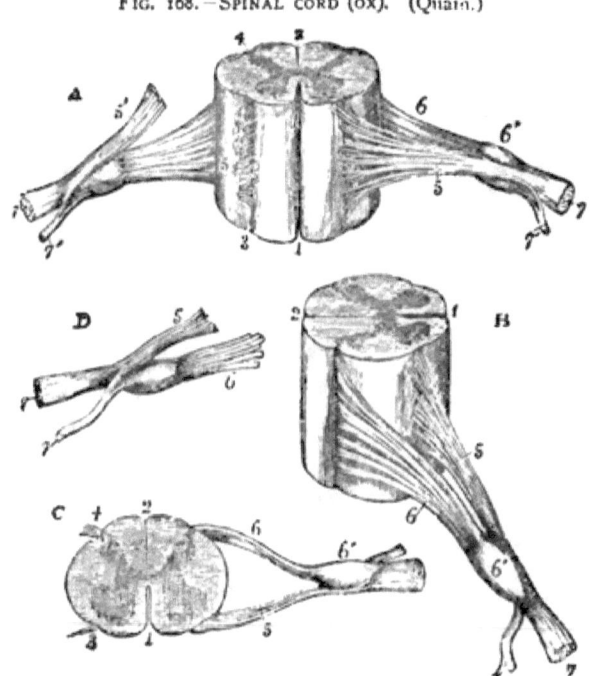

Fig. 168.—Spinal cord (ox). (Quain.)

A, antero-posterior view; B, lateral view; C, transverse section; D, union of the two roots of a spinal nerve. 1, anterior fissure; 2, posterior fissure; 3, origin of anterior root (5); 4, origin of posterior root (6); 6′, ganglion on the posterior root; 7, 7′, sensory and motor nerves.

while the tenth and last supplies the region of the urostyle and cloaca.

In addition to the cerebro-spinal nervous system thus briefly sketched there is another visceral or **sympathetic nervous system**, consisting of a double chain of ganglia connected by commissures to each other and to the cerebro-spinal nerves, and lying in the dorsal region of the cœlom, just beneath the vertebral column, close to the aorta. This system has under its control more especially the intestine and blood-vessels in relation thereto.

Histologically it will be necessary to glance at the distribution of the three elements of the nervous system—the

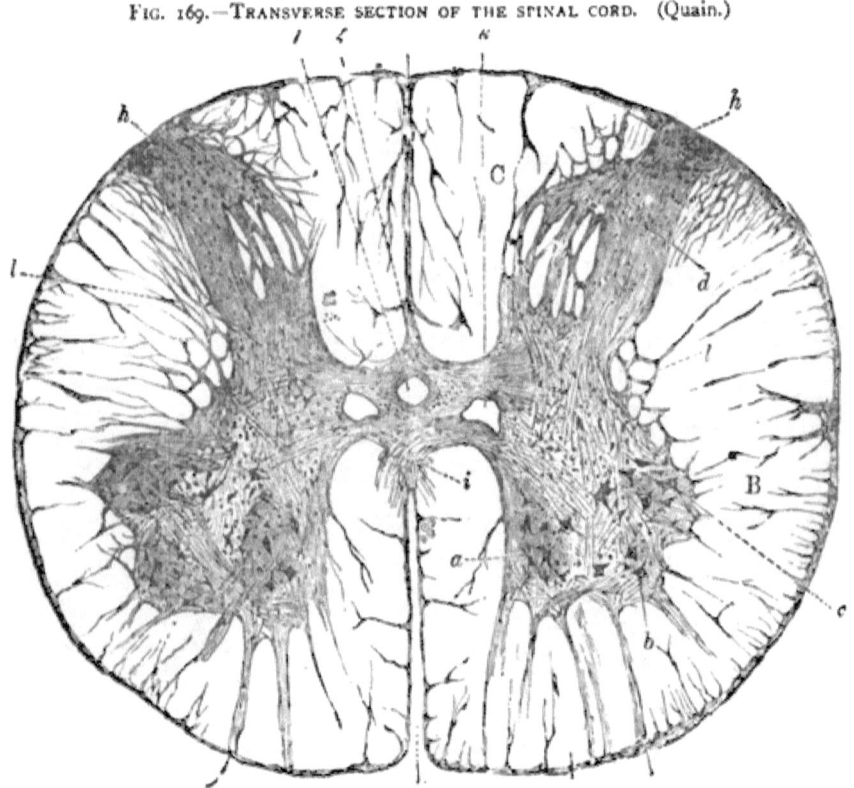

FIG. 169.—TRANSVERSE SECTION OF THE SPINAL CORD. (Quain.)

a, b, c, multipolar nerve-cells in the anterior horn of grey matter; *d*, posterior horn of grey matter; *e*, anterior fissure; *f*, central canal; *g*, posterior commissure of grey matter; *h*, exit of the posterior horn of grey matter; *i*, anterior commissure; *k*, canal in grey matter; *l, l* nerve-fibres.

nerve-fibres, nerve-cells, and connective tissue; and in order to do so it will be sufficient to examine a section of the cerebrum, a section of the spinal cord and of a spinal nerve.

Nerve-tissue with a preponderance of nerve-cells has,

from its appearance under the naked eye, been called **grey matter**; when the nerve-fibres are more abundant, or alone present, the nervous tissue is known as **white matter**. In both white and grey matter there is a considerable amount of connective tissue (**neuroglœa**) present.

A section of the cerebral hemisphere, or cerebellum, shows it to be composed externally of a layer of grey matter — that is, of nerve-cells and neuroglœa — and internally of white matter — that is, of nerve-fibres and neuroglœa. The cerebellum, optic lobes, and other parts of the brain present the same arrangement of elements. A careful examination of the sections of the frog's brain shows that there is a complicated series of spaces and channels in the interior, all of which are continuous with a canal which runs down the centre of the spinal cord.

If a section of the spinal cord be now examined the arrangement of elements will be found to be somewhat different. Here the grey matter occupies the interior and has roughly the form of an H, the central canal just alluded to piercing the middle of the cross-bar. The grey matter is said to have two anterior and two posterior horns, and if the section be taken at the origin of a spinal nerve it will be found that the two roots of the nerve are connected with the anterior and posterior horns respectively. The central canal is lined by ciliated epithelium. Surrounding the grey matter on all sides lies the white matter of the cord, consisting of nerve-fibres and connective tissue and surrounded in turn by the sheath of delicate connective tissue largely supplied with blood-vessels, which is continuous over the entire brain and spinal cord, and which is known as the **pia mater**. The pia mater dips down into the cord anteriorly and posteriorly almost to the transverse band of grey matter, thus nearly dividing the cord into two parts. These two clefts are known as the **anterior** and **posterior fissures**, and it is the mouth of the posterior fissure that gives the grooved appearance to the dorsal aspect of the cord. Externally to the pia mater is a strong protective sheath, which does not follow the pia mater into the fissures: to this the name of **dura mater** is given.

A **nerve** consists of a large number of ultimate nerve-fibres bound together by connective tissue. The connec-

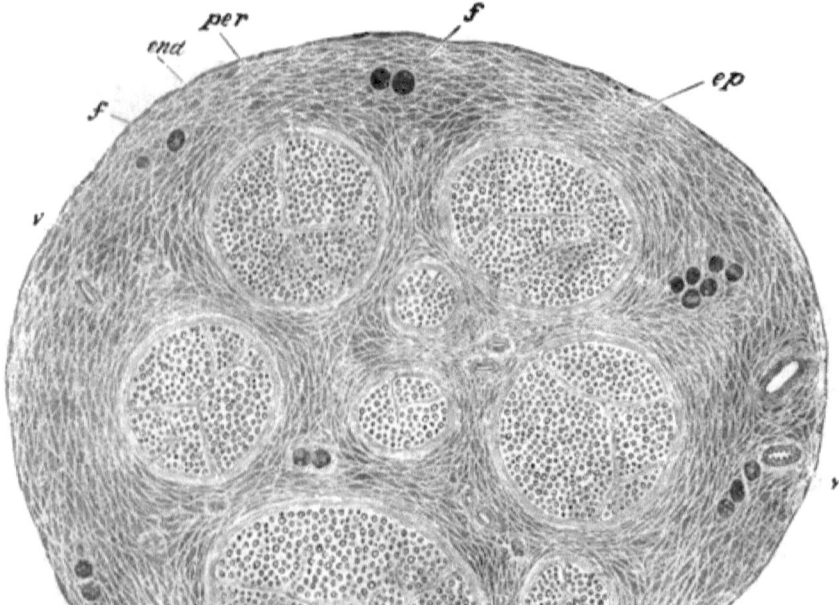

FIG. 170.—TRANSVERSE SECTION OF A LARGE NERVE. (Schäfer.)

v, v, blood-vessels; *end,* endoneurium; *per,* perineurium; *ep,* epineurium.

tive tissue receives different names according as it binds together ultimate nerve-fibres (**endoneurium**), simple bundles of nerve-fibres (**perineurium**), or compound bundles (**epineurium**). An ultimate nerve-fibre consists of an **axial cylinder** of nerve-fibrillæ, surrounded by one or two sheaths. The inner sheath, composed of a fatty substance,

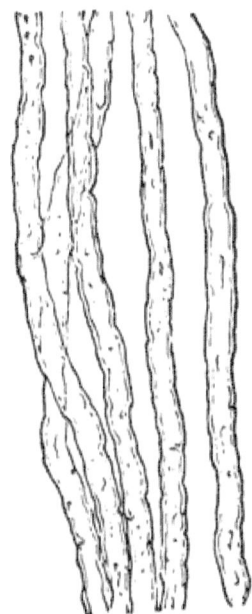

FIG. 171.—NON-MEDULLATED NERVE-FIBRES. (Schäfer.)

FIG. 172.—MEDULLATED NERVE-FIBRES. (Schäfer.)

is spoken of as the **medullary** sheath, and fibres which possess it are spoken of as medullated fibres. Many nerve-fibres, however, are non-medullated, and in that case possess only the outer sheath, or **neurilemma**, which corresponds to the sarcolemma of the muscle-fibre, and with which it is homologous.

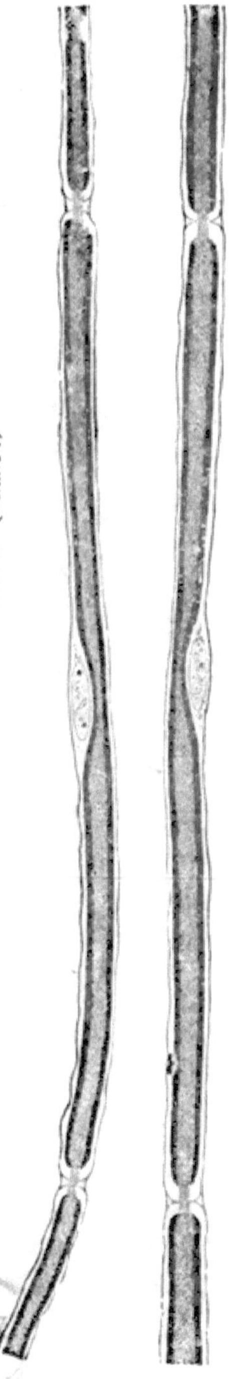

Nerve-cells are extremely variable in size and shape. They are, however, usually branched, and are termed **unipolar**, **bipolar**, or **multipolar**, according to the number of poles or branches they possess. The poles are continuous with the axial cylinders of nerve-fibres. The cells are naked, and the sheaths of the nerve cease before uniting with the nerve-cell.

Before leaving the nervous system it will be necessary to indicate briefly the **functions** of the various parts of that system. The brain, as a whole, may be looked upon as the grand centre for the originating and governing of the

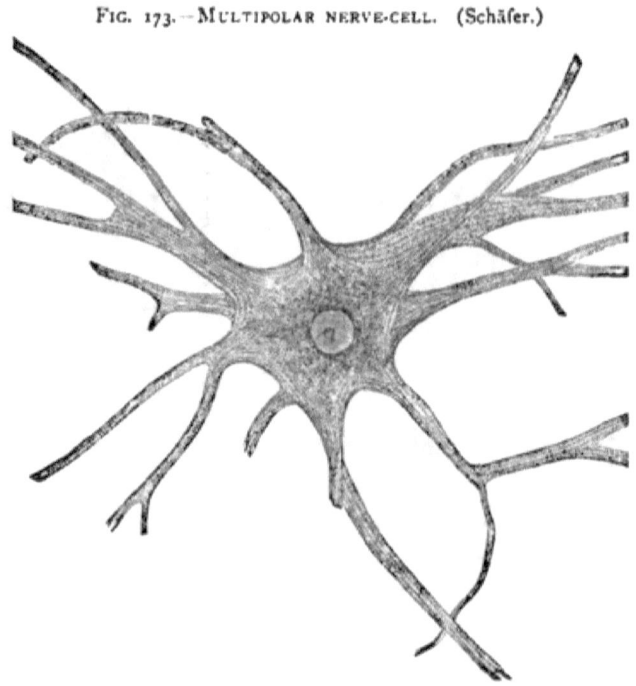

FIG. 173.—MULTIPOLAR NERVE-CELL. (Schäfer.)

various actions of the body, as well as for the reception of all impressions derived from the body itself or from the external world; whilst the nerves are the organs for transmitting these impulses and impressions from and to the brain, or sensorium. A little reflection will enable us to analyse the nervous messages into at least two chief classes—**centrifugal** or **motor impulses**, and **centripetal** or **sensory impulses**. To these, however, we must add impulses of at least two other kinds, viz. impulses governing the action of glands, and therefore called **secretory**, and those which regulate the phenomena of growth and nutrition of tissues generally; to these latter the name of **trophic** has been given. It is as yet doubtful whether secretory and trophic impulses pass by special nerves devoted to the transmission of such, or travel by nerves which are under other circumstances intrusted with the carriage of motor impulses. We know, however, that sensory impressions do have special nerves devoted to their transport, while motor nerves carry impulses which stimulate to action the muscles to which they are distributed; hence the names of **sensory** and **motor** applied to the **posterior** and **anterior roots** of the spinal nerves to indicate that messages from the outer world travel to the central nervous system by nerve-fibres which enter the cord by the posterior root, and that messages from the central nervous system pass outwards to the muscles (glands and tissues generally) by the anterior roots. Sensory fibres are sometimes spoken of as **afferent**, and motor fibres as **efferent**.

From analogy with the higher animals it is probable that the **cerebrum** has to do with the originating of voluntary actions and with the analysing of sensory impressions. The **cerebellum** is probably the centre for the co-ordinating of muscular movement, while the **optic lobes** and the **olfactory lobes** have to do with the two important sense-organs which the nerves originating from them supply, namely, the eye and the ear.

The **spinal cord** in the higher animals is, in all probability, chiefly a path for the transmission of impulses from the brain outward or from the nerves inwards, though it no doubt also has to do with the government of local movements or simple organic changes not requiring the special interference of the brain. These are known as **reflex actions**, and consist essentially of three separate phenomena, viz. (1) the transmission of a sensory impression along an afferent nerve to a nerve-centre; (2) a metabolic change taking place in the centre, which results in (3) the transmission of a motor or secretory impulse along an efferent fibre to the muscle or gland concerned. For example, the olfactory nerve is a sensory nerve; stimulations of the termination of that nerve in the organ of smell, say by means of the fumes of acetic acid, produces an effect on the nerve-centre (in this case the olfactory lobes) which we term a sensation—something perceived. In ordinary circumstances, i.e. when the brain proper does not interfere, an impulse

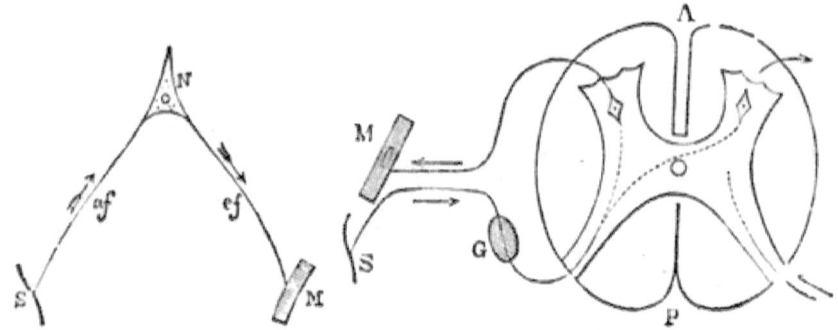

Fig. 174.—Diagram to illustrate reflex action. (Landois and Stirling.)

s, sensitive surface; G, ganglion on sensory nerve; a f, afferent or sensory nerve; e f, efferent or motor nerve; M, muscle fibre; N, nerve-cell; A, P, anterior and posterior aspects of the spinal cord. The arrows indicate the direction of the nerve-impulse.

originating involuntarily in the nerve-centre is carried along a secretory nerve (the glosso pharyngeal) to the salivary glands, causing them immediately to secrete a large quantity of saliva. Numerous instances might be given of reflex actions in different parts of the body; that just given may suffice to illustrate what is meant by the term. That these reflex actions are possible without the intervention of the brain is proved by the fact that even in a decapitated frog stimulation of the sensory-nerve terminations in the foot is at once followed by the withdrawal of the foot from the source of irritation.

We must now briefly touch on the terminations of the special sensory nerves connected with the senses of touch, taste, smell, hearing, and sight. First of all we may begin with the general statement that the ultimate fibrillæ of all these nerves are in the long run in direct connection with more or less modified epithelial cells.

Touch.—The organ of touch is the **skin**, and in it fine nerve-fibres are abundantly distributed, and their ultimate

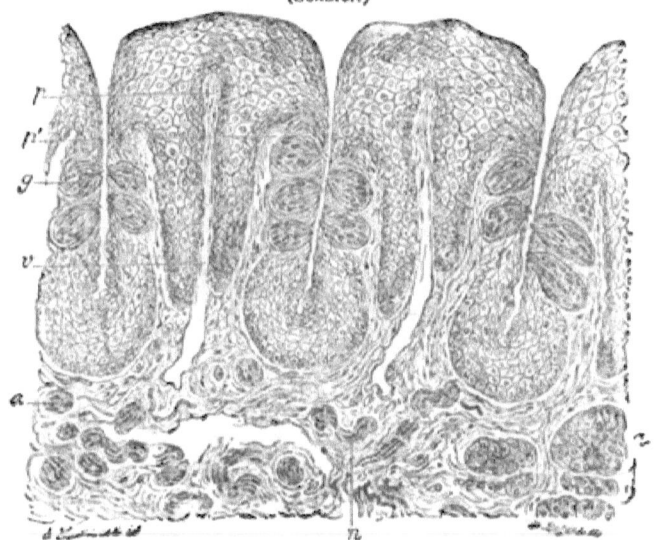

FIG. 175. CIRCUMVALLATE PAPILLÆ FROM THE TONGUE OF THE CAT. (Schäfer.)

a, n, transverse and longitudinal sections of nerves in the dermis; *v*, lymphatic in a papilla of the dermis, *p*; *g*, gustatory body, or taste-bulb.

fibrillæ lie in close relation to the epithelial cells which form the outer layer of the skin, although in the frog no special organs of touch have been discovered.

Taste.—The organ of taste, at least in the higher animals, lies in the **tongue**, and more especially in its posterior third, where there is a limited number of papillæ of very peculiar character. Each consists of a broad columnar projection of dermis and epidermis, surrounded by a groove or ditch: hence the name of **circumvallate** applied to these papillæ. On the sides of this groove are situated numerous flask-shaped depressions, formed of long stave-like epithelial cells, whose outer ends project freely into the vallum, while their inner ends are in communication with the axis cylinder of the glosso-pharyngeal nerve. Soluble substances introduced into the groove must of necessity stimulate the nerve-terminations through the epithelial cells.

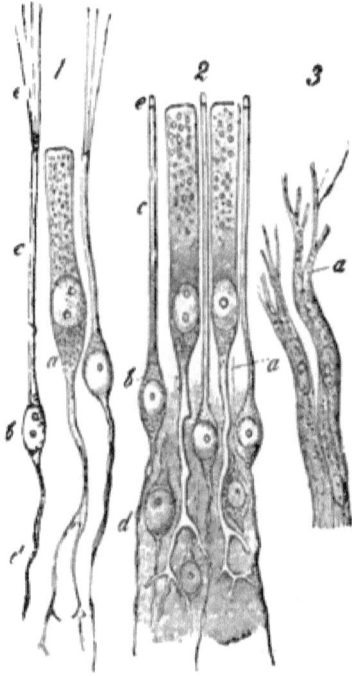

FIG. 175.—SENSORY EPITHELIUM FROM THE NOSE. (Schäfer.)

1 and 2, varieties of olfactory epithelium and supporting cells; 3, termination of the olfactory nerve.

Smell.—The sense of smell is located in the **nose**. The interior of the nasal capsule is ridged in such a manner as to largely increase the surface of the chamber-wall. The terminations of the nerves of smell are distributed over the mucous membrane covering the ridges, and their axis-cylinders end in long spindle-shaped cells, whose pointed free ends project from the surface of the membrane. Air bearing odoriferous particles enters the anterior nares and stimulates the nerve-terminations in its passage over the ridges projecting from the walls of the nasal capsule.

Hearing.—The organ of hearing is much more complicated, though fundamentally the same in principle as the sense-organs already described. Without entering into detail, it will be sufficient to say that the auditory or periotic capsule of the frog contains a cavity, lined by a membranous capsule, which fits it exactly. The membranous capsule, which takes the form of a partially divided vestibule with semicircular canals opening into it, is composed of a framework of connective tissue carrying modified ciliated epithelial cells. These cells are connected with the termina-

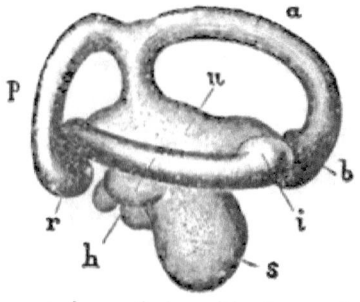

FIG. 177.—THE MEMBRANOUS LINING OF THE RIGHT INTERNAL EAR OF THE FROG FROM THE OUTER ASPECT. (Milnes Marshall.)

a, anterior vertical semicircular canal; *b*, ampulla or swelling on it; *h*, horizontal canal and its ampulla, *i*; *p*, posterior vertical canal and its ampulla, *r*; *s*, sacculus and *u*, utriculus, the two subdivisions of the vestibule.

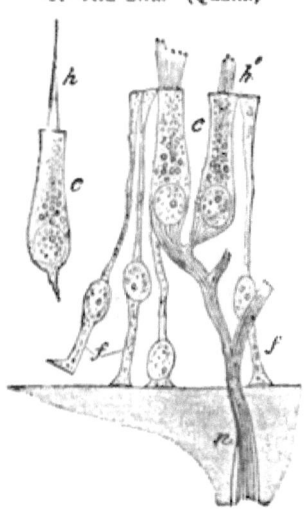

FIG. 178.—SENSORY EPITHELIUM OF THE EAR. (Quain.)

c, c, sensory cells; *f, f*, supporting cells; *n*, nerve; *h, h'*, cilia.

tions of the auditory nerve. The cavity of the capsule is filled with lymph into which the cilia of the cells project. The wall of the cavity is perforated at one point, termed the **fenestra ovalis**, which, however, is closed by a delicate membrane, to which is fastened on its outer side a small rod-like bone, known as the **columella**, whose outer end abuts against the **membrana tympani** already described as visible on either side of the skull behind the eyes. The intermediate chamber (or tympanic cavity) containing the columella communicates with the buccal cavity by a tube, known as the **Eustachian tube**, whose opening has already

Y

been referred to (p. 267). Vibrations of the air cause the membrana tympani to tremble in unison, and those tremblings are, by means of the columella and the membrane covering the fenestra ovalis, communicated to the lymph filling the inner ear, which in its turn stimulates the epithelial cells in connection with the terminations of the auditory nerve.

Sight.—The peripheral terminations of the nerve of sight are more complicated than those of the other sense-organs. The **eye** consists of a strong capsule of fibrous tissue, known posteriorly as the **sclerotic**, anteriorly as the **cornea**. The cornea is transparent, the sclerotic is white and opaque. The capsule is pierced behind by the optic nerve, and is kept in its socket and at the same time moved by six bands of muscle, four of which spring from the upper, under, and two lateral margins of the eye, whilst the remaining two are obliquely placed, one arising from the upper and outer margin, the other from the under and inner margin. The four muscles first mentioned are known as the **superior, inferior, exterior,** and **interior recti**, while the oblique muscles are spoken of as the **superior** and **inferior oblique** respectively. It will be remembered that no less than three out of the ten pairs of cranial nerves were distributed to the muscles of the eye. Their distribution is as follows:— the superior, inferior, and interior recti, and inferior oblique are supplied by the oculi-motor nerve (III.); the exterior rectus is supplied by the abducens (VI.); while the pathetic (IV.) nerve goes to the superior oblique muscle. Within the fibrous capsule there are two chambers, a large posterior and a small anterior. Lining the inner surface of the sclerotic is a highly vascular pigmented membrane, the **choroid**, which separates away from the sclerotic just where the sclerotic becomes continuous with the cornea. It there forms a diaphragm, named the **iris**, crossing the eye from side to side, incomplete, however, in the centre, where a rounded aperture is left, the **pupil**. Behind the iris lies a muscular

FIG. 179.—HORIZONTAL SECTION OF THE RIGHT EYE. (Quain.)

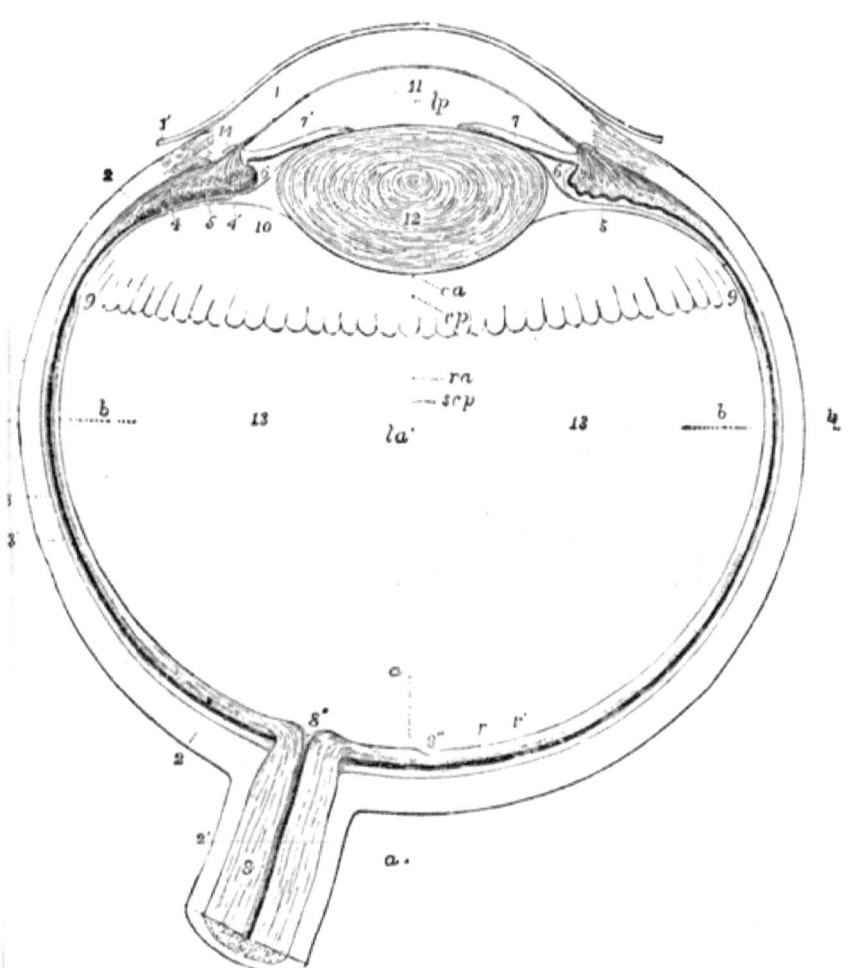

a, a, antero-posterior axis ; *b, b,* lateral axis ; 1, cornea : 2, 2′, sclerotic ; 3, 3′, choroid ; *r, r′,* retina ; 4, ciliary muscle ; 5, ciliary process ; 6, 10, 14, lymph canals ; 7, 7′, iris ; 8, b′, optic nerve ; 8″, point of acutest vision ; 9, crinated zone marking the anterior termination of the retina ; 11, anterior or aqueous chamber ; 12, crystalline lens ; 13, posterior or vitreous chamber.

zone, also continuous with the choroid, known as the **ciliary muscle.** That again is continuous with a ligamentous zone which supports the **crystalline lens.** The lens thus occupies the space immediately behind the pupil, and assists in separating the anterior from the posterior chamber of the eye. Lining the choroid is a very delicate membrane, composed partly of nerve fibres, partly of nerve-cells, arranged in a series of definite layers, supported by very delicate connective tissue. These nervous elements are the terminations of the optic nerve, which enters, as has already been stated, at the back of the optic capsule. The greatly modified epithelial cells, which form the true peripheral endings of the nerve, lie between this nervous layer and the innermost pigmented layer of the choroid, and

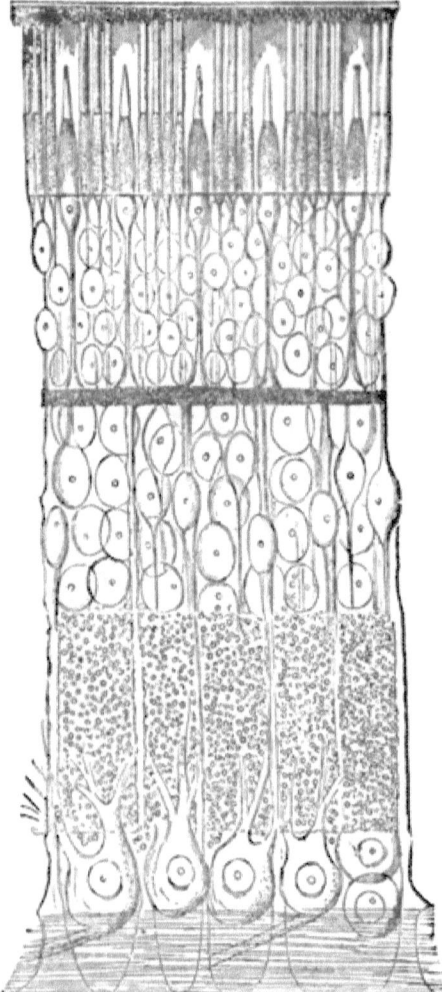

FIG. 180.—VERTICAL SECTION OF RETINA.
(Quain.)

The layer of rods and cones is shown abutting against the pigment layer of the choroid. Numerous granular layers follow, bounded by a layer of nerve-cells and fibres. The layer next the bottom of the page is that which is nearest the centre of the eye.

point towards, or rather have their free ends abutting against, the latter. The nervous layer and the terminal epithelial cells (named the **rods** and **cones** from their appearance) form the **retina**. Lastly the posterior chamber is filled by a gelatinous substance, the **vitreous humour**, while the anterior chamber similarly contains a more watery fluid allied to lymph, the **aqueous humour**. A ray of light transmitted through the cornea and aqueous humour is focussed on the retina by means of the crystalline lens. The curvature, and therefore the focussing power of the lens, can

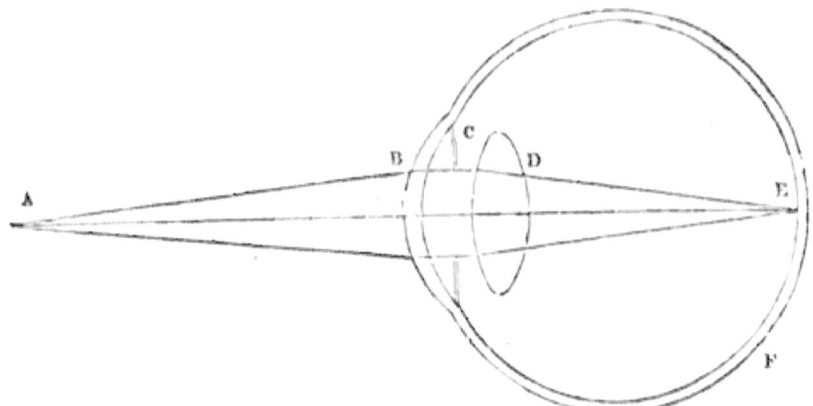

FIG. 181.—ILLUSTRATION OF THE METHOD OF FOCUSSING RAYS OF LIGHT ON THE RETINA. (Landois and Stirling.)

A, point of origin of rays; B, cornea; C, iris; D, lens; E, point of acutest vision; F, sclerotic.

be altered to suit rays coming from different distances by means of the ciliary muscle. The iris is also provided with radiating and circular muscle-fibres by means of which the size of the pupil can be altered so as to allow of the entrance of more or less light according to circumstances. The rays pass through the vitreous humour and penetrating the retina are reflected back from the choroid on the rods and cones. The excitement produced there is carried by means of the elements in the nervous layer of the retina to the optic nerve itself, and by that means to the brain.

We have now briefly surveyed the chief points in which one of the higher animals shows advance in organisation as compared with the types already discussed, so far as individual life is concerned. We have still left the organs concerned in the maintenance of tribal life, viz. the **reproductive system**.

This system is a comparatively simple one, though in the course of development considerable modification has taken place. The sexes are distinct. The **spermaria** (testes) in the male consist of a pair of white elliptical masses lying in close relation to the ventral surface of the kidneys and connected to these organs by mesentery (**mesorchium**), and bearing at their anterior ends lobed fatty masses, the **corpora adiposa** (fig. 157). The spermaria of the frog differ in one important point from the spermaria of the majority of animals, viz. in that the vas deferens or special duct for the conveyance of the sperms to the exterior is also the ureter. The mesorchium supports a large number of **vasa efferentia**, or efferent vessels, which transfer the sperms from the spermaria to the kidney, whence they escape into the cloaca by the ureter, which for that reason may be known as the **urino-genital duct**. (From a developmental point of view, however, the ureter is wanting, and the vas deferens carries the products both of the kidneys and spermaria to the exterior.)

In the female there are two **ovaria**, which at the breeding season are often of very large size, connected to the body-wall by peritoneum, and also provided with **corpora adiposa**. The walls of the ovaria are very thin, and, when the ova, which are of large size, are ripe, rupture readily, shedding their contents into the cœlom. The **oviducts** —which are quite unconnected with the ovaria—are of great length, and are stowed away in the cœlom in complicated coils. Each oviduct opens anteriorly beneath the lungs by a thick-lipped aperture, into which the ova find their way in a manner not understood. They are then forced down to the cloaca by the rhythmic contractions of the muscular fibres in the wall of the oviduct, while at the same time glands in the upper region of the duct coat the ova with an albuminous substance which swells readily in water. The ova, as they are shed from the cloacal aperture, are fertilised by sperms from the male.

Before describing the subsequent developmental changes which the fertilised ovum undergoes it will be necessary to glance at the origin and development of the sperms and ova themselves, and also at the changes which take place in the ovum before and in the act of fertilisation.

Both kinds of reproductive glands are at first precisely similar; they both originate from mesoblast (p. 249), and both consist of what is known as **germinal epithelium**.

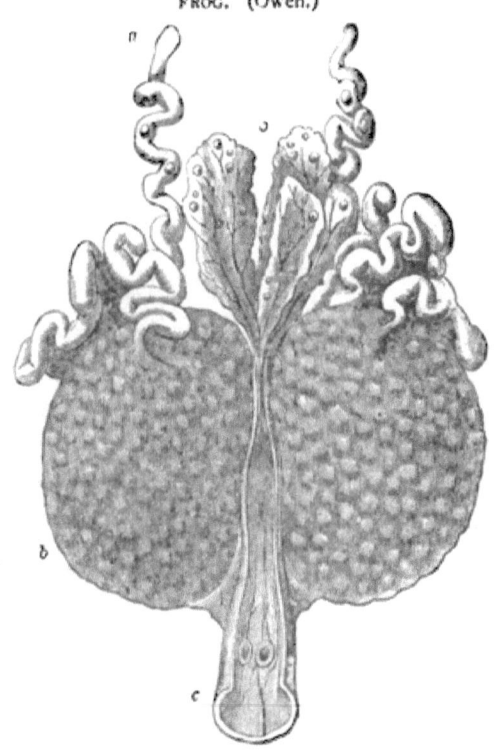

FIG. 182. — FEMALE REPRODUCTIVE ORGANS OF THE FROG. (Owen.)

a, oviduct; *o*, ovaries; *b*, swollen end of the oviduct with fertilised ova; *c*, oviducal outlets into the cloaca.

In the male this epithelium arranges itself in the form of a mass of convoluted tubules, which are bound together by connective tissue. The cells lining these tubules are **spermatospores**, or cells capable of forming sperms. Each sperm originates as a bud (**spermatoblast**) from the spermatospore, the bud or daughter-cell having its nucleus transformed into the head, while the cell-protoplasm becomes the vibratile tail of the sperm.

No tubules are formed in the ovarium; the outer cells of the **germinal epithelium** become transformed into the **ovarian wall**, while the central cells become **ova**. The ripe ovum differs from the germinal cell or primitive ovum in the possession of a cell-wall, the **vitelline membrane**, and in having a large development of oil-globules in one region, the pure protoplasm (with the nucleus) tending to aggregate towards one side of the ovum. Such an accumulation of fat-granules is known as **yolk**, and it is much more

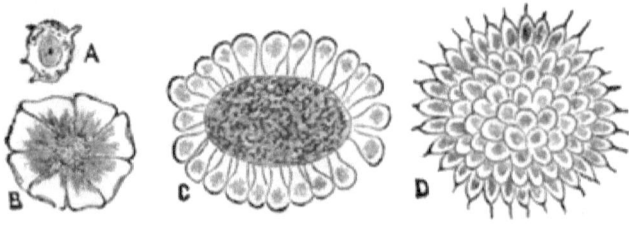

FIG. 183.—DEVELOPMENT OF SPERM IN THE EARTHWORM. (Blomfield)

FIG. 184.—SPERM OF FROG. (Owen.)

A, spermatospore; B, eight young spermatoblasts; C, numerous spermatoblasts; D, spermatoblasts developing into sperms.

abundant in the ova of some forms (e.g. the fowl) than in the frog. Before fertilisation takes place the nucleus of the ovum undergoes karyokinesis (p. 78) and segments, one half remaining as the nucleus of the ovum, the other half being extruded and forming the so-called **polar body** (fig. 186). A second polar body is then extruded in the same manner. Only one sperm fuses with the ovum, and its nucleus (known as the **male pronucleus**) unites with the new nucleus of the ovum (to which the term **female pronucleus** has been given). When the fusion is complete the ovum has been fertilised, viz. has become an embryo. Segmentation then commences, the entire ovum undergoing division. Two cells, therefore, result, one half of each, however, owing to the distribution of the yolk, being more protoplasmic than the other. Occasionally (as in the bird) the relative abundance of yolk and comparative absence of protoplasm in that section of the ovum prevent the segmentation being complete, that is to say, only the protoplasmic part of the ovum undergoes segmentation, while the yolk remains passive and acts as a store of food-matter for the embryo which will develop from the more protoplasmic section. When segmentation is complete, as in the frog, it is spoken of as **holoblastic**; when it is incomplete, as in the fowl, it is spoken of as **meroblastic**. The yolk portion of the frog's ovum divides much more slowly than the protoplasmic, so that as a final result of the division a mass of cells is formed, small and very numerous at the protoplasmic, large and fewer at the yolk end. This will be best understood by reference to fig. 187. The next change which takes place consists in the gradual covering of the large slowly dividing cells by the rapidly developing protoplasmic cells, until in the end the former become entirely hidden save at one spot, the **blastopore**. Although no actual invagination takes place as in *Amphioxus*, yet it is not difficult to see the homologies of the parts of the embryo, or the similarity of the phenomena in the two cases. The small-celled outer part is obviously **epiblast**

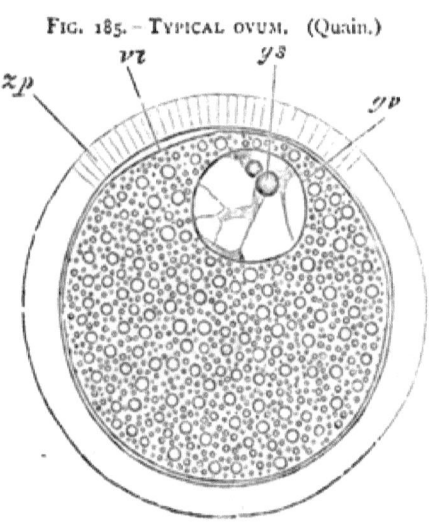

FIG. 185.—TYPICAL OVUM. (Quain.)

zp, cell-wall; vi, protoplasm with fat-granules; gv, nucleus; gs, nucleolus.

and comparable to the outer layer of the gastrula in *Amphioxus*, the large enclosed cells being comparable to the inner layer of the gastrula, though they do not take the same share in the formation of the alimentary canal as in the case of *Amphioxus*. The small **segmentation cavity** also is left for a time between the two layers in the frog embryo. This, however, soon becomes obliterated. The blastopore is present in both, though formed rather as a

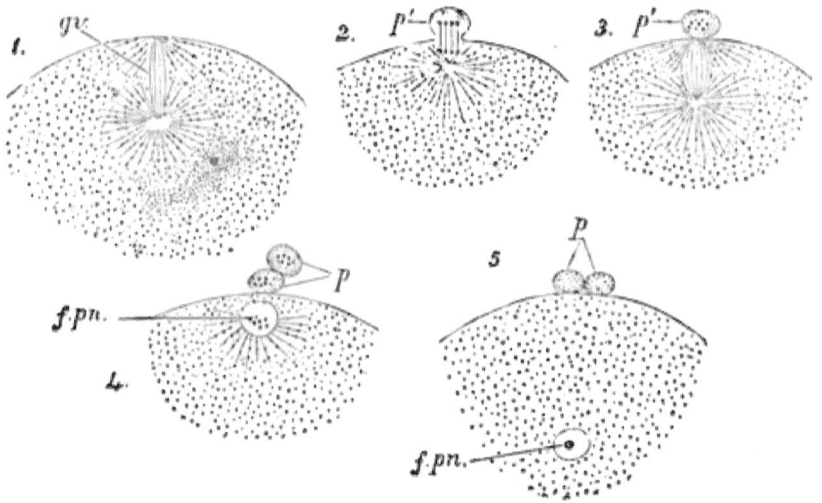

FIG. 186.—FORMATION OF POLAR BODIES FROM THE UNFERTILISED OVUM. (Quain.)

1, segmentation of nucleus and formation of nuclear spindle, *g.v.*; 2, 3, extrusion of first polar body, *p'*; 4, 5, extrusion of two polar bodies and formation of female pronucleus, *f.pn.*

consequence of the activity of the epiblast than as a result of the sinking in of the hypoblast. It is plugged up in the frog.

Before the epiblastic cells have enclosed the yolk-cells a ridge or lip of epiblast arises at the margin of the blastopore, and, pushing its way backward, roofs over a cavity whose floor is formed by the yolk-cells. This cavity is the **mesenteron**, and the layer of epiblastic origin which forms its roof becomes, therefore, **hypoblast**. At the same time between the epiblast and hypoblast above, and the epiblast and yoke-cells on the other side, several layers of cells are formed—the **mesoblast**. Lastly, the floor of the mesen-

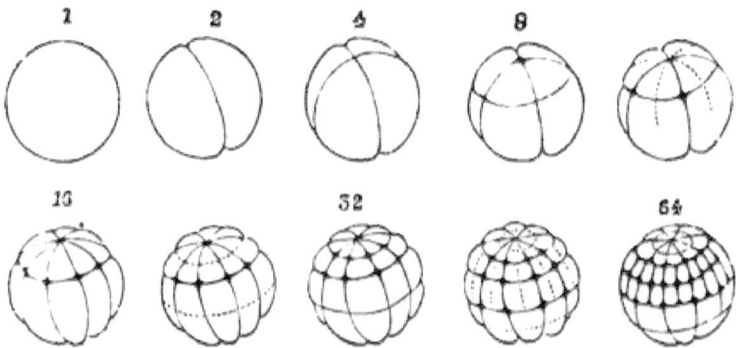

FIG. 187. STAGES IN THE DIVISION OF THE FROG'S OVUM. (Ecker.)

teron is formed partly of hypoblast cells derived from the superficial cells of the yolk, and partly of an ingrowth of epiblast. The only difference, therefore, at this stage between the embryo of *Amphioxus* and that of *Rana* lies in the possession by the latter of a quantity of food-yolk (afterwards absorbed), the presence of which to a certain extent alters the shape of the embryo and renders the stages in its development rather more difficult to follow.

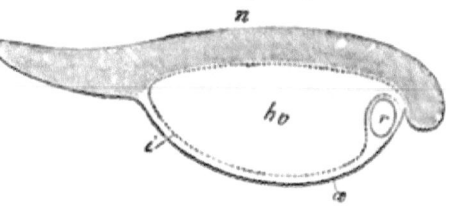

FIG. 188.—DIAGRAMMATIC LONGITUDINAL SECTION OF EMBRYO. (Owen.)

n, neuro-vertebral axis; *a, i*, layers of the abdominal wall; *r*, heart; *hv*, yolk.

It is unnecessary to follow the various changes in the development of the embryo in detail here; we may rather conclude this section by a brief consideration of the mode of origin of the system of the adult which shows the greatest amount of differentiation, viz. the nervous system and by summarising the very remarkable changes undergone by the embryo after it has been hatched.

The development of the brain.—The nervous system of the frog originates somewhat similarly to that of *Amphioxus*, save that in the former the neural canal is formed entirely by the laminæ dorsales. The anterior blind end of this canal becomes swollen so as to form three so-called cerebral vesicles, the walls of which become differentiated into the fore-, mid-, and hind-brains, while their cavities are represented by chambers already referred to as present in the fully developed brain. From the first cerebral vesicle a hollow bud is given off on either side to form the cerebral hemispheres, the vesicle itself becoming the cavity of the thalamencephalon; its cavity is known as the third ventricle. The walls of the second cerebral vesicle differentiate to form the optic lobes; its cavity becomes a narrow channel known as the iter. The walls of the hind-brain develop into the cerebellum and medulla oblongata, while its cavity, into which opens the iter anteriorly and the central canal of the spinal column posteriorly, is spoken of as the fourth ventricle.

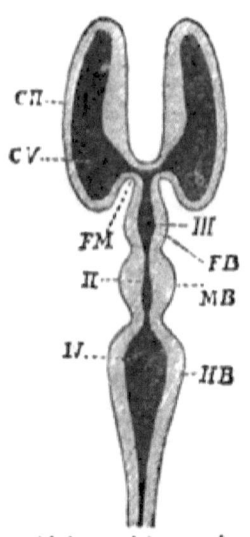

FIG. 189.—VENTRICLES OF THE BRAIN. (Jeffrey Bell.)

III, third ventricle; II, iter; CH, cerebral hemispheres; CV, their cavity; FM, passage from third ventricle to cavity of cerebral hemisphere; FB, fore-brain; MB, mid-brain; HB, hind-brain.

Metamorphosis.—The young of the frog after it has escaped from its vitelline membrane is known as a **tadpole**, and differs very markedly from the adult frog in the general contour of the body. The head is not well differentiated from the body, and there is a long tail, by the rhythmic contractions of which movements of the body as a whole are effected. There are at first no limbs. The mouth is round and sucker-like, and quite unlike the wide gape so characteristic of the adult. From the sides of the neck project three pairs of **external gills** (branchiæ), prolongations, in short, of the vascular membrane covering the branchial arches of *Amphioxus*. By them respiration is effected just as in that type, for the lungs have not yet been developed. Subsequently the gills become covered over by a fold of skin, though a communication with the exterior is still maintained late in embryonic life. Respiration is carried on by means of the gills, which are now

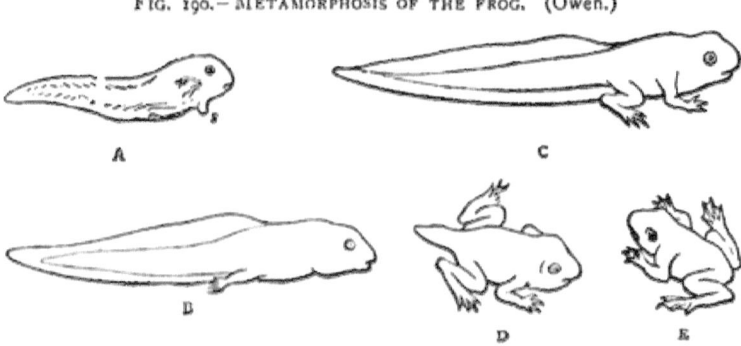

FIG. 190.—METAMORPHOSIS OF THE FROG. (Owen.)

much reduced in size and hidden beneath the fold in a sort of branchial chamber comparable with the atrial cavity of *Amphioxus*. The lungs are then developed as buds from the alimentary canal, and the blood-stream is carried to their walls by means of the pulmonary artery. The hindlimbs are the first to appear, springing from the origin of the tail. Concomitantly with the development of the hindlimbs the tail atrophies (i.e. becomes absorbed); the forelimbs make their appearance from beneath the membrane covering the branchiæ. The branchial slits close, and the gills atrophy also, the entire respiration being now undertaken by the lungs. Finally the frog becomes a truly carnivorous animal, for the tadpole is only partly so. This change involves a certain amount of modification in the length and character of the alimentary canal, for that organ in the carnivora is relatively shorter than in the herbivora.

The entire series of changes thus briefly summarised takes two to six months according to the temperature, being longer in cold and shorter in warm weather. The first fortnight or so of the embryonic life is spent within the egg-membrane; the metamorphosis, however, is gone through after hatching in fresh water.

It will be noted that that metamorphosis consists in the gradual alteration of a herbivorous aquatic animal, breathing of necessity by means of gills, into a carnivorous terrestrial creature, breathing by means of lungs though capable of enduring without injury prolonged immersion. The title of amphibian is therefore fully justified, and the early life-history of the frog thus forms one of the most interesting cases of development known to us, although in many respects special in its character and confined to the group of which it is a representative.

An examination of the embryonic histories of higher types, as we have already hinted (p. 53), shows many interesting transition stages, pointing to genealogical relationships with a primitive chordate type. The possession of branchial arches and clefts, a tail more or less rudimentary, certain transitory phases in the formation of the circulatory system, and such like, are here alluded to. For a detailed consideration of these and similar phenomena, and indeed for many details with regard to the structure and life-history of the frog itself, reference must be made to zoological textbooks. The above sketch of the organisation of the frog will have served its purpose if it show how from such a simple typical form as *Amphioxus* it is possible to derive an organism as complicated as that which we have been considering. We shall find in the next and concluding section that the main principles we have already laid down are true, not only morphologically, but physiologically as well; that, in short, the key to the understanding of the structure and life-history of animals, as of plants, is morphological and physiological differentiation of a primitively simple or generalised type.

SECTION III.—GENERAL PHYSIOLOGY OF ANIMALS.

In our study of plants we found it advisable to devote a section to a general survey of the subject of physiology, or the mode in which the various organs of the plant performed their functions, and the part each played in the general phenomena of life. In the preceding survey of the chief points in the organisation of the representatives of the Metazoa which we have chosen as typical, physiology has been incidentally dealt with in connection with morphology. A section may, however, with profit be devoted to a general summary of the principles of animal physiology in particular, and the comparison of animal with plant physiology.

We may begin our review by noting that the fundamental principles of plant and animal physiology are the same. In both we have an organism essentially composed of protoplasm, subdivided into cells which are again modified in various ways according to the special function or functions they have to perform. Protoplasm, in short, as already stated (p. 33), is a highly complex store of potential energy, in virtue of the possession of which the plant or animal is able to perform certain duties related to the maintenance, partly of tribal, partly of individual life. Since the phenomena which characterise animal life are manifested only as a result of the decomposition of some of these protoplasmic compounds, so that a certain amount of potential energy becomes kinetic, it follows that, as in the case of the plant, the physiology of an animal has two aspects: first, the anabolic or constructive aspect; and secondly, the katabolic or destructive aspect. In the former the formation of new protoplasm (nutrition and assimilation) has to be considered; in the latter, the disintegration of protoplasm and the various phenomena (locomotion, secretion, nervation, &c.) which take place in consequence of that disintegration are the subjects of consideration.

Anabolism.—The first great point of difference which may be noted between the physiology of the plant and that of the animal is the nature of the food-supply in the latter. In the plant (p 190) we found that the food consisted of chemical elements or exceedingly simple compounds, such as carbonic acid, water, salts of nitric acid, &c.; in the animal, though water and many simple salts are employed as food accessories, yet the essential food-stuffs are derived from already formed products of anabolism. In the long-run all animals are dependent (p. 49) on the plant world for food. Without the assistance of green plants the inorganic constituents found in the environment could not be built up, for the animal, as we have seen, has no power to integrate such simple bodies into protoplasm. The most it can do is to modify and assimilate already formed compounds, employing water and simple salts as accessories. The popular distinction, therefore, of animals into **carnivorous** and **herbivorous** is only superficially correct, since herbivors, on which the carnivors prey, are directly dependent on the plant world for food.

Anabolism in the animal may be said to consist of the following processes :—

(*a*) **Mastication.**—By the assistance of the teeth, tongue, and muscles of the buccal cavity in the higher forms, or by the gizzard or the masticatory organ of the lower animals, the food, whether it be animal or vegetal in its nature, is divided into small particles, enabling it thereby to be more easily acted on by the juices which are subsequently mixed with it.

(*b*) **Digestion.**—The primary object of digestion is, of

course, to render the food-particles soluble. For that purpose various secretions are poured into the alimentary canal from glands in its vicinity. The most important of these are saliva, gastric juice, intestinal juice, pancreatic juice, and bile. It may be convenient if we summarise the functions of these fluids and the action they severally have on the contents of the alimentary canal.

Saliva.—Saliva, though absent from the Amphibia, is so important a fluid that a notice of it cannot be omitted in a general sketch of animal physiology. It is a colourless, watery, but slightly viscid fluid, produced in abundance in certain glands situated in or near the buccal cavity. The essential constituent of saliva is a ferment, **ptya'in**, which has the power of transforming starch into sugar. Starch, being one of the substances already described as colloids, is incapable of being absorbed through an animal membrane, while sugar, being a crystalloid, may be so absorbed. Ptyalin, by changing starchy substances in the food into sugar, thus renders them soluble, while the water of the saliva dissolves the sugar so formed, which thus is rendered capable of subsequent absorption and assimilation. When food is introduced into the mouth, and the masticatory movements take place, the salivary glands are reflexly (p. 317) stimulated to secrete a copious supply of saliva, which in the process of mastication becomes thoroughly mixed with the food. All the digestive glands act in the same way, i.e. reflexly, the medium being a sensory or afferent nerve distributed to the mucous membrane of the alimentary canal, and an efferent or secretory nerve going to the secretory cells of the glands, the stimulation of which brings about glandular activity and a flow of the secretion.

Gastric juice.—The digestive fluid formed by the glands in the mucous membrane of the stomach-wall also contains one essential ferment, namely, **pepsin**, which in the presence of a small amount of hydrochloric acid (0·2 per cent.) transforms insoluble proteids into soluble substances known as peptones. The involuntary churning movements which take place in the stomach act in the same manner as the voluntary movements of the buccal cavity in promoting a perfect mixture of the gastric juice and the food.

The action of these two fluids, therefore, is to render two important constituents of the food, starch and albumin, soluble and capable of being absorbed through the walls of the intestine.

The food, or **chyme**, as it is termed, after being acted on by gastric juice, now passes into the intestine, where it meets with **intestinal juice**. This fluid is secreted from the Lieberkühnian follicles in the wall of the intestine, and appears to have much the same action upon the intestinal contents as the **pancreatic juice** has; we may simplify matters, therefore, by considering these together. The pancreatic juice contains three ferments, all important in their nature. The first and characteristic ferment of the pancreas is **trypsin**, which has the power of transforming proteids which have escaped the action of the peptic ferment into peptones—but here in an alkaline medium, while pepsin only acts in an acid medium. Further, the pancreatic juice contains a ferment which acts on fats or oils so as to transform them into an emulsion, in which the oil occurs in extremely fine particles; it then decomposes them into glycerin and their corresponding fatty acids (p. 28). Lastly, the fatty acid forms soaps with the alkali present in the juices of the pancreas and intestine. Pancreatic juice is also able to change starch into sugar should any be left over unacted upon by the saliva. Where salivary glands are absent, as in the frog, the pancreas is the only agent in this process.

Bile.—The character and functions of this fluid have been sufficiently referred to in connection with the liver (p. 280). We may briefly summarise its uses by saying that, while acting as a stimulant on the intestinal mucous membrane, it also assists the process of absorption by moistening the wall of the intestine and by acting as an antiseptic.

In the intestine also peristaltic movements (p. 277) perform the same function as the churning movements taking place in the stomach, viz. that of mixing of the food-stuffs and the digestive secretions.

(c) **Absorption.**—The third process in anabolism is absorption, or the reception into the circulation of the prepared food-substances. Absorption takes place partly in the stomach, partly in the intestine. The mucous membrane of the stomach and intestine contains an abundant supply of capillaries; the walls of these vessels, as has already been pointed out (p. 287), are only one cell thick, consequently the soluble peptones and sugar will diffuse readily into their interiors. In the intestine the area of absorption is largely increased by means of the villi, which, in addition to absorbing the food-stuffs just mentioned, also take into their interiors the emulsified fat. The oil-globules pass into the lacteals, which in turn communicate with the chief vessel of that system, the thoracic duct, which opens into the left vena cava near the shoulder.

(d) **Circulation.**—The food stuffs having been absorbed are now circulated, and in their passage through the body are altered in a variety of ways; for instance, in the liver the important starch-like body, glycogen, is abstracted from the blood and stored temporarily in the hepatic cells; the elements of bile are likewise extracted and stored in the gall-bladder or flow into the intestine directly, while probably urea and other products of metabolism are formed and pass away in the blood-stream to the kidney to be got rid of. In the lymph glands also the **chyle**, or alkaline nutritious fluid absorbed by the lacteals, no doubt undergoes important chemical changes. We have already (p. 288) referred in sufficient detail to the course of the blood-flow, and general physiology of the circulation. The action of the heart is a purely muscular one under government of the nervous system, while the muscular walls of the vessels assist in the circulation, and by their elasticity regulate the flow. There also the motor nerves (vasomotor) determine the degree of contraction of the circular muscle-fibres, and so govern the calibre of the vessel in question.

(*e*) **Assimilation.**—The final processes of anabolism which result in the formation of new protoplasm and the repair of tissue-waste are as yet much involved in mystery. No doubt the cells of the various tissues have the power of abstracting or selecting from the blood and lymph supplied to them the special substances which they require. Muscle-cells are thus no doubt able to select the proteids that are needed to form new muscle-cells, and, at the same time, the carbohydrates on which the evolution of muscular energy depends; saliva-secreting cells similarly seize on compounds required to form ptyalin, mucin, and the other constituents of saliva, and similarly for other glands. The nervous system also undoubtedly depends on the blood (the purest in the body) brought to it by the capillaries of the carotid arteries for those compounds needed to repair nervous waste. In the absence of detailed information with regard to the anabolic processes we may summarise the probable nature of these processes and those of katabolism by employing a convenient and probably in the main correct diagram as follows :—

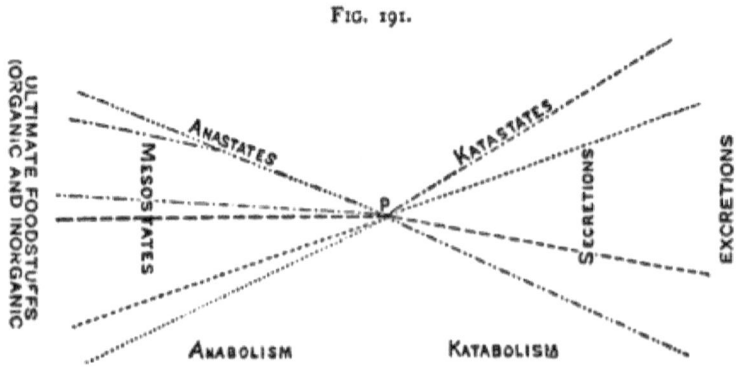

FIG. 191.

P represents the fully formed living protoplasm (animal) occupying the centre of two sets of diverging lines. On the left hand the ultimate food-stuffs are represented as being built up into intermediate products, which may be known as mesostates, while on the right hand protoplasm is represented as undergoing katabolism, where some of the intermediate stages are of service in the body (secretions) although ultimately they are all got rid of as katastates or excretions. Of course the same diagram might apply to protoplasm of green plants, although in that case the ultimate food-stuffs would be inorganic only. Combining both diagrams, and at the same time varying the character of the figure itself, we might graphically summarise the metabolism of both plant and animal in relation to the organic world thus:—

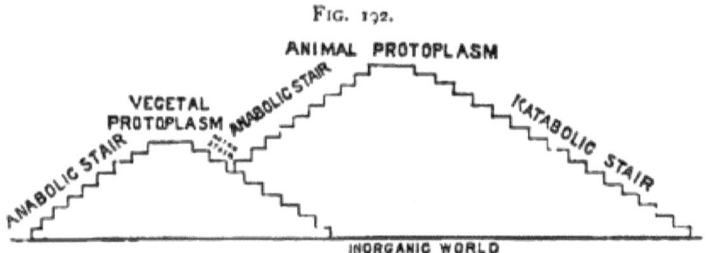

FIG. 132.

The diagram is, indeed, only a variation on that important scheme on which so much emphasis was laid at p. 49. The separate steps stand for anastates and katastates, while the anabolic stair for animal protoplasm is made to spring from near the top of the katabolic vegetal stair as indicating that the animal is dependent on the plant for food.

We must now glance for a moment at the results of the metabolism of animal protoplasm. The more important of these may be classified under growth, motion, nervation, heat, light, and electricity. Reproduction or the separation of sexual cells has already been sufficiently considered (p 52).

Growth in the animal as in the plant is due to the excess of repair over waste, of anabolism over katabolism. This anabolic excess is proportionally very great in the young, becoming less as maturity is approached. In the animal this early period may be divided into an embryonic stage spent inside the egg-membrane, and a postembryonic period, during which, as in the frog, metamorphosis may occur. Growth in the lower animals especially is frequently accompanied by **ecdysis**, or skin-casting, when the skin, whether soft as in the frog, or stiffened by a deposit of keratin (insects), or carbonate of lime (crustacea). is cast off and a new one is assumed. Ecdyses are concomitant with periods of more active growth.

Motion.—Motion is brought about by the contraction of muscle-cells in one direction; it is therefore definite. Indefinite motion in the higher animals is still represented by the amœboid movements of white blood-corpuscles and lymph-cells, &c.

A muscle contracts in response to a stimulus, usually nervous. Muscles are themselves irritable, for if the peripheral terminations of nerves be poisoned by curara, the muscles are still able to respond to a non-nervous stimulus, such as a prick from a needle or the application of certain chemical compounds, for example acetic acid. As we have already seen, the muscles of the body may be arranged in two categories: muscles which are intrinsically parts of organs, e.g. the muscles of the heart, alimentary canal, &c.; and muscles which are attached to hard parts, by the contraction of which motion of the limbs and trunk, or of the body as a whole, is effected. A single muscular contraction may be represented by a curve rapidly attaining a maximum, and more slowly regaining the abscissa. If, however, the muscular contraction be followed immediately by another before the first contraction has reached its maximum point, the total maximum contraction is considerably greater than the maximum which would have resulted from one stimulus alone. If a rapid succession of stimuli be applied to the muscle, an absolute maximum is at length reached. The muscle is then said to be in **tetanus**. The absolute maximum gradually falls as the muscle becomes exhausted.

Nervation.—While the rate of muscular motion is comparatively slow the chemical changes which take place in nerve-cells and nerve-fibres during nervous activity are extremely rapid. It has been calculated that a nerve impulse travels along a nerve at the rate of 200 feet per second. The rapidity of the metabolic processes in the brain is proverbial. The essential nature of these processes and of nerve motion is unknown.

Heat.—The ultimate form into which all other forms of energy become resolved is manifested more abundantly and can be studied more easily in the animal than in the plant. The temperature of the living body in the case of the higher animals varies, but the majority exhibit a uniform temperature of about 100° Fahr. In birds it is slightly higher. In the frog, however, the temperature of the body is that of the surrounding air. Hence the old-fashioned classification of animals into cold-blooded (e.g. fish, frogs), and warm-blooded (e.g. birds, mammals). Heat, as has been already stated, is the final results of katabolic processes taking place in the body; the more work done the more heat evolved, and the more food required to repair waste. Without entering into details on the subject of animal heat, it may be of interest to point out the important relationship that exists between the evolution of heat and the metabolic changes of the body viewed in relation to the constant variation in atmospheric temperature. In the case of a hot-blooded animal if the temperature of the air decrease, more heat-producing food (fats) must be oxidised to keep up the balance; if the temperature increase, less food is of course needed. If, on the other hand, the animal be cold-blooded and the temperature of the air decrease, metabolism is diminished; if the temperature of the air increase, metabolism is also increased. It will be seen that this relation depends entirely on the fact that the temperature of the warm-blooded animal is nearly constant, while that of the cold-blooded animal varies with the surrounding temperature within certain limits.

Light.—Many animals have the power of giving out luminous rays, which serve either to frighten away enemies or to guide them in finding their prey in the dark. Many fish, for instance, possess this power. This luminosity is known as **phosphorescence** (p. 209).

Electricity.—The existence of normal electrical currents in certain animal tissues, notably, muscle and nerve, has already been alluded to. These currents are particularly noticeable if the muscle or nerve be injured in any way. Further, a special electrical current, the so-called negative variation, is developed in a muscle or nerve on the application of a stimulus, and this electrical wave is the forerunner of the actual contraction, or of the nervous wave, and shows that certain metabolic changes are taking place preparatory to the actual contraction or the passage of the nervous impulse. The whole subject is, however, still under consideration, for the connection between the metabolic changes in the tissues and the electric currents is by no means clear.

CHAPTER XI.

HISTORY OF BIOLOGY.

In order to obtain a complete view, even though in outline only, of any science, it is necessary that some effort should be made to understand the chief stages in its history, the more noticeable features in its development. In the preceding chapters we have considered a few of the more important types illustrating the structure and physiology of the plant and animal kingdoms. No effort has been made even to sketch the principles governing the distribution of living organisms, nor have we entered at all into the great question of their etiology or genealogy. Under these circumstances it would be, of course, entirely out of place to mention any of the multitudinous systems of classification of plants and animals the knowledge of which was in old times, and is by some even yet, considered the aim and object of zoological and botanical study. We may, however, endeavour to obtain some conception of the gradual evolution, so to speak, of the science of biology out of a mass of isolated and disconnected observations, the collecting of which, as we have seen in the Introduction, forms the first stage in the development of any science.

Aristotle has been often termed the 'father of natural history,' and certainly he and his pupil **Theophrastus** in the fourth century B.C. may be looked on as the first collaborateurs of that vast catalogue of species to which the scientific expedition of **H.M.S. Challenger** (1872-76) has added only the latest chapter.

To the Greek naturalists and the few Romans who, like **Pliny** (23-79 A.D.), followed in their steps, belongs the honour of having laid that necessary foundation for future generalisation—the gathering of data. How great was the work they achieved can scarcely be better shown than by noting how men for centuries afterwards seemed to think that Aristotle had probed the secrets of Nature to the bottom; that there was, in fact, nothing more to learn; and that what he said must be true simply because he said so.

After these early natural historians—they can scarcely be called biologists in the sense in which we now understand the word—there comes a gap of nearly five hundred years before we meet with the founders of **Arabian medicine**, whose labours afterwards bore fruit in the great **medical schools of Bagdad and Cordova.**

Wise men were not wanting in those early days who saw that the study of animals was one which was likely to throw considerable light on the organisation of man himself, and therefore must tend in great measure to advance the art of medicine from what it was—a mere collection of recipes and conclusions founded on empiricism—to what it ought to be, a well-digested and connected system of treatment based on scientific generalisations arrived at by a careful study of the comparative anatomy and physiology of man and the lower animals. The work of the Arabian and Moorish doctors consisted in the generalising of what was known for present need; and though necessarily very small absolutely, yet relatively speaking the advance made was so great that it took six hundred years more before the advent of the great anatomists **Vesalius** (1514-1564), **Fallopius** (1523-1562), **Fabricius** (1537-1619), and their pupils marked the beginning of a new era of comparative morphology.

Nothing strikes one more forcibly in looking back over the history of the science of those days than the paucity of generalisations, which are at once the summation of work done and the basis for future effort. There were doubtless many reasons for this, but certainly one was the insufficiency of data. Vesalius and Fabricius were too earnestly engaged in mastering the details of mammalian anatomy to plunge into the sea of general Biology. It needed more students of Nature moulded on the Aristotelian type for work such as that; and yet it was not till the sixteenth century that **Gesner** (1516-1565) and **Cæsalpinus** (1519-1603) rose to supply the want. It was then that the lists of species compiled by Aristotle were found so defective, and the labours of these men and others of their school did much to increase the range of biological knowledge. But they did more; they attempted, and with wonderful success, to generalise on the observations they had made, and from a careful study of the material they had collected endeavoured to establish a more or less rational classification of plants and animals.

Biology was the last of the four great sciences to come into being. Astronomy, the most general of them all, was also the oldest. Physics and Chemistry were still in a transition state, and did not comprise a tithe of the array of facts and conclusions which are now included under these sciences. Yet just as Sociology, Anthropology, and the various sub-sciences dealing with the relationship of man to man are based on Biology which treats of him as an animal, structurally and functionally, so Biology itself is, as we have seen, based on the sciences of Physics and Chemistry. For that reason Biology had to wait for Physics and Chemistry to develop from the chaotic condition in which they were in the sixteenth century into the comparatively orderly and scientific department of knowledge which they became before the days of **Cuvier, Haller,** and **Bonnet.** Biology was in the bud; but it could not blossom until the physical and chemical sciences were in a fit condition to supply the necessary nourishment in the shape of suggestive ideas and generalisations of wide application.

That preparation had now been made. Kepler and

Galileo, Geber and Van Helmont, and all the host of physicists and chemists that the alchemical movement of the middle ages directly or indirectly gave birth to, had lived and left their mark. The telescope was revealing what was hidden in the sky beyond man's unaided vision, and the microscope was preparing, under the fostering genius of **Leeuwenhœck** (1632–1723), to tell him of the wonders that lay unknown at his feet. Although in the end of the seventeenth and the beginning of the eighteenth centuries we still meet with natural historians of the old school in the form of **Ray** (1628–1705) and **Willoughby** (1635–1672), **Buffon**, (1707–1788) and **Linnæus** (1707–1778), yet these famous writers were the last of their race, for a new epoch was dawning in the history of our science.

As might be expected, no attempt worth referring to was made in those early days to elucidate the nature of the origin and development of living things, nor was it possible in the condition of Geography and Geology to make even a start, in the great subject of distribution. Even function was not in those times treated separately from structure; no attempt was made to separate morphology from physiology. The *Histoire Naturelle* (1749) of Buffon and the *Systema Naturæ* (1736) of Linnæus were merely encyclopædias giving in the one case a popular, in the other a scientific, account of the animals and plants then known. At this point, however, we meet with a great advance, due perhaps as much to the introduction of the microscope into biological research as to anything else. Morphology and physiology began to separate from each other, and eager workers rapidly appeared in both subjects to raise the splendid monuments of intellect that we are able to look upon to-day.

Just as in the natural order of procedure in the examination of an animal or a plant we treat first of the organism as a whole, its appearance, habits, and so on, and then pass to a consideration of the structure and functions of the organs of which it is made up, then of the tissues composing these organs, of the cells, or component parts of the tissues, and, lastly, of the protoplasm or ultimate physical basis of life, so in the history of biology the progress has been in all respects similar.

As, year by year, hundreds upon hundreds of new species of animals and plants were added to the catalogues already in existence, and as naturalists with the help of the microscope and the scalpel dived deeper and deeper into their structure, it soon became a sheer impossibility for one man to master the entire range of biological knowledge—a feat easy enough in the days of Aristotle. Division of labour became necessary. One naturalist devoted himself to Botany, another to Zoology, still further specialising in some particular line research, morphological or physiological, as taste or circumstance dictated.

Thus **Laurent de Jussieu** (1748-1836) in Botany and **Baron Cuvier** (1769-1832) in Zoology laid the foundation-stone of morphology by their classic treatises, *Genera Plantarum* (1789) and *Règne Animal* (1817). About the same time **Haller** (1708-1777) and **Bonnet** (1720-1793) established on a true scientific basis the subject of physiology. With them Biology advanced from being a study of external form and habit to that of internal organisation and function. It was an easy step from that to the study of tissues, a step greatly aided by the continued improvement of the microscope. One prominent name, that of **Bichât** (1771-1802), stands out as the founder of histology, or tissue study, and histogeny, or tissue development, in his *Anatomie Générale* (1801).

Research could not, however, rest there. As the physicists improved their lenses, the biologists with their help were enabled to analyse tissues into cells. **Schleiden** (1804-1881) was the first by means of the improved technical appliances to perform that analysis in plants; a discovery which he followed up by a generalisation to the effect that all tissues were composed of minute saccules, to which he applied the name of 'cells.' **Schwann** (1810-1882) was similarly the first to apply the same generalisation to the tissue of animals, and so to aid in enunciating the cell theory on which modern morphological research for the most part rests.

Cells were found to vary greatly in size and shape, and a collection of similar cells formed a tissue. Every plant and every animal examined told the same tale. Organs made up of different kinds of tissues, tissues composed of collections of similar cells. Not only so, but every organism in the earliest stage of its existence was found to be composed of a single cell, which by division gradually became first a minute cellular mass, then by differentiation of cells a collection of tissues with different duties to perform, and finally an adult plant or animal, as the case might be, with tissues composed of different cellular elements united to form organs concerned in the maintenance of individual or of tribal life.

This takes us well into the nineteenth century, and its early years bring us face to face with all those names that we are most accustomed to associate with biological progress. **Geoffroy S. Hilaire** (1772-1840) and **Von Humboldt** (1769-1859) had begun their researches into the distribution of living organisms, and **Lamarck** (1744-1829), working on the material collected by Cuvier and the anatomical school of zoologists which he had founded, had made his guesses at the origin of living things; guesses which were destined in after years, in Darwin's hands, to become organised into the theory of evolution by natural selection.

Lamarck's generalisations were greatly in advance of the age in which he lived. To write a book in those days in support of the view that 'all species, including man, are descended from other species' was unlikely to lead to any other result than to arouse suspicion as to the sanity of the author. Lamarck, however, despite the risk he ran, published his views and earned the ridicule and contempt of his contemporaries and the posthumous applause of scientific investigators a century after. In 1835 **Dujardin** had taken the final step in the study of living things and had discovered the existence of a substance within Schleiden's cell-wall to which he gave the name of 'sarcode'; and **Von Mohl** (1805-1872) did the like service for plant-cells and named the granular gelatinous substance he found in the cell 'protoplasm.' Lastly, **Max Schultze** (1825-1874) identified the two substances as being the same, and thus struck the keynote of the science of Biology as we now understand it. For the adoption of a new name for the science which has grown out of, and has now absorbed the two older sub-sciences of Zoology and Botany, signifies more than a merely nominal union. It signifies the adoption of a unity of treatment in investigations into the morphology and physiology of plants and animals, a step parallel to and naturally following from the discovery of the identity of Dujardin's animal 'sarcode,' and Von Mohl's plant 'protoplasm' by Max Schultze.

No sooner had the morphologists performed their final analysis and discovered that all organisms were built out of protoplasm, well named by Professor Huxley 'the physical basis of life,' than the physiological school led by **Claude Bernard** (1813-1878), proceeded to study its functions, and ere long elucidated the great general principle that living protoplasm was constantly undergoing chemical changes; that these changes might be divided into two categories, viz. constructive or anabolic changes, leading to the formation of protoplasm, which thereby became a store of potential energy, and destructive or katabolic changes, resulting in the breaking down of the protoplasm and in the evolution of the stored energy in a kinetic or active form which manifested itself in the various phenomena of life.

Contemporary with these great leaders in biological thought, were many who devoted themselves to some special problem, or series of problems, such as the development of the embryo in the plant (**Robert Brown**, 1773-1858) and in the animal (**Von Baer**, 1792-1876); the diseases to which cells are liable (**Virchow**, 1820--——) ; the fertilisation of flowers (**Sprengel**, 1750-1816) ; and the like.

Lastly, in our own day, comes the evolution school, led by **Darwin** and **Wallace**, who, summing up the work of the past in the light of the present, simultaneously formulated an explanation of the structure and distribution of living things based on their genealogical relationships (1858). That the hypothesis of evolution by natural selection was enunciated by either of these men in its final form would be a statement both premature and unwarranted ; but that their theory was a true and workable theory, and a key to many, if not all, of the anomalies which had so puzzled the workers of the past, and driven them often to grotesque expedients by way of affording an explanation, is acknowledged by most, and has been proved to be so by the multitude of biologists who have spent or are spending their lives in adding some fragment of the unknown to the known. Foremost amongst these we may note the names of **Huxley, Agassiz, Balfour, Hæckel,** and **Gegenbaur** in Zoology, and **von Sachs, Sir Joseph Hooker, Herman Müller, Hoffmeister,** and **De Bary** in Botany.

It is of course quite impossible in this volume to give a detailed account of the work accomplished by these and countless others in recent years. This summary will fulfil its function if it serve to guide those who wish further information on the subject in selecting, out of the long catalogue of biologists who have made Biology what it is, those who may, without prejudice, be considered, if not as the leaders in the several subjects with which their names are associated, at least as representative types of the different schools in Biology ; which schools, however diverse their opinions and varied their methods, have at least one thing in common—the advancement of the science of Biology from a heterogeneous collection of isolated facts and observations to a homogeneous body of phenomena and laws, with the gradual evolution of the higher type from the lower, the more complex from the more general, as its guiding principle.

INDEX.

Absorption in the animal, 339; in the plant, 200
Acetabulum, 306
Afferent nerves, 317
Agassiz, 352
Albumin, 26
Albuminates, characters of, 26
Albuminoids, characters of, 26, 27
Aleurone, nature and uses of, 136
Alkaloids, vegetal, 209
Alternation of generations, 100
Amides, 204
Amœba, life-history of, 73
Amœboid motion, 33
— stage in *Protomyxa*, 59
Amphioxus, alimentary system of, 253; atrial cavity, 254; circulatory system, 255; cœlom, 257; development of the embryo, 260; excretory system, 256; external characters, 252; locomotory system, 258; nervous system, 258; protective system, 258; reproductive system, 259; respiratory system, 253; sense organs, 259; supporting system, 258
— and *Lumbricus* compared, 263
Amyloids, characters of, 27
Anabolism, 34; in the plant, 197; in the animal, 336
Analysis, 25
Anastates, 34
Anatomie Générale, 349
Angiospermæ, 144
Annual rings in wood, 180
Anterior abdominal vein, 291
Anthotaxis, 160
Aorta, 289
Apheliotropism, 212

Apical cell, 120
Apogamy, 100
Aqueous humour, 325
Arabian medicine, 346
Archenteron, 249
Archesporium, 109
Aristotle, 345
Aromatic substances, 209
Artery, structure of an, 286
Asci, 97
Ascospores, 97
Asexual reproduction, 52; in *Penicillium*, 95, 98
Ash of plants, analysis of the, 195; constituents of the, 190
Asparagin, 204
Assimilation, conditions of, 203; in the plant, 203; in the animal, 340
Astronomy, definition of, 3
Atmosphere, composition of the, 41
Atom, 9
Auricles of the heart, 285
Automatism of protoplasm, 34
Axial cylinders of nerves, 314

Baer, von, 352
Bagdad, medical schools of, 346
Balance of nature, the, 48
Balfour, 352
Bary, De, 352
Bast, 118, 147, 179
Bernard, Claude, 351
Bichât, 349
Bile, 280; functions of, 338
Biology, definition of, 4; position among the sciences, 5

BLA

Blastocœle, 231
Blastoderm, 173
Blastopore, 249, 290, 329
Blastosphere, 248, 260
Blastula, 231
Blood, 240, 255, 282
Bone, structure of, 297
Bonnet, 347, 349
Brachial plexus, 311
Brain, structure of the, 308
Bronchus, 293
Brown, Robert, 352
Buffon, 348

CÆSALPINUS, 347
Calcium, origin of and importance to the plant of, 193
Calyptrogen, 174
Cambium, 150, 179
Capillary, structure of a, 287
Carbohydrates, characters of, 27
Carbon, origin of and importance to the plant of, 190
Carbonic acid, absorption of, by the plant, 203; destiny of, 40; in the atmosphere, 42
Carnivorous plants, 213
Carotid artery, 289
Carpel, structure of, 162; development of, 166
Carpus, 305
Cartilage, 297
Causality, law of, 2
Cell, 29; cell-theory, 350
Cellulose, composition of, 61
Cell-wall, 31; thickening of, 149
Cerebellum, 308; structure of, 313; function of, 317
Cerebrum, 308; function of, 317
'Challenger,' H.M.S., 345
Chara, 83
Chemical change, laws of, 22; affinity, 19; compounds, classification of, 21
Chemistry, definition of, 4
Chlorophyll, composition, structure, and function of, 38; in *Hydra viridis*, 226
Choroid, 322
Chyle, 339
Chyme, 338
Ciliary muscle, 324, 325
Circulation, of water in the plant,

DOR

204; of sap, 206; in the animal, 339
Circumvallate papillæ, 320
Classification of organisms, 54
Clavicle, 305
Coagulation of blood, 283
Cœlom, 243, 249
Cœnosarc, 221
Coleochæteæ, 83
Coleorhiza, 177
Colour of flowers, 169
Columella, 321
Concentric fibrovascular strand, 120
Condyles, 301
Conjugation in *Spirogyra*, 80
Connective tissue, structure of, 275
Conservation of energy, law of, 15
Contractility of protoplasm, 33
Coracoid, 304
Corallineæ, 91
Cordova, medical school of, 346
Cork, 181
Cornea, 322
Corpora adiposa, 326
Cotyledons, 173
Cranial nerves, 310
Cranium, 301
Cross-fertilisation, 139, 168
Crystals, composition and occurrence of, 157
Cuvier, 347, 349
Cystolith, 157

DARWIN, 352
Death, 36
Decay, 36
Decomposition, 22
Dehydration, 22
Deoxidation, 23
Dermatogen, 173
Development, 36
Diastole, 73
Diatomaceæ, 72
Dicotyledonous type of plant, 178
Differentiation, 36
Digestion, 336
Dionæa, 214
Dissociation, 22
Distribution of organisms, 54
Division of labour, 55
Dorsal laminæ, 260, 332

Index.

DRO

Drosera, 214; structure of the leaf of, 215
Dujardin, 351
Dura mater, 314
Duration of plants, 174

EARTHQUAKES, 18
Ecdysis, 342
Ectocarpus, 91
Ectoderm, 221, 244
Ectoplasm, 29
Efferent nerves, 317
Electricity in plants, 210; in animals, 344
Elements and compounds, 9
Embryo, 53; of *Spirogyra*, 81; of *Penicillium*, 98; of *Polytrichum*, 108; of *Pteris*, 129; of *Selaginella*, 142; of *Lilium*, 171; of *Obelia*, 231; of *Lumbricus*, 247; of *Amphioxus*, 260; of *Rana*, 328
Embryo-sac, division of the nucleus in the, 167
Encysted stage, 60
Endoderm, 221, 244
Endodermis, 116
Endogenous origin of roots, 177
Endoneurium, 314
Endoplasm, 29
Endosperm, 138, 172
Energy, 11, 12; transformation of, 13; directly available sources of, 16; indirectly available sources of, 19
Enteron, 228
Epiblast, 231, 248, 329
Epineurium, 314
Eustachian tube, 267, 321
Excretions, 35
Exogenous origin of branches, 177
Eye, 259, 302, 322; muscles of the, 322

FABRICIUS, 346
Fallopius, 346
Fats, characters of, 27
Fatty acids, 28
Femur, 306
Fenestra ovalis, 321
Ferments in the plant, 206; in the animal, 337
Fertilisation, 53; in the Angiospermæ, 168

HAL

Fibrin, 283
Fibrovascular system, 102, 116, 146
Fibula, 306
Filum terminale, 310
Fission, 71
Flagellate stage, 61
Florideæ, 91
Flower, nature of the, 143; diagrams, 160; types, 144
Food of plants, 195
Food-supply of organisms, 47
Foramen magnum, 301
Formic aldehyde, 203
'Fructification,' 96
Fruit, nature of the, 143; structure of the, 174
Fucus, life-history of, 83; structure of the reproductive organs of, 85; structure of the thallus of, 84; germination of the embryo of, 88; differentiation of tissues in, 89
Fuel, 16
Fundamental tissue, 116, 134, 146, 178
Fungi, characters of, 91
Funicle, 123, 163

GALL-BLADDER, 279
Gametophyte, 132
Gases, solubility of, 42; absorption of, by the plant, 202
Gastric juice, 277, 337
Gastrula, 260
Gegenbaur, 352
Genera plantarum, 349
Geotropism, 212
Gesner, 347
Glenoid cavity, 305
Globulins, characters of, 25
Glomerulus, 296
Glycogen, 280
Gonophore, 227
Gravity, 7, 19
Growth, 36; in the plant, 210; in the animal, 342
Gymnospermæ, 142

HÆCKEL, 352
Hæmoglobin, 21
Hairs, forms of, 155
Haller, 347, 349

HEA

Hearing, structure of the organ of, 320
Heat, nature of, 14; mechanical equivalent of, 16; in the animal, 343; in the plant, 209; earth's internal, 19
Heliotropism, 212
Hilaire, S., 350
Histoire Naturelle, 348
Hoffmeister, 352
Holoblastic segmentation, 329
Hooker, Sir J., 352
Hotsprings, 18
Humboldt, von, 350
Huxley, 352
Hydra, 219; nerve cells of, 229; microscopic structure of, 224
Hydractinia, 221
Hydration, 23
Hydrogen, origin of, and importance to the plant of, 191
Hydrozoa, 219
Hygroscopic water, 201
Hyoid, 304
Hyphæ, 93
Hypoblast, 231, 248, 331
Hypocotyledonary axis, 174
Hypoglossal nerve, 311

ILIUM, 305
Individual life, 50
Inertia, 10
Infundibulum, 308
Intervertebral foramina, 310
Intestinal juice, 338
Intracellular digestion, 225
Inulin, nature and uses of, 156
Iris, 322
Iron, origin of, and importance to the plant of, 193
Irritability of protoplasm, 33
Ischium, 306
Isomerism, 22

JUSSIEU, De, 349

KARYOKINESIS, 78
Katabolism, 34; products of, in the plant, 208
Katastates, 34
Kidney, 295
Kinetic energy, 12

MAT

LACTEALS, 282
Lamarck, 350
Laminaria, 91
Latex, 182
Laticiferous vessels, 182
Leaves, arrangement of, 185; types of, 185
Leeuwenhœck, 348
Lens of the eye, 324
Lenticels, 182
Lieberkühnian follicles, 278
Light, nature of, 14; effect on organisms of, 45
Lilium, reproductive organs of, 157; structure of the flower of, 158; life-history of, 143; structure of the root of, 150; structure of the leaf of, 152; structure of the stem of, 145; structure of the floral axis of, 146
Linnæus, 348
Liver, structure of the, 279
Lumbricus, nephridia of, 236; clitellum of, 235; protective system of, 242; respiratory system of, 241; nervous system of, 244; reproductive system of, 246; cœlomic fluid of, 240; structure of the body-wall of, 244; purificatory system of, 241; cuticle of, 244; circulatory system of, 239; sense organs of, 245; circulation of, 240; alimentary system of, 236; hæmal fluid of, 240; differentiation of organs in, 234; locomotory system of, 242; external characters and habits of, 233; development of the embryo of, 247; nutrition of, 238; prostomium of, 235; renal system of, 241
Lungs, structure of, 291; development of, 293

MAGNESIUM, origin of, and importance to the plant of, 193
Mandible, 301, 304
Manubrium, 228
Manuring, 195
Mastication, 336
Matter, states of, 10; fundamental properties of, 7; constitution of, 9

Index. 359

Maxilla, 301, 304
Medulla oblongata, 308
Medullary plate, 260
Medusoid, reproductive organs of, 230; structure of a, 227; nerve-cells in a, 229; sense-organs of, 230
Membrana tympani, 321
Membrane bones, 304
Meristem, 120
Meroblastic segmentation, 329
Mesencephalon, 308
Mesenteron, 262
Mesentery, 242, 272
Mesoblastic somites, 249, 261
Mesoderm, 230, 244
Metabolism of protoplasm, 34; in the animal, 340; results of, in the plant, 209
Metacarpals, 305
Metameric segmentation, 249
Metaphyta, 64, 65
Metastasis, 206
Metatarsals, 306
Metazoa, 64, 66
Metencephalon, 308
Mohl, von, 351
Molecular motion, 11
Molecule, definition of, 8
Monocotyledon and Dicotyledon compared, 144
Motion in animals, 342
Motor nerves, 317
Mucous membrane, 267
Müller, Hermann, 352
Multicellular organisms, 64
Muscle, microscopic structure of, 273
Myelencephalon, 308
Myotomes, 258
Myxomycetes, 71

NASAL capsule, 302
Natural law, 1; phenomena, 1
Nectar, 209; glands, 184
Nectocalyx, 227
Nematocyst, 225
Nepenthes, 214
Nephridium, structure of a, 242
Nervation, 343
Nerve-cells, 315; structure of, 314; tissue, elements of, 313; fibres, medullated and non-medullated, 315

Nervous system, function of, 316; origin of, in Vermes, 232
Neurilemma, 315
Neuroglœa, 313
Neuromuscular layer of *Hydra*, 225
Nitrogen, origin of, and importance to the plant of, 191
Nitrogenous compounds, formation of, in the plant, 204
Non-essential elements in the ash of plants, 194
Notochord, 252; origin of the, 262
Nucleoli, 31
Nucleus, 30
Nutrition of the plant, 197

OBELIA, differentiation of zooids in, 222; structure of, 220; development of the embryo of, 231
Occipital segment of the skull, 301
Ocelli, 230
Oil glands, 184
Olfactory lobes, function of, 317
Omo-sternum, 305
Ontogeny, 53
Open fibro-vascular strand, 180
Optic tracts, 308; thalami, 308; lobes, 308, 317; chiasma, 308
Organ, definition of an, 37
Organs, classification of, 51
Osmosis, 199
Otic capsule, 302
Otocysts, 230
Ovarium, 85
Oviducts of *Rana*, 326; of *Lumbricus*, 246
Ovules, varieties of, 163
Oxidation, 23
Oxygen, absorption of, by the plant, 202; origin of, and importance to the plant of, 191

PALATINE, 302
Pancreas, structure of, 281; secretion of, 338
Pandorina, 83
Parasitic Fungi, 100
Parasphenoid, 302
Parenchyma, 102, 148
Parieto-frontal, 302
Parthenogenesis, 53
Pectoral girdle, 304

PEL

Pelvic girdle, 305
Penicillium, mycelium of, 93 ; life-history of, 93 ; reproductive organs of, 96 ; compared with *Fucus*, 97
Pepsin, 278, 337
Periblem, 173
Periderm, 181
Perineurium, 314
Perisarc, 221
Peristalsis, 277
Peritoneum, 272
Phalanges, 305, 306
Phelloderm, 181
Phellogen, 181, 182
Phloëm, 118, 134, 147, 179
Phosphorescence in the animal, 344 ; in the plant, 209
Phosphorus, origin of and importance of, to the plant, 192
Phyllotaxis, 160, 185
Phylogeny, 53
Physics, definition of, 4
Physiology of protoplasm, 31 ; of the plant, 189, 196 ; of the animal, 335
Pia mater, 313
Pineal gland, 308
Pituitary body, 308
Placenta, 123
Planula, 231
Plasmodium, 59
Plasmolysis, 200
Plerome, 173
Pleuron, 292
Pliny, 346
Polar body, 328
Pollen grains, structure of, 162, 166 ; development of, 169
Polytrichum, life-history of, 101 ; structure of the sporophyte of, 108 ; reproductive organs of, 104 ; structure of the gamophyte of, 101 ; structure of the embryo of, 108 ; compared with *Penicillium*, 112
Portal circulation, 288
Postcaval vein, 291
Potassium, origin of and importance to the plant of, 193
Potential energy, 12
Præfoliation, 121
Precaval vein, 291
Premaxilla, 303

RAN

Pressure, effect of, on organisms, 44
Proctodæum, 262
Prosencephalon, 308
Prosenchyma, 149
Protamœba, life-history of, 55
Proteids, 26
Protista, 55, 63
Protococcus, life-history of, 69
Protomyxa, life-history of, 57
Protonema, 104
Protophyta, 63
Protoplasm, morphology of, 29 ; varieties of, 38 ; composition of, 25 ; physiology of, 31
Protozoa, 63
Pseudopodium, 33
Pteris, structure of the sporangium of, 122 ; structure of the leaves of, 121 ; germination of the spores of, 126 ; structure of the rhizome of, 114 ; life-history of, 113 ; structure of the roots of, 120 ; structure and development of the embryo of, 129 ; ovaria of, 128 ; thallus of, 126 ; spermaria of, 127 ; summary of the more important conclusions in regard to, 130
Pterygoid, 304
Ptyalin, 337
Pubis, 306
Pulmo-cutaneous artery, 289
Pulmonary vein, 289
Punctum vegetationis, 212
Pupil of the eye, 322

RADIUS, 305
Rana, intestine of, 277 ; teeth of, 267, 270 ; stomach of, 277 ; tongue of, 271 ; skull of, 301 ; respiratory system of, 291 ; circulatory system of, 282 ; alimentary canal of, 265, 272 ; reproductive system of, 326 ; blood of, 282 ; heart of, 285 ; external characters of, 265 ; renal system of, 294 ; fore limb of, 305 ; development of the brain of, 332 ; development of the embryo of, 329 ; metamorphosis of, 332 ; sperms of, 327 ; ova of, 328 ; spermarium of, 326 ; ovarium of, 326 ; nervous system of, 307
Ranunculus, stem of, 178 ; leaf of,

185; root of, 184; flower of, 188
Raphides, 157
Ray, 348
Rectum, 279
Reflex action, 317
Règne Animal, 349
Rejuvenescence, 74
Renal-portal circulation, 291
Reproduction, 35, 52
Reproductive organs in *Rana*, development of, 327
Resin canals, 183
Respiration, 35; in the plant, 208; in the animal, 241
Retina, 325
Rhizoids, 103
Root cap, 120; hairs, 121
Rotation of crops, 195; of the earth, 19

SACCHAROMYCETES, 72
Sachs, von, 352
Saliva, 337
Salts associated with protoplasm, 28; absorption of, by the plant, 200
Saprophytic Fungi, 100
Sarracenia, 214; structure of the leaf of, 216
Scalariform vessels, 119
Scapula, 305
Scent of flowers, 169
Schizomycetes, 72
Schleiden, 349
Schultze, Max, 351
Schwann, 350
Science, methods of, 2
Sciences, 2; classification of the, 2
Sclerenchyma, 102
Sclerotic, 322
Secretions, 35
Secretory nerves, 317
Seed, structure of the, 174
Segmentation, 61; cavity, 231
Selaginella, leaf of, 134; root of, 135; sporangium of, 135, 141; cone of, 136; spores of, 137, 139; stem of, 134; sporophyte of, 132; alternation of generations in, 142; embryo of, 141; life-history of, 131
Self-fertilisation, 168
Sensitivity of plants, 213
Sensory nerves, 317

Sexual differentiation, origin of, 90; reproduction, 52
Sieve tubes, 119, 150
Sight, sensation of, 325; organ of, 322
Sinus venosus, 285
Skeleton, 297
Skin, 268
Smell, organ of, 320
Soil, composition of the, 196
Solar radiation, 19
Solubility of gases, 42
Somatopleure, 249
Somite, 235
Sorus, 123
Spectrum analysis, 4, 10
Spermarium, 85
Spermathecæ, 247
Sperms, development of, 247
Sphenethmoid, 302
Spinal cord, 252, 310, 313, 317; nerves, 310
Spiral vessels, 119
Spirogyra, life-history of, 76
Splanchnopleure, 249
Sporangium, 109 122, 162, 188
Spores, 95, 110, 124
Sporophylla, 123, 136, 158, 188
Sporophyte, 132
Sprengel, 352
Squamosal, 304
Stamen, structure of, 162; development of, 164
Starch, 155
Stem, increase in thickness of, 180
Sternum, 304
Stolon, 103
Stomata, 122, 153
Stomodæum, 262
Sulphur, origin of and importance to the plant of, 192
Supra-scapula, 305
Suspensor, 173
Sympathetic nervous system, 311
Symphysis, 306
Synergidæ, 170
Synthesis, 22
Systema Naturæ, 348
Systemic circulation, 288
Systole, 73

TADPOLE, 332
Tapetal tissue, 126, 165, 167
Tarsus, 306

Taste, organ of, 319
Temperature, effect of, on organisms, 43
Tentaculocyst, 230
Tetanus, 343
Thalamencephalon, 308
Thallus, nature of a, 77
Theophrastus, 345
Tibia, 306
Tides, 17
Tissue, definition of, 37
Tooth, structure of a typical, 270
Touch, sensation of, 319
Trachea, 293
Tracheæ, 119
Transition substances associated with protoplasm, 28
Transpiration, 205
Tribal life, 52
Trophic nerves, 317
Truncus arteriosus, 285
Trypsin, 338
Typhlosole, 237

ULNA, 305
Unicellular organisms, 63
Ureter, 295
Urinary bladder, 296
Urine, 296
Urino-genital duct, 326
Urostyle, 300

VACUOLE, 30
Vasa deferentia, 247; efferentia, 326

Vegetative multiplication, 35
Vein, structure of a, 286
Velum, 228
Ventricles of the heart, 285
Vernation, 121
Vertebra, 299
Vertebral column, 299
Vertebrata, characters of, 263
Vesalius, 346
Vessels of the plant, 149
Villi of the intestine, 278
Virchow, 352
Vitreous humour, 325
Volcanoes, 18
Vomer, 302

WALLACE, 352
Water, absorption of, by the plant, 200; currents, 18; percentage of, in protoplasm, 28; power, 18
Willoughby, 348
Wind currents, 18
Wood, 119
Work, 12

XIPHI-STERNUM, 304
Xylem, 119

ZOOID, 221
'Zygospore,' 81

www.ingramcontent.com/pod-product-compliance
Lightning Source LLC
Chambersburg PA
CBHW020315240426
43673CB00039B/808